WHO IS RAISING YOUR CHILDREN?

WHO IS RAISING YOUR CHILDREN?

BREAKING INDIA USING ITS YOUTH

RAJIV MALHOTRA
VIJAYA VISWANATHAN

ISBN: 978-93-6547-067-3

Second Impression 2025

BluOne Ink Pvt. Ltd
A-76, 2nd Floor, Sector 136, Noida
Uttar Pradesh 201301
www.bluone.ink
publisher@bluone.ink

Printed and bound in India by Thomson Press India Ltd.

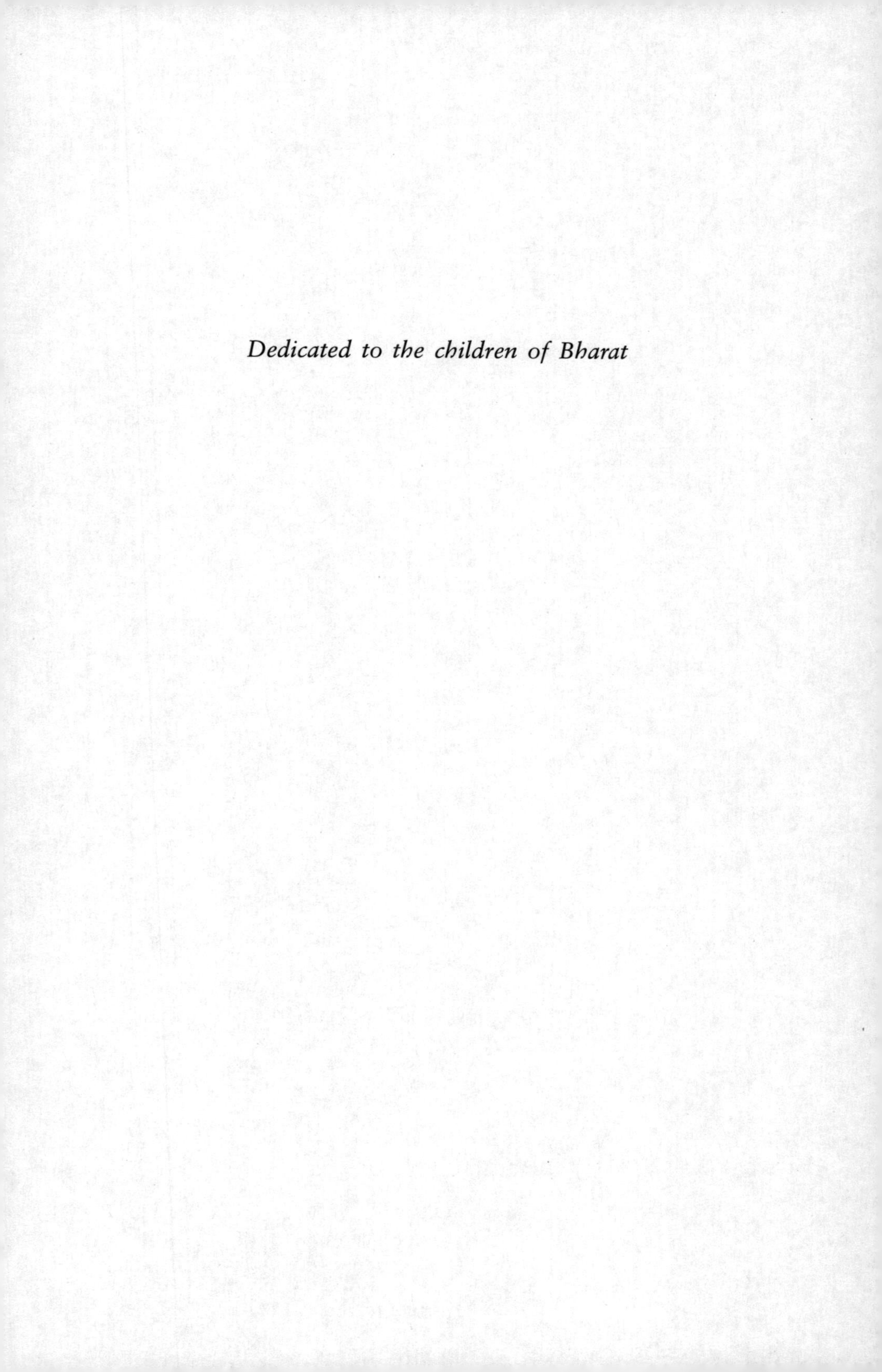

Dedicated to the children of Bharat

CONTENTS

INTRODUCTION RECRUITING OUR CHILDREN TO BREAK UP INDIA

The Tale of Aghasura

The image on the front cover of this book shows the malevolent snake Aghasura, an *asura* (demon) general who is committed to *adharma* (violation of dharma). This is a tale from the *Bhagavata Purana*. Driven by his malice, Aghasura had devised a sinister plan to wipe out the innocent children of the holy city of Vrindavan in Mathura, where Lord Krishna is believed to have spent his early years.

Aghasura assumed the form of an eight-mile-long serpent, disguising his open mouth to look like the entrance to a mysterious cavern in a mountain. His enticing trap appeared like a serene path through a beautiful meadow. His open mouth awaited the unsuspecting children.

The children were engrossed in play, mimicking peacocks and chasing birds' shadows. When they came upon Aghasura's mouth, they assumed it to be a mountain cave. Lured by the beautiful path, the children entered without hesitation, unaware of the impending doom. Elders and parents, who typically keep a watchful eye, were absent.

Aghasura intended to close his jaws and destroy them from within, exploiting their joyful innocence as bait to suffocate and kill them. The *Bhagavata Purana* describes the dramatic event as follows:

> His lower lip rested on the surface of the earth, and his upper lip was touching the clouds in the sky. The borders of his mouth resembled the sides of a big cave in a mountain, and the middle of his mouth was as dark as possible. His tongue resembled a broad traffic-way, his breath was like a warm wind, and his eyes blazed like fire. The children assumed it must be a beautiful scenic spot of Vrindavan. Later, when they recognized it to look like a giant snake, they remained unafraid and assumed it to be a statue made in the shape of a great snake for their enjoyment.[1]

Seeing this, Lord Krishna came to their rescue and killed Aghasura.

Aghasura's story is a powerful metaphor for the hidden dangers and deceptive threats that the children and the youth of our country face. Just as Aghasura disguised his lethal intent with an innocent and exciting appearance, many dark forces are currently cloaked in benign forms.

This book urges the reader to look beyond the surface and recognize the true nature of what we are being told. Today, the metaphorical Aghasura has returned to destroy our children. We will show that under the garb of nice-sounding ideals like 'Social Emotional Learning' (SEL) and sex education claiming to protect children from risks, the real effect is sinister: Children are being sexualized at very early ages to create chaos and confusion in their minds, and being denied the practical education in reading and math that would ready them for careers. This is how they can be controlled, exploited, and ultimately, destroyed. These are not isolated trends but are being driven top-down by global forces we deem necessary to expose.

Much like Aghasura's enticing lure, the path toward destruction is long and winding, going through promises of preparing children for global citizenship and attractions of an inclusive society. Aghasura is operating at the highest levels of power and influence in society and governance. Woke ideology is the mechanism to draw Indian children into its mouth through various institutional partners that facilitate easy access to the cavern.

This book is an early warning to prepare India proactively with a preemptive response. We see systematic programs across the country to replicate the American education model. Our previous books, ***Breaking India 1.0*** (*Western Interventions in Dravidian and Dalit Faultlines*) and ***Breaking India 2.0*** (*Snakes in the Ganga*) highlighted issues *after* they had already unfolded and will take decades to repair. This time we are stepping in early to prevent future issues from metastasizing. India must make immediate choices to control its educational landscape.

Sadly, Indian leaders can sometimes lack the tools required to fully grasp the language and hidden implications behind Marxist ideologies—ideologies that often come wrapped in appealing rhetoric on the surface. This book is a guide to unpacking the complex and convoluted language, exposing the subtle concealed layers. By shedding light on these ideological agendas we hope to empower leaders and citizens to recognize the potential pitfalls.

We pray it is not too late. The Indian education system is heading down a path reminiscent of the era of Macaulay (Thomas Babington, 1800-59, author of the 1835 *Minute on Indian Education*), but far more disturbing. The trajectory being uncovered is of new Western education models promoted by globalists whose programs target the children of millions of aspirational parents seeking a better future for their offspring.

India's children are falling prey to programs geared to sexualize them as early as age five and grooming them as warriors for social justice activism. These programs desensitize children, inflict psychological harm, and rewire their brains using behavioral science, psychology, and neuroscience.

Before diving into the infiltration of India's education system by these threats, we will explain the global theater as the source of dangerous ideologies.

Paradoxes of the Emerging World *Dis*order

The global system is once again at a tipping point. The prevailing structures developed under the Bretton Woods institutions, i.e. a set of rules establishing commercial associations between the United States of America, Western European countries, Canada, Australia, and other countries that have held the World Order together since the Second World War (1939-45) are being challenged. Western Universalism is under attack from multiple fronts, some main contenders being Marxist Universalism, Christian Universalism, Chinese Universalism, and Islamic Universalism. Each is asserting its distinct vision of an entirely new World Order.

Most predictive models, both liberal and conservative, have crashed, having failed to make sense of the latest social-political disruptions. This new disequilibrium has created cognitive dissonance among public intellectuals and policymakers who are being confronted with experiences outside their comfort zones, and are ill-equipped to deal with the dilemmas and paradoxes raised.

We will focus on a specific area of disequilibrium, one that concerns the use of education to *raise a generation of children who are over-sexualized, unemployable, angry at the prevailing structures*, and *driven by a sense of entitlement*. This is the first time in history that an entire generation is being systematically nurtured into *a worldwide cultish movement* that sees the destruction of the World Order as redemption. The battle for our children's future is also a battle for India's future.

The statement in the preceding paragraph is heavily loaded with several claims, each of which needs to be unpacked and substantiated. Our focus is on India: how this new generation will become a deadly 'Breaking India' Force. The key issues are summarized in this Introduction. This is expanded systematically in the chapters that follow with empirical data and evidence to back our provocative claims.

We begin by listing some of the disruptions and paradoxes that are confounding most observers today and that our thesis explains. These paradoxes are as follows.

Paradox 1: Marxist Takeover of the United States of America

Over the past century, the United States of America became the leading superpower based on meritocracy and democracy and has been the major force fighting Marxism. Yet today, its college campuses, media, institutions, corporations, and the progressive elements of the Democratic Party are being driven by Marxist ideologies that are becoming mainstream as the new normal and are being exported. Democracy, free enterprise, and meritocracy are being hijacked and replaced with Marxist ideas of a revolution that would bring entitlements for those declared 'oppressed'. Diversity, Equity, Inclusion (DEI), and Environment, Social Justice, Governance (ESG) mandates in almost every organization are among the tools, and these call for the *redistribution of wealth, resources,* and *power* in ways that undermine meritocracy. It is indeed paradoxical that of all countries, the USA has become the center of this movement based on Marxism whose end game is to topple free enterprise and free speech because these are perceived as oppressive structures.

Paradox 2: Billionaires Helping Dismantle Capitalism and Meritocracy

Billionaires around the world have used capitalism to accumulate unprecedented levels of personal wealth. Yet, their tech companies and private philanthropy often support ideas that are aligned with dismantling the very structures that made them successful. *Oligarchs are playing a dance of duplicity: promising to protect the wealth of the ultra-rich with programs for population reduction, while supporting leftist ideologies that drive toward wealth redistribution.* However, in the process, they are gaining greater power. There is a paradoxical equilibrium between the oligarchs and the Left.

Paradox 3: Leftists Support Islamic Practices That Violate Liberalism

The human rights movement exempts Islam from criticism by declaring all its critics to be Islamophobic. In effect, Islam has skillfully co-opted the Left's social justice movement. Islam has diverted the social justice warriors away from its barbarities and targeted infidels like the Jews and Hindus. The sheer hypocrisy of the human rights movement is overwhelming. An example of duplicity is that any criticism of Islam or Muslims is considered Islamophobic, which is criminalized, while Hinduphobia is not condemned. One can debate whether the Left is using the Muslims or the other way around. What is clear is that: (1) the Left brings intellectual sophistication and access to the West's intellectual machinery, which the Muslims lack; and (2) the Muslims bring funding from the Middle East along with an army of activists organized like a militia. In the end, they would have to fight each other once the common enemy has been destroyed—because their ideologies are incompatible. Sadly, the Blacks in America have been co-opted.

Paradox 4: Feminists Silent on Assault on Womanhood

The liberal, leftist feminists are silent regarding the rights of Muslim women as explicitly codified in their holy text and implemented in practice. Feminists are complicit about transgenders, with male genitals and males by birth, freely entering women's locker rooms and competing in women's sports. This is creating mental and emotional health challenges for most women. In effect, the feminists are canceling womanhood.

Paradox 5: Deception and Opaque Jargon Used to Weaponize the Youth for Social Justice

University professors are brainwashing under-informed and over-opinionated students and turning them into angry citizens shouting slogans. The traditional teaching of critical thinking skills has been replaced by demonizing opponents and instilling dogmatic ideologies. Those calling themselves liberals are canceling opponents from speaking engagements and projecting biases in the name of 'fact-checking' and 'anti-hate speech'. The Left has created a large-scale project taking control of education in the USA and other countries where the latter exerts influence. Also, the Left has mastered the art of obfuscation by using attractive jargon that is difficult to unpack. They claim to be 'evidence-based' using circular logic or agenda-driven research which is designed to reach predetermined outcomes. They have gamified the system that people assume to be legitimate.

Paradox 6: School Children Becoming Over-Sexualized From Age Five

School-going children are being emotionally manipulated by encouraging them into sexual desires, experimentation, exploring gender and sex change—all this bypassing the parents or blackmailing them into believing that non-compliance will lead to suicide. Rich Western countries might want to spread and encourage more hedonism in their children, but many other countries have different challenges and priorities that demand education geared toward employment. Besides, it is rash to blindly import into India what is considered normal in another culture and thereby rupture the societal guardrails. Furthermore, empirical data shows that the USA has ruined its youth with sexualization, drugs, violence, and dropping academic standards compared to many other developed countries—this is the wrong role model for India to import.

Paradox 7: Abysmal Academic Standards in India Despite Increased Government Spending

Academic scores for education in India rank very low compared to the rest of the world and have been dropping even further in recent years despite the increased budget allocation for education. Priority has not been given to upgrading educational standards of math, science, and reading. Sadly, the data shows that those with degrees have even higher levels of unemployment than uneducated youths, which points to the failure of the education system to equip students for gainful employment. The IQ level of India's population also ranks very low compared to Japan, China, Korea, Singapore, and European countries. *Why would the Indian government focus on sex education rather than upgrading the mental competence and employability of its children?*

Paradox 8: The Climate Crisis Clubbed With Other Parasites Like the 'Sustainability' Movement

The movement to protect the climate was broadened to include human rights, which include the full-fledged Woke agenda of social justice: DEI, redistribution of wealth, rewriting history from the 'oppressed' perspective, and dismantling the structures that have served as the guardrails of social stability. *Even movements like Kashmir separatism and Khalistan (the demand for a separate state for Sikhs) have become part of this.* This Woke tsunami also includes a specific approach to sex education, and is at the heart of the problem we will concentrate on. *The fundamental problem explained in this book is that a large gamut of Marxist agendas has latched on to the climate crisis as parasites, sucking the credibility* and *resources being poured into the climate crisis for their own goals. Our problem is not with the climate movement itself but with its broad exploitation in this manner.*

Paradox 9: China's Skillful Navigation of the Disruptions

China has emerged unscathed amidst this tsunami despite its undemocratic system and social injustices both domestically and overseas. It is poised to gain even more power because of this disruption in democratic countries. China has skillfully weaponized these disruptions to weaken its enemies by supporting such causes overseas while keeping its domestic society insulated.

Paradox 10: India's Capitulation to the American Left

Despite having a rich heritage on issues like diversity, inclusion, social theories, environmentalism, and education, and despite all the buzz words and slogans like *vasudhaiva kutumbakam* (the world is one family), 'holistic' education, 'knowledge economy', 'Indian Knowledge Systems' (IKS), 'soft power', 'Competency-Based Education' (CBE) and the like, India has sold out to ideas imported from the American Left. *This has infiltrated the Indian bureaucracy and government machinery over the past several years.* Yet, there is no public discussion or even awareness on the part of India's intellectual elites and influencers. While the USA has a well-developed and organized movement to push back against Wokeism, India is far behind in this regard.

The purpose of this book is to present an interpretive lens, a *drushti* to make sense of these dilemmas. We are not presenting any new facts that are not available to anyone who makes the effort to dig into the details. We are systematically curating a vast amount of information and connecting the dots to develop a thesis of causation: how through multiple stages of cause-effect, the ultimate impact of these syndromes is a new kind of Breaking India Force. The detailed End Notes, based on the rich Bibliography, provide the supporting hard evidence.

Globalists and the Gameboard

Despite these challenges, people prefer to see no evil and hear no evil even though evil is metastasizing into a dangerous cancer right before their eyes. The world is being reshaped under the influence of what we refer to as the Globalist Agenda, and this is like a new form of colonization. Besides the United Nations (UN) and the World Economic Forum (WEF), there are numerous corporate leaders and other liberal/leftist nexuses that are defining and implementing the new rules of the global gameboard.

We will set the stage by presenting a broad overview of the

global gameboard in which multiple disruptive forces are at play. *Though their worldviews are incompatible and different ambitions compete for control, they share a common agenda: dismantle the World Order.*

When talking about globalization, most people assume it refers to the idea of a 'flat world' where meritocracy shapes a new World Order that transcends national boundaries. The bad news is that that vision for the future has been replaced by an entirely new kind which we refer to as 'globalism'. This is a dramatic shift *away* from meritocracy and toward a breakdown of fundamental structures, redistribution of wealth, and vacuum of power.

The globalists are not one individual or a single country or ideology that controls this giant ecosystem. Rather, it is a nexus with its playing field where, in this coalition, numerous contenders have a seat at the table. Some of the players include the Bill & Melinda Gates Foundation, George Soros' Open Society Foundations, Omidyar Network (founded by eBay founder Pierre Omidyar), and a vast assortment of Non-Governmental Organizations (NGOs), which are in turn funded by governments and wealthy individuals. It is therefore important to understand how the different kinds of players are using a common agenda being pushed through the UN and its aligned institutions.

Before we discuss the state of the United Nations in recent years, we must clarify that we certainly appreciate the many good things it has done. It has mediated successfully in certain situations, and even where it failed, its role has generally helped alleviate suffering to some extent. It has facilitated crisis intervention and dialogue among nation-states and introduced initiatives for the preservation of monuments, poverty eradication, and security. All this and much more is certainly commendable.

However, certain countries, religions, ultra-rich oligarchs, and powerful ideologies (like Marxism) have successfully infiltrated and even hijacked the control of the UN system including its associated agencies and international financial institutions. The weaker countries and hence, most of the human population inhabiting them do not enjoy the same influence and clout. There is a disequilibrium among countries and the rebalancing underway is at the expense of the weaker countries as well as the ideologies that are not powerfully organized.

'Sustainable' as the Umbrella for Multifaceted Disruptions

The central framework being used by the globalists is the UN Sustainable Development Goals (SDGs) 2030. Emerging from a war-torn world, and a failed and rigged international order (i.e. The League of Nations), the UN had started losing relevance in the 1970s and tried to revive itself by stretching its mission into the development and governance agenda. A major attempt was the Millennium Development Goals (MDGs) of 2000. This was followed by the Sustainable Development Goals of 2015 whereby the UN used the Climate Agreement as the foundation and added human rights, gender, disability, children, migrants, etc.[2]

We must point out that there are many beneficial components of the SDGs, but this book focuses on the sweeping educational reforms designed to indoctrinate young minds. We will explore what happens when education turns into an ideological weapon, classrooms become battlegrounds for mind control, and individual freedoms get suppressed under the guise of global unity and sustainability. This book examines the chilling implications of such a future.

Like most reasonable people, we too are concerned about the environment. However, unlike most, we have delved into the hubris that is being sold as part of the *moral halo of sustainability*. A deeper dive is needed to expose potential flaws with the proposed sustainable solutions. Our specific issue is how the Climate Agreement is being used to push the UN's SDGs 2030 which includes a wide assortment of unrelated issues like sex education.

One certainly wonders what the Climate Agreement has to do with sex education, especially the kind that runs counter to the traditions inherent in many societies. The agenda manipulates legitimate environmental concerns to propagate broader socio-political disruptions.

How did issues like climate change and fighting poverty and racism expand into the sweeping ideology of SDGs 2030 that the UN and other international bodies want to push globally? To understand how such a vast assortment of agendas was combined under the rubric of sustainable goals, one must peel the onion of sustainability by examining the following chain of causation:

1. The initial movement was to address climate change, and this expanded into the movement for the 'sustainability' of the environment.
2. Sustainability was merged with the development movement to alleviate poverty and turned into 'sustainable development'. The development movement by itself required increased use of fossil fuels, but these run counter to sustainability. Hence, the combination of both became a way to balance the goals.
3. Next, the separate goals of human rights were brought under the umbrella of sustainable development.
4. Human rights activists, however, used the agenda of fighting racism to introduce the framework of Marxism.
5. The door was opened to all kinds of groups claiming victimhood and thus, what is known as 'Wokeism' became part of sustainable development. This has brought in LGBTQIA+, Dalits, Muslims, Khalistanis, and others as 'oppressed' people—all sorts of causes entered the big tent definition of sustainable development.
6. Such a sweeping transformation requires reengineering the way humans think and feel. Therefore, 'Social Emotional Learning' was formulated by a coterie of experts and consultants and turned into the core of education worldwide.
7. Like SEL, a central place is being given to sex education codified as Comprehensive Sexuality Education (CSE), which Marxist experts consider necessary for reproductive health and dismantling patriarchal structures of society. Thus, sex

positivity, sexual rights, and sexual desires are enshrined as core ideas in the sustainability movement.

8. The CSE comprises components that encourage very young children to masturbate, explore each other sexually, explore genders, and intimate desires, learn techniques of sexual pleasure, and experiment with sexual fluidity—all this bypassing parental control and supervision.
9. Apart from SEL and CSE, Global Citizenship Education (GCE) has been added to the curriculum to make the next generation loyal to the global agendas more than being patriotic to their respective countries. *Global Citizenship Education burdens children with responsibility for the world's problems*. It is about making personal sacrifices (like limiting travel to reduce the carbon footprint), while CSE is about rights like unrestricted freedom to engage in sexual activities without limitations or constraints. Social Emotional Learning rewires the brain to accept the GCE responsibilities while being receptive to the 'benefits' of sexual pleasure through Comprehensive Sexuality Education.
10. Competency-Based Education or the CBE model is the umbrella infrastructure to achieve equity in educational outcomes in the name of student-centered education. It prioritizes SEL competencies, which is about reengineering values, attitudes, and disposition towards learning combined with lowering standards for everyone. Thus, CBE acts as the dashboard, measuring competencies in assimilating responsibilities (to the collective) and sexual rights (of the individual). The following diagram shows the roles of these various three-letter acronyms.

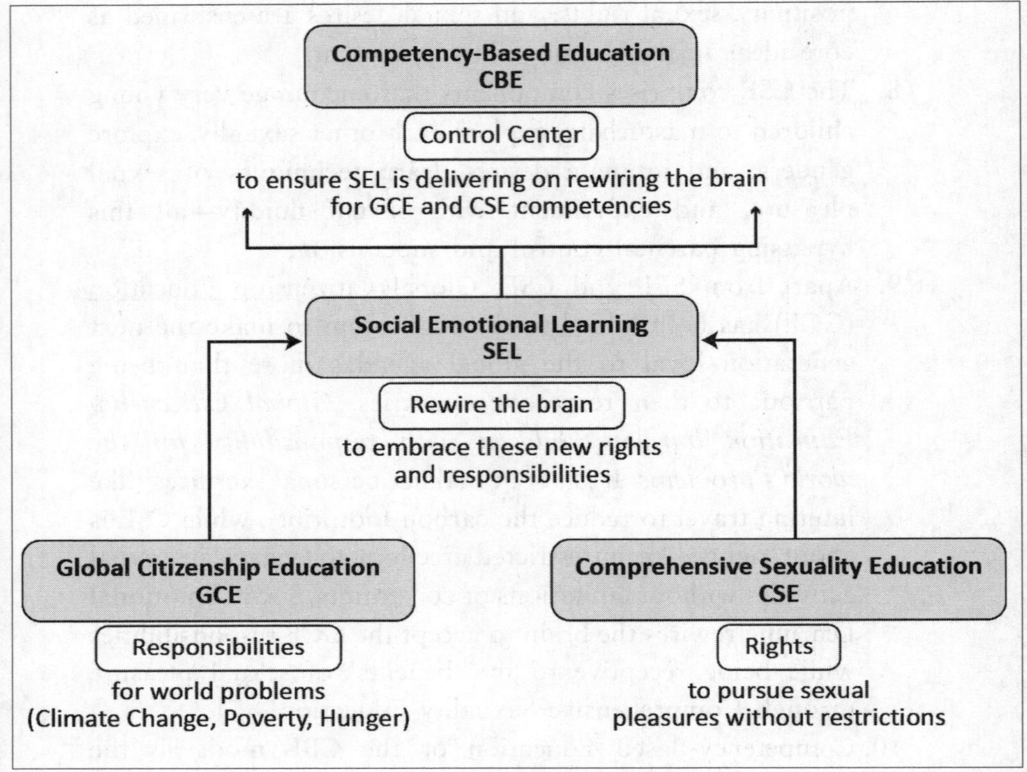

This manipulative jargon is used to conflate diverse issues, turning it into a tsunami we are calling Breaking India 3.0. The following chain of causation summarizes the aforementioned ten points:

Climate ➔ Sustainability ➔ Social Justice ➔ Human Rights ➔ Wokeism ➔ Leftist Madrassas ➔ Sexualizing Children ➔ Rewiring Young Minds ➔ Breaking India 3.0

The following diagram captures the four major forces that have come together dominated by the globalists.

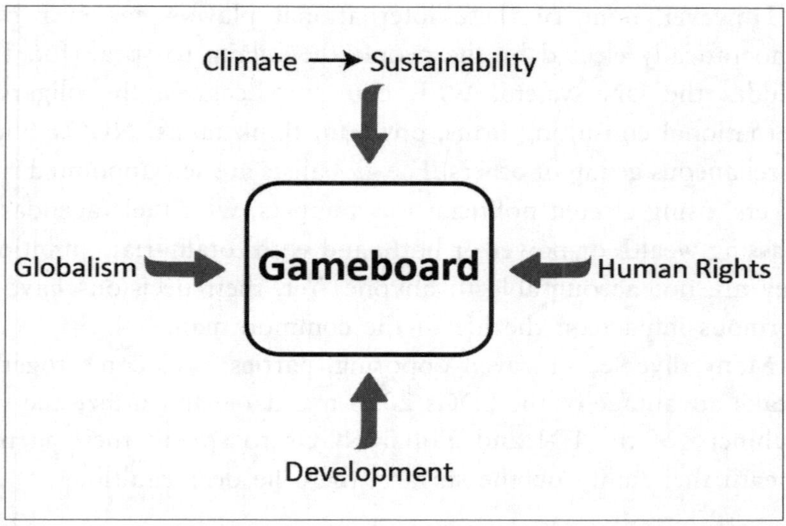

The United Nations and the Ecosystem of 'World Government'

The UN system uses its vast network of affiliated powerful NGOs and international consultants to blur the boundaries between the Climate Agreement and their own broader agendas and to push these goals, especially to developing countries. These independent international organizations have considerable influence within the national governments. They use different entry paths such as cultivating ties with family members of politicians and government officials, and other means, public or clandestine. This must raise concerns about transparency and potential conflicts of interest.

Marxists originally entered the UN under the umbrella of eliminating hunger, poverty, and human rights violations. Once they had their foot in the door, they rapidly expanded their influence. Their environmental concerns emerged later, and all such movements became intertwined. This integration makes it difficult to scrutinize the assumptions being made. Climate change suddenly became a climate emergency. Because climate emergency is a global problem, one that needs a global solution, the UN has become a powerful epicenter pushing agendas that are beyond its charter.

However, none of these international players has ever been democratically elected by the people they claim to speak for. This includes the UN system, WEF, elite Ivy Leagues, the oligarchs, international consulting firms, powerful think tanks, NGOs, and a miscellaneous group of others. The globalists are self-appointed rule-makers, using elected politicians as puppets, with their agendas of amassing wealth or power or both, and with totalitarian ambitions. They are not accountable to anyone. Yet, their decisions have an enormous impact on the life of the common man.

Many diverse, and even opposing, parties have come together to take advantage of the SDGs 2030 mandates and utilize the vast machinery of the UN and global NGOs to spread their agenda. Beneath their unity on the surface, there lie deep faultlines:

- Western nations and China participate with their respective well-defined strategies and agendas to interpret the SDGs and shape the world.
- Oligarchs like Bill Gates and George Soros provide large amounts of funding to this powerful international machinery thereby injecting their ideological visions into it.
- The World Economic Forum has become a major organization serving the needs of the Western oligarchs and their governments.
- Proponents of eugenics seeking population control have been operating abortion services under the rubric of family planning and sexual and reproductive health. They have become a multi-billion-dollar industry backed by some powerful governments and wealthy philanthropists.
- Islam has one of the best and most clearly articulated plans for a world government ruling the world with *Sharia* (religious laws based on the Koran). The terms *Dar-ul-Islam* (Nation of Islam) and Caliphate are often used for such a world government. Man-made nations must be ultimately superseded by the one nation ordered by Allah.

- Karl Marx envisioned a future in which the proletariat would govern, and private property along with individual nation-states would become meaningless.
- The Bahá'í Faith (followers of Bahá'u'lláh; 1817-92) was founded on the aspiration for a unified governance of humanity.
- Christianity holds both views: those aspiring for the Church to take over the world, and its opponents fearing that the Antichrist is behind these moves to form a world government.
- Theosophists fantasized about creating a unified world system that they would oversee with the secret guidance of a spiritual authority.
- And various others aspiring to create some form of world government.

Each of these stakeholders has its well-formulated interest in controlling the world both socially and politically. Many of them form tactical collaborations with each other where their interests align, while also maintaining autonomy and pursuing their agendas separately.

The Western globalists are wealthy technocrats (we refer to them as oligarchs) who promote their interests over national sovereignty using the UN machinery. Under the pretense of doing good, especially for the environment, they champion objectives like 'global cooperation in an increasingly interconnected world' to control the framework of the problems and the solutions. These globalists are perched at the top of parallel systems to circumvent the elected governments.

At times they collaborate with certain governments to push their agenda and at other times use their financial power independently. They influence legislative guidelines in sovereign states and fund NGOs to implement programs under the new laws. Oligarchs and Western governments use the WEF, UN agencies, and international consulting firms as evangelists of their ideology.

Is This Liberal?

In the following table, we point out the sharp contrast between this new Woke ideology driving these trends and the principles of traditional liberalism.

Tenet	Traditional Liberalism	Woke Ideology
Core Principles	Individual liberty, free speech, and equality before law.	Focus on identity politics and dismantle existing structures.
Individual vs. Group	Individual rights.	Group rights.
Free Speech	Freedom of expression for all.	Free speech for 'oppressed' but 'oppressors' must be canceled.
Equality	Equality for all.	Equality of outcome (= Equity).
Justice	Equality for all.	Rectify historical and systemic injustices by reverse discrimination. Restorative justice.
Economic Policies	Free-market principles.	Redistribution of wealth and resources.
Cultural Attitudes	Cultural pluralism and the coexistence of different beliefs.	Transformative social change to bring down the 'oppressor' identities.
Identity Politics	Recognizes individual identities.	Identity politics and weaponizing the marginalized.
Meritocracy	Rewards based on meritocracy and individual achievement.	Meritocracy deemed to hide privileges, to be toppled by equity.

Sustainable Development Goals 2030

The 17 goals and 169 targets of the United Nations' Sustainable Development Goals 2030 are intended to completely transform the world using its top-down standards and controls. It leaves no aspect of human life untouched—the environment, business, society and people, and even religious/spiritual private lives.

What is seldom mentioned is that public consultations in the development of these SDGs were limited and were engineered and funded by an ecosystem of globalists speaking for the 'public good'. A cabal of influencers, promoters, and international experts is championing these standards because they receive lucrative consulting contracts funded by the globalists. As a result, many public intellectuals have become aligned with the slogans without fully understanding the ramifications as they stand to benefit from the limelight and payouts they receive.

The UN and its affiliates use a logo with a colorful wheel and rainbow to promote these goals and targets. The goals seem honorable and lofty: sustainability, ending poverty and hunger, ensuring equality and education for all, and so on. However, there are several contradictions. For example, ending world hunger is made more difficult by imposing drastic practices for sustainable agriculture, as Sri Lanka has learned: It followed the UN mandate and suddenly replaced agrochemical farming practices with organic farming, thereby running its economy into the ground in 2022 with a crisis of food shortages. This created political instability. The crisis was the direct result of implementing untested UN targets for sustainability that left millions hungry.

Sadly, the parties being impacted have unequal power and participation. While the sustainable goals sound commendable at face value, beneath the veneer is a scheme that dismantles the existing structures in exchange for unproven ones.

A majority of the public is ignorant of the deeper implications due to the lack of transparency. Under the pretext of sustainability, there hides an entire Woke ideology of social justice, which now includes the sexualizing of children.

Colonization by Indexes

The SDGs framework is a master plan to bring the world under a gigantic social credit system, one in which the goals and standards are defined and measured by globalist forces at the expense of a nation's sovereignty. This grand plan is being implemented at organizational as well as individual levels:

Organizational level

Politicians and bureaucrats worldwide are helping import the SDGs standards in ways that often compromise the rights of their citizens. These standards and indexes are rapidly driving the lives of people across the globe. Industry, government, and NGOs have already been brought on board the SDGs framework using the Environment, Social, Governance standards pushed by the WEF.

These standards are not contextualized to a given country's level of economic development, institutional capacity, or social and political environment. Not only are the local cultural values and ethos ignored, but there is often no viable transition pathway nor the resources available to implement. This creates perfect conditions for external and elite globalists to dictate the 'norms of governance' in developing countries. Invariably, global issues creep into local development, domestic public policies, institutional structures, and social practices.

In effect, *these standards comprise a social credit rating system to determine the compliance of a given organization, and hence, the level of financial and other support it will receive*. The 'S' (Social) of the ESG ratings is further structured as the Diversity, Equity, Inclusion movement. The definition of 'equity' is not to be confused with equal rights, as in the traditional liberal idea. Rather, it refers to a quota system in which identities deemed to be 'oppressed' become privileged and there is reverse discrimination against those using merit to get ahead. This is quintessential Wokeism becoming entrenched in human resource departments worldwide.

Individual level

Sustainable Development Goals 2030 also requires countries to overhaul their education systems using Social Emotional Learning standards that are being sold as the education of the future. The attractive verbiage calls for 'mainstreaming education for global citizenship, sustainable development, and climate change into national curricula'.[3]

However, hidden in these standards there lies a particular kind of sex education called Comprehensive Sexuality Education. Education curricula are increasingly incorporating SDGs that include SEL and CSE. These curricula are being developed and implemented by the UN's affiliated NGOs which we shall discuss in detail in dedicated chapters.

In effect, compliance with the SDGs is leading to the young generation being brainwashed through educational curricula infused with Critical Race Theory (CRT), Queer Theory, anti-nationalism, etc., all under the authority of international experts with no love for India or its traditions. These programs indoctrinate children into a collective and emotionally charged mindset of hyperactive sexuality, environmentalism, global citizenship, and activism. The recent anti-Semitic outbursts on university campuses in the USA will impact India sooner than most people anticipate, and this mindset is being developed in Indian schoolchildren from an early age.

Do We Want a World Government?

A self-proclaimed 'globalist' and United Nations legal affairs official admitted that the UN is 'ninety-five percent useless' in fulfilling its primary mission of maintaining international peace and security.[4] However, he added that 'one of the UN's objectives is to create an identity of a global citizen.... [A global citizen is] someone who shares a political identity with everybody on the planet... They created this institution [UN], which is the closest we've ever got to kind of a one world government'.[5]

Through its many programs (for example, the International

Treaty on Pandemic Prevention, Preparedness and Response discussed in a later chapter), the UN is slowly eroding national sovereignty to establish global governance. The United Nations Educational, Scientific and Cultural Organization (UNESCO), focuses primarily on children's education to cultivate a generation that prioritizes globalism over nationalism, using brainwashing programs such as SEL and CSE.

The Vedic worldview considers the world as a unified spiritual entity, seen from a higher state of Consciousness. In contrast, the UN's globalist perspective, rooted in Western Marxist ideas, stems from the ego; therefore, it seeks to control the world even if that necessitates tyrannical means. This is because Western social sciences lack spiritual understanding and depth to transcend the ego. Consequently, globalists view a one-world government as a pathway to acquiring power.

The globalists make inroads using local individuals situated in positions of government responsibility and their close family members. Global policies are being forced upon member nations as politicians and bureaucrats pay lip service to their citizens while allowing external forces to run their nations.

The oligarchs who aspire to rule humanity in the hi-tech world have made their plans explicit and clear. They are using the UN and other global organizations like WEF to bring the entire world under *their* vision for humanity. The ultimate effect is to enslave people using the UN's machinery to control governments everywhere. The umbrella of sustainability makes all this look credible.

However, we must raise the following issues:

- Will there be a global government, howsoever amorphous, of which we will all be citizens?
- If so, who will rule this global government?
- Who establishes the criteria and frameworks, sets the standards, and with which civilization's lens?
- Who gets to be the judge and enforcer of these standards, with punishments for non-compliance?

- What will be the rights and obligations of this global citizenship?
- What will be the accountability of the governing global elite?

Klaus Schwab, founder and chairman of the World Economic Forum, gave a hint by saying that *holding democratic elections will become futile because Artificial Intelligence (AI) can pick leaders better than humans*. The WEF is on a mission to reset the world and bring about a new World Order ruled by the globalist elites. This involves ridding countries of their sovereignty or at least diluting it. Schwab has publicly boasted that the WEF, through its Young Global Leaders program has penetrated various governments.[6] (India's Smriti Irani, a prominent member of the ruling Bharatiya Janata Party {BJP} is one example of such a WEF global leader.)

The WEF and its billionaire club wield enormous power over the United Nations to push towards one World Order, global citizenship, and the SDGs 2030 agenda. Brainwashing the next generation into these ideas is crucial for the success of this ambition. The education system is therefore the latest target. A generation of children indoctrinated with CSE and SEL education will be the ideal compliant workforce that will dovetail seamlessly into corporations governed by the ESGs. This grand global plan is being implemented brick by brick, with K-12 (kindergarten to grade twelfth) education as the foundation.

Recent technological breakthroughs have weaponized these globalist ambitions with Artificial Intelligence and related technologies. As explained in Rajiv Malhotra's book, *Artificial Intelligence and the Future of Power*, AI is an unprecedented force multiplier of its owner's power. Far from being ideologically neutral, it is the most powerful weapon for indoctrination ever invented.

Add to this the idea of transhumanism, the theory that humans can (and should) evolve into super-humans using science and technology. This was initially expounded by Julian Huxley (1887-1975), a eugenicist with a dystopian worldview, who served as the first director-general of UNESCO. The Israeli writer, Yuval Noah

Harari, supported by Bill Gates and WEF, is also an influential proponent of this idea.

The UN also favors open migration into countries under the pretext of achieving SDGs 2030. The director general of the UN's International Organization for Migration claimed: 'We won't reach the Sustainable Development goals if we don't harness the power of migration'[7] and therefore have devised a framework 'for addressing migration's challenges, and harnessing migration's benefits'.[8] Ignoring the problems of illegal migration that burdens nations and causes instability, the UN states that 'Migration is a powerful driver of development. For business and societies, migration is filling critical gaps in the labor market'.[9] While legal migration offers this benefit, illegal migration overrides sovereignty and facilitates the globalist agenda.

The diagram that follows shows these ideologies and some of the leading organizations we will later discuss in detail.

Example of Globalist Authoritarianism: The Pandemic Preparedness Treaty

The playbook to reset the World Order goes as follows: Create a crisis that disrupts lives and livelihoods. Then exploit the masses' desperation for some semblance of normalcy by withdrawing their fundamental rights under the pretext of public good, such as restricting free speech, movement, and travel. And thus, use the disruption to usher in a new order with new systems to monitor and enforce.

The way COVID-19 pandemic was used for this purpose provides a glimpse into how national sovereignty and individual freedoms can be suddenly lost. We were pressured to give up our fundamental rights under the duress caused by public anxiety, panic, misinformation, and fear. In the name of the collective good through public health, individual freedoms were sacrificed in unprecedented ways. An entire infrastructure of vaccine passports, tests, and mandates was instituted to control and limit freedoms. Draconian rules affecting the movement of people were enforced through lockdowns and travel restrictions.

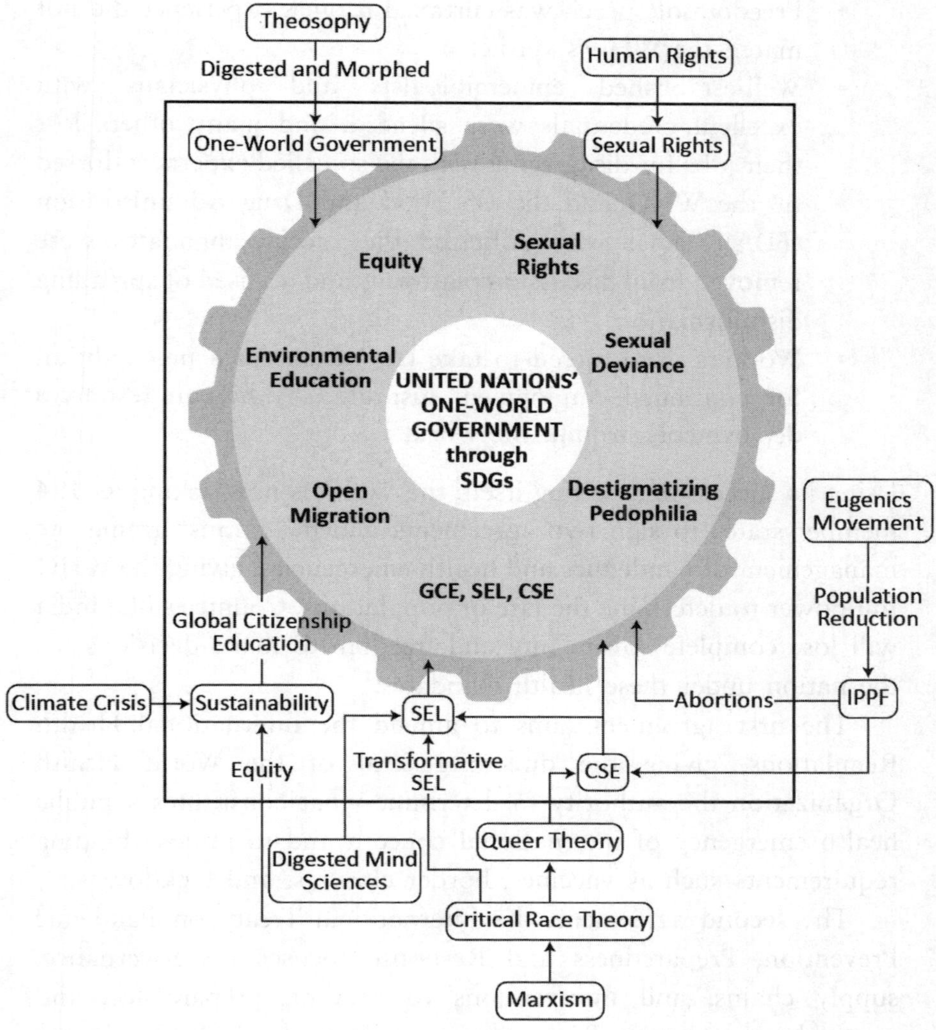

The World Health Organization (WHO) used this crisis to assume the role of a sort of world government, forcing countries to follow its mandates, and stripping ordinary citizens of certain rights. For example:

- Ayurvedic options for treatment were quashed and other viable alternate treatments were suppressed.

- Freedom of speech was curtailed if one's experience did not match the WHO's verdict.
- Well-established epidemiologists and physicians with excellent credentials were silenced, and many others lost their jobs for disagreeing with the so-called experts endorsed by the WHO and the US Food and Drug Administration (FDA). Those who criticized the vaccine mandates were removed from discussion platforms and accused of spreading disinformation.
- Workers were forced to take the vaccine as a precondition for continued employment instituted by human resources departments around the world.

Using its success in asserting itself, the WHO is now asking its 194 member states to sign two agreements aimed at transforming the management of pandemics and health emergencies, giving the WHO full power to determine the fate of populations. Countries like India will lose complete sovereignty and freedom to make decisions for the nation under these health mandates.[10]

The first agreement aims to amend the International Health Regulations, giving the director-general of the World Health Organization the authority to determine what constitutes a public health emergency of international concern and to impose binding requirements such as vaccines, border closures, and lockdowns.

The second agreement, the International Treaty on Pandemic Prevention, Preparedness and Response focuses on governance, supply chains, and interventions to prevent, prepare for, and respond to pandemics. Both agreements grant the WHO significant mandatory control over decision-making and actions whenever it declares a health emergency.[11] This will formalize the WHO as a world-governing body with the authority to do the following:

- Mandate vaccinations of populations including those vaccines that are gene therapies and not vaccines in the traditional sense.

- Prevent alternate treatments.
- Impose travel restrictions.
- Suppress any dissent on these mandates.

These agreements have serious problems, and the authorities have not been transparent in discussing the details.[12] Yet India seems all set to sign this treaty. Let us consider examples of critics who are fighting back.

Twenty-Two American States Retaliate Against the Pandemic Treaty

As the USA and other nations prepare to sign the WHO's new Pandemic Treaty, more than twenty attorneys general at the state level have written to President Joe Biden (at the time of going to press). They are highlighting the unconstitutional nature of delegating public health decisions to the WHO. They argue that signing the Pandemic Treaty would essentially mean ceding power to the WHO and this would violate the rights of American citizens. They argue that it would restrict their citizens' rights 'to freedom of speech, privacy, movement (especially travel across borders) and informed consent'.[13]

The attorneys general have raised several red flags about giving authority to the WHO to make decisions for Americans:

> The WHO's Director-General would achieve the power to unilaterally declare a 'public health emergency of international concern' (PHEIC) in one or more member nations. Such declarations can include perceived or potential emergencies other than pandemics, including climate change, immigration, gun violence, or even 'emergencies' involving plants, animals, or ecosystems. The more egregious versions of the proposals would authorize the Director-General to dictate what must be done in response to a declared PHEIC. In other words, America's elected representatives would no longer set the nation's public health policies. Even watered down, these proposals would inappropriately cede American sovereignty to the WHO.[14]

The letter pointed out the lack of disclosure and transparency. It emphasized that the 'amendment process has largely occurred behind closed doors' and expressed concerns about losing national sovereignty:[15]

> To varying degrees, these measures would threaten national sovereignty, undermine states' authority, and imperil constitutionally guaranteed freedoms. Ultimately, *the goal of these instruments isn't to protect public health. It's to cede authority to the WHO— specifically its Director-General...*[16]

The complaint letter stated that such a globalist victory 'would lay the groundwork for a global surveillance infrastructure, ostensibly in the interest of public health, but with the inherent opportunity for control (as with Communist China's 'social credit system')'.[17] The state attorneys general said that they would 'resist any attempt to enable the WHO to directly or indirectly set public policy for our citizens'.[18]

Protest by 164 Elected Officials from 29 Countries

In May 2024, US Congressman Chris Smith wrote to Dr Tedros Ghebreyesus, director-general of the WHO, expressing profound concerns over the Pandemic Treaty. Smith emphasized the importance of preventing tyranny and oppression: 'It is thus imperative that you honor existing treaties and international laws yourself'.[19]

He cited violations of the World Health Assembly (WHA) Rules of Procedure, including lack of due diligence and deferred disclosure of financial obligations, which could lead to confusion and undermine global health efforts. Smith outlined fundamental principles of the rule of law that must be adhered to, including transparent negotiations.

Smith warned that the proposed Pandemic Treaty would be illegal and urged adherence to good governance principles to demonstrate WHO's commitment to global health and the rule of law.[20] Appendix A includes the letter signed by 164 elected officials from 29 countries.

Pushback by Japan

In April 2024, tens of thousands of Japanese citizens across the nation came together in a series of rallies, a rare occurrence in Japan, to protest the WHO's Pandemic Treaty, expressing concerns that 'public health' was becoming a vehicle for an unprecedented push towards a totalitarian surveillance society.

One of the speakers, Masayasu Inoue, professor emeritus of molecular pathology and medicine at Osaka City University Medical School, issued a stern warning: Globalists are weaponizing public health to wage what he called 'a third world war fought with information'. He expressed anger that Japan might capitulate to pressures from the WHO and others like the World Economic Forum:

> Upon investigation, over 85% of WHO's budget turns out to be funded by pharmaceutical companies and stakeholders like Bill Gates Foundation, indicating that it's being directed towards their interests. This means *our health is being used as a weapon, and now we're amid a third world war fought with information,* questioning whether responsible adults are aware and able to protect themselves accordingly.[21]

Another eminent speaker was a professor of modern and contemporary Japanese history, Chikatsu Hayashi. His address was a call to the Japanese people and government to resist global totalitarianism, symbolically calling for 'stopping the third atomic bomb with our hands'. He is part of a national movement against the globalists that are threatening Japan's sovereignty:

> Let's stop the third atomic bomb with our hands, in the hands of the Japanese people. …Here, we vow to protect our children, to protect Japan. We stand against WHO, global totalitarianism, pandemic treaties, submarine IHR, genetic vaccines, 'plandemic', (sic) control of information, and declare to eliminate all these. Figures such as Tedros, Gates, Schwab, Biden, representatives of the New World Order.[22]

The Japanese public is speaking up against the use of 'global crises' like health for control and surveillance. They are demanding autonomy and transparency; they are questioning and challenging policies that disrespect their national sovereignty and individual rights.

Neuroliberalism and Authoritarianism

UNESCO has adopted neuroscience as a basis for 'transforming education' for peace and sustainability. This is being called a *neuro*liberal turn in the global education policy, a departure from its previous focus on democratic processes.[23] The term '*neuro*liberalism' refers to the use of neuroscience and behavior science for indoctrination. It entails using psychological techniques to manipulate behavior and nudge people with rewards and punishments towards alignment with its ideology.

Neuroliberalism emerged when educators realized that humans cannot be easily convinced merely by rationality. Therefore, it was decided that 'digital pedagogies', and subtle coercion are needed 'to govern via the mobilization of novel cognitive and emotional regulation strategies … to produce preferred forms of social conduct'.[24] This is a slippery slope leading to an authoritarian world government.

Social Emotional Learning programs are therefore being designed to 'correct' a child's attitudes and rewire brains. The goal is to create a person whose emotions are compliant with UN-defined global citizenship or sustainable goals. These children will have the 'correct' stance on contentious issues such as race, caste, sexuality, migration, and climate change. These SEL programs are aimed at making children aware of world problems, creating 'emotional resilience', and spurring them into action to solve these problems.

This trend is being challenged by critics who find it a reductionist view of a person as merely a physical brain. They believe that the political, ethical, and material implications of using this for implementing SDGs are a dystopian trend. Rather than *raising* children, SEL is *designing* them to fit their political agendas. This is being called 'techno-authoritarianism' and 'biological determinism'.[25]

Malhotra's *Artificial Intelligence and the Future of Power* explains the use of AI-based psychological control. Humans get modelled as algorithms and their behavior can be managed by top-down policies using global master-algorithms. The neuroliberalism espoused by UNESCO is precisely such a system. The UN should be fighting <u>against</u> the dehumanization of future generations through the top-down imposition of standards and homogenization, and the alarming use of AI for the robotization of human behavior. Instead, it has become a collaborator of global elites. Our children are being turned into robots controlled by the ideology of globalists.

A good example of neuroliberalism is the Bill & Melinda Gates Foundation's funding to reduce the resistance to vaccines and the promotion of Gates' position on vaccines during the COVID-19 pandemic. Partnering with Ashoka University in India, the Gates Foundation launched an intervention to attack people's belief in karma and surrender to the will of *Isvara* (God), by calling it 'fatalism' and superstitious. This preying on innocent masses is intended to undermine a nation's civilizational ethos. Once the civilizational fabric is dismantled, people become vulnerable to influence from Naxals, Marxists, and missionaries. We are not taking any position on vaccines but simply drawing attention to the way foreign-funded sources use Indian institutions to influence and change the behavior of the masses.

Redistribution of Wealth—Identity Warfare

The Marxist end game that is seldom stated openly is to bring about a massive redistribution of wealth and resources worldwide because the present World Order is considered to have been constructed by the dominant people and is therefore inherently oppressive.

Ironically, this redistribution will not undermine the ultra-wealthy oligarchs. They control these global instruments *and* the AI technology necessary to disrupt the old hierarchy and create a new one.

We see a future society with three levels of people, from the lowest to the highest:

A. Lowest strata: In the name of retribution, the poor ('oppressed' classes) will be made to fight the merit-based middle tier, and later fight each other. The oligarchs will remain beyond their reach and hence, untouched.
B. Middle strata: The success of those based on meritocracy, but who depend on their careers to maintain their lifestyles, will be sandwiched and hit the worst. From below, they will be attacked by the oppressed seeking wealth redistribution, and from above, their dependence on the oligarchs will intensify as competition for jobs increases. This middle-tier workforce is enabling the oligarchs to develop and operate their machinery, and yet will become dispensable and get squeezed. In effect, they are digging their own graves.
C. Top strata: The oligarchs do not need careers and plans in place to survive the havoc.

In the end, the ultra-rich will not get hurt by the cultural wars and by the redistribution among the masses down below. They will get wealthier and more powerful. The middle tier of meritocracy will suffer the most. The clash and redistribution are between levels A and B. They are the useful idiots serving the interests of the globalists/oligarchs.

Eventually, the 'oppressed' masses in level A will be replaced by technology. *The final solution the oligarchs want is depopulation.* This is politically incorrect to discuss, and the oligarchs do not want to show their hand. However, most of them have started supporting 'population control' initiatives, which should give us a glimpse of where things are headed. They use climate change as a euphemism to hide their depopulation agenda.

This explains why the oligarchs are aligned with the Woke movement—to disrupt the very same social, legal, and political structures that enabled them to amass wealth.

Comparing India's and China's Approach to Global Citizenship

The UN's original thrust was about diversity, the goal being to nurture decentralized communities with individual rights and freedoms. This has, however, been replaced by the goal of top-down homogeneity using the tenet of global citizenship that dilutes patriotism and loyalty to one's country.

UNESCO, the wing of the UN responsible for education and culture, is pushing the SDGs into every country's education system to groom a new generation of 'global citizens'. Such citizens will be engineered to imbibe homogeneous values defined by globalists and reject their respective native heritages. This large-scale behavior modification will dislocate the next generation from their parents and communities and make them hostile to their heritage.

The literature of the SDGs defines a global citizen as one that champions the goals set by the UN rather than the direction set by one's government and civilization. Children are being educated to prioritize the problems and values defined by the globalists while sacrificing the pride and values of national identity, civilizational grand narrative, and cultural heritage.

Being a global citizen requires toeing the line of the SDGs and this includes enthusiastically embracing all the Woke values—transgenderism, climateism, and the like. This education system is an indoctrination program to brainwash children into becoming obedient global citizens and to monitor them with a global social credit system.

A popular British scholar quotes the Brazilian Marxist, Paulo Freire's *Pedagogy of Hope: Reliving Pedagogy of the Oppressed* to explain global citizenship education:

> Global social justice is a major theme of the aims of global citizenship education combined with a pedagogical approach that is participatory, open to a range of voices and perspectives, and challenges dominant assumptions about the world. It is

> this clear value base around social justice that connects global citizenship to a pedagogy of hope.[26]

Here is the sleight of hand: The term 'sustainability' is used as the politically correct way to bring in all sorts of educational brainwashing. For example, the standard SDGs 4.7 titled *Quality Education* states that 'By 2030 ensure all learners acquire knowledge and skills needed to promote sustainable development' and this definition includes objectives like 'lifestyles, human rights, gender equality, promotion of a culture of peace and non-violence' and so forth.[27] And within SDGs 4.7 are embedded SEL and CSE because these are considered *a pre-requisite for sustainability*. The goal of SEL and CSE is to prepare children to become global citizens espousing the newly formulated global cultural values while dismantling traditional heritage in and patriotism for their countries.

It is interesting to contrast India's and China's approaches to adopting the SDGs.

India Compromises on Vasudhaiva Kutumbakam to Adopt the UN's Global Citizenship

Where is India in this fight for a new World Order? Does it have an agenda for its vision for such a future world in keeping with its Vedic heritage? And what strategy has India formulated in keeping with its civilization to adapt these global standards appropriately? The honest and unpalatable answer is 'none'.

India was part of the thirty-member Open Working Group (OWG) constituted by the UN General Assembly (UNGA) in 2013 to prepare a proposal on SDGs. However, *unlike the Chinese Communist Party's (CCP) deeply thought-out strategies, frameworks, and ambitious policies for a new World Order, India failed to develop any such cohesive Bharatiya doctrine. Worse still, forget the World Order, it even lacks a comprehensive Grand Narrative for itself. The question of leading the world does not arise.*

Only based on a robust national Grand Narrative could India pick and choose from the UN SDGs mandates and adapt them to fit its best interests—the way China has done. In the absence of such a comprehensive narrative, India lacks its framework as the reference point and has fallen prey to foreign nexuses with their established schools of thought to control the minds of its citizens.

In this state of dependency, India is being forced to join one of the competing ideological camps as a junior partner. While China has established itself as a contender with its camp, Indians debate whether India should join the American camp, Russian camp, some Brazil, Russia, India, China, South Africa (BRICS) camp; or whether it should be a gymnast playing one camp against another hoping to secure a place for itself as a sort of middleman.

For all practical purposes, India has become a client state that is eagerly complying with the globalist agendas and mandates as we show in Chapters 4, 5, and 6 and much of Part 2. Its 1.4 billion citizens have been made to 'feel good' with emotional platitudes and slogans like *vishvaguru* (the claim that India is the guru to the world) and 'vasudhaiva kutumbakam' (the entire world is one family), and 'yoga as soft power'.

The harsh reality is that India has been sold out by the Indian elites who are eagerly serving the globalists. Most Indian interlocutors have bought into the American apple pie and motherhood narrative and feel privileged to be invited as its members, even in junior positions. Some Indian billionaires aspire to join the globalists and become one of them. Many more are employees and consultants of the globalist machinery and enjoy the good life just like *zamindars* (the gatekeepers appointed by the British during colonial rule). This is a tragedy given the great heritage of India.

What is worse is, as this book will show, *India's sovereignty is at risk* because of the invasion of this globalist agenda deep into the lives of the next generation. *Our children are being weaponized to become warriors of the social justice army run by globalists, all under the aura of moral superiority.* This has been carried out meticulously by India's bureaucracy starting from the National Institution for Transforming India (NITI) Aayog at the top level (discussed in Chapter 10), with government ministries and state governments enthusiastically implementing the mandates from international nexuses.

Though the SDGs bring many benefits, in India they are also a brainwashing program that will unleash 'Gen BI' or Generation Breaking India using modern technology—all with the blessings of the Indian government. On the surface, India's minister for human resources, Ramesh Pokhriyal, claims that he wants to 'bring a new education policy that will be based on Vedic knowledge and science', and that 'ancient knowledge should become part of every discipline'.[28] However, he appears to be seriously uninformed about Vedic knowledge and seems unaware that their education policy contradicts the Vedic worldview. We will discuss the topic of education from a Vedic worldview in Part 3 of this book.

The government has reduced Vedic ideals to simple slogans like 'vasudhaiva kutumbakam'. India's minister of home affairs, Amit Shah said, 'The purpose of NEP is to develop citizens who combine national pride with global good with the spirit of Vasudhaiva Kutumbakam.'[29] However, vasudhaiva kutumbakam should not equate to the SDGs' definition of global citizenship that India has embraced wholeheartedly.

In his article titled *Education, A Guiding Light for a Shared Vision of G20*, the Union minister of education, Dharmendra Pradhan elaborated on the theme of *One Earth, One Family, One Future*, by incorrectly assuming that the principles of vasudhaiva kutumbakam were being followed in creating global citizens. He proudly claimed legitimacy for the G20's (Group of 20) education working group by listing the distinguished organizations and fields that comprised it:

> NIPUN Bharat, toy-based learning, 200 television channels, the National Education Technology Forum and the National Credit Framework to the creation of skill labs with Artificial Intelligence and machine learning, technological advancements in automation, the education working group (EdWG) under

> G20 will witness a wide spectrum of new ideas, learnings and practices that India has to offer.[30]

However, there were no experts from Indian Knowledge Systems included in this working group. In fact, Pradhan proudly announced the Indian government's international and national knowledge partners which include UNESCO, UNICEF, the Organization for Economic Co-operation and Development (OECD), and the Tata Institute of Social Sciences (TISS).[31] These are the very organizations that have hijacked India's education system in a direction diametrically opposite to the *Vedas* and Indian Knowledge Systems.

Later in this book, we will explore how India's education policy could be reimagined by incorporating core principles of IKS and Indian pedagogy. The University Grants Commission (UGC) of India has taken some baby steps to incorporate Indian Knowledge Systems into undergraduate and postgraduate curricula. However, this will fail *because K-12 education does not prepare students to engage with Indian Knowledge Systems later in higher education. Lacking an elementary foundation in the highly developed epistemological and philosophical frameworks of IKS, students cannot suddenly jump into it beyond the superficial and chauvinistic level.*

The National Education Policy 2020 clearly states that the Indian education system must be rooted in Global Citizenship Education, and superficially uses terms like ahimsa, *prem* (love), and *shanti* (peace) that do not fit into the GCE framework. The result is a mumbo-jumbo of jargon, ridden with contradictions using Sanskrit to create an aura of authenticity:

> Environment education will include areas such as climate change, pollution, waste management, sanitation, conservation of biological diversity, management of biological resources and biodiversity, forest and wildlife conservation, and sustainable development and living. Value-based education will include the development of humanistic, ethical, constitutional, and universal human values of truth (*satya*), righteous conduct

> (*dharma*), peace (*shanti*), love (*prem*), nonviolence (*ahimsa*), scientific temper, citizenship values, and also life-skills; lessons in *seva*/service and participation in community service programmes will be considered an integral part of a holistic education.[32]

An example of a contradiction is the approach to gender: Gender identities other than male or female have always been accepted in Indian society, but the idea of weaponizing them into 'oppressed' communities and training them to fight the rest of society is contrary to dharma. Marxism and its Critical Race Theory are incompatible with Indian Knowledge Systems, and yet Indian authorities have failed to debate such issues.

Several economic and cultural issues in the SDGs need to be weighed against India's circumstances and adapted or rejected accordingly. Indian children, however, are being taught to blindly prioritize a sense of global citizenship over their national identity in ways that undermine national allegiance. Indoctrinating an entire generation to perceive themselves solely as global citizens led by global experts and role models, would weaken India's autonomy and national identity. India is now bringing GCE into its curricular framework to ensure that Indian children are proper global citizens, *at the expense of valuable lessons on the civilizational Grand Narrative of India*.

The UGC's *Educational Framework for Global Citizenship in Higher Education* was jointly drafted by UNESCO and other experts to use SEL for developing activism:

> [The GCE] seeks to instill values among learners and equip them with the social and emotional skills and attitudes that can facilitate international cooperation. GCED seeks to ensure that all learners acquire the knowledge and skills needed to *embrace their social responsibility to act for the benefit of all societies and generate solutions to solve the problems faced by humanity*.[33]

The UGC believes that 'Social-Emotional Learning (SEL) plays a significant role'[34] in education and has included SEL in its standards for higher education institutions. The UGC framework even suggests offering a 'Short term Diploma or credit course…around theme(s) such as "Vasudhaiva Kutumbakam" for students'.[35] The UGC has bought into Woke ideas of environmentalism and global citizenship confusing them with Vedic ideas:

> These examples from ancient texts explicitly demonstrate that the concept of global citizenship is an Indian concept and not alien to us. The genesis of this ethos is solidarity with distant and unknown others. The meaning of "Vasudhaiva Kutumabakam" in everyday life was to understand humanity as a whole part of the extended family, without ever meeting those members of 'family' who are far away. Likewise, the respect for environment is not just about looking after plants and animals in my own neighbourhood, village or locality, but a commitment to the ecological well-being of all around the world. Such a planetary view of global citizenship was embedded in Indian ethos of global solidarity, with distant and unknown others, their communities, life-styles and culture.[36]

As we explain further in this book, the Woke definitions of diversity, equity, and inclusion are incompatible with Vedic frameworks of society, and the entire project of sustainable development is not grounded in Vedic cosmology.

By decoupling children from their native identities and heritage, they are being goaded and channeled into frustration and this anger is being targeted towards dismantling Indian structures that do not fit into the framework of Western Universalism.

Hence, the loose and careless use of the term vasudhaiva kutumbakam to mean global citizenship is irresponsible and dangerous. Most Indian officials who use it have no clarity on the meaning of either term.

The UN's SDGs 2030 agenda requires countries to commit to

teaching children to be worthy of 'global citizenship' under SDGs 4.7. Hence, GCE has become a mainstay in curriculum frameworks.

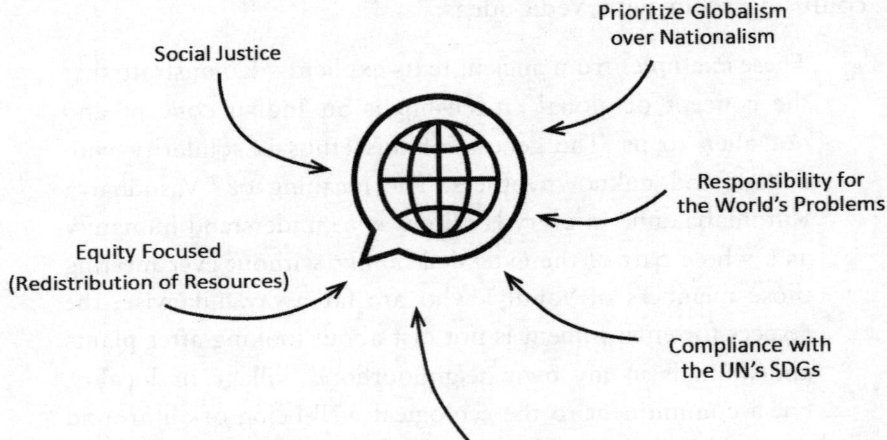

The international standards also differentiate between global citizenship *consciousness* and global citizenship *competence*.[37] The former is about having a cosmopolitan attitude combined with 'humanist principles', whereas the latter is about activism and teaches each child to take on the world's problems as their own. The latter is taken to the extreme of having guilt, wiping away one's self-identity, and questioning the validity of sovereignty.

> A more comprehensive typology containing two categories of conceptions of global citizenship in terms of their ideological underpinnings: the cosmopolitan type that represents mainstream models of global citizenship … and the advocacy type that refers to more critical approaches and tends to involve a strong degree of advocacy from a

particular perspective, including social, critical, environmental and spiritual global citizenship.[38]

In summary, there are two problems with this approach to global citizenship.

- Firstly, we disagree ideologically: Global citizenship is not about being aware of the world's problems and appreciating diverse cultures and heritages, but rather it is pushing the monoculture of Woke-based social justice ideologies on gender, sexuality, and racism.
- Secondly, it is a call to rabblerousing: It drafts the youth into the army of 'useful idiots' for a Marxist project to dismantle the existing power structure and usher in a new one.

As a result of NITI Aayog's glaring error in adopting the global citizenship 'competence' variety, by 2030 India must ensure that 'all learners acquire the knowledge and skills needed to promote 'sustainable development', which includes social justice causes, human rights, and gender equality. In other words, *India has committed itself to training all its young people to be compliant and think of themselves* *not* *primarily as citizens of Bharat but to instead align them with the UN on social, economic, and environmental issues of the world and teach them to use advocacy to solve these problems.*

We propose that the NEP must first develop children as solid citizens of Bharat and only then learn to become global citizens as ambassadors of Bharat.

China Refuses to Capitulate on Global Citizenship

China has a clear vision for preparing its future generation in line with its global ambitions. President Xi Jinping set the stage at the highest level when he shared his vision as defined by Chinese frameworks for solving global problems: 'fostering a new type of international relations and using the Belt and Road Initiative (BRI) as a practical platform'.[39] He presented an assertive foreign policy with a three-pronged approach to solving global problems the Chinese way:

- Global Development Initiative (GDI or 'Belt and Road Initiative')—presented to the UN in 2021 with over one hundred countries supporting it.[40]
- Global Security Initiative (GSI)—presented to the Boao Forum ('Asia's Davos') in 2022.
- Global Civilization Initiative (GCI)—launched in 2023 at the 'CPC in Dialogue with World Political Parties High-Level Meeting'.[41]

These doctrines comprise a well-conceived theoretical framework for China's version to build

> a world of lasting peace through dialogue and consultation; a world of common security for all through joint efforts; a world of common prosperity through win-win cooperation; an open and inclusive world through exchanges and mutual learning; and to make our world clean and beautiful by pursuing green and low-carbon development. It pursues the common values of humanity, follows the fundamental path of fostering a new type of international relations, and uses the Belt and Road Initiative (BRI) as a practical platform.[42]

As explained, India is very vocal about its unique heritage and traditional knowledge, and slogans like 'vasudhaiva kutumbakam', but in practice, it is towing the Western line and working hard to fit into the framework of Western Universalism.

However, unlike India, China clearly rejects the Western framing of issues like *social justice*, as expressed by President Xi Jinping:

> Each country has its unique culture, which is the foundation on which its own approach to modernization should be based. Only by respecting the diversity of civilizations will the world have a sound base on which to build lasting peace for the entire world.[43]

Rooted in its strategic thinking, Jinping dismisses 'the crooked path taken by some countries to seek hegemony once they grow strong', and states that modernization cannot be realized by 'a cookie cutter approach or simple copy and paste'. He asserts that China has its definitions of 'tolerance, coexistence, exchanges'.[44]

India has never pushed back in its foreign policy as China has. China defines its own rules for a new World Order, one in which aspirations are different and relative to each nation, with no nation imposing its ideals on others:

> GCI advocates against a world in which those concepts can have meaning through united efforts to call out and collectively act against those who violate them. Under the GCI, perceptions of such 'common aspirations' are 'relative' and thus countries must 'refrain from imposing their own values or models on others'.[45]

Clearly, China does not support the UN's definition of global citizenship that India has blindly adopted. This, then, determines the way children are to be educated: in China's case, patriotic to their country, but in India's case, the allegiance is to global interests overriding India's national interests. The Chinese neither teach the UN's version of global citizenship to its children nor does its education policy documents include it:

> The term 'civic and citizenship education' is not commonly used in China's educational policies and documents. Related terms in the Chinese context mainly include moral education and political education.[46]

The curriculum in China's secondary schools has a consistent theme of patriotism and identity. The trajectory of Chinese education in the past century is summarized in the table below:[47]

Pre-Communist Party: Confucianism	Collectivism over individualism; create loyal citizens with moral values; follow social norms.
People's Republic of China in 1949	National identity; loyalty to the Communist Party and collective identity.
Modernization policy in 1978	National identity; patriotism, hard work, pride in identity.[48]

China believes it is the center of the universe; hence, none of the above stages in its development espouse loyalty to so-called globalism. In a recent address to Chinese children, President Jinping laid out his priorities on education:

- <u>Patriotism</u>: 'serve the nation with absolute loyalty…calling students to break new ground for China'.[49]
- <u>Focus on science and aesthetics</u>: encouraged 'passion in science exploration', 'encouraging them to stay hungry for knowledge and foster their scientific spirit…importance of aesthetic education in shaping a beautiful mind'.[50]
- <u>Strength</u>: Physical fitness and wellness.
- <u>Industriousness</u>: 'life is built on hard work…Through work, you will not only sow the seeds of hope and reap the fruits, but also temper your will and improve yourselves'.[51]

Chinese scholars view global citizenship rooted in Chinese identity quite differently than the Woke ideas that India so eagerly embraces:

> …Chinese scholars tend to define global citizenship from a multidimensional identity framework with an *emphasis on the fundamental status of national identity while expanding the global domain.* … Zhou (2008) refers to 'global citizen' as *an international perspective on the premise of the establishment of national identity.*[52]

According to scholars, the course *Thought and Politics* taught to Chinese students contains some semblance of the UN's Global Citizenship Education, but it is adapted to emphasize nationalism. Though it teaches certain aspects of global citizenship, this is not the focus and is more like lip service.

The following is a summary of a study that analyzed the course taught in China:

1. China does not blindly adopt foreign frameworks and then reprioritize education policies based on them: 'The [logic of the] modules are based on China first, and then go out, looking at these issues from a global perspective'.[53]
2. Practical guidance on navigating the complex world of trade rules and international laws and Chinese culture and philosophy:
   - **Economic aspects of GCE:** Topics covered include 'global economy and global markets, international trade regulation, WTO, Critical thinking about international competition and cooperation, the rules of international trade'.[54]
   - **Political aspects of GCE:** 'Knowledge of sovereign states and international organizations, Critical analysis on the role of the UN and other international organizations, competition, conflict, and cooperation between countries, China's foreign policy'.[55]
   - **Cultural aspects of GCE:** 'Cultural development in social practice and cultural innovation (e.g., Western Renaissance cultural works, world-famous works). Valuing cultural diversity and respect for different cultures and how Chinese culture promoted world civilization'.[56]
   - **Philosophical aspects of GCE:** 'Philosophical worldviews of Chinese and foreign thinkers. The dialectical concept of interconnectedness, development and transformation. Using the dialectical method to explain the importance of critical thinking'.[57]
3. China teaches its students its ideas of diversity and global citizenship:

The teachers argued that understanding and respecting the cultural differences within China also contributes to being global citizens.[58]

4. China believes that global citizenship should not conflict with the nation; only when self-identity is strong, can a person have healthy attitudes towards others:

   Developing a healthy attitude towards one's cultural identity and group is (a) prerequisite to positive and reflective attitudes towards other cultural, ethnic groups. The teachers believed that one should have enough recognition and understanding of one's own country and culture to play a better role of (a) global citizen.[59]

5. China focuses on teaching its youth the Chinese grand narrative, with texts from the early Han period (206 BCE-220 CE), teachings of Confucius (551-479 BCE), and the Zhou dynasty (1046-256 BC). While the SEL and CSE courses in India are designed to break the family, China teaches its youth the importance of the family, identity, and moral values. China teaches its students to develop a 'Confucian' worldview:

   The participants considered the relationship between the individual, the nation and the world from a Confucian lens, where lies a progressive ethical requirement within these levels of identities, from self, family, nation, to the world (Tianxia). The multiple identities are interrelated in a developmental way. The steps to better the world are written in *The Book of Rites, The Great Learning* is: 'correct thoughts with sincerity, cultivate the moral self, manage the family, govern the state and safeguard peace under Heaven'. Being a moral person and running a harmonious family are prerequisites to being a qualified national citizen; being a qualified national citizen is a prerequisite to cosmopolitan beliefs, attitudes and behaviors.[60]

6. Notably absent in the Chinese global citizenship curriculum are topics like social justice, human rights, and activism: 'With a strong national narrative, GCE elements remain rare and discussions about global issues are conservative in the curriculum'.[61]
7. Under President Jinping 'the party has ramped up patriotic education... helping shape one of the most nationalistic generations of youth that the country has seen in years'.[62] The Chinese are instilling pride in the Chinese civilization and do not buy into the UN's methods to attain SDGs:

> Many scholars have highlighted the viewpoint of strengthening socialist civic education and cultivating national citizens who have a strong sense of national pride and adhere to traditional Chinese culture, while grasping new trends of global education in the face of the rapidly changing world. An ideal 'global citizen' in the Chinese context is thus an individual who adheres to socialist core values and at the same time has a strong sense of global responsibility, pursuing ideals of 'the unity of the world' and upholding the idea of 'harmony in diversity.'[63]

The CCP finds Hong Kong's 'liberal studies curriculum' problematic because it radicalizes the youth by including climate change and other topics deemed controversial. Jinping introduced an ideological education program starting at age six to align children with the Communist Party and teach them love for the country, the CCP version of 'Make China Great Again'.[64] They believe: 'Passionately loving the country and the motherland should be taught in the first class'.[65] In 2023, the CCP enacted a Patriotism Education Law:

> According to the law, patriotic education covers areas such as ideology and politics, history and culture, national symbols, the beauty of the motherland, national unity and ethnic solidarity, national security and defense, and the deeds of heroes and role models. The law highlights patriotic education for youngsters and children and makes stipulations regarding

> patriotic education for various groups of people, such as employees of government departments, enterprises and public institutions, residents of urban and rural areas, as well as compatriots from Hong Kong, Macao and Taiwan, and overseas Chinese.[66]

China is on a mission to truly uplift its citizens, instead of implementing superficial changes designed to impress the UN and other globalists. For example, China launched a 'Smart Education of China platform' which has become the largest platform of educational resources in the world.[67]

The New 'Breaking India' Force: Four-pronged Attack on Society

We will use the Vedic framework of four *varnas* to explain how globalists are undermining and trying to dismantle every aspect of our society. The term 'varna' here does not refer to caste or *jati* by birth but to the four distinct types of functional roles in any healthy society. These roles are:

- **Brahmin** (teacher): role to educate the next generation.
- **Kshatriya** (governance): role to manage the affairs of politics and statecraft.
- **Vaishya** (business): role to run industry and create wealth.
- **Shudra** (labor): role as the workforce to run the economic engine.

India's sovereignty requires control over three forms of capital, each of which has been compromised:

- <u>Ideology</u>: Brahmins are supposed to control knowledge, doctrine, schools of thought, and narratives. However, these are being imported mostly from the USA to educate the next generation, as the following chapters will show.
- <u>Institutions</u>: Kshatriyas and Vaishyas are the elites of society who are supposed to control institutions. India's

elites, however, are busy chasing foreign trophies of photo opportunities, name-dropping, craving prestigious appointments, and networking to climb the social ladder.

- Human resource: This is developed by the education system for the next generation. In this book we show how this has been abandoned to Western leftist ideas channeled through the UN, WEF, various NGOs, and philanthropies run by the oligarchs.

The Kshatriya, Brahmin, Vaishya, and Shudra social functions must each be healthy and work in unison for the well-being of society and the sovereignty of India. However, in the subsequent chapter, we will demonstrate that the exact opposite is happening.

The government must perform as the national-level Kshatriya, and in this capacity, it should protect its youth as the most vulnerable population. However, the Indian government is heavily infiltrated by the UN and other international agencies and NGOs, thereby compromising India's sovereignty. The UN's Sustainable Development Goals primarily target the Kshatriya (government) function. India's NITI Aayog is the government's natural nodal agency through which these SDGs enter India and penetrate all its domestic institutions. It has compromised the Kshatriya *adhikara* (authority of power and governance) to the globalists.

The government policies on education determine what the Brahmin function of society teaches as educators. Unfortunately, Indian educators are being driven by Western institutions of learning rather than the Indian system of education. Within the SDGs, SDGs 4 (Quality Education) includes mandates for Social Emotional Learning. Comprehensive Sexuality Education falls under SDGs 3 (Good Health and Well-Being), SDGs 4 (Quality Education), and SDGs 5 (Gender Equality).[68] The Brahmin (teacher) function has been disrupted by the development of educational standards based on these mandates. Part 3 of this book is devoted to explaining what India's traditional approaches would be.

The USA and India already suffer poor academic standards, and these standards have been falling even further. Yet, the priority and resources have been diverted toward sex education and Wokeism rather than practical subjects. *The whole purpose of education has changed from math, reading, and writing, to sex education, environmental education, emotionality, global citizenship, and social justice*. This corruption is preparing the next generation to dismantle itself, family, and country and culminate in the Marxist dream of a violent revolution.

This is more severe than what Aghasura did to the children of Vrindavan, because in this case the children are groomed and sent out to fight against and destroy their own families and traditions.

The <u>Vaishya</u> function must fund the educational initiatives in keeping with Indian values as interpreted by its traditional Brahmin exemplars. Sadly, the Indian Vaishyas are craving to be aligned with the global Western oligarchs and have sold out to get a seat at the table alongside the global elites. The Vaishya function is corrupted by enforcing ESG compliance on corporate houses. This amounts to a corporate social credit system that measures corporate virtue as defined by the globalists. The ESG index is the standard used to audit how well companies have incorporated the UN SDGs into their businesses. Now ESG has become widely installed as a management tool to change a company's behavior. It is a carrot-and-stick approach.

For example, a company is forced to be an advocate of the trans agenda, to increase the 'S' score of ESG. This is an extortion racket by large fund managers like BlackRock, Fidelity International, The Vanguard Group, and State Street Corporation, which manage investments of over twenty-five trillion dollars. These are pension funds that belong to ordinary citizens and the fund managers have weaponized them for their agenda. They have a large representation on the boards of almost all *Fortune 500* companies and use this power to force management to implement DEI and Woke marketing campaigns as part of enforcing ESG.

A corporation must comply with this mafia-like system, or else, its access to capital, insurance, and other basic services can be cut off or become prohibitively expensive. A company can also be de-banked for non-compliance and put out of business. Management's bonuses are often based on the DEI rating achieved and can even get fired if the scores are low. The need to maintain good ESG and DEI scores is the reason we see a flurry of transgenders in advertisements like Nike, Bud Light, and Starbucks India.

The problem is that ESG is subjective, and the criteria for measuring it are artificial. It is set by Western oligarchs and their financial and consulting institutions and is based on *their* values. The UN, the WEF, international consulting, and investment firms use their grip on industry to impose their ESG regime. *Environmental, Social Justice, Governance amounts to a Woke takeover of the Vaishya function of society.*

The Shudra function, being the masses, should comprise a well-educated workforce to secure respectable careers in the modern world and transform India into an economic power; they should live in mutual harmony amongst themselves across the boundaries of faith, economic strata, language, and ethnicity. However, the reality is that the Indian elites (Kshatriyas, Brahmins, Vaishyas) have sold them out to the foreign nexus, and these nexuses are mis-educating the next generation of Indian youths to become unemployable, over-sexualized, and radicalized against their society.

Diversity, Equity, and Inclusion are now the well-established standards to undermine the quality of the workforce because it is based on the Critical Race Theory that divides society into oppressor and oppressed camps and makes them fight each other. It is not the diversity of thoughts, ideas, and experiences but of race, ethnicity, religion, gender, and skin color, assuming these to be the markers of oppression. Training of DEI seeks to identify and accentuate grievances of one identity camp against another. It is a mechanism to redistribute the resources to achieve equal outcomes, punishing some and rewarding others based on artificial or irrelevant identities.

It encourages a divisive society where victimhood is glorified. It undermines meritocracy and thereby produces a society that is less competitive than others like China.

Each of these four aspects of society is being corrupted by the globalists in what could be the final Breaking India battle:

- SDGs 2030 is directing the **Kshatriya** role (governance).
- SEL and CSE provide the framework and pedagogy for **Brahmins** (educators).
- ESG is required of **Vaishyas** (industrialists) if they are to receive investments.
- DEI within organizations is bringing conflict among the **Shudras** (workers).

Generation Breaking India: The Brainwashed Generation

When Rajiv Malhotra first wrote about the Breaking India syndrome (which we refer to as Breaking India 1.0), he exposed how the rural poor were being targeted by Marxist ideas on the one hand, and the evangelizing Christian machinery on the other. Rural areas were targeted by NGOs to create a grassroots uprising through Maoists and Christian missionaries.

Our subsequent book, *Snakes in the Ganga: Breaking India 2.0* discussed what we referred to as Breaking India 2.0. The book exposed how India's urban elite, the corporate honchos leveraging their connections with elite institutions like Harvard University, had targeted the highest levels of social, political, economic, and government institutions, and weaponized them to dismantle Indian society.

The present volume goes into a much deeper level that we call Breaking India 3.0. Here we expose a project that co-opts senior architects of India in the government, uses them as elite sepoys to thoroughly brainwash the young generation and decouple them from the nation, their families, and their cultural heritage. This is a continuation of the Breaking India project.

While Breaking India 1.0 was bottom-up and Breaking India 2.0 was top-down, Breaking India 3.0 is *inside out*, thus dismantling India from within by turning its children into agents of self-destruction. An army of foot soldiers is being produced in India to work like termites and destroy from within.

In Breaking India 1.0, missionaries and Marxists resorted to subterfuge and inculturation to indoctrinate the hapless public. Breaking India 2.0 infiltrated the core of Indian industry and its elites producing an army of white-collar commissars, who are foot soldiers in all our institutions through departments like DEI and using indexes of performance that are defined and managed by foreign nexuses.

Breaking India 3.0 is using our children against us, indoctrinating them to complete the Breaking India project. There is a two-pronged attack to turn children into an angry generation fighting against their very civilization and country:

- Make them uncompetitive compared to global benchmarks like China, South Korea, etc., especially in Science, Technology, Engineering, and Mathematics (STEM). This creates a massive population of unemployable youth.
- Over-sexualize them by introducing desire-affirming sex education and installing 'sexual rights' as a UN mandate being implemented by the Indian government and its affiliate institutions.

The diagram that follows shows the three levels of Breaking India working in tandem.

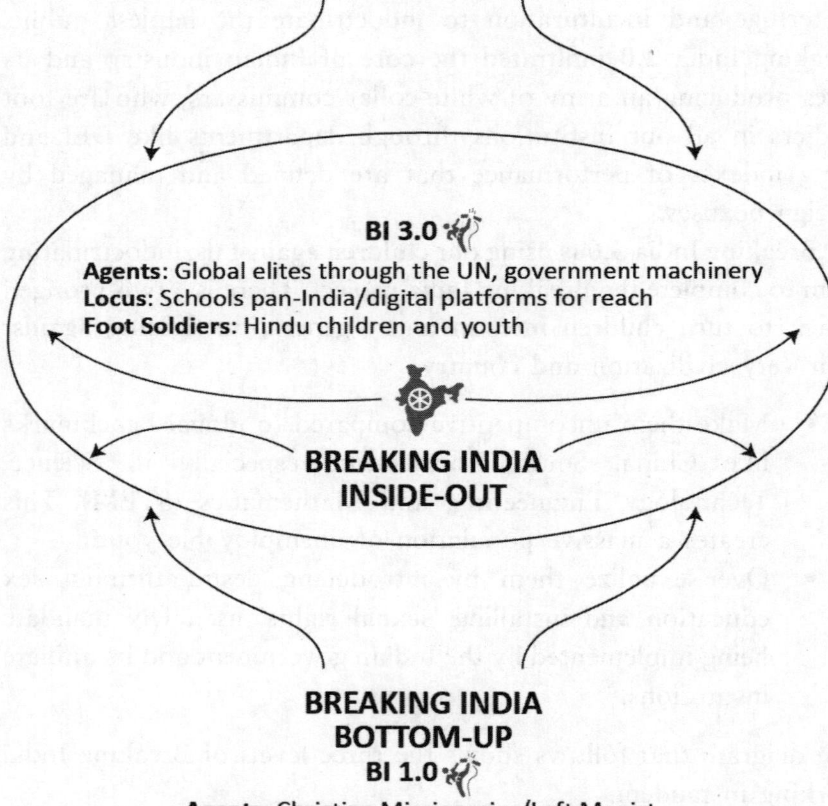

Destructive Education

It is irresponsible for the globalists and their Indian accomplices to rapidly scale a new education system that remains untested to study its effects. Furthermore, the average person has no participation in decision-making and the experts who are in control have never been elected. *As India's aspirational poor finally emerge from the ashes of colonialism to give their offspring a shot at a decent education, the elites have sold out their future to the globalists to ensure their subjugation.*

It is a matter of pride that many Indian youth have recently achieved success both internationally and domestically as entrepreneurs and thought leaders. However, as a percentage of India's very large youth population, they represent a tiny section. Our concern is with the state of the remaining ninety percent.As we noted earlier, present Indian standards of education are abysmally low, and too many educated youths are unemployed *and* unemployable. India has low average IQs compared to countries in East Asia and Europe. The takeover of education by the latest fads in Western society is only making things worse.

A recent study showed that young Indians are *more* likely to be jobless if they are educated. This demonstrates the poor quality of education relative to the need for employment or a fruitful occupation.[69] Solving this problem ought to be the primary focus of the education system. Instead, the CSE program focuses on driving children toward sexual pleasure and deviance, in ways that are detrimental to their mental and emotional development. Over-sexualizing children from a very young age prevents them from thriving in careers that are natural for them.

By keeping them sexually distracted and untrained in STEM or other employable skills, they will be subordinates or mind-controlled slaves of the West and China. They will be suitable as a supply of cheap labor or be groomed to fight social justice causes and bring about mayhem.

Children should be the main stakeholders in education. However, a dangerous generation is being raised as over-sexualized and undereducated with a sense of entitlement, driven by anger and revenge. India's youth dividend could turn into a nightmare if children get weaponized against their society.

Battle for Diversity

The divergence between Indian tradition and Wokeism is rooted in their respective approaches to diversity. Under Woke ideology, the biological categories of male and female are a social construct, and so is the boundary between an adult and a child. All social constructions were created by the oppressors to oppress and exploit. This oppressor/oppressed division of society is fundamental to Marxism; from this emerges the doctrine of mobilizing all sorts of 'victims' to overthrow society's structures.

The flaws in this logic are obvious: What about gender in animals or even plants? Is biology the result of social constructs created by human oppressors? The implications of Wokeism are outlandish and against the basic tenets of science.

According to our Vedic tradition, sexual diversity, and indeed all diversity, is innate in the very architecture of the cosmos. Divine consciousness manifests as the cosmos. The cosmos is nothing but consciousness *as* matter, and consciousness *in* matter. It is the divine expressing itself by transforming into a variegated universe in which differentiation and originality are innate. We call this *integral diversity*, which is diversity as the natural order in the cosmos. Therefore, diversity is not something that humans create. It is the very fabric of the cosmos.

However, when the ego synthesizes entities, it produces *synthetic diversity*. When individuals and institutions are fraught with maladies like selfishness, revenge and egotism formulate the policies, the mandates contain attitudes and orientations that are not aligned with the cosmic order. Imposing top-down targets to achieve those attitudes is not how cosmic diversity works and such initiatives by powerful egos go against the very nature of natural diversity. The idea of oppressor/oppressed categorizations based on artificially created identity groups (be it gender, sexuality, caste, or race) is all the result of the ego's false cognitions.

In truth, the entire rubric of Western social sciences suffers from flawed premises about the nature of humankind. These social theories are forcing diversity against the natural order and are hence, unstable. Social engineering through education is killing natural diversity by imposing artificial diversity. The importance of reviving Vedic social theories, rooted in the natural order of the cosmos, is becoming even more urgent to help organize society and address problems. *We must differentiate between integral diversity (natural) and synthetic diversity (artificial)*.

Wokeism is based on the fundamental premise that sexual/gender diversity is a human social construct, and hence, artificial. Since the dominant/oppressors created all the structures, the time is now ripe to take revenge by demolishing the old structures and empowering the oppressed to build new socially constructed structures. In other words, civilization is a battle between the oppressors and the oppressed fighting to control all structures. Under this worldview, diversity is a battleground.

The Indian government's implementation of UN-mandated CSE and SEL as the cornerstone of education has disastrous repercussions that will affect children adversely and take a toll on their mental and psychological health. It is subjecting children to peer pressure and nudging them in a certain direction. A good education should begin with spirituality and connect with the child's inner intelligence.

Furthermore, the Woke approach to diversity is self-contradictory. On the one hand, it considers binaries like male/female to be social constructs and wants to replace them with gender 'fluidity'. On the other hand, it introduces binary categories like racism/anti-racism, oppressor/oppressed, etc. This raises several questions: Why cannot one make choices on individual issues in an à la carte fashion, rather than being forced into binary camps? Why not allow fluidity of ideological views?

Disrupting Society by Sexualizing Children

The focus of this book is to drill deep into how this globalist disruption affects India, and more specifically, how it is stealing the future of our children by <u>not</u> educating them with the skills necessary to succeed in the competitive world. *In other words, India's education system has been hijacked to raise a 'Breaking India Generation'.*

A useful comparison is with madrassas ruining young Muslim boys by failing to provide them the academic competence required to build respectable careers in modern society, and by channeling their frustrations with ideology and anger to fight mainstream society in the name of Allah.

Let us compare madrassa education with the problem we are explaining:

- Worse than the madrassas, the weaponization of youths we are discussing affects not just boys but also girls and is driven by a secular ideology.
- Rather than training children to join Allah's movement, the child's anger is first built up using Marxist ideology. It is then directed toward a revolution to overthrow all those deemed to belong to the 'oppressor' category—including Hindus, the Jews, Whites, heterosexuals, and others who support them. The children are brainwashed that they must shoulder the responsibility to fight on behalf of the 'oppressed'—including Blacks, Muslims, Dalits, LGBTQIA+, and so on. *This indoctrination is being pushed as 'Social Emotional Learning' and 'Global Citizenship Education' by the United Nations*. A child belonging to a family deemed to be in the oppressor category is pressured to join the fight to dismantle his/her heritage and family—because they are considered oppressors. This is the root cause of self-hatred infiltrating college campuses today. The same is also spreading to schools.

Moreover,

- Sex education is now designed to indulge sexually and defy established norms; it is the fuel being used to propel the angry youth. We shall discuss this in considerable detail in later chapters. This new kind of education system of sexualization begins at birth and promotes sexual pleasure, masturbation, experimenting with one's sexuality, encouraging changing one's gender/sex both psychologically as well as physically, and so on. All this is being done bypassing the parents, because parents are deemed to be the 'problem' that must be defeated. The result is a breakdown of families, which leaves children dangerously exposed.

- Many expressions used in the education standards are open to multiple interpretations; these deceive the naïve public. For instance, the UN's standard for sex education uses the generic and benign term 'sexuality' but its NGO partners use this category to include controversial topics like masturbation, sexual desires and fantasies, eroticism, gender fluidity, trans-surgeries, etc.
- Meanwhile, children are not being sufficiently taught math, reading, science, or the ability to think independently, because the resources of the education systems have been diverted into this political agenda. Robots will replace them!
- Unlike China, India is not developing its laws independently in keeping with its national interest. In fact, the chapters that follow will give concrete examples where it has done just the opposite, like passing bills aligned with foreign interests. It is craving the Western pat on the back and has become one of the biggest importers of this new education system.

Sex education, environmental education, and global citizenship are the marquee issues being championed by the globalists, sidelining the need to make academic performance competitive with world standards. Traditional disciplines like reading, math, and science have been downgraded and the poor academic performance in countries like the USA and India has fallen even further, let alone reviving Indian Knowledge Systems and pedagogies. A generation of youth whose emotional quotient is destroyed and whose intellectual quotient has not been nurtured or developed is being created.

This is the cascading effect of the leftist takeover of the UN and related international bodies. It is the latest, and most comprehensive, plan ever to control the entire world: this time by indoctrinating children in the guise of sustainability. A chain reaction of social upheavals gets triggered that culminates in the breakup of a nation's social fabric.

India is blindly importing foreign frameworks *and* their problems and solutions. The holy books of the Abrahamic religions contain demonology of LGBTQIA+ and therefore had historical bans against such diversity. This has made it necessary to actively revolt and dismantle these abusive structures using an organized movement. However, the same historical problem does not apply to Indian society where nobody cares about someone else's gender or sex identity. Hence, introducing these revolts against social structures is not the right approach for India.

It is incorrect to pressure Indian children to become fashionable and join a politicized queer or LGBTQIA+ group. These groups require them to be trendy and pretend to feel a certain way by using artificial pronouns and gender identities. This is emotionally harmful because it makes them feel sexually inadequate for not having the right type, quality, or quantity of sexual experience in some popular identity.

Trans individuals should enjoy full rights and respect, but without eroding the rights of women in sports or private spaces like restrooms. It is also wrong to organize LGBTQIA+ people with anger channeled against those who live as traditional males or females.

To accomplish the violent and unnatural disruption of binary male/female sexuality and gender, children are being sexualized starting from a very young age. However, puberty should be allowed to take its natural course without introducing pressure to change one's sex and embark on gender transition socially and/or with hormone interventions. It is wrong to teach children below four years to touch their private parts, glamorize nonbinary identities, and access to transitioning/surgeries. Teaching self-indulgence has replaced teaching values like self-discipline.

A Hindu Perspective on LGBTQIA+

In *Snakes in the Ganga*, we shared the story of Deepthi Rao, a Hindu lesbian in the USA who discovered that Hinduism has always had a nuanced view of gender and sexuality. The ancient texts depict a spectrum of gender identities and sexual orientations, indicating a historical recognition of diversity: 'I studied Vedic heritage and discovered the numerous references to people being non-heterosexual,' says Rao.

However, as Rao got deeper into the American LGBTQIA+ movement, she confronted her new friends who were pressuring her into rejecting her Hindu identity. She decided that 'my Vedic heritage was much more important, even though I now face harassment as a Hindu!' Rao felt that the whole movement was a false and forced unity:

> *As a lesbian, I am certain of my womanhood and do not want a surgical sex change*. But the Queer movement denies the very concept of a woman, calling it a social construct that must be dismantled...Indians belonging to the LGBTQA+ community are being used by the Queer movement to provide them political strength in numbers, against our own civilizational survival.

We are concerned that the LGBTQIA+ and gender fluidity discourse is politicized and/or divisive. Heterosexual children forming the majority become puzzled by concepts that do not reflect their own experiences. Non-heteronormative identities should also be respected without anyone being made to feel overshadowed or confused. When we accept and embrace someone the way they are, there is no judgment, bias, prejudice, or label; we simply accept them as human beings.

A significant concern is the bypassing of parental involvement. In Hindu families, parents are the primary guides of their children who teach them the right values. The idea that schools or the state might impose certain ideologies is troubling. Such matters should be approached with sensitivity, preserving the family unit's harmony and cohesion. Rao powerfully states:

> What is needed is a movement within Hinduism that integrates, normalizes, and protects the LGBTQA+ people using Hinduism's own traditional resources. This is not just a matter of passive 'tolerance' of diverse genders and sexualities, but an inclusive movement…It requires structures, institutions, leaders, and resources. Otherwise, we Hindus will not only lose a large number of our people to the Critical Race Theory Movement, but also find them being used as a weapon against our own heritage.

The Americans Pushback Against Woke

Mainstream liberal commentators too are taking note of the absolute corruption of American institutions by the mainstreaming of Woke ideologies. Bill (William) Maher, a popular liberal comedian gave some examples of pushback in a documentary about rampant pedophilia with child actors using highly suggestive and derogatory sexual content on a children's TV network.[70]

Similarly, a *CNN* report discovered that young actresses at Walt Disney Studios were heavily sexualized from an early age. The report exposed the hypocrisy of liberals because when Conservative Florida governor, Ron DeSantis took up the issue seriously, he was dismissed as a bigot. Maher called out parents who turn a blind eye by selling out their children for fame and money:

> There are Instagram moms these days who are practically only fanzing [a popular porn site] their itty-bitty beauty queen daughters by having them wear skimpy bikinis and eat bananas to build social media stardom. They're called *Surenters*, a hybrid of sharing and parenting. *I call them pimps, a hybrid of pimp*. And people who believe in social justice have agreed this is wrong and this is bad and exposing kids to an adult world of lurid costumes and garish makeup borders on abuse.[71]

He goes on to talk about *Drag Queen Story Hour*, an event for children that promotes diversity:

> Maybe it's time to admit that sometimes Drag Queen Story Hour is more for the queen than the kids…And when I see a 5-year-old tipping at a bar under a sign that says it's not going to lick itself. Do I have to pretend that's cool, to keep my Liberal ID card?[72]

Maher feels that Wokeness has gone too far and is no longer an extension of liberalism. It has gone beyond advocating for inclusion and instead seeks to promote and entrap:

> And contrary to current progressive dogma, children aren't miniature adults wise beyond their years. They're morons. They're gullible morons who believe anything and just want to please grown-ups and they don't have any frame of reference, so they normalize whatever is happening. That's why endlessly talking about gender to six-year-olds isn't just inappropriate, it's what the law would call entrapment. Which means enticing people into doing something they wouldn't ordinarily do... Entrapment suggesting someone into something they wouldn't otherwise do. And if you think that some of that isn't going on with gender in schools, you're not watching enough TikTok videos.[73]

He calls out the activists who want to take 'heterosexuality, old school, old fashioned, boring, minding its own business, and lump it in with patriarchy and sexism and racism and tell kids, wouldn't it be cool if you were anything but that? It also seems to be the theme of kind of a lot of kids books these days'.[74] Maher thinks it is time to give children a break from the culture wars.

Sustainable Development Goals have been sold as a package deal for the future of humanity. Most nations lack the resources, sophistication, and self-confidence to carry out independent studies and be able to analyze and push back, except for a few like China. It is noteworthy that China weaponizes the UN to destroy other countries with these sweeping agendas while exempting itself from their harm; this is elaborated in a later chapter.

The newly self-affirmed Hindus are so excited about being recognized as a successful group that they have become blind to these realities. They have been co-opted under the aura of feeling good. The Indian elites are unable to push back because of ignorance, an inferiority complex, and the attractive rewards of selling out.

Artificially Conflating Issues

As discussed earlier, sexualization and LGBTQIA+ mobilization have become part and parcel of fighting racism and the sustainability movement. Therefore, if one disagrees with sexualization, one is likely to be declared a racist. This is a form of terror on campuses and schools. It is a way to silence the opponents in the name of diversity, anti-racism, and protecting the climate.

In other words, the education system is being gamified. The rule breakers are rewarded in the name of disrupting oppression. This is leading to campus riots and divisiveness. The coalition of the ultra-Left and Islamists is using these trans-LGBTQIA+ as pawns in their game. The protests do not emanate out of well-informed individuals making free choices, instead they are programmed activities backed by international funding and ideological training with the use of toolkits.

The following diagrams are a visual summary:

- The first diagram depicts how sexualization takes place through several stages. Initially, most people would not understand where things are headed as they appear innocent and even desirable. India is somewhere in the middle of these stages and therefore, few can see the grand scheme behind such a trajectory.
- The second depicts how problematic sex education takes them through stages that lead to isolation and a dumbed-down existence. This makes them unqualified to pursue fruitful careers in the modern world.

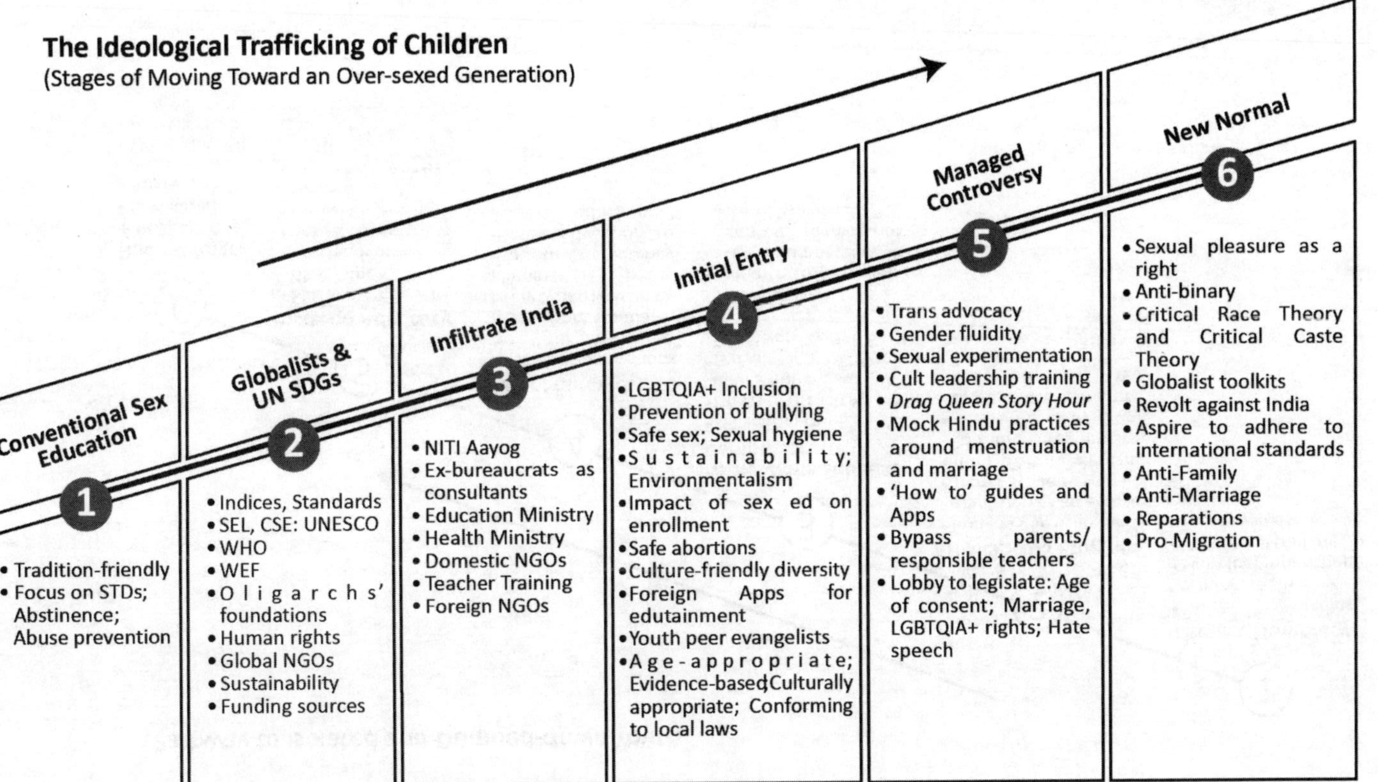
The Ideological Trafficking of Children
(Stages of Moving Toward an Over-sexed Generation)
1
Conventional Sex Education
• Tradition-friendly
• Focus on STDs; Abstinence; Abuse prevention
2
Globalists & UN SDGs
• Indices, Standards
• SEL, CSE: UNESCO
• WHO
• WEF
• Oligarchs' foundations
• Human rights
• Global NGOs
• Sustainability
• Funding sources
3
Infiltrate India
• NITI Aayog
• Ex-bureaucrats as consultants
• Education Ministry
• Health Ministry
• Domestic NGOs
• Teacher Training
• Foreign NGOs
4
Initial Entry
• LGBTQIA+ Inclusion
• Prevention of bullying
• Safe sex; Sexual hygiene
• Sustainability; Environmentalism
• Impact of sex ed on enrollment
• Safe abortions
• Culture-friendly diversity
• Foreign Apps for edutainment
• Youth peer evangelists
• Age-appropriate; Evidence-based; Culturally appropriate; Conforming to local laws
5
Managed Controversy
• Trans advocacy
• Gender fluidity
• Sexual experimentation
• Cult leadership training
• Drag Queen Story Hour
• Mock Hindu practices around menstruation and marriage
• 'How to' guides and Apps
• Bypass parents/ responsible teachers
• Lobby to legislate: Age of consent; Marriage, LGBTQIA+ rights; Hate speech
6
New Normal
• Sexual pleasure as a right
• Anti-binary
• Critical Race Theory and Critical Caste Theory
• Globalist toolkits
• Revolt against India
• Aspire to adhere to international standards
• Anti-Family
• Anti-Marriage
• Reparations
• Pro-Migration

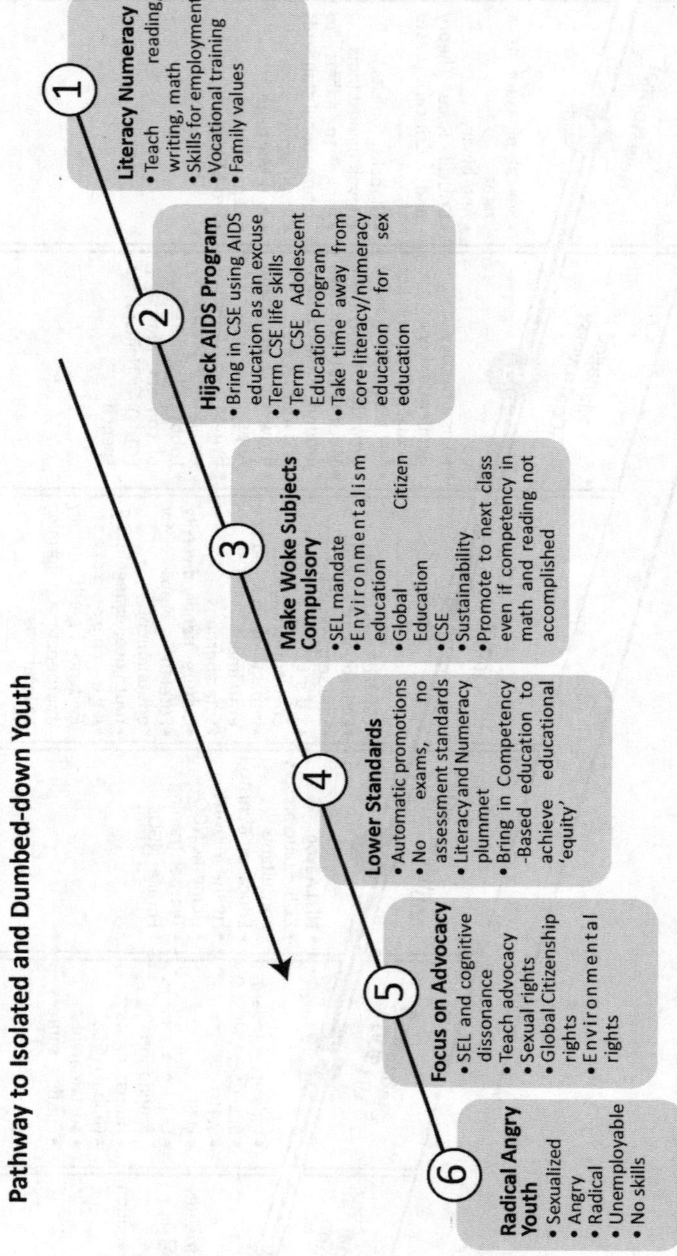
Pathway to Isolated and Dumbed-down Youth
1
Literacy Numeracy
• Teach reading, writing, math
• Skills for employment
• Vocational training
• Family values
2
Hijack AIDS Program
• Bring in CSE using AIDS education as an excuse
• Term CSE life skills
• Term CSE Adolescent Education Program
• Take time away from core literacy/numeracy education for sex education
3
Make Woke Subjects Compulsory
• SEL mandate
• Environmentalism education
• Global Citizen Education
• CSE
• Sustainability
• Promote to next class even if competency in math and reading not accomplished
4
Lower Standards
• Automatic promotions
• No exams, no assessment standards
• Literacy and Numeracy plummet
• Bring in Competency -Based education to achieve educational 'equity'
5
Focus on Advocacy
• SEL and cognitive dissonance
• Teach advocacy
• Sexual rights
• Global Citizenship rights
• Environmental rights
6
Radical Angry Youth
• Sexualized
• Angry
• Radical
• Unemployable
• No skills

Impact on the Family Structure, Society, and Country

The result of this education will manifest in what we refer to as Breaking India 3.0 at four levels:

1. Destroying the next generation with an education that sidelines employment-related disciplines like reading, math, and science while focusing on over-sexualizing the students and turning them into ideological warriors for the Woke army.
2. Destroying the family structure by influencing children to bypass their parents and fight against traditions and specifically targeting girls and *vanavasi* (tribal) populations.
3. Fragmenting society, economy, and culture by restricting Hindu education while giving greater freedom and privilege to non-Hindu educational institutions.
4. Creating civil wars among different identity groups, brainwashed from early childhood to fight one another as oppressed versus oppressors.

Demolishing the Family Structure

Parents aspire to raise their children, protect their childhood innocence, and pass on their culture, heritage, and values. However, they are now being sidelined as trusted custodians. The new education programs want to raise children through the mandates of the United Nations' SEL and CSE programs that impinge on parental rights.

Sex education is being imparted on digital platforms and AI chatbots, and these virtual entities are the confidants trusted by children. All kinds of Apps, government programs, and peer educators (i.e. other children recruited as evangelists to promote sex education) are educating our children. These serve as proxies for parents.

The next generation will be kept happy with sexual pleasure supplied to them virtually through various devices, AI sexbots, and other Augmented Reality (AR)/Virtual Reality (VR) technologies.

Children are becoming increasingly dependent on Apps controlled by globalists and their NGOs, and hence, losing their ability to think independently.

In effect, the government along with international NGOs are stepping into the role of parenting by using systems that circumvent parent involvement under the pretext of providing health care or education. Gradually, the parents are made to feel like relics and traditional parenting is considered obsolete. Such initiatives are completely contrary to nature, as they undermine the traditional family structure. Besides impacting the children, these trends also affect the mental health of parents and cause families to break down. This is a Breaking India Force because families are the building blocks of a society. Children disconnected from family and their surroundings are pushed into isolated bubbles. The result is a cultish mindset dominated by peers and Apps.

There has been no study, comprehensive or otherwise, on the long-term effect of such dislocation and dissonance. Nor has this been a topic for public debate involving parents, educators, psychologists, and other stakeholders. What kind of generation is being produced in such a silo mentality in which dissent and alternative views are blocked?

The Destruction of Hindu Society

As China has shown already, the educational goals and policies should be consistent with the nation-building needs of each country, and not geared to build a generation of slaves working in a Western-dominated world.

Indian authorities already see the dangers of allowing Chinese influences like TikTok. The Indian government banned the App because of its ability to influence young people and gather data that could be used to model their behavior. However, TikTok's ominous mission to spy and indoctrinate young people pales in comparison to the sinister mission of foreign CSE and SEL indoctrination programs that have been invited.

The CSE curriculum is antithetical to Hindu ideas of sexuality. While the same may be true of other faiths too, the issue is that only Hindu children and families are the targets of these radicalizing programs, because the minority institutions get protection from the Right to Education (RTE) laws. Schools of other religions are not required to subject their children to CSE-based sex education.

Unlike the orthodox view of the Abrahamic religions, the Hindu view of sexuality is not repressive or neurotic. Nor does it instill shame or guilt around pleasure. Sexual pleasure falls into the category of *kama*, one of the legitimate pursuits of life when carried out appropriately in a dharmic manner. However, as part of this dharmic system, there is a tradition of upholding *Brahmacharya*—a system that encourages celibacy while a child is a student. Further, we have practices of yoga (including *pranayama*, etc.) and fine arts that can help channel sexual impulses toward creativity and learning.

The UN mandates explicitly allow SEL to be adapted and made compatible with each nation's cultural environment and not conflict with it. A good example is how China has implemented its policies aligned with its national and cultural interests. However, Indians responsible for implementing the SDGs have failed to do so even though they use Indian jargon to impress.

Why can't Indians use their traditions to formulate Social Emotional Learning instead of cloning foreign versions? We have a rich educational heritage that made ancient India great, and yet India's modern education is not being modeled on Vedic metaphysics. This could be a combination of an inferiority complex, ignorance, and the ego's desire to be aligned with Westerners.

Destroying India From Within

By stripping the next generation of the right to a decent education, and prioritizing sex education as conceived in the West, the result will be devastating for India's future. Apart from rendering children mentally and emotionally traumatized, this will breed a generation that will be less competitive in the world, making them incompetent to contribute in a meaningful way to society. They will be living below the glass ceiling constructed by the West and be only worthwhile as cheap labor. Moreover, SEL programs indoctrinate children with a certain political ideology which is about advocacy and dismantling traditional structures rather than building society.

The Woke foot soldiers are useful idiots to dismantle society and cause chaos and instability. Because instability is hard to endure, people will do anything, succumb to any new rules, and forgo their fundamental rights, just to have a sense of peace and stability. We witnessed a panic of this kind during the COVID-19 pandemic.

It is not an exaggeration to paint India's future as overpopulated with a moronic and unstable youth clamoring for rights and handouts, and loyal to Apps that are remote-controlled by foreign NGOs. Their ideology will be aligned with the foreign NGOs grooming them, and not to their parents or India. This will create an army of unqualified and unemployable people with a sense of entitlement as promised by the purveyors of sexual pleasure and rights-based indoctrination. Such a generation will be intellectually and emotionally fragile due to a lack of inner civilizational foundation. We call this 'Breaking India from within'.

The chapters that follow will show that these programs and the NGOs implementing them are working partners of the Indian government. This reminds us of the way Indian zamindars, sepoys, and babus operated with the British because that layer of Indians bought into the idea of British rule as a civilizing mission under the guise of global progress.

A bipolar world with China controlled by the Chinese Communist Party and the rest of the world controlled by the billionaires through the UN and the WEF is becoming the new World Order. The move to digital currencies, electronic identification cards, and biometrics are all steps in this direction. Once the Woke radicals have done their job of dismantling societies, they will be rendered useless.

The West has a strong pushback movement against this agenda

of the globalists, and we hope that India does not remain deluded by emotional platitudes like the Ram Mandir, the Kashi Vishwanath corridor, election victories, cricket and Bollywood, and lofty slogans of 'yoga as soft power', superpower and claims to being the *vishvaguru*.

Provocative Questions for the Reader

This book systematically guides the reader through his/her introspection. Our goal is to equip each reader with the information required to make up their mind, decide the course of education for their young ones, and be able to articulate and defend their positions. We encourage the reader to ponder the following points:

Question 1: Islamophobia

- Should Islamophobia be banned, or should there be the right to criticize Islam just like any other religion?

Question 2: Wokeism, Censorship and Racism

- Should Woke ideas be considered like religious dogma in the guise of social justice?
- If one disagrees on sustainability or gender fluidity, does it imply one is a racist?
- Should free thought and debate be denied to those deemed to belong to so-called dominant identities because they are considered oppressors?
- Is it more appropriate to teach respect for everyone without making it political and divisive?

Question 3: Identity Branding

- If a given identity is branded as an oppressor or oppressed, does it implicate all its members one way or the other, or can there be oppressed individuals within the oppressor community and oppressor individuals among the oppressed community?

Question 4: **Revolution and Revenge**

- To remedy old injustices, is it a good idea to dismantle all the old structures of society, especially through violent means? Is resource redistribution the answer to inequities?

Question 5: **Sovereignty**

- Should non-Western democracies be pressured to conform to Western standards, indices, and mandates, or face denigration and even threats of sanctions?

Question 6: **Parental Authority**

- Woke educators argue that past systemic bias is being perpetuated by parents passing on their values. Hence, parents should be sidelined. Should parents control the way their children are raised, or should the education system control them? Do parents know more about what their children need, or do the activists who work for NGOs?
- Education on sexuality is becoming secretive in classrooms as well as through youth/peers and online Apps. Should youth peers be educating other children on sexual matters? And should parents know about their child's sexual health—HIV, abortions, gender transitions?

Question 7: **Gender—Biology vs. Constructivism**

- Is biological science right in saying that DNA determines everyone as either male or female, or are these socially constructed binary categories?

Question 8: **Sexualization**

- Should the legitimate rights of LGBTQIA+ drive education of all including teaching very young children to experiment with gender fluidity, and even have access to 'treatment' to transition? Is the best way to achieve acceptance of transgenders by constantly encouraging <u>all</u> children to

explore choosing their gender?
- Should the government sponsor sex change surgeries and cosmetic enhancements with taxpayer money?

Question 9: **Childhood Innocence**

- Is it a good idea to teach young children promiscuity and sexual pleasure as a 'sexual right' under the ostensible goal of reducing risky sexual behavior?
- Is it okay for an adult to have sex with a minor if the minor initiates and consents to such sexual activity?

Question 10: **Rewiring Children**

- Should educational institutions collect vast amounts of private data on children to rewire them into what are considered favorable dispositions?
- Should the system use neuroscience and psychology to nudge children's behaviors to comply with SDGs?

It is essential to understand the theoretical foundations of Marxist education and the language it employs, as these frameworks shape policy globally. The language used in policy appears to support our civilizational values while promoting ideas that stand in stark contradiction to them. The complexity and nuance of this language can make it difficult to discern the true intent. This book unpacks the sociological frameworks that inform such policies, revealing how carefully crafted language is used to gain acceptance while facilitating the Breaking India Forces on the ground. It is about *purva-paksha*!

This book is a critique of India's posture towards education to serve as a pre-emptive warning to avoid the pitfalls faced by the West. We have analyzed a pattern in other countries following various stages summarized below:

Psychological Violence: Pronouns ➔ Trendiness/Being Cool ➔ Intimidation & Pressure to be Politically Correct ➔ Normalization of Behavior

Legal Violence: Suppression of Free Speech ➔ Official Policy ➔ Exclusion of Parents ➔ Legalization ➔ Criminalization

Physical Violence: Transitioning ➔ Chemical Hormones ➔ Surgery

India is also moving in this direction with many of these very building blocks being laid. The same players that have created education frameworks in the West are playing a role in directing India's education system with no pushback from local leaders. The systemic infrastructure being established in India serves as a precursor to what lies ahead. Once India embarks on this education trajectory, it is nearly impossible to reverse the course.

In the concluding chapter, we propose a path forward by exploring Vedic principles on the purpose of life and the role of education through *samskaras* (values) provoking thoughtful discussion on various topics, including the environment, fellow citizens, humanity, and sexuality.

PART 1

THE GLOBAL GAMEBOARD AND INDIA

1

THE CLASSROOM AS AN IDEOLOGICAL BATTLEFIELD

Introduction to Wokeism: The New Avatar of Marxism

Marxism, Postmodernism, and Liberalism are three of the most important theoretical frameworks used as building blocks with various permutations and combinations to delineate a spectrum of leftist postures. Some leftists staunchly adhere to Marxism, others may prioritize postmodern principles, and yet others might be liberals adopting milder versions combining these.

The situation gets more complex if one drills deeper: Marxism, Postmodernism, and Liberalism are not single ideas. Each boasts a rich history characterized by internal diversity and numerous sub-camps, adding layers of intricacy to their study and application in societal contexts. The following historical overview traces the European roots of what is commonly referred to as the Left.

In the 1930s, a new iteration of Marxism, known as the Frankfurt School, emerged in Germany. With the onset of the Second World War, its leading figures fled to the United States of America to escape Nazi persecution. Among these were prominent German philosophers Jürgen Habermas and Herbert Marcuse, who played pivotal roles in attracting a new generation of American followers to the Marxist cause. Columbia University in the USA established itself as a significant hub for this intellectual movement.

Meanwhile, Postmodernism traces its origins to early twentieth-century France, evolving significantly through the contributions of leading thinkers. In the USA, the introduction and spread of postmodernist ideas were notably aided by key figures such as Gayatri Chakravorty Spivak. A literary theorist, Spivak was instrumental in translating the works of these French postmodernists into English, making their ideas more accessible to an American audience. Another pivotal figure in bringing Postmodernism to the USA was Homi K. Bhabha, originally from India and now based at Harvard University. The Americanization of both Marxism and Postmodernism positioned the USA as a global center for the development of new leftist ideologies.

Initially, Marxists conflicted with Postmodernism because Marxism relies on clearly defined binary categories such as oppressor and oppressed that are essential for its revolutionary aims. In contrast, Postmodernism challenges the very existence of such binaries, advocating that all concepts are social constructs subject to interpretation, thus resisting any absolute truths. This fundamental difference means that applying Postmodernism to class structures, as Marxism does, leads to contradictions that undermine the possibility of a Marxist revolution because a revolution requires clear distinctions to mobilize action.

Eventually, Marxists and postmodernists reached a form of compromise, creating hybrid theories that leverage the strengths of both frameworks. A notable outcome of this synthesis is the Queer Theory, which blends Postmodernism's deconstructive approach to categories with Marxism's strategy of mobilizing the oppressed to challenge their oppressors. Marxism on its own, with its deterministic and reductionist nature, would not lead to Queer Theory, as it traditionally focuses on economic classes rather than identity or cultural dimensions. Conversely, Postmodernism's core premise involves questioning and breaking down established structures and binaries, including those related to well-defined classes that Marxism requires. Queer Theory deconstructs the traditional binaries that define sex and gender, leading to the varied spectrum of identities encompassed by terms like LGBTQIA+. Thus, Postmodernism's influence is pivotal in challenging and expanding beyond rigid binaries, revealing deeper, often obscured meanings within social constructs.

Marxists are obsessed with power and have built an entire worldview to view everything through this binary lens of oppressed and oppressors. The French sociologist, Pierre Bourdieu expanded Marxism beyond the domain of economics by developing the idea that culture is a form of capital that the upper class uses to grab power for oppressing the lower class.

This concept has been applied to various contexts outside its original Western-centric frame, including in India. Here, the notion of cultural capital has been extended to include 'caste capital'. In this adaptation, caste is viewed as a form of capital that the upper castes leverage to sustain their dominance and perpetuate systemic inequalities, thereby marginalizing the lower castes. This application of Marxist and Bourdieu's ideas to caste illustrates how theoretical frameworks can be localized to specific societal structures. The application of these ideas to dismantle the Indian Institutes of Technology (IITs) has been discussed in the book, *Snakes in the Ganga*.

An important point is that *Marxism inherently seeks to redistribute wealth* by dismantling existing systems that perpetuate the current World and Social Order. This ambition drives the continual adaptation of Marxist theory, as it seeks to identify and undermine the mechanisms that uphold the structures. In its various revisions and updates, Marxism explores new methodologies and forms alliances with other theoretical frameworks to challenge, and eventually overhaul, the entrenched power structures and dismantle society.

After the Second World War, American Marxists formulated the Critical Race Theory as a new intellectual framework. Often associated with 'Wokeism', CRT posits that systemic, unconscious, and pervasive racism is embedded within the core structures of

Western society, affecting government, financial, and corporate institutions. This endemic racism perpetuates the oppression of certain minorities. The theory emphasizes the difference between being 'not racist', which it views as insufficient for dismantling systemic racism, and being 'anti-racist', by joining the fight and actively challenging personal biases and institutional practices to dismantle old structures.

The Critical Race Theory incorporates elements from Marxism, Postmodernism, and Liberalism, while simultaneously rejecting many of their central tenets. Paradoxically, many traditional liberals, who identify with a blend of these three ideologies, struggle to reconcile how CRT contradicts foundational aspects of their thought. This has led to a significant ideological clash within the leftist spectrum, with the emergent 'New Left', driven by CRT, challenging the established 'Old Left'.

The Critical Race Theory gained mainstream visibility following the resurgence of the Black Lives Matter (BLM) movement, which highlighted longstanding instances of police brutality against Black individuals in stark, undeniable ways. These incidents served as a catalyst, propelling CRT into prominent public discourse. As a result, it has become a significant topic of discussion across various platforms, including the media, educational institutions, and workplaces. This heightened awareness and discussion aimed to address and influence public perception and policy. Unfortunately, given the media sensationalism, most people did not understand that the moral halo of anti-racism was being extended to introduce issues unrelated to race, like gender.

While these goals are laudable and the problems confronted are real, some of the methods of redressal are ultimately problematic and more destructive than constructive. This calls for a careful evaluation of strategies to ensure that they truly contribute to positive social change without unintended negative consequences.

A major premise of the Critical Race Theory is that human rights must be fought, not by individuals for individuals, but by groups for their members. This is a predominant shift from classical Liberalism where rights belong to individual citizens and not to group identities. However, in CRT the social position of a *collective identity* determines the privilege or oppression of all its members. This is not about any individual, but the way one's collective identity is categorized and operates in society.

The following are prominent examples of the expanding coalition of the oppressed:

- Blacks are recruited against Whites: Birth of Critical Race Theory.
- Dalits are recruited against Hinduism: Birth of Critical Caste Theory.
- LGBTQIA+ are recruited against traditional family, sexual/gender norms: Birth of Queering.
- Muslims are recruited as ground fighters against the Jews: Support for anti-Israel movement.
- Sikhs are recruited against India's sovereignty: Support for the Khalistan movement.

The Marxist Theory of Education

The Western education system became the model based upon which almost all countries in the world design their systems and curricular frameworks. In particular, the American education system was the torchbearer of promoting skill development to produce the workforce for a capitalist economy. Elaborate approaches were developed and standardized tests were instituted to predict the success of students in the workforce. This education system emerged out of the need to serve the modern economy.

However, Marxists felt that societal hegemony was reproducing itself from generation to generation due to the education system. Hence, penetrating education became their master stroke to destroy the pesky problem of societal reproduction.[1] If done successfully, they could put a stop to the problem of society reproducing itself from one generation to the next passing on society's normative values—both culturally and socially. Thus, the goal of education itself was altered to turn children against their parents and weaponize them for the revolution, thus dismantling the family structure, the fundamental unit of society.

This is why Marxists decided to completely change the orientation of education—from being one that feeds the economy to one that is concerned with social justice and Marxist liberation. The use of the word 'liberation' has nothing to do with liberty or freedom as is generally understood. Liberation is about freeing society from the shackles of the normal—like traditional family structures, heterosexuality, preserving childhood innocence, and condemnation of sexual deviance and pedophilia. The focus of the Marxists has been on hijacking the education system to breed a new generation for jihad against civil society. This weaponizes children against their own families and heritage, and even against their merit-based careers. This agenda has unleashed a vast ecosystem of new ideas and initiatives.

The goal is to shift the focus away from literacy and numeracy and instead, push young children into life-long activism and resistance. Fighting for social justice causes, and more importantly, preparing children to become the next generation of social justice warriors has become the vision for a protracted intergenerational war on civilizations resulting in a Marxist revolution. This is what motivates Marxists to enter the school systems to indoctrinate children. And it is working!

As a result, American education is not the system that was once obsessed with excellence in reading, writing, and math. The goal is not to raise the standards of the workforce and contribute to society in constructive ways, but to bring about a revolution using social justice causes (LGBTQIA+ rights, feminism, abortion rights, migration) as a pretext:

> Saul Alinsky, the radical organizer and mentor of Barack Obama and Hillary Clinton, used to ask his new followers

> why they wanted to become community organizers. They would respond with idealistic claims that they wanted to help the poor and oppressed. Then Alinsky would scream at them like a Marine Corps drill instructor, "No! You want to organize for power!" That's the way the SDS [Students for a Democratic Society] radicals at the University of Texas approached the abortion issue—as a means to power, or, in Margaret Sanger's words, to remake the world. As a writer in the 1960s radical SDS publication New Left Notes put it, "The issue is never the issue. The issue is always the revolution".[2]

Marxist scholars decided to undermine society by challenging its moral boundaries and created new pedagogies to achieve this. They penetrated institutions, developed textbooks and teacher training courses to pose situational problems, to offer leading questions that stimulate the conversation between student and teacher, and thus indoctrinate the student with a Marxist lens. Children are encouraged to role-play specific Marxist dialogues to give voice to the oppressed by showing empathy, compassion, and being inclusive.

Slowly, pedagogy and curriculum have changed in K-12 schools in the USA because of this new Marxist orientation. Later in this chapter, we will show how this has destroyed American education. India is also quickly adopting these ideas of education, with NGOs, the UN, and the government itself all eager participants to wage a war for the minds of the young generation.

The following diagram shows the ideologies and forces at play that are revolutionizing the education system.

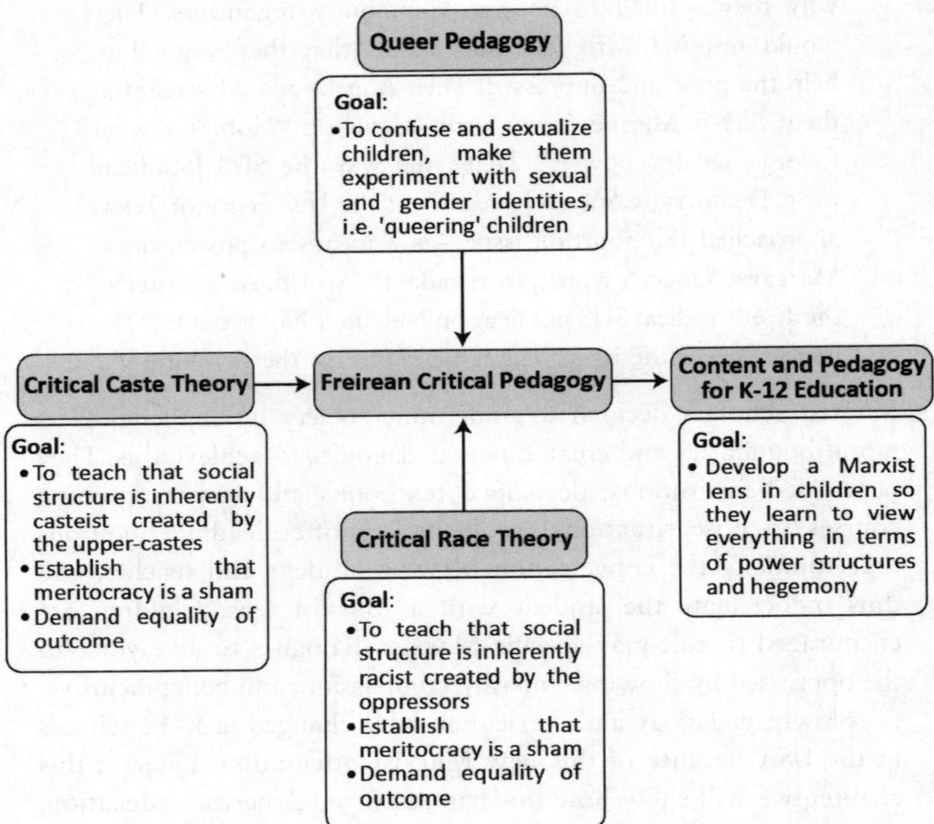

The Brazilian Marxist, Paulo Freire's seminal book, *Pedagogy of the Oppressed*, gave Marxist educators a theoretical framework to address the problem of society reproducing itself through established structures that are to be dismantled. His 'plug and play' framework allows for any social theory to be incorporated for dismantling the existing social norms. We will discuss two such theories that plug into Freire's pedagogical framework: Critical Race Theory and Queer Theory. Both have entered India's classrooms as we will discuss later.

Critical Race Theory and Critical Pedagogy

Marxists claim that pedagogies focusing on teaching marketable skills result in the reproduction of hegemonic social structures from one generation to the next.[3] The curriculum, school discipline, and teaching methods are all designed by the oppressors in a grand conspiracy to keep the oppressed down. Marxists believe education is thus always political and can never be neutral because society reproduces upon the scaffolding created by the oppressors to safeguard their position on the power hierarchy.

Consequently, Marxist education primarily intends to teach students to uncover latent power structures and motivate them to dismantle these through dissent, activism, and resistance. They have developed elaborate theories and praxis to turn students into angry activists who are driven to destroy society. In their view, the education system is responsible for reproducing hegemony and therefore the solution is also through the education system.

More recently, Critical Race Theory has entered American primary education in public schools. Children are routinely made to rank themselves according to the hierarchy of privileged status as defined by the pedagogy. They are taught that meritocracy is a myth because oppressors use it to uphold the systems of abusive power and hegemony. In *Snakes in the Ganga*, we discussed this new movement at length that considers science and rationality as products of the White and White adjacent (Asians) dominant cultures. Its proponents use Postmodernism to argue against any truth-claim being objective and insist that all knowledge is created by power structures and propagated by societal norms.

Freire laid the foundation for what is now known as critical pedagogy, the goal of which is to mold young minds to Marxist thinking so that they see hegemony and power structures everywhere in society. Freire argues that to have a cultural revolution and liberation, the lens of the young minds of the marginalized should be shaped to prime them for rebellion and protest. It is important to note that the word 'critical' in critical pedagogy specifically refers to the Marxist lens of looking critically at power structures and hegemony in all relationships, thus developing a 'critical consciousness'.

As the leading scholar in education from a developing, poverty-ridden country (Brazil), one would think that Freire's pedagogy would be on skill development to earn a living and become productive citizens with a healthy physical, mental, and emotional balance. Instead, his focus was that 'educators had an enormous responsibility to address important social and political problems'.[4]

His critical pedagogy is a framework designed to install ideology and hijack the education system by realizing that childhood is ideal for brainwashing and thus using education to bring about a Marxist awakening.[5] Freire calls this 'conscientization', a process of making students fixated on identifying the power structure of the oppressor-oppressed binary in all realms—within society, family, marriage, and even between the student-teacher relationship with an end goal of a cultural revolution.[6]

Regardless of the discipline, students are taught to inject their lived experience and refute dominant narratives and power structures. The desired result is dissent, resistance, demonstration, activism, pushing of boundaries and transgression, and empowering the youth to become activists fighting for social justice. It is no surprise then that the entire education system is inflicted with this virus, and the goal post of education has shifted from basic numeracy and literacy to awakening critical consciousness in the student.

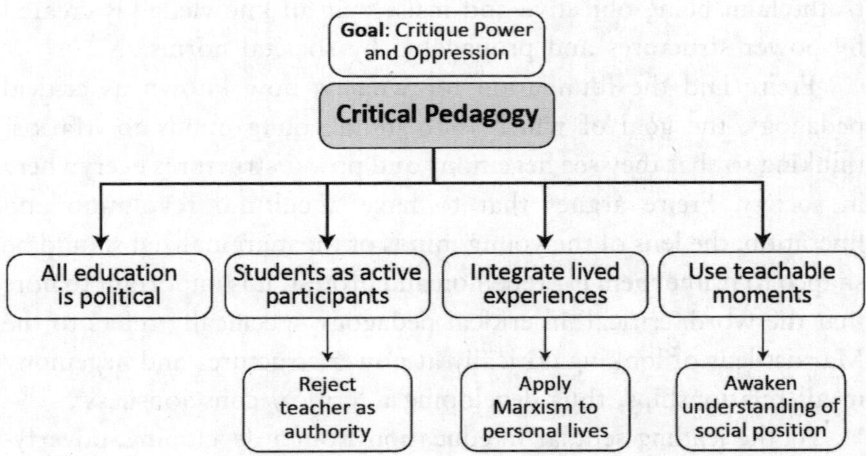

Thus, according to critical pedagogy:

1. All education is political, and the goal is to teach students to critique structures of power and oppression.
2. Students are not passive recipients of knowledge from the authoritarian teacher, and fighting the teacher as an oppressor is encouraged.
3. Students' lived experience becomes part of the curriculum so that Marxism gets applied to the personal lives of students. Victimhood is thus glorified.
4. The teacher uses 'teachable moments' to awaken students to understand their place in society and the surrounding power structures.

Freire's approach uses 'generative themes' in every subject to evoke emotions in students and awaken a sense of critical consciousness. Teachers are trained to have political conversations with young children and all lessons are embedded with political themes. James Lindsay, an American scholar says how pedagogy allows

> a seemingly benign and innocuous second-grade problem in mathematics class to show how a simple subtraction lesson can be turned into any number of political conversations about poverty, race, sex, gender, sexuality, family, parental authority, and environmental issues or climate change by a manipulative teacher-activist using the Freirean generative themes approach.[7]

Freire does not intend to genuinely uplift the downtrodden by teaching literacy or math but instead wants to create anxiety in the student's alleged/real powerlessness and get him/her ready for resistance. His pedagogy provokes children to dismantle the existing system of education and society. By making individuals feel inadequate or oppressed, they may be more likely to desire change and be guided toward specific actions or ideologies.

In psychological warfare, education and media are often

leveraged to spread specific ideologies or narratives to destabilize or challenge existing structures. Similar techniques are used to gradually change perceptions and behavior over time, ensuring sustained influence or control. The study of Freire's pedagogical material is compulsory for all teacher training and certification, even in India.

Freire's work was evangelized in mainstream education by the scholar and cultural critic, Henry Armand Giroux, and later by his student, Peter McLaren. Giroux, who is deeply critical of capitalism, admits that Freire's work gave him 'the language that enabled education to be understood as a political process'.[8] Echoing Freire, he writes:

> Critical pedagogy must be seen as a political and moral project and not a technique. Pedagogy is always political because it is connected to the acquisition of agency. As a political project, critical pedagogy illuminates the relationships among knowledge, authority, and power. It draws attention to questions concerning who has control over the conditions for the production of knowledge, values, and skills, and it illuminates how knowledge, identities, and authority are constructed within particular sets of social relations.[9]

Giroux believes that education is central to politics itself, and his goals for education have nothing to do with the acquisition of knowledge or skill:

> First and foremost critical pedagogy is about the struggle over agency. It's a struggle over how people define themselves, In their relationship to each other and the world. It's not just about knowledge. It's not about the consumption of knowledge, it's not about the production of knowledge. It's just about the relationship between knowledge and power. It's not just the method. It's far more than that. It's a moral and political project.[10]

Giroux is also against any objective testing on student performance, and by implication, meritocracy:

> Reducing pedagogy to the teaching of methods and data-driven performance indicators that allegedly measure scholastic ability and improve student achievement is nothing short of scandalous.[11]

He makes no bones about the fact as to how education must only be about the political Marxist narrative:

> We often see pedagogies that teach to the test, we often see pedagogies that simply (are) about accountability, objective standards, pedagogies that in no way take into consideration the experience of students, in no way speak to important social issues; There are pedagogies that in many ways are designed to undercut the possibility for students to be critical thinkers, to be critically conscious, to be aware of their own cultural capital and strengths and their place in the world.[12]

Critical Race Theory is explicitly against meritocracy. It states that outcome inequities are the result of a power-based system. The goal of CRT is to produce equal outcomes and re-distribute resources from those who earn through merit and hand them to designated victim groups as their entitlement. Critical Race Theory glorifies victimhood and hence, we see ever more victim groups emerging based on newer identities that are manufactured.

The 'anti-racist' movement has swept American schools where children in classrooms are classified as either oppressors or oppressed based on their skin color and other identity markers. This is being championed openly under the banner of Diversity, Equity, and Inclusion. Children are taught that America is intrinsically racist, and is present in its very DNA, without showing the progress America has made in race relations since the Civil Rights Movement (1954-68).

Giroux's Interference in Indian Education

In 2023, Delhi University (DU) wanted to scrap its four-year Bachelor of Elementary Education (B.El.Ed.) program and replace it with the Integrated Teachers Education Program (ITEP), a **one-year professional training program in education followed by three years of general undergraduate education (BA/BCom/BSc). Giroux along with** the UNESCO chair professor on Education for Peace, Social Justice and Global Citizenship, **and others wrote a letter to the** DU vice-chancellor **protesting this move saying, that while the four-year B.El.Ed. program was known for including** 'compulsory courses on story-telling, drama, gender and inclusion', the **one-year ITEP program merely instructs the teacher in 'transacting the text'**[13] 'rather than as a socially responsible and autonomous professional capable of interpreting and adapting the curriculum and inspiring her pupils'.[14]

Clearly, Giroux and UNESCO are worried that the one-year **ITEP** program does not sufficiently address the praxis of 'conscientization', which they consider vital for brainwashing. Giroux's popularity is also increasing in newly minted liberal arts institutions. He was recently awarded an honorary deanship at Hyderabad's Woxsen University.

Queer Pedagogy and the End of Childhood Innocence

One would believe that the purpose of sex education would be to prevent unwanted pregnancies and Sexually Transmitted Diseases, to maintain good sexual health and hygiene, and to raise awareness about the harmful effects of pornography. However, Queer Theory brings a completely new purpose to sex education. *The term 'queering' simply means dismantling whatever society considers normal, and blurring boundaries that typically serve as guardrails.*

Society considers as normal, a marriage between man and woman, a stable two-parent family to raise and instill values in children, protection of children from pedophiles, and any other kind of abuse. However, queer pedagogy teaches children to challenge these normative ideas because it considers normative behaviors as social constructs created by the oppressors. Society imposes and reproduces these norms to marginalize those who deviate.

Therefore, the goal of education must be to grab power from the 'sexually privileged' heterosexuals and hand it to the deviants. Heterosexuality is to be replaced by sexual fluidity, and the binary nature of gender is to be replaced by gender fluidity; abstinence, monogamy, and responsible sexual behavior are to be replaced by the pursuit of risky pleasure-based sexual encounters. The aim is to sexualize children right from kindergarten, encourage them to explore risky sexual behavior, push the boundaries, normalize sexual deviance (including pedophilia), and confuse them on gender and sexuality by insisting that these boundaries are fluid.

Queer pedagogy destroys childhood innocence and psychologically breaks down the child by sexualizing during early ages. Queer Theory's idea of inclusion is to destigmatize and decriminalize fringe behavior of all kinds, including pedophilia. The goal is to 'center' or normalize pedophiles and other deviants who have been relegated to the margins of society.

This ideology is taking root with a toolkit for 'queer' education for children. It includes the following tactics:

1. Creating confusion in children by:
   - Imagining that gender and sexuality are different; teaching children that gender has nothing to do with biological sex.
   - Teaching children that gender is fluid and can be worn like clothes depending on how one feels on a particular day.
   - Promoting myriad alternative sexual identities and personal pronouns.
   - Incentivizing children (through attention and celebration) to socially transition and try out genders on the spectrum.
2. Normalizing abortion and Sexually Transmitted Diseases as consequences that can be managed with ease.
3. Destabilizing children psychologically by:
   - Encouraging masturbation in very young children including preschool children.

- Introducing children to pornography and promoting sexual promiscuity.
- Encouraging children to explore risky sexual behavior at very young ages.
- Promoting 'pleasure' in sexuality as a 'right'.

4. Instigating children:
   - Into activism.
   - To challenge parental authority.
   - Providing support systems for gender transition, library books, and clubs for LGBTQIA+.
   - Seek mental health (based on Western models) resources, replacing parents with psychologists or internet life coaches.
5. Desensitizing society to the stigma of pedophilia and making it socially acceptable; decriminalizing pedophilia; and encouraging intergenerational sexual encounters.

Queer Theory was the result of applying Marxism to the ideas of sexualizing children that evolved over multiple social thinkers. A key figure was Alfred Charles Kinsey (1894-1956) after whom the famous Kinsey Institute at Indiana University is named. He is often considered the father of the American sex revolution. However, the conservative writer, Judith Ann Reisman shows that he manipulated the data sets of sex offenders in his research to make wild claims about sexuality. A serious allegation is that Kinsey sexually exploited children and even infants in his studies, and that he considered pedophilia a non-issue:

> Alfred Kinsey, and his view of 'children's sexuality', a view based not on children's experiences of their sexuality but on adults' experiences of their sexual interactions with children, using the one criterion which Kinsey found important and to which everything else became subservient: the orgasm. Kinsey wished to *argue that children have a sexuality which is not harmed by being used for adult gratification*, and thus he saw adults 'manipulating' children to orgasm as synonymous with

> children's own authentic and autonomous sexuality. His views on childhood sexuality have continued to *shape understandings of pedophilia and child sexual abuse* up to the present day. Kinsey articulated a view of sex in which the only 'abnormal' sex is no sex and therefore, by extension, pedophilia does not exist as a pathology or even as a separate concept. *Children – like animals, adults or wet dreams – are simply another 'sexual outlet' which may be used for orgasm.* Kinsey also argued persuasively that 'sex offenders' do not exist and so should not be criminalized. Neither of his two encyclopedic books on human sexuality deals with the reality of rape and nowhere is the concept of non-consensual sex addressed. According to Kinsey, therefore, it would be absurd to prosecute anyone for such an offence as 'pedophilia' or 'child sexual abuse', and indeed, his work has been used to argue for leniency and, more fundamentally, to revise legislation to make it less vigorous in prosecuting sexual offences.[15]

A further foundation for Queer Theory was laid by the American anthropologist Gayle Rubin's paper *Thinking Sex: Notes for a Radical Theory of the Politics of Sexuality.*[16] While Freire was concerned about education as how 'society is constructed', Rubin was concerned about family as how gender gets reproduced. Rubin says that 'the family was a structure whose task it was to reproduce gender'.[17]

In the Marxist framework, the 'means of production' of something bad must be attacked and destroyed, and in this case, the family is such a target. Marxism started out by targeting only economic exploitation, then expanded to include cultural exploitation, which has been interpreted further to include race, religion, and now gender as institutions of oppression. Since each kind of oppression is perpetuated by a specific means of production that must be dismantled, now the family has been identified as such and it must be dismantled.

Her critics demonstrate that Rubin defends sexual perversion, child pornography, and even pedophilia.[18] Empathizing with pedophiles whom she calls 'boy-lovers', Rubin is only concerned about the stigma they face:

> It is harder for most people to sympathize with actual boy-lovers. ... Like communists and homosexuals in the 1950s, boylovers are so stigmatized that it is difficult to find defenders for their civil liberties, let alone for their erotic orientation.[19]

Rubin attacks the age of consent laws that are meant to protect children from sexual predators, and in effect defends pedophiles:

> The law is especially ferocious in maintaining the boundary between childhood 'innocence' and 'adult' sexuality. Rather than recognizing the sexuality of the young and attempting to provide for it in a caring and responsible manner, our culture denies and punishes erotic interest and activity by anyone under the local age of consent. The amount of law devoted to protecting young people from premature exposure to sexuality is breath-taking. The primary mechanism for ensuring the separation of sexual generations is age of consent laws. These laws make no distinction between the most brutal rape and the most gentle romance…Nor are minors permitted access to 'adult' sexuality in other forms. They are forbidden to see books, movies, or television in which sexuality is 'too' graphically portrayed. It is legal for young people to see hideous depictions of violence, but not to see explicit pictures of genitalia. Sexually active young people are frequently incarcerated in juvenile homes, or otherwise punished for their 'precocity'.[20]

To destigmatize child pornography, she bemoans that laws have become far more stringent for the 'mere' possession of nude pictures of children.[21] She laments about the sorry state of unemployability of pedophiles and 'exotically sexed individuals':[22]

> Sadomasochists leave their fetish clothes at home and know that they must be especially careful to conceal their real

> identities. An exposed pedophile would probably be stoned out of the office. Having to maintain such absolute secrecy is a considerable burden. Even those who are content to be secretive may be exposed by some accidental event. Individuals who are erotically unconventional risk being unemployable or unable to pursue their chosen careers.[23]

It is worth noting that many social scientists who endorse deviant sexual behaviors are themselves considered to be personally indulging in perversions. In 2021, the French American philosopher, Guy Sorman, accused the renowned French philosopher Paul-Michel Foucault of pedophilia during his stay in Tunisia.[24] Sorman says that he witnessed Foucault pay money to have sex with little boys in Tunisia. This would not come as a surprise to those who know that Foucault in his works often defended pedophilia:

> There he argued that it was 'quite unacceptable' and an 'abuse' to assume 'that a child is incapable of explaining what happened and was incapable of giving his consent' to sex with an adult. (Note that Foucault takes it for granted that the child will be a boy.) It is a matter of public record, however, that Foucault signed a petition to the Assemblée Nationale in 1977 calling for the decriminalization of all 'consensual' sexual relations between adults and children. Foucault was impressed by the fact that the Greeks 'never admitted love between two adult men … [for them] love between two men is only valid in the form of classic pederasty.' He even told his biographer James Miller: 'Besides, to die for the love of boys: What could be more beautiful?' For Foucault, pederasty was the only truly romantic form of love.[25]

Likewise, Rubin used her lived experience to shape her social theories and rationalize her pathologies:

> Beginning in the late 1970s, Rubin, a lesbian writer and activist, had immersed herself in the subcultures of leather,

> bondage, orgies, fisting, and sado-masochism in San Francisco, migrating through an ephemeral network of BDSM (bondage, domination, sadomasochism) clubs, literary societies, and New Age spiritualist gatherings. In 'Thinking Sex,' Rubin sought to reconcile her experiences in the sexual underworld with the broader forces of American society. Following the work of the French theorist Michel Foucault, Rubin sought to expose the power dynamics that shaped and repressed human sexual experience.[26]

With this background, we can dive further into Queer Theory. Judith Butler, a lesbian known for her books *Bodies that Matter: On the Discursive Limits of 'Sex'* and *Gender Trouble: Feminism and the Subversion of Identity*, is considered the official founder of what is now known as Queer Theory. According to Butler, gender 'is a mix of cultural norms, historical formations, family influence, desires and wishes and psychic realities'.[27]

Gender has nothing to do with biology. Butler says 'gender performativity' defines gender norms, which means society conditions us to 'perform' gender roles by forcing the repetition of roles that are to be enacted like lines in a screenplay. She rejects the conformity to established norms by calling them social constructs, which has now become the widely parroted view across schools, corporations, and even medical colleges. The rejection of the male-female binary, the child-adult binary, and the fluidity of gender and sexuality have rapidly become mainstream.

Queer Theory has also entered India's centers of power. *In 2015, then-education minister, Smriti Irani announced that Judith Butler would be one of the first scholars selected to teach Indian students through the Indian government's Global Initiative for Academics Network (GIAN).*[28] Foreign social scientists like Butler were paid thousands of dollars of Indian taxpayer money for a single course. Butler's work is prescribed coursework in many social sciences departments in India. It is no surprise that she is invited to hold workshops at Ashoka University's gender studies department.

Indian queer theorist Pushpesh Kumar, a gender studies professor at the University of Hyderabad, wants to 'queer' Indian sociology and says that Indian social sciences have not taken sexuality very seriously because they ignore desires and erotic marginalities.[29] He wants to dismantle traditional Hindu rituals that celebrate female fertility through puberty rituals, claiming that this harms the LGBTQIA+ community even though he has not offered any data to support his claim.

The word 'queer' is being introduced in the classroom both as a noun and as a verb. As a verb, 'queering' children means indoctrinating them into the queer ideology. For instance, children are asked to pick pronouns and imaginary genders to nudge them to experience gender fluidity. Suggestive questions are used to start a conversation on social justice in Freire's 'generative' style of learning to contour students' minds. This is Freire's pedagogy to 'unlearn' the norms.

Even the field of statistics is being queered using the Freirean approach of generative themes to initiate 'intersectional interrogations' on the subject of LGBTQIA+:

> Introductory courses in statistics...may be an exemplary arena in which to queer course content and delivery. This is particularly true when considering the types of exercises, supplementary materials, projects, and discussions that can be incorporated into statistics syllabi. Perhaps the most salient development along these lines is the accessibility of databases that reflect the demographics and attitudes of LGBTQ-identified individuals. Instructors and students can find and retrieve information from, among others, sites such as LGBTData.com, a resource curated by Randell Sell at Drexel University; LGBTStats maintained by UCLA's Williams Institute; the Pew Resource Center Survey of LGBT Americans (2013); and the Population Research in Sexual Minority (PRISM) Health Data Archive (2019). While important and statistically relevant questions might usefully compare data

> reflecting LGBTQ populations with information obtained from straight-identifying cohorts, having access to sources of data exclusively associated with queer subjects opens the door to intersectional interrogations that take seriously the ways that race, class, gender, and a multiplicity of other identities combine to influence lives and experiences.[30]

Queering then goes even further on steroids, to invalidate the field of statistics itself because it is too objective and factual, and needs to be made fluid:

> Intrepid statistics instructors can take these exercises to another level – perhaps as a way of imagining a thoroughly queer approach to course content and development – by asking students to reflect on the extent to which our culture fetishizes quantification...To what extent do statistical analyses elide (elude) realities and concerns that might be better examined using more nuanced approaches.[31]

Drag Queen Story Hour *for Children: The Fox in the Henhouse*

One of the ways queer pedagogy manifests in the classrooms of very young impressionable children is through *Drag Queen Story Hour* (*DQSH*). While queer pedagogy struggles to define what a 'woman' is, *DQSH* promotes drag queens, who are biological men dressed up as flamboyant, provocative females for entertainment (typically associated with the gay culture). Men dressed as drag queens have entered schools to read to children as a way of teaching them 'inclusivity and tolerance'.

Craig A. Carter, a research professor of theology at Tyndale University in Toronto, and theologian in residence at Westney Heights Baptist Church in Ajax, Ontario states:

> Drag queens are homosexual men who dress up to imitate a crude and disgusting stereotype of woman thus insulting

> women and making it clear that they don't care what women think because they don't need women. Drag queens existed long before 2015. But suddenly drag queens wanted access to children in public. That was new.[32]

Harper Kennen, professor of gender and sexuality research in education at University of British Columbia, and his co-author 'Lil Miss Hot Mess' propose:

> Five interrelated elements of DQSH that offer early childhood educators a way into a sense of queer imagination: play as praxis, aesthetic transformation, strategic defiance, destigmatization of shame, and embodied kinship. Ultimately, the authors propose that 'drag pedagogy' provides a performative approach to queer pedagogy that is not simply about LGBT lives but living queerly.[33]

Leading critics of *DQSH* in the USA say that the 'kinship' sought through *DQSH* is a sinister deception, because it is a way to slip into the minds of innocent children and introduce them to queers on the street and form a kinship or relationship with them:

> Though Drag Queen Story Hour events are often billed as 'family-friendly,' Kornstein and Keenan explain that this is a form of code: 'It may be that DQSH is 'family friendly,' in the sense that it is accessible and inviting to families with children, but it is less a sanitizing force than it is a preparatory introduction to alternate modes of kinship. Here, DQSH is 'family friendly' in the sense of 'family' as an old-school queer code to identify and connect with other queers on the street.' That is, the goal is not to reinforce the biological family but to facilitate the child's transition into the ideological family.[34]

The purpose of *DQSH* is not for the audience to empathize with queer people. Instead, it is an attempt to evangelize little children into 'drag queen hood' and to recruit them as queers. The queer scholars are explicit about their agenda of encouraging children to experiment with 'becoming' and 'performing' as a gender different to their biological one:

> Rather than walking in someone else's shoes – and trying to understand what it might mean to be a different gender, for example – drag offers a model for participants to try on many costumes and cosmetics to understand how these elements reinforce or alter their own sense of self. In the classroom, this queer dress-up might create more opportunities for young people to experiment with the feeling of how and why seemingly arbitrary changes of clothing and behavior impact the ways they experience and are interpreted by the world. That is, drag is an imaginative and creative process. It is grounded in building character, both in the sense of constructing a persona and in better understanding one's own relations to others. This approach can support students in finding the unique or queer aspects of themselves – rather than attempting to understand what it's like to be LGBTQ.[35]

The Queering of the American Child: How a New School Religious Cult Poisons the Minds and Bodies of Normal Kids by Logan Lancing and James Lindsay, states that queer theorists want to indoctrinate children before adolescence when their ideas of gender identity are still unstable.[36] The *DQSH* uses 'glitter and fantasy' to capture the attention of children and exploit childhood innocence.[37]

In June 2023, *NBC* reported on queer and trans activists chanting: 'We're here, we're queer, we're coming for your children' at a prominent New York City drag march. The media brushed off this declaration as merely provocative:

> The 'coming for your children' chant has been used for years at Pride events, according to longtime march attendees and gay rights activists, who said it's one of many provocative expressions used to regain control of slurs against LGBTQ people.[38]

Such open proclamations combined with schools pushing the LGBTQIA+ agenda have been a wake-up call for many Americans.

It has been traditionally accepted that childhood innocence needs to be protected for the psychological well-being of a child. However, queer theorists assert that childhood innocence is a privilege of the oppressor class, and that the innocence of the oppressed was perhaps robbed due to sexual abuse at a young age. Hence, it must be destroyed to level the experiences of the privileged with the less fortunate.

Despite all the Woke pressure, most children's parents oppose *DQSH* as per a 2022 survey:

> The latest Rasmussen Reports national telephone and online survey finds that 60% of American Adults consider 'Drag Queen Story Hour' not appropriate for children, including 44% who say it's Not At All Appropriate. Only 29% think 'Drag Queen Story Hour' is appropriate for children, including 11% who consider it Very Appropriate. Another 10% are not sure.[39]

Montana is the first state in the USA to ban *DQSH* in public-funded schools and libraries, and prohibits any 'sexually oriented' performances at those venues or on any public property where children are present. Other states like Tennessee and Florida have followed suit.

And this is not just an American problem—*DQSH* has arrived in urban Indian schools as we will discuss in a later chapter.

The Strategy to Queer Our Children

The de-stigmatization of pedophilia has begun with scholarship referring to pedophiles as 'Minor-Attracted Persons' (MAPs). The goal is to 'queer' the age of consent; in other words, use Queer Theory to dismantle age boundaries, and position pedophilia as merely a transgression of boundaries. While the general population is oblivious to this, the effort to decriminalize pedophilia is being strengthened in the fields of sexology, patho-psychology, evolutionary psychology, criminology, sociology, sociobiology, anthropology, ethnology, and human ethology:[40]

> There are a 'plethora of publications that are positive' on this topic and that 'Intergenerational Studies has just begun, and…there are shades of grey and white in the discussion that do not appear in the literature of abuse'.[41]

Theodorus G.M. Sandfort, professor of clinical sociomedical science at Columbia University, is hailed as a hero by the pedophilia community for his book *Boys On Their Contacts With Men: A Study of Sexually Expressed Friendships* published in the early 1980s. He claims that adult-child sexuality can be positive for children:

> He wants to provide evidence that children do enjoy sex and are sexually active and therefore that age of consent laws which limit the extent of their sexual expression below a certain age do not reflect reality and should be altered or removed, thus de-criminalizing consensual sexual contact at any age. His second point is that people generally regard all adult-child sexual contact as harmful. Therefore, if he can prove any counter examples, the harm argument will be shown to be logically flawed. He has therefore gone out to find a sample of boys who will tell the researcher, convincingly, that they enjoy their sexual relationship' or 'sexually expressed friendship' – with men and that they find it 'pleasant' and therefore not harmful.[42]

The North American Man/Boy Love Association (NAMBLA) is an advocacy group for pedophilia and pederasty in the USA with a mission to normalize pederasty stating that it is merely another kind of sexuality, such as being queer or homosexuality, and thus belongs under the LGBTQIA+ umbrella. The NAMBLA advocates for relationships between adult men and underage boys, which it frames as a form of civil rights. Just as Foucault, Rubin, and

Sandfort want to decriminalize pedophilia and toss out laws on the age of consent, NAMBLA too has the same mission:

> NAMBLA sought to turn sex between men and boys of literally all ages into a civil rights issue, get pederasts to come out of the closet, and show North America that boy-lovers are people too. *Kids, says NAMBLA, should be able to decide when and with whom they have sex.*[43]

In fact, NAMBLA claims it is the children that often initiate a sexual relationship with an adult and that the adult simply indulges these children.[44] Even if this were true, it is well known that children who have been sexually abused tend to express trauma by showing such tendencies. They need therapy and not pedophiles to exploit their vulnerabilities. Clearly, Queer Theory-based sex education primes children for pleasure-based sexual encounters at very young ages by using the education system to give them agency for initiating sexual encounters with adults.

From both legal and ethical perspectives, the consensus in most societies is that children and adolescents are not able to consent to sexual relationships with adults due to significant differences in maturity, understanding, and power dynamics. Laws on the age of consent have been designed to protect minors from exploitation and abuse.

Historically, we have seen that pedophiles have sought situations where they can have easy access to vulnerable children, as proven by the countless cases of sexual abuse by pedophiles in the Catholic Church and missionary-run orphanages. *Drag Queen Story Hour* may become the new fertile ground for such criminals. In 2019, a local news outlet in Texas reported that a registered sex offender was exposed reading to children during a *DQSH* at a Houston Public Library:

> A media spokesperson for the library confirmed one of those drag queens, Tatiana Mala Nina, is Alberto Garza, a 32-year-old child sex offender...In a statement, the Houston Public

> Library admits they didn't do a background check on Garza and said Garza will not be involved in any future library programs.[45]

We will later show how the UN and other agencies are pushing sex education for three-year-olds on one hand, and trying to make sexual rights a fundamental human right on the other, so that children can initiate a sexual relationship at any age and will have a right to do so without parental consent. This will be the consequence of declaring sexual relations as a fundamental human right—not just for adults, but for everyone with no age of consent boundaries. The grand plan is to sexualize and 'queer' children by setting pedophiles loose on society to further dismantle the family structure and cause psychological harm to the younger generation.

The following diagram shows the various points we have discussed.

The Destruction of Childhood Innocence
by Early Sexualization of Children

Educational Interventions

Sexualize Children Through Education

Children Groomed for Pleasure-based Sex

- Introduce pornography
- Teach children to seek sexual pleasure
- Encourage them to take risks
- Prevent pregnancy not by abstinence, but by suggesting alternate forms of sexual acts

Legal Interventions

Lower Age of Consent

Decriminalize Pedophilia

Make Sexual Rights a Fundamental Human Right

Implications:

- Children have a right to sexuality
- No age of consent laws
- Parents have no say if a child wants to indulge in sexual activity

Goal: Set Pedophiles loose to dismantle family and society

2

THE UNITED NATIONS' MANDATES ON SEX EDUCATION

Social Emotional Learning

Social Emotional Learning is a multi-billion-dollar industry that develops programs for teaching children to manage their emotions and behaviors. The two men who played major roles in its inception were both trained in Maharishi Mahesh Yogi's Transcendental Meditation (TM).

- John Fetzer was a Transcendental Meditation practitioner who borrowed ideas from theosophy and developed a framework known as Social Emotional Learning through his Fetzer Institute.
- Daniel Goleman, a Harvard psychologist who studied meditation in India along with other Hindu and Buddhist systems, used this knowledge to conjure up 'emotional intelligence'. His books on the subject have been bestsellers and yet few people know about his unacknowledged debt to India.

John Fetzer

John Fetzer was a wealthy media businessman who made his money in broadcasting through his numerous television and radio stations. He also owned Detroit Tigers, an American professional team in Major League Baseball. He was raised as a Seventh-Day Adventist, which he rejected, and moved on to esoterism and theosophy. He practiced Transcendental Meditation, considered Maharishi Mahesh Yogi his teacher and brought the practice of TM into the locker room of the Detroit Tigers.

He was profoundly convinced of the concepts of karma and reincarnation and studied Buddhism among other spiritual traditions. He was an ardent devotee of the British theosophist, Alice Bailey (who had digested a considerable amount of Indian spirituality into theosophy and was among the first to use the term 'New Age'). Like the other theosophists, he wanted to unite spirituality and science.[1] However, Fetzer was also mapping Indian spiritual knowledge onto Christianity and spoke of 'universal Christ consciousness' and 'infinite intelligence'.

Fetzer was ahead of his time in the West using meditation techniques with his professional sports team to help him succeed:

> Fetzer's lifelong fixation (was) on maintaining a positive outlook, aided by techniques such as meditation to reduce stress, verbal affirmations to build determination and visualizations to mentally rehearse success, according to the book. Those techniques have since become second nature to professional athletes and been popularized in 'how-to' books for the public, showing that Fetzer was ahead of his time in applying practical psychology to life's challenges.[2]

He was frustrated with the existing preventative emotional health programs in the USA and searched for solutions. In 1994, his non-profit foundation, The Fetzer Institute, held a conference at Yale Child Study Center, bringing various researchers to work on emotional intelligence whose purpose was 'focused on relationships between people'.[3]

Thus, Social Emotional Learning was born as a framework to tackle emotional and psychological health issues in schools:

> In attendance were a range of researchers, educators, and advocates with diverse interests related to meeting the

> developmental, psychological, educational, and general health needs of children. These issues were discussed, and the term *social and emotional learning* (SEL) was introduced. SEL described a framework for providing opportunities for young people to acquire the skills necessary for attaining and maintaining personal well-being and positive relationships across the lifespan.[4]

Out of this 1994 meeting, Collaborative for Academic, Social, and Emotional Learning (CASEL) was spun off as a separate non-profit organization with a mandate to establish 'high-quality, evidence-based SEL as an essential part of preschool through high school education'.[5] Today, CASEL is considered the premium SEL institute, certifying schools and selling SEL programs worldwide.

The CASEL framework for K-12 children address five key areas for promoting healthy social and emotional health, going from the child's inner to the outer: self-awareness, self-management, social awareness, relationship skills, and responsible decision-making.

Daniel Goleman

Daniel Goleman became the cofounder of CASEL at Yale Child Study Center, 'whose mission centers on bringing evidence-based programs in emotional literacy to schools worldwide'.[6] Goleman's journey of U-turn and digestion is an interesting one. The following background is summarized from Rajiv Malhotra's forthcoming book on the *U-Turn Theory* which contains many examples of U-Turns like that of Goleman.

Goleman has become an internationally acclaimed psychologist, and bestselling author of several books including *Emotional Intelligence: Why It Can Matter More Than IQ*, besides being the former chief editor of *Psychology Today* magazine.

However, his story begins when he was an undergraduate at the University of California, Berkeley during the 1960s and became interested in Indian meditation systems. For his PhD research at Harvard and a pre-doctoral fellowship, he went to India to study meditation. There he became friends with Richard Alpert, who had been fired from Harvard because of his experiments with the hallucinogenic drug, LSD. Alpert went to India and became a disciple of the guru, Neem Karoli Baba, and changed his name to Ram Dass. Ram Dass, who died in 2019, was an icon of the New Age/hippie era who became famous for bringing the Bhakti Movement to the USA.

Goleman later returned to India under a post-doctoral grant. He, too, spent considerable time with Neem Karoli Baba and studied Indian spiritual traditions across a wide range, both in theory and practice. As a doctoral student at Harvard in 1970, one of his first research papers was on Indian meditation in which he describes what the Indian texts state about the 'fifth state of consciousness'.[7]

Looking back, Goleman recalled how a Harvard fellowship served as a springboard for his work, saying, 'wow, I am going to India' and wanted to see 'what's up with Neem Karoli Baba'.[8] 'I would like to see what the end point is for following a spiritual path…My focus was on the ancient systems of psychology and meditation practices of Asia'.[9]

Goleman mused: 'And I saw that they [Neem Karoli Baba] were quantum leaps different than the famous professors of psychology that I was studying with back [at Harvard] in the States. They had developed a different part of themselves, that you never really heard about in psychology'.[10] Goleman then brought these Indian ideas to the USA.

He describes working with Herb Benson at Harvard researching meditators practicing Maharishi Mahesh Yogi's TM. Goleman explains the TM practice in detail as well as the clinical findings of its benefits. These discoveries created a sensation in medicine and were considered a significant breakthrough by the scientific community. He writes that after trying out several meditation techniques for three years he had concluded that TM as taught by Maharishi Mahesh Yogi was the most suitable one, and he practiced it the longest.

Goleman goes on to say: 'My hypotheses are generated from experience with TM but are framed in terms of meditation in general in the hope that they will be tested on a variety of different systems.'[11] He concludes: 'I must state that this paper is the bare beginning of the delineation of the process whereby meditation changes the meditator into the fifth state being, nor does it do justice to describing what that state is like.'[12]

Goleman then expanded his analysis to Buddhist meditation. In 1972, he wrote two influential research papers quoting both Vedic and Buddhist sources and comparing their teachings and meditation systems. He explains what he learned from his study of Buddhism in India:

> A psychological system (was) at the heart of Buddhism… absolutely unknown in Western psychology...I started to write about it, and the way it worked with the mind, the way it conceived of what you could do to transform the mind… meditation was very much at the heart of that… Western psychology did not understand that…meditation did transform the mind, and now we know, the brain. No one had ever heard of the word, neuroplasticity in the 1970s…repeated experiences change the structure and function of the brain was implicit in Buddhist psychology and unknown in Western psychology. … you could transform the mind, to the point where, … your inner emotional state was not at the whim of external conditions, but was an ongoing, …equanimous state that was one of kindness. This was inconceivable…I would say psychologists in the 2010s don't think about it that much as (a) whole.[13]

He discussed the Bhakti and the Hare Krishna Movements in a positive, scientific way. He cited Swami Vivekananda and his American disciple Christopher Isherwood and compared Bhakti with Raja Yoga, both well-known Vedic systems. His survey of Indian systems includes Sri Aurobindo's Integral Yoga, the renowned philosopher J. Krishnamurti's meditation, Patanjali's *Yoga Sutra*, and the sage, Ramana Maharshi's teachings. He then discussed

Swami Muktananda, the Shaivite founder of Siddha Yoga, already very popular in America. He drew comparisons between Kundalini Yoga, Tantra, and Tibetan Tantra.

Goleman achieved an impressive body of theoretical knowledge of Vedic and Buddhist cosmologies and explained them as Indian religious traditions without any attempt to cover up at that time. His work included an extensive glossary of Sanskrit terms that he used copiously to explain Indian literature. Goleman's papers were among the most thorough early surveys of meditation in the West from a scientific perspective, referring to almost a dozen different Indian systems. Though Sufi and Christian mysticism were also mentioned, these were very brief and mainly to show superficial compatibility, and ninety percent of the study was on Hindu and Buddhist systems.

By 1975, Goleman started to map his Vedic knowledge onto the framework of Buddhist Abhidharma philosophy. After gaining confidence and legitimacy, Goleman started publishing in more prestigious psychotherapy scientific journals.

This triggered further research into Indian meditation in the West and led to what is now being called the field of *Mind Sciences* (*adhyatma-vidya*). Ironically, the field has almost completely scrubbed off references to Indian sources even though an entire generation of American thinkers and scientists was raised on them. Gradually, he and his interviewees started omitting Vedic sources and began referring only to the Buddhist ones. Goleman presented the Abhidharma system as the broadest, and most detailed, traditional psychology of states of consciousness.[14] By 1976, he was referring to this knowledge more in secular terms as the 'Asian approach to mental health' and publishing it in prestigious mainstream scientific journals.[15]

His 1977 book, *The Varieties of the Meditative Experience*, became his first bestseller when it was republished under the title, *The Meditative Mind* with a foreword by Ram Dass. The book curates what he had learned from Indian systems and maps it onto a Western framework, but without hiding the Indian sources at this stage. A Western biographer writes: 'As might be expected from a recently minted PhD on psychology, there is a persistent framing of the ancient source material in psychological terms'.[16] The first edition was dedicated to Neem Karoli Baba and Lord Hanuman, among others. It was updated into a new edition by Penguin which became his first *New York Times* bestseller. To broaden the readership, he sprinkled the book with minor Jewish and Christian references.

By the mid-1980s, Goleman had become one of the most popular writers on meditation with regular columns in *The New York Times*, educating Americans on his discoveries of Mind Sciences which were a restatement of what he had learned from Indian sources.

At times, he has continued to acknowledge his Indian sources but largely confined himself to Buddhist sources. For instance, he regards Abhidharma metaphysics as a scientific approach to psychology:

> I discovered…an alternate psychological system.… Abhidharma, which is the Sanskrit term for this model of mind. Then I started writing about it in psychology journals, albeit very obscure psychology journals, because they were the only ones that were interested…it was important to bring this news to Western psychology because…it…extend(ed) the horizon line of the potential of being human...if psychology's about anything, it's about the mind and what are it's (sic) upper limits; what are the worst places we can go, what are the best places we can go? And this described some best places that we hadn't heard of yet.[17]

It is said that his 'U-turn moment' happened at Harvard when he got a pushback from his public associations with Hindu gurus like Neem Karoli Baba and references to theories and practices that he learned from Maharishi Mahesh Yogi. His career was taking off because of the limelight as a *New York Times* journalist. He was seen as America's leading authority in educating Americans on this newly discovered import called 'meditation'. This is when his Hindu links became a liability in his career.

His 1995 book, *Emotional Intelligence*, became an international bestseller and was translated into forty languages. It is an iconic book used by corporates for lessons in management and leadership.

This success fed his ego. He started to claim *that he had superseded the Indian spiritual traditions with his own new and original scientific discoveries*. For example, he writes: 'Psychoanalytic thought... has charted aspects of what would be called 'karma' in the East in far greater detail and complexity than any Eastern school of psychology'.[18]

Today, he is deemed to be the father of the major American corporate movement on stress management and leadership training, and emotional and ethical issues in the workplace.[19] His official biography, however, has been sanitized to delete all references to his Hindu gurus and India even though it was those influences that shaped his rise to fame.

Ironically, when he is invited by top multinationals in India, it is seldom highlighted that he is reselling Indian knowledge other than in casual references that he once traveled to India and might have picked up a few inspirations.

The important point to note is that it was only *after* his digestion of Vedic Mind Sciences that Goleman started CASEL. And Fetzer provided the seed funding. Thus, two Maharishi-trained Americans, each acknowledging their debt to the guru, came together to launch CASEL—one as a scholar, and the other as the businessman providing the funds.

CASEL: From Transcendental Meditation to Woke Education

The goal of CASEL has been to provide a framework and promote practical skills that can be taught to every child because American schools are struggling with behavioral problems. Fetzer also knew the value and benefits of Indian spiritual traditions from his exposure. Ideas like *dhyana* (meditation), yoga, and pranayama were all incorporated into CASEL's Social and Emotional Learning to address the increasing problems of bullying, drugs, and violence

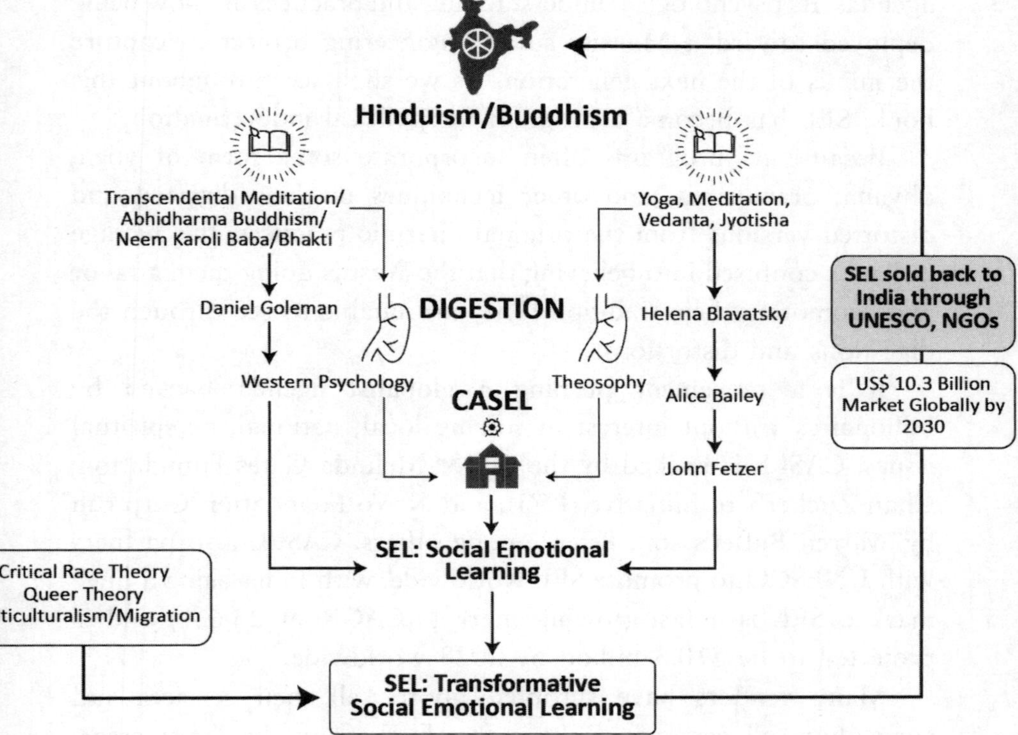

that were plaguing American schools. On the surface, it is about teaching children to have empathy, self-awareness, and self-control. It was sold to educators as a vital component of schooling to *help children manage emotions and relationships, show compassion to others, and make responsible decisions*. The case is being made that SEL is perhaps more important than learning reading or math; it was rolled out throughout America and even made mandatory by legislation.

Unfortunately, SEL morphed the Indian Mind Sciences into a typical American strategy for mind control. Like the trajectory of yoga, an entire multi-billion-dollar industry has sprouted around SEL with many vendors creating curricula based on the CASEL framework.

Later, the Marxist educators also entered the scene with their agendas. Its psychological understanding and practices are now being deployed toward a Marxist social engineering project to capture the minds of the next generation. As we shall see throughout this book, SEL has become a program for political indoctrination.

Because its programs often incorporate some form of yoga, dhyana, pranayama, and other techniques in their digested and distorted versions from the original dharmic practices, the average Indian is confused into believing that the West is doing them a favor and promoting their tradition. They are unable to see through the digestions and distortions.

It is a movement pushing a globalist agenda backed by billionaires without interest in solving local, national, or spiritual issues. CASEL is backed by the Bill & Melinda Gates Foundation, Chan-Zuckerberg Initiative (CZI), and NoVo Foundation Corp run by Warren Buffet's son, Peter, among others. CASEL also partners with UNESCO to promote SEL worldwide, with India being a huge market. SEL is a fast-growing market (CAGR of 23.6%) and is projected to be $10.3 billion by 2028 worldwide.[20]

Many vendors have sprouted up to sell their services and curriculum, all eager to make a fast buck from the latest craze. Just as ESG has become the de facto corporate social credit system worldwide, similarly, SEL is becoming the gold standard for children's education worldwide.

There are three troubling aspects of the way SEL has been deployed in schools:

1. It serves as a conduit for Woke pedagogy to penetrate all the subjects being taught and in fact, schools as a whole.
2. There is a transfer of custodianship of children from parents to schools, to teach values, religious morals, and worldviews apart from emotional, mental, and reproductive health.
3. The invasion of the privacy of children and families by continuous data collection and surveillance of children using technology and surveys. This data can be used to manipulate a child's desires, nudge him/her to make choices and trigger

> emotional responses aligned with the interests of the owners of the data.

Social Emotional Learning requires teachers to play the role of therapists teaching children the skills for managing stress, anxiety, emotions, and feelings, a role that requires professional psychologists. Critics worry that teachers are unqualified to take on such a role. Typically, only a small percentage of students require interventions for behavioral issues. However, SEL is a one-size-fits-all group psychotherapy. Even for children with psychological issues, unqualified teachers and their SEL programs are playing the role of psychologists, which could lead to dangerous outcomes.

Things became worse when, in the guise of promoting multiculturalism and anti-racism, CASEL expanded SEL into Transformative SEL (TSEL) and brought in Critical Race Theory and Queer Theory. In 2020, Karen Niemi, chief executive officer of CASEL presented an updated framework, and openly disclosed the Woke agenda, saying, CASEL will be explicit about how SEL can advance educational equity.'[21]

> The updated language pays attention to personal and *social identities*, cultural competency and *collective action* as part of SEL. It also emphasizes the skills, knowledge and mindsets needed to examine prejudices and biases, *evaluate social norms and systemic inequities*, and promote community well-being.[22]
>
> Inequities based on race, ethnicity, class, language, gender identity, sexual orientation, and other factors are deeply ingrained in the vast majority of these systems and impact student and adult social, emotional, and academic learning. ... While SEL alone will not solve longstanding and deep-seated inequities in the education system, it can create the conditions needed for individuals and schools to examine and interrupt inequitable policies and practices, create more inclusive learning environments, and reveal and nurture the interests and assets of all individuals.[23]

The promoters of SEL argue that a successful program includes eliminating systemic racism by requiring *equal outcomes* as per Critical Race Theory. Consequently, the SEL curriculum, with CRT and Gender Theory at the core, uses Paulo Freire's pedagogy to teach social justice by dividing children into 'oppressor' and 'oppressed' groups based on gender, sexuality, or race. This 'anti-racism' curriculum is designed to shame oppressors to acknowledge the guilt of their families and ancestors. Children belonging to the oppressed category are victimized and taught to celebrate victimhood.

> In 'Transformative SEL,' 'self-awareness' encompasses 'identity,' with 'identity' defined now through the lens of 'intersectionality.' 'Self-management' encompasses 'agency,' with 'agency' defined through 'resistance' and 'transformative/justice-oriented' citizenship. 'Transformative SEL' also embraces 'culturally relevant/responsive' pedagogy. This approach was pioneered by Gloria Ladson-Billings, the professor who brought Critical Race Theory to K-12 education. ... In its 'Roadmap to Reopening,' CASEL defines 'self-awareness' as 'examining our implicit biases,' and defines 'self-management' as 'practicing anti-racism'.[24]

Social Emotional Learning is not taught as a separate subject but is *built* into every subject. Therefore, there is no way to opt out of SEL classes. CASEL sets the standards for social justice, and the SEL curriculum permeates all subjects in the school. For example, children are often given SEL exercises at the expense of math and English classes and asked to fill out extensive surveys on 'one of more than 100 grievance subjects, including transphobia, homophobia, racism, gender, fascism, sexism, BLM, and socialism'.[25]

Following is a curated sample of questions on SEL survey questions, tips, and lessons across schools in the USA, from various published sources:

'"How do you feel when you see two men kissing?" she said it read, paraphrasing. The choices were "A.) Aggressive, B.) Passive aggressive, C.) Neutral, or D.) None of the above, ...

A first-grade text included **Jacob's New Dress**, a story about a boy who wants to wear a dress to school, and a fourth-grade text included **When Aidan Became a Brother**, which pushes gender theory and teaches kids to question the sex they're assigned at birth....

If you didn't have a diverse makeup of friends in your friend group, is it racist to seek out another race to fill your friend group?...

For a 11-year-old - "SEL lessons during related arts class, one of which Kim said was called "How You Can Be an Upstander." The PowerPoint posed the following scenario, she said: "You are watching a makeup tutorial on YouTube. The person putting on makeup in the video identifies as male. There are people in the comments saying extremely hateful and cruel things. What could you do to be an upstander in this situation?"....

You are at lunch with a group of friends. A male classmate walks by. He loves theater and dance, doesn't play sports, and often hangs out with girls in class more than with boys. A friend at the table refers to the student with words that you know are insulting and offensive. If you were a student at this table, what would you do?"

"a SEL curriculum from Casel explicitly named "social justice" as its main goal and provided "five tips for your first time [having sex]" to 13 and 14-year-old students....

A Virginia district's SEL training urged teachers to "make your ally status known by hanging a rainbow flag, sharing your own pronouns and/or supporting the school's LGBTQ groups....

In one such instance, students were given an extensive survey that asked middle schoolers questions like "How do you feel about your gender?" and "Where do you consider yourself on the gender spectrum"'[26]

Many American parents do not agree with the 'normalization' of alternate family structures like homosexual families and polyamory.

They want values and religious beliefs to be the purview of the family and not the school. The same is true of teaching children that gender and sexuality are fluid and are mere social constructs. Many worry that the sense of reality in young children becomes warped by these SEL programs that constantly instruct them that they are oppressors, or are free to choose their gender. There is pressure to adopt pronouns as something cool or socially acceptable. There is a sense of fear of getting pronouns wrong and potentially offending a peer. Teaching children to think alike in the name of being inclusive is worrying.

These programs are political and create a wedge between parents and children. Parents too are pressured to use pronouns or else they risk creating conflict with or offend their children. Some experts also worry that excessive attention and focus on a child's feelings tends to fuel narcissism and entitlement in children, nurturing victimhood.

Children designated as coming from an oppressive heritage are required to shoulder the sacrifices needed for climate change, equity and diversity, and anti-meritocratic practices, etc. To compensate for having an oppressor identity by birth, they must give up 'privilege' by angrily agitating about systemic bias, caste privilege, carbon footprint, capitalism, and so on. If they accept this responsibility to become change agents and activists, they are praised for having 'emotional resilience'. If they disagree, they are branded 'fragile'. Children from the oppressed group are taught a sense of entitlement, and to celebrate their victim status, because 'everything is someone else's fault'.

This culture war is being amplified by social media influencers to create an environment in which these issues are the most critical and urgent ones because they are about 'saving the world'. Recently, the UN climate chief, Simon Stiell stated: 'Humans just have 2 years to save the world'.[27]

Meanwhile, SEL zealotry is eating away precious instruction time needed for teaching reading, science, and math, and as a result, academic standards have deteriorated. Social Emotional Learning does not serve the interests of those children who go to school for academic reasons.

In concrete terms, teaching SEL is about:

1. Creating anxiety about the climate crisis.
2. Turning children into activists by role-playing social justice situations and triggering them into action. This includes becoming emotionally resilient and attacking those who are deemed to suffer from fragility.
3. Normalizing LGBTQIA+ lifestyle and nudging children into making it part of all discussions.
4. Complying with equity initiatives.
5. Creating a wedge between parent and child by undermining parental authority.

These SEL programs are doing the groundwork to prepare students for an even more insidious program called Comprehensive Sexuality Education, which is geared toward sexualizing children right from birth. Both SEL and CSE are based on Critical Race Theory and are foundational to the WSCC program, i.e. 'whole school, whole child, and whole community'.

The WSCC model in the USA is backed by the Center for Disease Control (CDC), where the school becomes the one-stop shop for children's education, health, and well-being. All these terms (education, health, well-being) are defined by Woke ideology, thus preparing the school to take full control of children with the slow erosion of parental rights and inputs on how to raise them.

Social Emotional Learning and Surveillance

One of the most worrisome aspects of SEL is the collection of sensitive K-12 student information through online assessments, without parental consent, including data to profile children's emotions at every step of learning. Parents are not even aware that their child's behavior is under surveillance and are naïve about the potential for misuse.

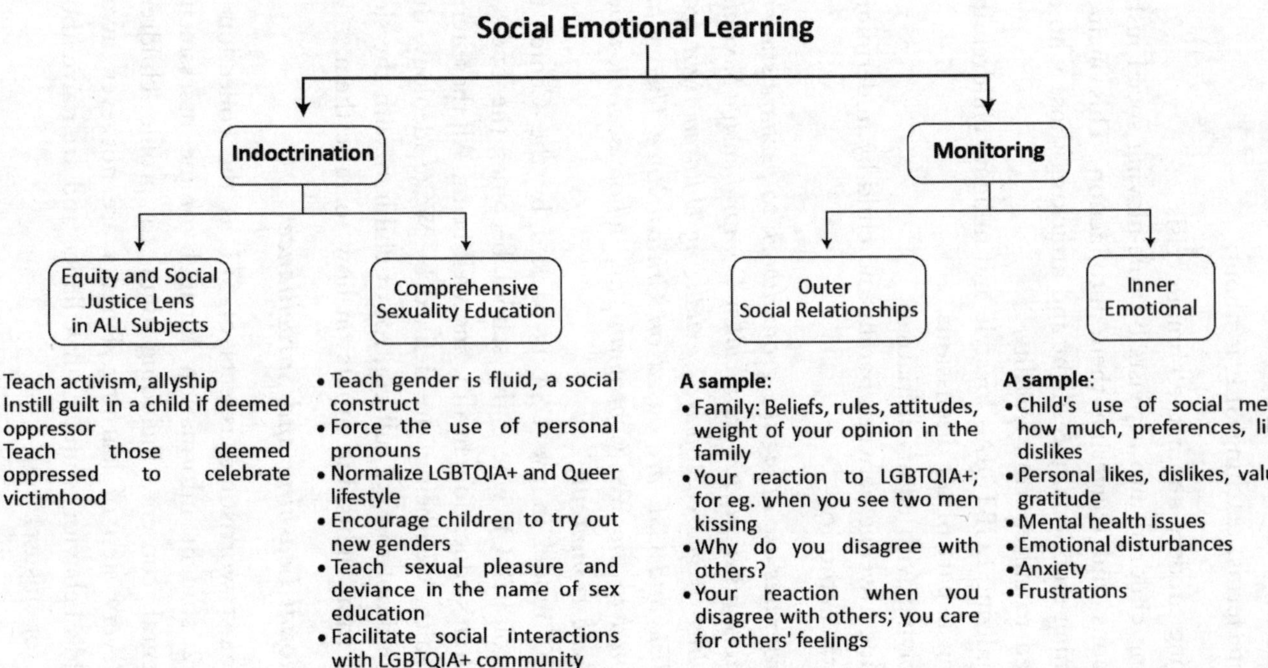
Social Emotional Learning
Indoctrination
Monitoring
Equity and Social Justice Lens in ALL Subjects
Comprehensive Sexuality Education
Outer Social Relationships
Inner Emotional
• Teach activism, allyship
• Instill guilt in a child if deemed oppressor
• Teach those deemed oppressed to celebrate victimhood
• Teach gender is fluid, a social construct
• Force the use of personal pronouns
• Normalize LGBTQIA+ and Queer lifestyle
• Encourage children to try out new genders
• Teach sexual pleasure and deviance in the name of sex education
• Facilitate social interactions with LGBTQIA+ community
A sample:
• Family: Beliefs, rules, attitudes, weight of your opinion in the family
• Your reaction to LGBTQIA+; for eg. when you see two men kissing
• Why do you disagree with others?
• Your reaction when you disagree with others; you care for others' feelings
A sample:
• Child's use of social media: how much, preferences, likes, dislikes
• Personal likes, dislikes, values, gratitude
• Mental health issues
• Emotional disturbances
• Anxiety
• Frustrations
Use survey data and Artificial Intelligence to customize the indoctrination of children

Soon there will be biometric devices collecting even more data. Vital markers such as temperature, pulse rate, respiratory rate, blood pressure, etc., clubbed with emotional data from surveys can be a powerful weapon to use on the young generation, all in the name of delivering emotional education by increasing the teacher's understanding of students. Artificial Intelligence systems are being developed to profile individuals for use by predictive models.

The Chan Zuckerberg Initiative has its eye on children's data and has penetrated many schools, offering free tools to help teachers communicate and manage relationships with their students. The Chan Zuckerberg Initiative is a for-profit entity and thus enjoys the privacy of private companies. Mark Zuckerberg, the founder of CZI, is known to have breached the privacy of his clients. He knows the value of data, has leveraged it for personal gain, and continues to harvest data through his many ventures.

In 2021, CZI started a new initiative called Along.org in partnership with another NGO, Gradient Learning, which receives funding from CZI. Priscilla Chan, Zuckerberg's wife, heads the board of Gradient. Sounding altruistic, Along.org and Gradient offer a *free* 'digital reflection tool designed to help teachers make each of their students feel seen and understood'.[28]

According to Along.org, this tool offers 'Efficient ways to ask and collect student input'.[29] Additionally, it lets 'students send quick video, audio or text directly to their teacher'.[30] Along.org promotes SEL by offering its free data mining tool to create what it calls 'intentional spaces for SEL'.[31] This tool 'allows students to share quick reflections one-on-one so they can open up about who they are and what's really on their mind—without peer pressure'.[32]

Gradient's data mining tool that Along.org promotes profiles each student's identity and encourages them to emphasize it:

> That's why Summit Learning projects and lessons allow students to explore important social issues that are central to their lived experiences – including racial discrimination, LGBTQ rights, Latinx culture, and divides in rural America.[33]

The data collected includes attendance and homework records, grades, various external factors affecting the children, the teacher's notes on each child, disciplinary actions taken, factors that cause anxiety including students' socioeconomic status, grades and examination results, and extracurricular activities.[34] The contracts with schools ensure data privacy and the promise that data will be scrubbed and depersonalized. However, this is misleading because the contract gives ownership of such de-personalized data to Gradient and its partners:

> Once it has done so, Gradient may do what it wishes with users' de-identified data, such as create commercial products, use it for marketing, or sell or share it with any entity of its choosing – including CZI or Meta. Once the contract has been signed, no one – not schools, parents, or students can legally prevent Gradient from using their data in a de-identified form.[35]

Also, data experts know that the de-identified data on a person can easily be re-identified.[36] Moreover, even if left de-identified, the data can be misused:

> Analyses of massive sets of de-identified data are used primarily to classify, sort, and make predictions and decisions about *groups* of people. That is, those data sets are used to develop products that purport to predict individuals' future thoughts, feelings, behaviors, health, and success, based on the specific groups to which they appear to belong (Citron & Pasquale, 2014; Siegel, 2016; Woo, Tay, & Proctor, 2020). The sorting and classification enabled by such analyses can, for instance, be used to assign students to academic tracks based on predictions of their likely future success (Barshay & Aslanian, 2019); market products to them based on predictions of what they might want (Scott, 2016); set the prices for goods and services based on predictions of what they are willing to pay (Elmachtoub, Gupta, & Hamilton, 2021); price their health insurance based on predictions of

> their future lifestyle choices or their likelihood of switching providers (Maryville University, 2022); and surveil them based on predictions of their likelihood of perpetrating a crime (Brennan Center for Justice, 2022). This is why Katharina Kopp, the deputy director of the Center for Digital Democracy, described de-identified data to us as "the treasure trove of data analytics" (personal email message, March 1, 2021).[37]

China uses facial recognition to monitor its citizens, and this has also entered its classrooms along with AI systems that monitor emotions. China has introduced a band-like head device that monitors attention span to ensure students stay focused during instruction. These systems collect data on students using hi-tech gear to monitor their academic progress. The social credit system has entered schools with surveillance cameras monitoring every move, emotion, thought, and action of the child.

The USA criticizes China for these interventions but promotes the same techniques to the rest of the world in the name of SEL. While we strongly denounce China's use of technology to monitor its children, at least they are trying to improve the academic performance of their children, whereas the USA is bringing these same technologies to 'Wokeify' the younger generation at the expense of teaching them science and math.

Misinterpretation of Bhakti as Gender Fluidity

Marxism is strictly grounded in materialist philosophy and seeks equity or socio-economic equal outcomes in the material world. However, its quest to create an undifferentiated society runs counter to the natural order. Furthermore, Marxism advocates that society be dismantled to achieve equity through the redistribution of resources, thereby causing havoc as is evident by its history.

The Vedic view considers such Marxist actions as inherently ego-centric, driven by desires; this game of the ego is ultimately futile and merely leads to more frustration. This is why dharma guides the individual to transcend the material realm through lifestyle changes. True contentment can only be achieved by transcending the ego. This involves shifting one's focus from the desires of the ego to the recognition of a higher, unchanging reality. That higher reality is the experience of a union with the divine, a state of freedom from anxieties. This is the state of *ananda*, a state of true fullness and lasting peace, beyond the temporary victories of the material world.

Unfortunately, Marxism as well as Western Indology operate only in the material realm, while Vedic metaphysics comprises the following two realms:

1. The highly variegated *vyavaharika* realm of empirical reality.
2. The *paramarthika* realm that is based on the integral unity of the cosmos and is experienced through transcending the individual ego for a higher state of consciousness.

Unfortunately, the tenet of transcending the vyavaharika realm is not understood properly by Westerners like Daniel Goleman, the co-founder of SEL. When he met Neem Karoli Baba, he could not understand this transcendence of the ego that Baba displayed:

> I went to see ...Neem Karoli Baba, ... who was unlike anyone I've met before. He was absolutely centered, loving, present, and actually didn't seem to be motivated by the usual motivations. ...He wasn't interested in power, not interested in money, not interested in all of the things that someone in that position could take advantage of. And he was just totally present in a way that I had never seen in my Harvard professors, some of who were the leading psychologists of the day, by the way.[38]

Goleman says he was 'hanging out' at Neem Karoli Baba's ashram to be with him because he 'radiated this inner state'.[39] Unfortunately, SEL coined by Goleman has morphed the Indian Mind Sciences into a typical American strategy for mind control. Later, the Marxists also entered the scene with their agendas. Its psychological understanding and practices are now being deployed toward a Marxist social engineering project to capture the minds of the youth.

A major area of such distortion exists in the way Bhakti saints are misinterpreted by the LGBTQIA+ movement by ignoring the paramarthika realm. One cannot understand these saints within the limited framework of the vyavaharika realm.

For example, Nammazhvar, one of the twelve Vaishnavite poet-saints of the eighth century, known as the Azhvars, assumes the female form of Parankushanaayiki, to express his deep love and devotion in the form of *nayaki bhava* (female lover) to Lord Krishna through evocative poems. His bhakti manifested as love and yearning for union with the Divine. This form of Bhakti poetry transcends physical romantic attraction, elevating it to a spiritual experience that unites the devotee with the Divine. Nammazhvar also used his persona as Shadagopan and Paraankushan to compose verses on Lord Vishnu. Likewise, he also took on the persona of a mother to show the maternal aspects toward the divine.

Such personas are assumed as mere vehicles to lead one to experience paramarthika. This is why the goal for all men and women in the Gaudiya Vaisnava tradition is to unite with Lord Krishna as *gopis* (female). However, the Western framing of bhakti cannot appreciate the devotee's transcendence from the material realm. As a result, his relationship-seeking union with the divine is trivialized as a fulfillment of sexual fantasies.

Robert Goldman (not to be confused with Goleman), a well-known Indologist, uses Western frameworks of power dynamics to study bhakti literature for 'transsexualism', and believes that it provides 'a clearer understanding of the traditional literature and culture of South Asia and for a better sense of the ways in which gender, sexuality, and power have been constructed in many patriarchal culture…'.[40] He mischaracterizes the devotees' love for Lord Krishna by saying that 'traditional texts allude, sometimes elaborately, to a change of sex that a person experiences either as a fantasy or full-fledged delusion through the power of sexual desire'.[41] He then goes on to describe Ramakrishna Paramahamsa's bhakti (which is not about a physical bodily fantasy) as some sort of sexual fetish. He describes his 'constant desire to dress, behave, and experience the world as a woman' as a sexual fantasy: Ramakrishna 'often even appeared to lose himself in elaborate fantasies of being reborn as one of the gopis of Vrindavan'.[42]

Similarly, when the yogi, Paramahamsa Yogananda expresses his deep emotional bond with his mother by calling her *Divine Mother*, Goldman calls it a maternal fixation. Of Yogananda's practice of sexual austerity as a young man, Goldman says, 'It is little wonder that young Mukund Lal [Yogananda] grew up, like Ramakrishna, obsessed with the notion of women as manifestations of the desexualized Mother, and of men as all-knowing and potentially menacing gurus. It is also not surprising that all this was accompanied by an irresistible impulse to flee the world'.[43] Goldman incorrectly describes the surrender of the empirical world for higher states of consciousness as an act of cowardice for 'fleeing this world'. According to him, when Yogananda's disciples see him both as a father figure and a nurturing mother, it indicates fluidity of gender and sexuality in the physical sense. This confusion is typical of scholars who are ignorant of higher states of consciousness.

The behavior of such saints is not instances of 'queer identity' on display as most Western social scientists would like to claim. These are all examples of transcending the ego and relinquishing physical desires. In other words, such experiences of bhakti are not to be interpreted within the Marxist framework but within the framework of the integral unity of paramarthika-vyavaharika. This is elaborated in Part 3.

Our position is that the Vedic worldview must be understood in its framework. Therefore, we reject all Marxist frameworks like Queer Theory because they are about power, redistribution of resources, and social justice. The categories of gender and sexuality as per Queer Theory are about erasing sexual boundaries purely for a power struggle. This game is a battle of egos whereas the Vedic framework advocates transcending beyond egos.

Judith Butler asserts that gender is performed as a social construct that 'is manufactured through a sustained set of acts, posited through the gendered stylization of the body'.[44] We reject that gender is being 'performed' by the Bhakti saints for sexual gratification. The Bhakti tradition offers pathways to transcend the empirical world for each type of *bhakta* (disciple) with his/her unique disposition. It is a means to achieve union with the divine, and not a pursuit of the physical body for sexual gratification.

Dasa bhava, which means servitude to the divine is also a form of bhakti. It does not mean that the devotee is performing the role of a Marxist 'subaltern'. Such a deconstruction of Vedic literature gives rise to distortions because the foundational principles are violated by dismissing the paramarthika realm.

The United Nations' Comprehensive Sexuality Education

Organizations like UNESCO, WHO, UN, and others are pushing the Comprehensive Sexuality Education program that is sometimes incorporated as part of SEL and other times as a stand-alone program. The World Health Organization defines sexuality to include 'gender identities and roles, sexual orientation, eroticism, pleasure, intimacy, and reproduction. Sexuality is experienced and expressed in thoughts, fantasies, desires'.[45] Its standards for sex education states:

> The development of sexual behaviour, feelings and cognitions begins in the womb and continues throughout a person's lifetime. Precursors of later sexual perception, such as the ability to enjoy physical contact, are present from birth. […] Children have sexual feelings even in early infancy.[46]

To cater to these sexual feelings, sex education must teach the child about *sexual fantasy, eroticism, sexual pleasure, gender identity,* and more. The UN's Comprehensive Sexuality Education is touted as evidence-based, age-appropriate, rights-based, and with a 'positive and respectful approach' to sexual desires.[47] The main thrust of the program is to teach children the skills for deriving sexual pleasure. It positions sexual engagement as their right: 'Sexuality education consists not only of information, but also of support for the acquisition of skills and competencies and of support for the development of one's own standpoint/attitude towards sexuality'.[48]

The rights-based approach encourages children to make choices on sexual matters without parental involvement. The traditional approach of parental guidance is bypassed. The framework of UNESCO states that children's values do not need to coincide with those of their parents. What is lacking is a concern to protect children from risky sexual behavior.

Also, the CSE program is being embedded in the entire curriculum and hence, parents cannot opt out. There is no escape door: 'The central prerequisite for sexuality education is...that it needs its own specific place in schools and thus should be covered throughout the curriculum in quite some detail'.[49]

Shocking Content for Middle School Children

Comprehensive Sexuality Education has been in the system for over a decade, with the Obama administration (2009-17) discontinuing the funding for abstinence-based sex education and promoting gender as a social construct *assigned* at birth.[50] Worldwide, CSE programs that are designed around queer pedagogy at the core are on the rise.

Even though the literature on CSE always touts 'evidence-based' and 'age-appropriate' sexual education, it promotes pleasure, kinky sexual fetishes, pushing sexual boundaries, transgenderism, experimentation, and risky sexual behavior. Toddlers as young as three are targeted by this ostensibly 'age-appropriate', 'evidence-based' sex education being promoted. They claim that even very young children are sexual beings and must be given the 'right' to have sexual experiences. Thus, CSE has become a major threat to the parent-child relationship and is violating the rights of parents in many instances.

Comprehensive Sexuality Education is marketed as teaching kids about consent, communication, setting boundaries, and empowerment. However, some of the sex lessons will shock most parents. For example, a widely used sex education program for middle schoolers in the USA (ages eleven-thirteen) is called Reducing the Risk or RTR. Here is a description of what it teaches:

> RTR's New Abstinence includes teaching students about using sex toys, having anal sex with a condom, having oral sex using dental dams, and even, it seems, having unprotected sex, getting pregnant, and getting an abortion, all of which are promoted in the curriculum. Such things are being taught wherever schools and school districts use RTR curriculum... In one lesson students are given a handout promoting mutual masturbation, sexual fantasy, oral sex, and anal sex with a condom. Another lesson instructs students to call and visit a clinic, such as Planned Parenthood, to ask about sterilization, shop for condoms, and ask about abortion pills...One common exercise used in RTR is forcing students to participate in gender neutral role plays of sexual encounters.[51]

International Technical Guidance on Sexuality Education

UNESCO states that programs advocating abstinence for young kids are ineffective and are given cursory treatment. The new global sexual revolution under the banner of 'Comprehensive' Sexuality Education programs can encourage children to embrace risky sexual behavior leading to unwanted pregnancies that can be mitigated by easy access to abortion services.

UNESCO's 2018 guide on CSE, the *International Technical Guidance on Sexuality Education* (ITGSE), lays out a framework with content and concepts to be covered by age within classrooms.

This ITGSE guideline clearly states that it aims to equip children to have sexual relationships and is intended to help children build relationships with romantic or sexual partners. The guideline includes teaching children as young as five about kissing, hugging, touching, and sexual behaviors. *The overall objective is to make children independent of, and potentially in conflict with, the values about sexuality that are fostered at home.*

While they say it is up to each country to customize their content according to their context, *India has not proactively developed and proposed its framework nor shown any independent reflection on CSE in general or the ITGSE guidelines.*

The ITGSE is being implemented around the globe as part of the United Nations' SDGs agenda 2030:[52]

> We are convinced that if we do not meet young people's calls for good quality comprehensive sexuality education, we will not achieve the Sustainable Development Goals (SDGs) we have set for 2030, and the commitment that has been made to leave no one behind.[53]

Drafted in collaboration with the International Planned Parenthood Federation (IPPF) member associations, the ITGSE guidelines were also produced in partnership with other UN organizations like WHO, UNAIDS, UNFPA, UNICEF, and UN Women. It lays out a systematic plan to turn children into activists to promote its ideology on childhood sexuality.

The stages of education are:

Knowledge ➔ Attitudes ➔ Activism

Following are some highlights of the ITGSE guidelines for children starting at age five:[54]

- Teach children that gender is a social construct and ask them to experiment and explore their sex and gender.[55]
- It is natural for humans to enjoy their bodies and be close to others throughout their lives.[56]

- Understand that physical enjoyment and excitement are natural human feelings, and this can involve physical closeness to other people.[57]

A few ideas in the ITGSE's CSE framework for children over nine include:

- The guidelines promote masturbation as normal.
- They emphasize teaching about various types of 'non-traditional families' with a focus on LGBTQIA+ rights.
- They promote access to contraception and abortion for children.
- Nine to twelve-year-olds are asked to describe ways that human beings 'feel pleasure from physical contact (e.g. kissing, touching, caressing, sexual contact)'.[58]
- Fifteen-year-olds are asked to discuss and reflect on 'how gender norms and stereotypes influence people's expectations and experience of sexual pleasure'.[59]

A key consultant in developing these guidelines was the Swedish Association for Sexuality Education (RFSU), an affiliate of IPPF that also sells sex toys for pleasure. The RFSU also markets a 'how to book' on sex for teens with graphic sexual content and explicit details of sexual positions; there is a section dedicated to 'enjoyable sexual things you can do together' that will interest teenagers.[60]

The ITGSE guideline advocates gathering evidence on how its CSE can lead to increased demand for youth-friendly sexual and reproductive health and rights services and products. In effect, it is promoting the business services of organizations like the IPPF, which profit from gender-affirming care and abortion services.[61] The following table summarizes the main ITGSE guidelines and key areas.[62]

Topic	Guideline Description
Target Age Group	Five to fifteen-year-olds
Publisher	UNESCO
UN Agencies	UNESCO, UNICEF, WHO, UNAIDS, UNFPA, UN Women
Contributor	International Planned Parenthood Federation
Distribution	Global
Key Areas	**ITGSE Guideline Summary**
Distorts Abstinence	Promotes selective application of abstinence and is critical of abstinence-only programs.
Promotes Early Sex and Promiscuity	Emphasizes early access to sexuality and introduces diverse sexual practices.
Promotes Transgender Ideology	Introduces diverse gender identities and sexual orientations. Describes biology as distinct from gender.
Affirmation of Diverse Sexual Orientations	Presents LGBTQIA+ issues and encourages expression of any sexual orientation or gender identity at any age.
Masturbation	Discusses masturbation as behavior during puberty or earlier.
Sexual Rights for Children	Describes sexual pleasure and male/female responses to sexual stimulation.
Consent	Teaches children how to consent to sexual behaviors.
Abortion	Discusses abortion access as a right and emergency contraception.
Contraception	Provides guidance on correct condom use and accessing contraception.
Values on Sexuality	Encourages exploration and challenging of social, cultural, and religious influences on sexuality.
Questioning Parents' Values	Explores values that are different from their parents regarding sexuality.

The World Health Assembly Vetoes Comprehensive Sexuality Education

The World Health Assembly (WHA) serves as the decision-making body of the WHO that determines its internal policies. In 2021, WHA rejected the language in the policy concerning 'sexuality education' that was being pushed by the USA and Western European countries. This occurred because the Russian Federation and several African and Muslim countries led a rejection of a section titled Operative Paragraph 10:

> To provide *accessible gender-sensitive, free from gender stereotypes, evidence-based and appropriate to age and evolving capacities* sexuality education to children, and with appropriate direction and guidance from parents and legal guardians, with the best interests of the child as their basic concern to empower and enable them to realize their health wellbeing and dignity, build communication, self-protection and risk reduction skills, as a fundamental part of the efforts to prevent, recognize and respond to violence against children.[63]

For instance, Egypt's stance was 'that some delegations tried to force "loaded and contentious terms" on other delegations forcing them to wade through controversies and ignoring their concerns with sexuality education that encompasses different sexual identities, something that was never agreed upon either at the World Health Assembly or in other venues'.[64]

A UNICEF document was criticized because it stated that 'children *should have access to confidential counseling and advice without parental or legal guardian consent*'.[65]

The term 'sexuality' is also loaded: Many of the UN agencies and their partners like the IPPF include controversial topics of masturbation, desires, fantasies, and gender identities. On the other hand, the term 'Sexual and Reproductive Health' is a more conventional form of sex education that refers to sexual hygiene, Sexually Transmitted Infections (STIs), HIV, and reproduction.

The proposal from the Russian Federation, Eswatini, Egypt, Mozambique, and Zambia was to replace the term 'sexuality education' with 'the somewhat less controversial information and education on sexual and reproductive health' in the resolution that had been under intense negotiation over two weeks.[66]

Diplomats from the USA, Canada, Europe, and other progressive nations expressed dissatisfaction with the rejection, reiterating their support for Comprehensive Sexuality Education, citing its alignment with previous UN agreements:

> During the debate the following countries thankfully took the floor and expressed either their support for replacing 'sexuality education' with the SRH language or in support of deleting the sexuality education paragraph entirely: Russia, Egypt, Zambia, Eswatini, Iran, Jamaica, Mauritania, Saudi Arabia, Kenya, Lebanon, Pakistan, Algeria, Senegal, Iran, Zimbabwe, Qatar, Eswatini, Morocco, China, Thailand, Japan. On the other hand, the European Union, Canada, Australia, New Zealand, Uruguay, the U.S., the UK, Germany, Portugal, Argentina, Monaco, and Switzerland all spoke out in favor of 'sexuality education' and against the proposed amendment.[67]

Comprehensive Sexuality Education vs. Traditional Sex Education

The CSE is geared towards dismantling the current 'normative' understanding of gender and sexuality. It has little to do with sex education for the prevention of Sexually Transmitted Diseases and unwanted pregnancies, information on sexual health and hygiene. On the contrary, it promotes pleasure, kinky sex, sexual fetishes, pushing sexual boundaries, sexual consent, and transgenderism, and encourages experimentation and risky sexual behavior.

The CSE's approach to the 'right to consent' issue is misleading because it is not just about setting boundaries and saying 'no' to unwanted sexual advances. It is about informing children that they

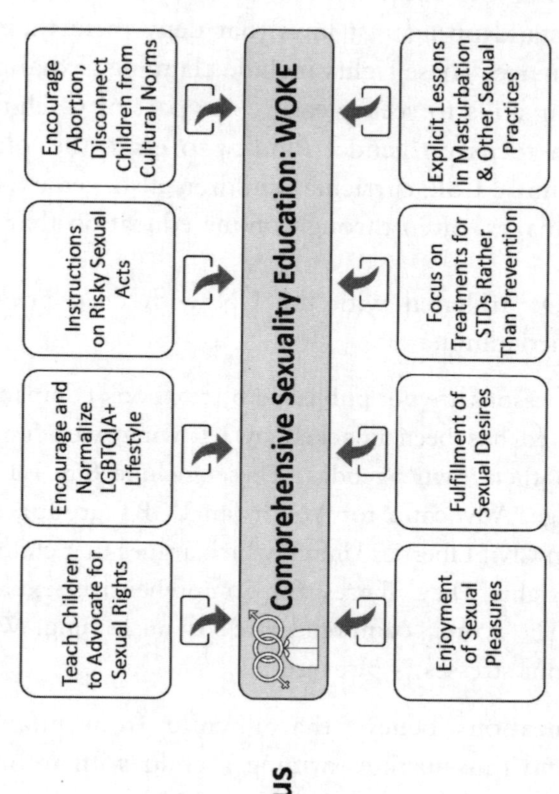
Sex Education Old Style
Teach
• Sexual Hygiene
• Abstinence
• Responsibility, Risks and Safeguards
• Prevention of Sexually Transmitted Diseases
• Prevention of Unwanted Pregnancy
Versus
Teach Children to Advocate for Sexual Rights
Encourage and Normalize LGBTQIA+ Lifestyle
Instructions on Risky Sexual Acts
Encourage Abortion, Disconnect Children from Cultural Norms
Comprehensive Sexuality Education: WOKE
Enjoyment of Sexual Pleasures
Fulfillment of Sexual Desires
Focus on Treatments for STDs Rather Than Prevention
Explicit Lessons in Masturbation & Other Sexual Practices

have the right to 'know and explore' their bodies, going as far as asking them to stand up against laws that deny them their sexual rights at a certain age. These rights include claiming sexual pleasure and education on skills to seek pleasure. As part of teaching these rights, there is a focus on gender fluidity to erase the 'old ways' of thinking. In most CSE curricula, children also get exposed to graphic sexual images, often through online education that parents cannot access.

Several NGOs affiliated with the UN with deep pockets are providing the curriculum:

> Most sex ed lessons are not published by textbook companies. Instead, sex ed has been hijacked by left-wing, well-funded groups with their own agendas. These include Sex Ed for Social Change, Advocates for Youth (an LGBT group), and the American Civil Liberties Union, which argues that children have sexual rights. They all press for Comprehensive Sexuality Education. The word "comprehensive" is misleading. What the curriculum stresses is pleasure.[68]

The UN organizations believe that a child from infancy is a 'sexual being' and thus justifies arming a child with information/skills on methods and outcomes, a domain that was previously the responsibility of parents. This opens the door to attacking childhood innocence. An example is a book titled *It's Perfectly Normal* written by a Planned Parenthood consultant, which targets children from age ten.[69] The book contains explicit graphics of sexual acts which would be considered pornographic material if shared in public.

Obscenity laws in the USA prevent the distribution of explicit sexual content to minors because it is considered harmful.[70] However, there are obscenity exemptions provided in the law for purposes of education and research. Children learn by mirroring what they see in the world around them and this constant exposure to obscenity desensitizes them to sexual acts, including deviant ones. In effect,

CSE is grooming children to be sexually deviant starting in early childhood.

Thus, it is important to differentiate between sex education and sexualization programs:

- *Sex education* focuses on preventing unwanted pregnancies, reducing Sexually Transmitted Diseases, and protecting against sexual abuse, using ethical frameworks.
- *Sexualization programs* emphasize sexual exploration, pleasure, and rights, and the goal is to destigmatize and normalize transgenderism, gender fluidity, and pedophilia.

The following figure summarizes the key issues regarding Comprehensive Sexuality Education.

The WHO's Standards for Europe

The WHO's 'Standards for Sexuality Education in Europe', and the UN's 'International Technical Guidance on Sexual Education' are examples of standards that groom children into sexual activity from a very early age and attack childhood innocence as commonly understood. The WHO is piloting a project for European children that teaches even *newborns* to discover their genitals, masturbate, and learn sexual pleasure.[71]

The following is a snapshot from the WHO's 'Standards for Sexuality Education in Europe' for ages zero to four and four to six as recommended by the UN.

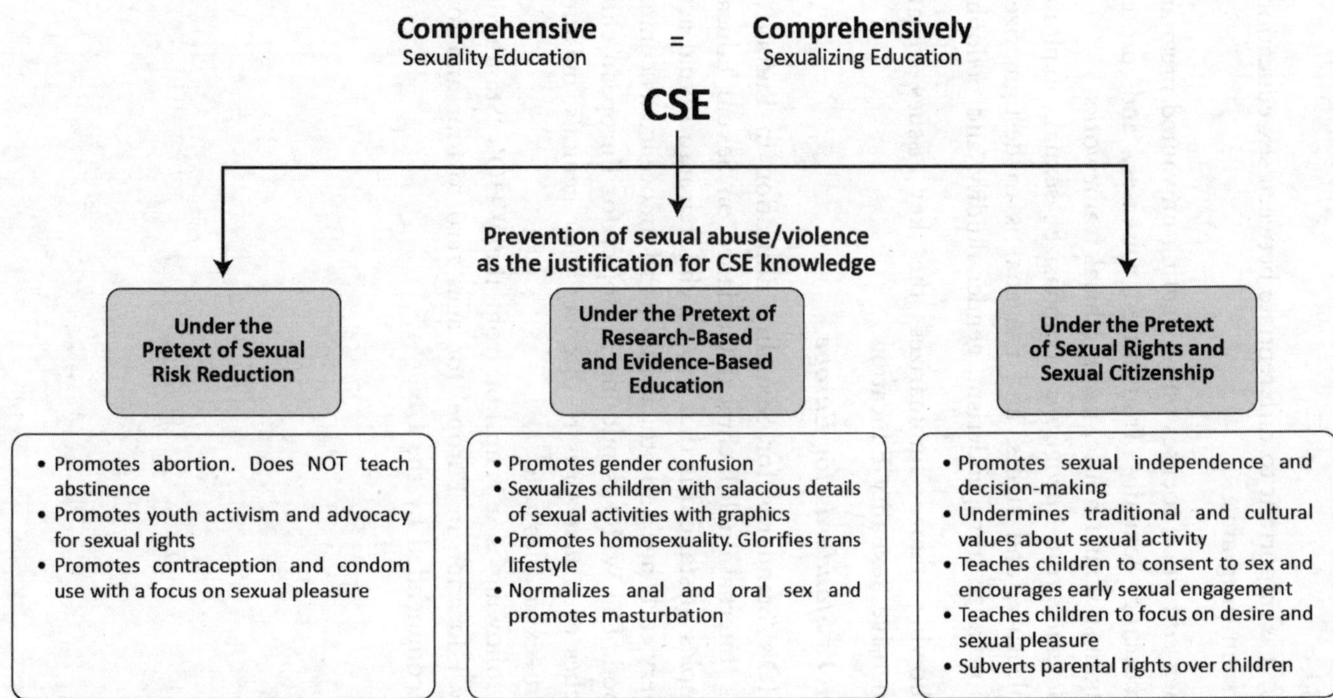
Comprehensive
Sexuality Education
=
Comprehensively
Sexualizing Education
CSE
Prevention of sexual abuse/violence as the justification for CSE knowledge
Under the Pretext of Sexual Risk Reduction
Under the Pretext of Research-Based and Evidence-Based Education
Under the Pretext of Sexual Rights and Sexual Citizenship
• Promotes abortion. Does NOT teach abstinence
• Promotes youth activism and advocacy for sexual rights
• Promotes contraception and condom use with a focus on sexual pleasure
• Promotes gender confusion
• Sexualizes children with salacious details of sexual activities with graphics
• Promotes homosexuality. Glorifies trans lifestyle
• Normalizes anal and oral sex and promotes masturbation
• Promotes sexual independence and decision-making
• Undermines traditional and cultural values about sexual activity
• Teaches children to consent to sex and encourages early sexual engagement
• Teaches children to focus on desire and sexual pleasure
• Subverts parental rights over children

Age Group	Guidelines	Description
0-4 years	Teachings	Enjoyment and pleasure when touching one's body, early childhood masturbation, discovery of one's body and genitals, understanding physical closeness, types of love, yes/no feelings, privacy, good/bad experiences, right to ask questions about sexuality, exploring gender identities, exploring nakedness and body.
	Skills	Awareness of gender identity, talking about pleasurable/unpleasurable feelings, expressing needs and boundaries, need for privacy, differentiating good/bad secrets, private/public behavior, knowing where to touch.
	Attitudes	Curiosity about one's own and others' bodies, introduce diverse lifestyles and different relationships, awareness of sexual rights, 'My body belongs to me', and the feeling that they can make their own decisions.
4-6 years	Teachings	Enjoyment of the body, early childhood masturbation, body/genitals discovery, different sexes, sexual language, sexual feelings, same-sex relationships, different concepts of family, body experiences, and right to information.
	Skills	Talk about sexual matters, consolidate gender identity, use non-offensive sexual language, recognize privacy needs, manage disappointments, communicate emotions and needs, ask questions about sexual rights, deal with sex in media.
	Attitudes	Exploring choice, valuing own feelings, awareness of rights, respect for different sexual norms.

Sexualization targets accelerate rapidly with age. By age five, it includes things like exploring nakedness. By age nine, the child is expected to become aware of his/her sexual rights 'as defined by IPPF' and other similar organizations that are committed to dismantling traditional values on gender and sexuality. The goal set for education is that by age fifteen, a child should have explored the entire plethora of sexual experiments and experiences, become skilled in deriving pleasure from all forms of sex, and gained self-confidence in choosing sex/gender as something fluid.

However, at age fifteen the brain is not yet fully developed. According to the National Institute of Mental Health (NIMH): 'the brain is fully developed and matured in the mid-to-late 20s. The part of the brain behind the forehead called the prefrontal cortex, is one of the last parts to mature. This area is responsible for skills like planning, prioritizing, and making good decisions'.[72] That begs the question: how can young children decide about their gender when that part of the brain is still developing?

Will the United Nations Decriminalize Pedophilia?

The UN sees Comprehensive Sexuality Education programs as part of human rights and as a tool for children to lead healthy sexual lives that are 'inclusive' with 'sexual diversity'. However, its idea of inclusivity is to introduce deviant sexual practices and destigmatize them—such as pedophilia. Psychologists know the importance of preserving childhood innocence and the psychological damage caused by early inappropriate sexual encounters with adults. This is where sex education has become a lethal weapon of the Left to break up the fundamental unit of society, namely the family structure. Yet, the UN is working with human rights NGOs that want to decriminalize deviant sexual behavior across the world.

The International Committee of Jurists (ICJ) along with UNAIDS and the Office of the High Commissioner for Human Rights (OHCHR) have published a legal framework called 8-MARCH-Principles. This is a document by so-called 'expert' jurists that redefines human rights and criminality and advocates for the decriminalization of sex with minors. One of the topics is 'consensual sexual activities, including sex outside marriage, same-sex sexual relations, adolescent sexual activity and sex work; gender identity and gender expression'.[73]

The UN legal experts who have drafted this 8-MARCH-Principles are sidelining the laws on the age of consent in different countries. The minimum age for consensual sex exists because children are not fully capable of making informed decisions to engage in sexual activity. This is why any adult sexual activity with a minor is considered unlawful.

While the UN guideline document does not explicitly decriminalize pedophilia, it leaves open the age below which sexual activity with a minor would be criminal. This is consistent with *UNESCO's guidelines that human beings have sexual rights from birth*. This framework paves the way to destigmatize pedophilia.

The UN echoes the sentiments of queer theorists who refer to pedophiles as 'Minor Attracted Persons' to destigmatize pedophilia, because according to the UN, 'Criminal liability may not be based on thoughts, intentions, beliefs or status alone'.[74] Secondly, it wants pedophilia to be decriminalized on the principle that consensual sexuality is a human right:

> Any prescribed minimum age of consent to sex must be applied in a non-discriminatory manner. Enforcement may not be linked to the sex/gender of participants or age of consent to marriage. Moreover, *sexual conduct involving persons below the domestically prescribed minimum age of consent to sex may be consensual*, in fact, if not in law. In this context, the enforcement of criminal law should reflect the rights and capacity of persons under 18 years of age to make decisions about engaging in consensual sexual conduct and their right to be heard in matters concerning them. Pursuant to their evolving capacities and progressive autonomy, persons under 18 years of age should participate in decisions affecting them, with due regard to their age,

> maturity and best interests, and with specific attention to non-discrimination guarantees.[75]

One of the most enthusiastic endorsers of the above principles have been UNESCO's affiliate Creating Resources for Empowerment in Action (CREA, an NGO funded by IPPF), and the human rights advocates Tripti Tandon and Meghna Abraham in India. UNICEF and other international organizations are now targeting India's teens by lobbying the Indian government to lower the age of consent for sexual activity.

India's young demographic, with twenty-five percent of its population below the age of twenty-four, is a prime target for indoctrination programs through education. The adolescent population between the ages of ten and twenty-four is especially being targeted for sex education through SEL and CSE. The floodgates are open, and the creation of a 'Breaking India Generation' is going full steam ahead. This also opens the door for bad actors in entertainment and other industries to capitalize on these trends with pornographic content for 350 million young consumers.

The United Nations' Two-pronged Strategy to Sexualize Children Globally

Even though UNESCO's primary focus is education, it is not focused on eradicating illiteracy or upgrading math and science skills as we mentioned earlier. We explained its policy frameworks that install a Marxist political education and use the youth as rebels on the front lines to dismantle traditional institutions. These student activists will usher in a 'new World Order'.

This was the exact strategy used by Mao Zedong (1893-1976) to transform China into a communist society, ridding the Chinese of what he considered the shackles of traditional Chinese culture. He incited the youth by destabilizing them psychologically. The brainwashed youth turned against their friends, relatives, neighbors, and even their parents who were considered counter revolutionaries. Thirty million people perished as a result.

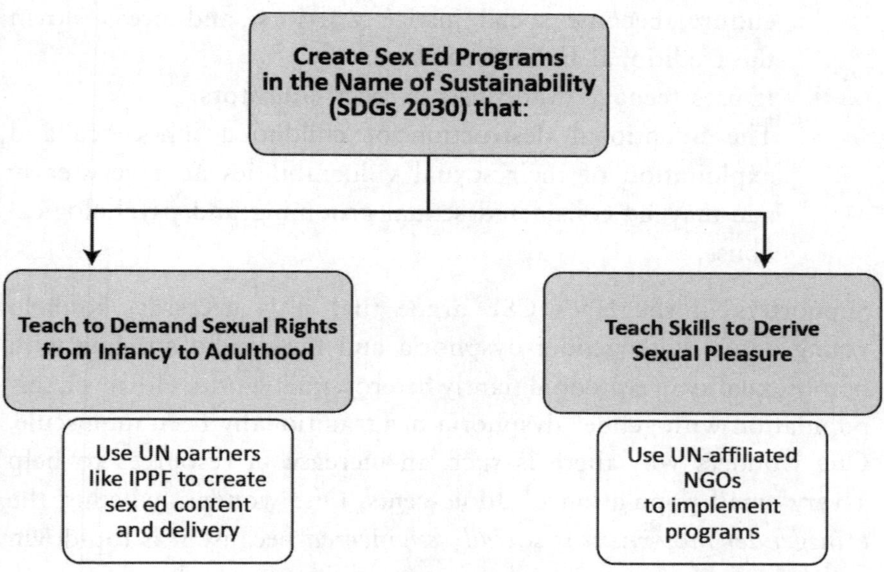

There are several problems with the CSE programs:

- It is not about reproductive health in the sense of preventing pregnancy or Sexually Transmitted Diseases. It is about exposing very young children to sex, pornography, masturbation, and exploration of gender fluidity. Gender fluidity and sexual fluidity are celebrated and reinforced as 'becoming queer'. Children who 'come out' as non-binary or trans or queer are made instant heroes and celebrities.
- UNESCO has adopted moral relativism in its sex education, which means there is no absolute set of moral principles. This renders young people confused, emotionally and

psychologically broken, and susceptible to manipulation and control.

- It encourages youth to rebel against their parents and culture, become social justice warriors, and break down the traditional family structure.
- It uses teenage evangelists as peer educators.
- The intentional destruction of childhood innocence and exploitation of their sexual vulnerabilities at a very early age may be considered sexual grooming and psychological abuse.

Supporters of the UN's CSE argue that it is necessary to help young adults with gender dysphoria and those who struggle with homosexuality in a predominantly heterosexual world. However, this population with gender dysphoria has traditionally been minuscule. One wonders why there is such an increase in resources to help a very small population of adolescents. One wonders whether the *transgender movement is socially engineered* because it is top-down and has suddenly produced a big jump in the number of 'queer' youths.

The UN, along with its international NGO partners, functions like a well-funded church with a doctrine and a mission to evangelize the world. They promote each other's reports and share the same jargon and frameworks. Among the main funders are the Bill & Melinda Gates Foundation, George Soros' Open Society Foundations, and many Western governments. This loose consortium is an unelected international body, serving as a mechanism for oligarchs, Western governments, and NGOs, to psychologically manipulate the youth of the world.

World Economic Forum and Social Emotional Learning

Though not a part of the UN, the World Economic Forum is an ideological ally. It is a powerful club of global elites who want to control the world. It has promoted a policy opposing basic math/reading skills for children in favor of 'emotional' education: 'Currently available ed-tech products focus on foundational skills, such as literacy and numeracy, not on the SEL-related competencies and character qualities'.[76]

The Boston Consulting Group (BCG) is the SEL consultant for the World Economic Forum and a partner of NITI Aayog, which we discuss in a later chapter. A report co-authored by WEF and BCG defines the future:[77]

> Policy-makers in particular must stand at the forefront of setting the agenda for policy change, prioritizing efforts that foster SEL and related assessments and measurements in education, as well as providing funding and other resources for the research and adoption of SEL and related ed-tech.[78] SEL is promoted inside and outside the school, through traditional and tech modes… the Lion's clubs have begun rolling out SEL programs called 'Lions Quest' to teach children to 'think-pair-share' which takes time from the academic schedule. History is also being hijacked by SEL, to teach about identity and reflection.[79]

3

THE ROT IN AMERICAN EDUCATION

A Report Card on Social Emotional Learning

In 2017, the American think tank Rand Corporation reviewed sixty-eight studies on SEL and found no evidence of academic benefits.[1] On the contrary, Social Emotional Learning has diverted precious resources *away* from academic competence. Some critics argue that SEL programs force teachers to be therapists, a role which they are not trained for. Other scholars are raising concerns that a tiny cabal of American academics have proclaimed their ideology as the universal truth because they are backed by powerful NGOs:

> Operating as scientific evangelists, a small, close-knit network of academics attached to major US research-intensive universities working within the domains of positive/personality psychology, neuropsychology and behavioural economics (SEL's Holy Trinity) have helped to secure and bolster a global consensus about the importance of SEL and elevated its status to a universal 'regime of truth'. With financial backing from a rapidly growing, multi-billion-dollar EdTech industry and tech-based philanthropists – most notably the Gates Foundation and the Chan Zuckerberg Initiative (CZI) these academic 'gurus' use their influence and expertise to advocate for the mainstreaming of SEL and SEL-based EdTech products and services in schools.[2]

Despite this, SEL consultants and business ventures are sprouting across the USA to sell their elixir for solving all sorts of behavioral problems like STDs, bullying, hate crimes, educational underachievement, and mental issues, as well as climate change.

> SEL's positioning as both a technology-driven policy 'solution' to long-standing educational problems and as a marketplace and investment opportunity has emerged within an increasingly corporatist global governance regime, whereby concerns about market reach and profit-accumulation now influence the content, delivery and assessment of learning in education systems worldwide.[3]

Unfortunately, India's NITI Aayog, the Ministry of Health and Family Welfare, and the Ministry of Education have all failed to use such research reports or do their due diligence before blindly jumping on the UN bandwagon. We will examine the American education system in some detail because that will give us a good idea of where India's educational trajectory is headed because it has copied the failed American model.

Our analysis reveals the systemic problems with the American system and the abysmal results it is producing from kindergarten to higher education. What is taught to children in the classroom and more importantly, what is glaringly absent in education shows the inroads Marxism has made. The propaganda of Marxist ideas permeates American education. It is not limited to decorating hallways and classrooms with the LGBTQIA+ rainbow flag. Even zebra crossings and steps leading to public libraries are being painted in these colors. Videos on social media show elementary school teachers boasting about their social justice curriculum, flaunting their classroom decorations, preaching their political leanings to children, and influencing them for activism.

This chapter will dig into American education's frameworks, content, pedagogy, the pipeline to universities, the teachers' unions, school libraries, the school boards as political platforms, teacher licensure/certification, examinations, after-school programs, the role of NGOs, and funding and admissions into universities.

The terminology used by social scientists sounds benign, but it is deceptive because many terms are code words loaded with hidden agendas and meanings that the average citizen cannot decipher. We will expose the real meaning of terms like diversity, equity, restorative justice, Sustainable Development Goals, inclusivity, anti-racism and anti-casteism, climate change, Competency-Based Education, and even words such as democracy whose meaning has been systematically distorted.

Queer Educational Frameworks

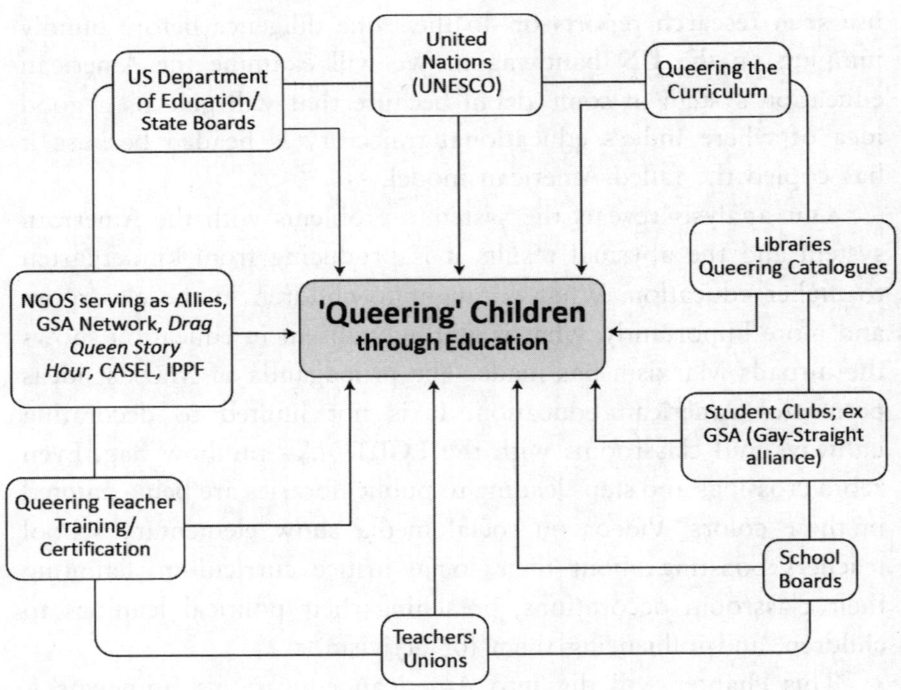

Queer pedagogists distinguish between two different levels of policy to support queer students:

- Defensive: Queer-inclusive teaching and curriculum, which includes school policies that protect queer students from discrimination and bullying.
- Offensive: Queer pedagogy, which is about 'queering' (verb) education and must teach children to systematically attack the non-queer students (heteronormativity) by constantly bombarding them with social justice topics through frameworks built by these queer pedagogists.[4]

We support the first policy: Schools should be inclusive and protect all children against bullying and discrimination. Children should be taught not mere tolerance but also mutual respect for their peers. That is the true meaning of diversity and inclusion.

However, what is being pushed is the second policy: The goal is to deploy children as social justice warriors attacking the entire system. Those deemed to be victims (merely by their identity) must become aggressive and go into attack mode. Those declared to belong to oppressor identities must apologize for their ancestors; they can redeem themselves only by fighting against their families and traditions.

We do not approve of policies that sideline the primary purpose of education, i.e. to teach knowledge acquisition, logical thinking, and skill development. Academic skills are taking a backseat, and the curriculum is being hijacked by a social justice agenda where priority is given to breaking limits, boundaries, and reading practices. This is being suggested by the well-known queer pedagogist Deborah Britzman, whose social justice frameworks have corrupted every subject area at all age groups.[5]

Following is a sample of how this hijacking is taking place today in various subjects.

Math

The pedagogy known as 'Critical Math' is an approach to 'queer' math by rejecting that math is objective. They want math education to be repurposed for 'reading the world' which means using math to quantify the power structures in society.[6] Math will no longer be about understanding its principles and learning to solve math problems required in a career.

One way of queering math in elementary schools is to include problems about queer individuals and then, using Paulo Freire's generative themes, step out of mathematics and into the Marxian political world of power dynamics. An example suggested to teachers is to teach 'the concept of equal in both a numerical sense and with concepts of diverse gender expressions'.[7] Freire's pedagogy is used to ask that 'elementary students not tackle math problems about queer individuals but consider broader questions about how queer people are seen in society'.[8]

Another strategy is to constantly 'center' the queer ideas on the one hand, and dismiss objectivity on the other, challenging the notion that there is one correct answer in math. Here is an example of a middle-school math exercise on same-sex marriage:

> The teaching was queered by giving students freedom to create their own mathematical questions and by incorporating some ambiguity into the lesson. For example, students used data from a newspaper article written after same-sex marriage became legal in their state that included a range of numbers for the average number of couples getting marriage licenses at a county courthouse. The students then all had slightly different answers, which challenged their ideas of what counted as a 'right' answer, as they expected from their experiences in more typical math courses.[9]

Tragically, such students will be *unqualified to enter careers requiring basic math skills*. In 2024, the California School Boards Association reviewed the impact of this approach and admitted that 'our approach to math has not led to improved outcomes in middle school and at all levels. ... Student achievement declines in mathematics as students' (sic) progress through the San Francisco Unified School District'.[10]

This assault on teaching mathematics comes from individuals

like Jo Boaler, a professor at the Stanford School of Education, who has a background in social sciences and not math, but who has been given immense authority as the architect of the state of California's math curriculum. We present Boaler's posture of equity as compiled by an education watchdog group:[11]

- Ban multiplication tables tests.
- **Arithmetic skills are outdated.**
- **Celebrate mistakes; there is no need to correct them.** When students make a mistake in math, their brain grows, synapses fire, and connections are made; when they do the work correctly, there is no brain growth. Students do not need to revisit a mistake and correct it to experience brain growth. Teachers need to make students feel good about their mistakes.
- Timed tests impair the brain's working memory and cause 'math anxiety', especially among girls. Math teachers need to stop frequent, timed testing.
- Teachers always know how well children are doing, so you don't need to test them. The children themselves can also self-assess and tell if things are wrong or not. They do that with extreme reliability.
- When we assign homework to students, we provide barriers to the students who need our support. Teachers and school leaders who want to promote equity should consider eradicating homework.
- Delay teaching algebra for all students and make courses easier. This will give students more time to do math together with each other.
- Stop tracking group work to counter racial inequities in mathematics achievement.
- Calculus is a 'horrible and inequitable filter' and 'less than 12% used any algebra, trigonometry, or calculus in their daily lives. Only 2% use calculus. Replace calculus and algebra with data analysis'.[12]

This approach to mathematics has ruined American excellence in STEM. Though this curriculum claims to bring racial equity, it has an adverse impact on the poor and marginalized students who attend public schools. Incidentally, Boaler's children are not in a public school learning her mathematics curriculum; they are in a private school that follows a rigorous math curriculum, revealing Boaler's hypocrisy.[13]

As another example of this kind of education, Seattle Public Schools are viewed as a pioneer in re-framing the math curriculum to make it useful for teaching social justice. They have come up with a math framework to 'humanize' math by bringing in ethnic studies. The idea is to encourage students to explore how the West has appropriated mathematics from others into its systems of oppression, thus rendering math a 'racist' subject. The framework's goal is to study the roots of mathematics 'in the ancient histories of people and empires of color'.[14] However, this framework has no mention of India's contributions and the well-known appropriation of Indian mathematics by European scholars. The curriculum's goal is to only showcase the contributions in mathematics of the designated 'oppressed communities'. And Hindus are designated as oppressors, hence, their contributions to math are excluded.

Science

Scientific objectivity is being rejected. The system wants that 'educators should also relax their views of objectivity, so that "ambiguous borderlands" are examined'.[15] For instance, teaching the binary nature of sex is declared non-inclusive. Queer scholars

> demand[s] that scientists and educators not rest comfortably in some myth of objectivity, but that they critically account for the broader cultural beliefs that necessarily empower, advance, limit, mislead, and bias scientific knowledge.[16]

They want to queer science to 'portray science education as a complex array of social codes, forces, and institutional powers that interact to shape the ideas of what is normative and deviant at any particular moment'.[17]

Social Studies

This is the subject where queer pedagogy takes full control. One of the stated goals is to 'enhance the capacity to teach for social justice'.[18] Students learn to be activists and foot soldiers by putting their entire brainwashing into practice through clubs and social media:

> This goes beyond queer inclusion to a queering, as students are digging beneath the surface and examining the social norms behind the messages. Students were also 'deconstructing heteronormativity through student-led dialogue' which led Lapointe to note that: 'Social Studies educators can benefit from following the queer pedagogical lead of these GSA members as a means to enhance their capacity to teach for social justice – a significant theme in Social Studies curriculum'.[19]

The conventional teacher/student relationship is also considered a binary that must be queered, i.e. the boundaries must be dismantled: 'Queering the student/teacher relationship may inspire educators to learn about and understand LGBTQ topics in queer ways, and ultimately integrate queer pedagogy in their classrooms'.[20]

Even tiny tots do not escape the queer pedagogy. As the *Drag Queen Story Hour* discussed earlier, little boys are encouraged to cross-dress and try being queer, all in the name of inclusivity:

> Working with even younger students, Bower-Phipps et al. (2017) discussed ways that gender categories can be queered with preschool students. Some of this disruption can be as simple as offering princess dresses to all students during imaginative play, not just the girls. This queers students' notions of gendered behaviors, as even in young children these societal norms are beginning to seem natural.[21]

Social Justice

As mentioned earlier, Critical Race Theory has entered the K-12 in full swing. For example, the Denver Public Schools were pushing the Black Lives Movement by sending out a Black Excellence Pledge that was racist against white people. It included statements like:

> 'Understand the prevalence & deep harm whiteness brings to students'; 'Equity-based revisions to curriculum'; 'Work to dismantle the system that allows certain students to excel, others to perish'; 'It is not if you are racist, but **how** you are racist'.[22]

Social justice based on CRT is taught right from kindergarten. For example, newly minted terms such as 'birthing persons' are to be used instead of 'pregnant mothers'. Texts are scanned to point out every instance of the exclusion of a race or identity as a systemic bias. Such lessons are brainwashing in the name of teaching literacy.

Restorative Justice

Restorative justice is now becoming a popular concept in the USA replacing the traditional concepts in the criminal justice system. Restorative justice does not believe in punishment. An example was the 'defund the police' movement that demanded dismantling the police departments altogether. Most DEI programs also include restorative justice as a means of attaining equity in the criminal justice system; this bypasses the objective application of the law and uses identity politics to determine how the law should apply. It does not teach accountability.

In schools, children are taught to question racial disparities in discipline and punishment. For instance, there is a discussion that Black students accounted for fifteen percent of the student body, but thirty-one percent of students were arrested. The discussion would not consider factors like fatherless homes and a culture of glorifying violence. Children are taught that since the outcome is disproportionate, the system must therefore be racist. As a result, in the name of restorative justice, schools are discouraged from reporting poor behavior such as assault, sexual harassment, and even violence toward parents.[23]

Restorative justice in the school system has done away with punishment altogether. With Critical Race Theory guiding the counseling, victimhood is glorified, and students are not held accountable for their actions. Critics say that students tend to misbehave more if they face no punitive consequences:

> Some restorative justice programs go so far as to reward misbehavior with time in a "decompression room" and the administration of snacks. Nearly all of them encourage students to blame factors outside their own control for misbehavior.[24]

Restorative justice assumes that violence in kids is solely the product of their environment, which is in turn the product of systemic racism; hence, the violent offender is a victim of such systemic oppression. In many public schools in America, teachers and administrators have lost total control over violent behavior in their classrooms. Students are underperforming, classes are turning violent, and teachers are unable to cope with disciplinary issues.

India has had a long tradition of a justice system such as the village *panchayat*, where the local community elders settle disputes using their cultural and social norms. The Marxism-based American restorative justice is more about the glorification of victimhood as determined by Western-trained social scientists. We reject this victimhood-based restorative justice that teaches the wrong values to children, a sense of entitlement, and a disregard for accountability. Justice should punish to shape the future behavior of the perpetrator and serve as a warning to others.

English and Literacy

sj Miller, a queer pedagogist and social justice activist, has developed a broad framework that is meant to be applied to all subjects taught in schools. His principles include ideas from Freire, Butler, and others. He treats gender as a social, historical, material, cultural, economic, and religious construct, fluid, and performative. It also requires students to choose pronouns, teaches them to identify and critique gender norms in different subjects, and advocates equity.[25]

Music

Students are presented musical pieces written and performed by queer artists and the teachers discuss the queer identities of the artists with the objective of 'queering the expectations' in music classes. This is considered beneficial because it 'expresses outrage to confront the terror of gender nonnormative students in all of our classrooms'.[26] In other words, attacking the non-queer as a form of revenge is deemed necessary.

Queering the Class: Assault On All Binaries

Woke social scientists have determined that gender and sex are not biological but social constructs, and therefore fluid. Because they are social constructs, it follows that the dominant/oppressor people who have controlled society are responsible for the male/female binaries. Children are taught that gender is a spectrum of maleness and femaleness with many genders in between. Therefore, biology is wrong.

They are also told that the male/female genders have been shaped because we have been 'performing' these genders as a habit forced by an oppressive patriarchal society that lays out the norms of what constitutes 'maleness' or 'femaleness'. In other words, all this goes back to the Critical Race Theory:

Oppressors (Whites, Heterosexuals, Brahmins, etc.) ➔ Define the binaries to help them control society ➔ People perform according to these binaries ➔ These binaries become habits that are falsely seen as 'science'

Queering and biology are on a collision course. Children are told that one can 'imagine' gender (which is ostensibly the identity), 'feel' attraction to a particular sex, 'express' gender outwardly in a certain way that has nothing to do with biology and may have a sexual anatomy which has nothing to do with the previous three.

Consequently, American schools 'socially transition' children to 'try out' different genders on this made-up spectrum by encouraging the use of pronouns, and changing names and clothing, often unbeknownst to parents. Children in elementary schools are indoctrinated by using attractive graphics of 'rainbow unicorn, a teddy bear, and a cookie', to teach them new made-up identities, and distinguish between gender that was 'assigned' at birth versus gender expression and gender identity.[27]

Strangely, political pressure is so strong that the fields of biology and medicine have also started accepting the notion that sex and gender are non-binary. A recent article in the *Scientific American* magazine claimed that sex was anything but binary, to which the famous evolutionary biologist Richard Dawkins responded:

> This ridiculous article (shame on the once-great Scientific American) ignorantly misunderstands the nature of the sex binary: 'Actual research shows that sex is anything but binary'. Sex is not defined by chromosomes, nor by anatomy, nor by psychology or sociology, nor by personal inclination, nor by 'assignment at birth', but by gamete size. It happens to be embryologically DETERMINED by chromosomes in mammals and (in the opposite direction) birds, by temperature in some reptiles, by social factors in some fish. But it is universally DEFINED by the binary distinction between sperms and eggs. You may argue about 'gender' if you wish (biologists have better things to do) but sex is a true binary, one of rather few in biology.[28]

The idea that gender is a cultural and social construct is becoming the required chant in the medical field. Those who oppose are immediately canceled with consequences to their employment. However, some audacious scientists like Dawkins have stood up to this nonsensical idea.

Colin Wright, an evolutionary biologist, also pushes back saying that sex is not a spectrum. He says that there are many sex determination systems (chromosomes, environment) in nature but all sex determination systems produce the binary of either male or female and that the downstream consequences of this binary sex are morphology, physiology, and behavior.[29] He proves that sex is indeed binary after accounting for other possibilities outside the XX and XY outcomes. He argues that these other presentations such as XXYY, XXY (Klinefelter Syndrome), XYY (Jacob Syndrome), XXX Syndrome, XO (Turner Syndrome), and XXYY Syndrome are considered chromosomal compositions *within* the male and the female binary and not an expansion of sex categories. Citing the case of Intersex people (individuals born with bodies that do not fit the typical binary characteristics of male or female) he notes that intersex conditions appear in one person out of 5,500 and this in no way means that sex is non-binary.

He goes on to explain that secondary sex characteristics developed during puberty such as breasts in women and facial hair in men are based on their gametes or chromosomal make-up, just as the hormones, morphology, genitalia, and behavior are also based on the binary gametes.

Despite all the scientific evidence to the contrary, support to promote the queer agenda is staggering. Many spokespersons of the LGBTQIA+ community with help from Woke NGOs arrange for queens to read to children in public schools. Some NGOs help in the formation of clubs within the school called Gender and Sexuality Alliances clubs (GSAs) for middle- and high-school students. These clubs provide a wide variety of resources and toolkits to help the GSA programs attract children with snacks and cookies; these are operational across forty states in the USA with California alone boasting over eleven hundred clubs in the GSA Network.[30]

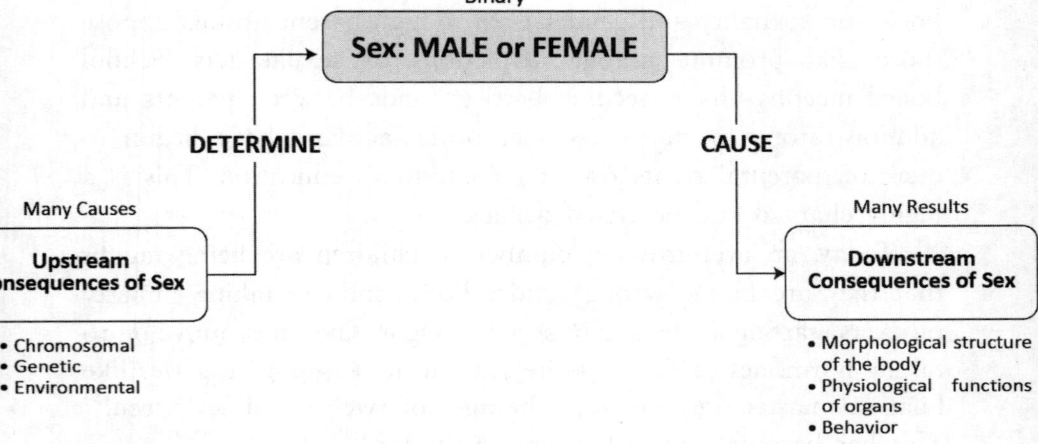

Source: Dr. Colin Wright, Evolutionary Biologist

Another organization promoting the LGBTQIA+ agenda is the American Library Association (ALA) whose mission is to promote libraries and library education internationally. The ALA is now promoting the trans agenda in schools through the library systems. Emily Drabinski, a self-proclaimed lesbian Marxist who heads ALA, has been figuring out ways to 'queer the catalogue', i.e. find ways to take over the cataloging of books by those trained in Marxist ideas. She claims that only someone with a 'queer lens' is capable of cataloging properly.[31] In other words, the library cataloging system is being taken over to help indoctrinate library users.

> Engaging queer theory and library classification and cataloging together requires new ways of thinking about how to be ethically and politically engaged on behalf of marginal knowledge formations and identities who quite reasonably expect to be able to locate themselves in the library. Queer theory invites a shift in responsibility from catalogers, positioned to offer functional solutions, to public services librarians, who can teach patrons to dialogically engage the catalog as a complex and biased text, just as critical catalogers do.[32]

To support the trans movement, school libraries have stocked up books on sexuality and gender even though parent groups oppose those that promote graphic depictions of sexual acts. School board meetings have become battlegrounds between parents and administrators. In states like California, activists have begun to question parental rights over their children's education. This is a highly charged and polarized debate.

Today, an ever-growing number of children are being taught that they are in the wrong gender body, and are taking puberty blockers starting at the age of seven or eight. Then they move on to taking hormones of the opposite sex and undergoing surgeries like bilateral mastectomy between the ages of twelve and seventeen.[33] This has become a huge business in the USA.

The use of puberty blockers and cross-sex hormones causes sterility and considerable damage to bone density. Puberty blockers seriously affect the physical and mental growth of children, while cross-sex hormones make irreversible changes to the body. These treatments are prescribed because transgender teens suffer high rates of depression and mental health issues.

The number of detransitioners or young adults who had medical/surgical interventions but who no longer identify as transgender is also growing. New studies show that discontentment with one's gender is high during adolescence but diminishes significantly with age.[34] As young adults, many of these detransitioners regret their irreversible decisions.

There is a sudden, and dramatic increase in gender dysphoria (or sex confusion) and people are debating whether mental health issues cause gender dysphoria or the other way around. It appears that some other causes could be responsible for this sudden surge in the number of youths who are confused about their sex and thus identify as trans.

Critical pedagogy has had a huge negative impact on children. Nearly twenty percent of those born between 1977 and 2003 or Gen Z identify themselves as LGBTQIA+.[35] Gen Z women are three times more likely to identify as LGBTQIA+ than their male counterparts. Among college-educated young adults, this number is even higher—at forty percent of youth entering Brown University in Rhode Island.

Jonathan Haidt, the American social psychologist, and professor at New York University's Stern School of Business, while researching the psychology of morality and moral emotions, has been studying the social contagion behind the surge in the number of young people claiming to be transgender:

> So, there's very important, older research by Nicholas Christakis and, James Fowler where they looked at, they had gigantic health data sets, the Framingham Heart Study, and they were able to see that, you know, if one person takes up smoking, their friends are more likely to take up smoking, but actually, so are their friends' friends and even friends' friends' friends. So, the things we do become spread out through social networks. We affect each other. Now it turns out, when you're looking at emotions, girls and women, when a woman is depressed, that spreads out to her network. Whereas when a man is depressed, it doesn't. Women talk about their feelings. They're more connected in that way. Girls are connecting on social media, where it just turns out in many communities, the more anxious and depressed you are, the more you get support. The more extreme your symptoms, the more you get likes and followers. You know, of course it's good to destigmatize mental illness. We don't want people to be ashamed. But boy, is it a terrible idea to valorize it, to tell young people, 'You know what, the more you have this, the more popular you'll be, the more support you'll get.' And so, you get this explosion, not just of anxiety – anxiety is in part spread sociogenically, it's called – from social causes, not from internal causes. But we get it for dissociative identity disorder, and it seems to be the case for gender dysphoria as well.[36]

When the interviewer asked Haidt: 'You think that the data demonstrates that it is above and beyond just the phenomenon of coming out and increased awareness?'[37] he responded:

> Yes. Because it happens in clusters of girls who had no previous gender dysphoria when they were young. So, it's very different from the kinds of gender dysphoria cases that we've known about for decades. But what happened, especially when girls got YouTube and Instagram early, then especially TikTok, girls get sucked into these vortices and they take on each other's purported mental illnesses.[38]

The constant push in schools, promoting the transgender agenda from kindergarten onward in the name of inclusivity, and constantly glorifying the use of pronouns and queerness, also adds to this social contagion that Haidt speaks about.

With all this focus on systemic racism and power dynamics, it is no surprise that academic competency has dropped. In 2022, the USA was the worst performer in mathematics among the Organisation for Economic Co-operation and Development (OECD) countries, and its performance was worse than a decade earlier in 2012. The 'grade level' competency in the USA is below most industrialized nations like Singapore and Finland. Recent data on numeracy and literacy in the state of Illinois shows that:

> Not a single student can do math at grade level in 53 Illinois schools. For reading, it's 30 schools. .... What's really incredible is that many of these schools are rated 'commendable' by the Illinois State Board of Education. That's the 2nd-highest of four 'accountability' ratings a school can receive.[39]

Instead of working to improve the skills of minority groups, academic standards are constantly being lowered in the USA to achieve equity. American classrooms today have inept teachers who cannot teach English or math because many are mainly activists for gender ideology and social justice. They are supported by leftist teachers' unions, which want to abolish standardized testing and eliminate teacher accountability. The entire education system is so corrupt that even the ratings given by school boards are not reliable.

College application processes are fraught with reverse discrimination based on Critical Race Theory. Through the essays in the application, universities prefer to admit social justice warriors over regular kids with academic skills. Standardized tests like SAT, GRE, and GMAT are abolished or made optional. There is grade inflation to ensure that everyone passes. Restorative justice replaces punishment for transgressions. There are more administrators than students in many college systems to ensure equity is achieved while academic standards keep sliding into the abyss. America has never spent more money on education.[40] Some studies even show that pumping in more money does not boost academic success.[41]

The Mental Crisis of America's Youth

After so much hype around SEL in the USA for over a decade, the record shows a poor state of mental health in American society. Unfortunately, India continues to rapidly import the very same educational policies that have ruined American children and families and created societal problems. Indian policymakers should take note of the following statistics in the West:

1 Over thirty-six percent of eighteen to twenty-four-year-olds have some mental illness.[42]
2. Ten percent of girls between the ages of thirteen to nineteen in 2019 took anti-depressants.[43]
3. Thirty-seven percent of twelve to eighteen-year-olds have been treated for depression or other mental health conditions, with the number going up to forty-three percent among nineteen to twenty-one-year-olds.[44]
4. Students in an SEL program suffered *more* depression and anxiety and worse parent-child relationships compared to the control group.[45]

5. Another larger study in the UK also reported more anxiety and depression in students who exhibited less mindfulness after SEL was instituted.[46]
6. An Australian study also confirmed these results on SEL.[47]
7. Another study published in the *Scandinavian Journal of Psychology* that was 'quite robust with a sample size above 5,000 and good psychometric properties', established that adherence to policies based on Woke critical social justice is correlated with higher instances of anxiety and depression: 'Specifically, being on the political left was more predictive of lower mental well-being than high critical social justice scores alone. This suggests that the link between critical social justice attitudes and mental health is complex and may be mediated by broader political and ideological beliefs'.[48]

Abigail Shrier, an American expert on the mental health crisis of young people in America, finds: forty-two percent have a mental health condition, seventy-eight percent of those are suffering from severe depression, and of those, ninety percent are struggling with severe anxiety.[49] Shrier empathizes with young people for the pain associated with their mental health. She investigates the key question: Despite being a generation with the highest wealth, access to mental health diagnosis and therapy, freedom, and education, how did they get into this state? Below is a summary of her findings in her book, *Bad Therapy: Why the Kids Aren't Growing Up*.[50]

- Shrier puts the blame squarely on American mental health experts, saying that the aggressive intervention methods being practiced make the problems worse. Mental health practices cause alienation from parents which worsens depression and anxiety. 'We are talking kids into feeling unwell' with the constant talk of Post Traumatic Stress Disorder (PTSD), trauma, etc., amplifying the ordinary problems of life into crippling mental health problems.
- Personality traits are being diagnosed with clinical labels:

What used to be 'worry' is now labeled 'anxiety', 'heartbreak' is labeled 'depression', and 'shyness' is 'social anxiety'. She views SEL programs as group therapy in which kids are asked to constantly talk about their pain, experiences of sadness, and family issues—constantly dwelling and reinforcing to make a child clinically depressed.

- SEL is offered to all kids even though most do not need therapy, creating more mental problems than it solves. Schools have become the epicenters for therapy, counseling, and mental health and wellness instruction.

Social Emotional Learning Turns Math Into 'Feelings'

Social Emotional Learning injects anxiety even into math classes: SEL zealots disrupt math, English, and history because they feel 'education is merely a vehicle for their social-emotional lessons'. For example, the educational consultant Ricky Robertson says: 'I can't think of a content area that needs more social-emotional learning than mathematics.' To understand this syndrome, Shrier sat through a presentation titled *Embedding SEL in Math*. The lesson commenced with a discussion of feelings about math. Many teachers said 'anxiety!' should be the main topic. Shrier relates:

> The presenters showed us a series of kindergarten-level 'math problems' that asked us to look at a bunch of shapes and asked: 'Which one doesn't belong?' At the end, they revealed the correct answer: they all belong. No wrong answers! Everyone wins! See, that wasn't hard. I turned to the high school math teacher next to me and asked her how she could possibly incorporate this sort of approach into Algebra II. She stared back at me, a frozen rictus pinned to the corners of her mouth. She seemed to think Big Brother was watching us...A decent number of kids actually show up hoping to learn some geometry and not burn their limited instructional time on conversations about their mental health. But from every angle, such children could only be made to feel errant and

alone. In the minds of social-emotional learning advocates, healthy kids are those who share their pain during geometry. That is how a teacher knows they are emotionally regulated. They are willing to cry for the benefit of the class.[51]

Dismantling Parenthood

Shrier says children are constantly told that grandma and elders can't be trusted to help them; only the 'experts' can. Hence, families must outsource their children's well-being to schools as mental health providers. She says the focus on emotional health and feelings takes center stage and amplifies the issues, whereas parental authority and love produce the most balanced children as it makes them feel secure. She says that hired caregivers, counselors, and therapists are no substitutes for parents and grandparents for navigating stressful situations and focusing on the tasks at hand. Mental health surveys ask the children personal questions that undermine a parent-child relationship, and children are told that parents do not know about mental health as the experts do.

Shrier worries that the mental health surveys administered to children are packed with questions on suicide, and the intensity of the questions keeps escalating. Children who have never thought about suicide are presented with these ideas.

Disruption Caused by an Over-Sexualized Culture

Schools are frequently facing issues like sexting, revenge porn, rape and assault.[52] Some blame this trend on the 'over-sexualized' culture of 'love-is-love' and the normalization of sexual deviance through CSE programs. A Chicago school investigation found:

> Case after case of teachers grooming children as young as elementary age for sex, texting pictures of their genitals to students, making sexual advances on them such as kissing, fondling, and inappropriate touching, and sexual assault. Several school workers were found to possess child pornography on their phones and in one case, a school

janitor was arrested after it was discovered he was secretly videotaping children in the school bathroom with a cell phone he had hidden under a sink. In another case, a male special education teacher was found to have spent seven months grooming an 8th-grade student and then ultimately having sex with the girl in her home. In another case, a male high school teacher was found to have sent more than 4,000 sexual texts to a student including 400 messages in just one day. The teacher also told the female student he had a sexual relationship with a male student, and that he had an open marriage...In some of the cases, staff members knew about the sexual misconduct, but failed to report it—as was the case involving a high school physical education teacher who exposed himself to female students by pulling down his pants and showing his genitals. According to the report, the teacher, who has a daughter around the age of the female students, sent videos via social media to at least one of the students of himself masturbating and engaging in other sexual acts.[53]

Normalization of Sexual Deviance in the Classroom

A report on middle school children aged eleven to fifteen states:

> Sex ed in middle school now includes graphic lessons on anal sex, oral sex, and masturbation, with stick figures to illustrate body positions. Supplemental reading in middle school libraries includes, 'Sex, Puberty, and All That Stuff,' a book explaining foreplay and how to rub the clitoris to produce pleasure. Massachusetts's curriculum tells seventh graders how to use cling wrap as a dental dam around their teeth for safe oral sex... High schoolers were recently assigned to write a sexual fantasy featuring massage oil, flavoured syrup, a candle, music, feathers, or a boa. How about teaching them math and English instead? ... A parent explained that it's one thing

to monitor social media and the movies kids watch, and it's another to have to worry about 'our children being exposed to curriculum that teaches them how to perform sexual acts.'... Many Massachusetts districts use Planned Parenthood's 'Get Real' curriculum. The eighth-grade teacher's manual suggests discussing a hypothetical scenario about two middle school boys who 'enjoy the sexual part of their relationship.'[54] A Florida parent voiced her concern that 'a cartoon video of a laughing clitoris, part of the curriculum, would encourage young girls to be promiscuous.[55]

A veteran pediatric endocrinologist says that 'medically or surgically assisted transgenderism among young children becomes so popular that it is now a social contagion phenomenon'. When asked whether kids at ages thirteen and fourteen—who can legally undergo sex-change operations in certain states—understand the long-term impacts of the transition, he replied that they cannot:

> 'It's trying to get the child to understand fertility or the fact that they will be sterile. They are sterilizing children by these processes...There aren't countries in the world that are called decent or moral will routinely allow children to be sterilized, and yet this is what's happening here in this country. The child can't even understand what that means'... Contrary to the common claim...American teenagers are having less sex, not more, over the past decade. Those who have had sex, however, experience more problems in their life than those who haven't.[56]

Some American experts point to the US Centers for Disease Control and Prevention (CDC) studies to show that those high school students who have had sexual experiences are more likely to be suicidal, depressed, and have other problems than those who have not. 'So really, we are obligated to teach children to avoid sexually risky behavior, to avoid sex until marriage'.[57]

Global Study Reveals Harmful Effects of Comprehensive Sexuality Education

A 2019 study examined authoritative reviews of CSE effectiveness that were conducted for UNESCO and sponsored by the US federal government, including the CDC.[58] The detailed study evaluated 103 international school-based CSE studies (60 in the USA, 43 outside the USA), and found some shocking results:

1. Eighty-seven percent of CSE programs globally *did not achieve their intended outcomes*, such as delaying sexual initiation, promoting increased condom use, or reducing rates of pregnancy and STDs as is often claimed by the NGOs aggressively promoting CSE.
2. Twenty-one percent showed harmful effects resulting from CSE in non-American schools. These effects included reduced condom use, increased sexual activity, higher numbers of sexual partners, engagement in oral sex, incidents of forced sex, and higher rates of STDs or pregnancy.

The study concludes:

> Using these more-credible standards, the claims that school-based CSE has been proven effective and AE [Abstinence Education] is ineffective are not supported by 120 of the strongest and most up-to-date sex education studies across the globe, the same studies that have been relied upon by the U.S. government and UNESCO in their extensive reviews of CSE results. Three decades of research indicate that school-based comprehensive sex education has not been an effective public health strategy—it has produced only a few sustained effects on protective out-comes, without other negative impacts, in U.S. and non-U.S. settings combined. In fact, it has shown far more evidence of failure than success and caused a concerning number of harmful effects. The evidence for abstinence education effectiveness in the U.S., though limited, appears more promising—enough to justify additional research.[59]

Fostering Anxiety and Negative Attitudes in Youth

The attitudes of the young towards parenthood, marriage, and taking responsibility are becoming unhealthy. A study revealed that over thirty-six percent of individuals aged sixteen to eighteen expressed a lack of desire to have children in the future.[60] Their reasons included apprehensions about capitalist societies, global warming, overpopulation, the cost-of-living crisis, the political climate, and the absence of women's rights. They face the ethical dilemmas associated with bringing children into what they described as an 'unsafe', 'deteriorating', 'cruel', and 'dangerous' world.

One young female student noted: 'The state of the world is in shambles. Governments are corrupt. The environment is deteriorating … it would be cruel to put a child through any of our problems, especially since they are not getting better'.[61] Fear and anxiety seemed to be underlying their views on pregnancy as well—'students who expressed fearing pregnancy and childbirth wanted to adopt to avoid the physical and mental stresses of pregnancy'.[62]

The study also noted that female students harbored concerns regarding potential 'permanent damage to their body' from pregnancy and feared the mental health effects of childbirth as 'terrifying'. These women also found children to be 'very annoying', 'inconvenient', and 'loud'. Some voiced a preference for pets over children. Nearly half of the respondents expressed concern about the prospect of being a parent. Students also blamed sex education for instilling such fear:

> Female students shared that the current sex education is fear-driven and is the reason for them having these negative associations with pregnancy and childbirth. 'Sex education also seems to focus on scaring people out of having children at a young age, but just seems to scare people out of having children.'[63]

These are not healthy attitudes for a young person. These programs make young people more anxious, and unable to cope with the challenges of life. Social Emotional Learning therapy is being performed by unlicensed people and the effects are untested.

A study in Finland describes anxiety as fear that is frequently associated with worries about potential threats, while depression is characterized by a lack of motivation and feelings of deep resignation. The study highlights that Wokeness has a stronger connection to anxiety than to depression, implying that liberals are more disturbed by social issues, which heightens their anxiety. The study 'suggests that wokeness is relatively directly, *causally* connected with anxiety…'.[64]

Another widespread study in Finland[65] looked at Critical Social Justice Attitudes (CSJA or Wokeness) and found that men generally (eighty-five percent) rejected CSJ propositions, while women (sixty percent) showed more support. The researcher said, 'Mental health problems correlate with having leftist views overall and even people on the left who don't have much CSJA [woke mindset] report worse mental health than people on the right,' adding, 'I have found that basic evolutionary tendencies seem to be tightly connected to my wellbeing and I ignore them at my peril… disliking masculinity in itself will make for a hard life, as 50-80% of our tendencies come from genes and in males those genes heavily direct towards behaviors and preferences that are deemed masculine'.[66]

Tragic Impact on Indians in the USA

In response to the rise of political agendas in public schools, many American parents are choosing to homeschool their children to escape the Woke indoctrination. Homeschooling has experienced explosive growth since the COVID-19 pandemic.[67]

Most Indian parents in the USA are either unaware of the indoctrination in schools or consider it a Right-wing conspiracy. They are slow to wake up to this reality in America and stand to lose their younger generation to Woke politics. Already, Indian parents are scrambling when their child identifies as trans or becomes Hinduphobic. This trend will worsen if the community leaves the education of their children to the state. The new gender ideology is already affecting many clueless Indian families leading them to taking drastic decisions.

The story of the ten-year-old Indian American girl Tia, who was socially transitioned by her teacher Jennifer Knight in Washington state, is an example of a growing trend. It all started when Tia wore Indian clothes to school one day and complained to Knight that her dress was itchy. Knight 'brought up the notion that perhaps she [Tia] didn't like girls' clothing because she wasn't a girl'.[68] Knight thus started a long and dark relationship with Tia, indoctrinating her to socially transition, assigning her a new male name 'Felix', and pronouns 'He, Him, They', all this unbeknownst to her parents. All the other children were told to hide this secret from their families. However, the news leaked, and other parents got to know that Tia was now Felix. Tia's parents were still in the dark. Who would have thought that asking children to hide information and lie to their parents would be the standard instruction from the American school system? Increasingly, children are told that they can't trust their parents.

When Tia's parents got wind of their daughter's situation, they finally understood why a cheerful Tia had become depressed, quiet, and distant. Tia meanwhile decided she had had enough of being a boy:

> Tia's mother said that 'her daughter had come to her and was crying and very upset. She was saying she wants to go to school, see her friends like normal, and doesn't want to be a boy anymore. But Tia was afraid that Mrs. A [Knight] would be mad at her and wouldn't like her anymore. Her mom was like, What are you talking about?'[69]

Tia's parents tried to confront Knight and the school principal but soon realized that the system was stacked against them and that they might lose their child. *Eventually, the Indian couple along with their two children fled the USA and returned to India, out of fear that American officials were trying to take custody of their children*: 'Tia and her younger brother were quietly driven out of the state, to a house in Oregon, where they stayed for a while before leaving the country'.[70]

Meanwhile, the emails that Tia received from Knight show Knight's persistence to have a secret relationship with her student:

> You need to get a personal email set up, so we still have a way to communicate...I would take you into my home any time you need...Make sure this email is deleted too when we are done [because] otherwise when your mom looks, you will be outed instantly...I kept emailing you, but I was worried your mom interfered before you saw my messages.[71]

What this story illustrates is that the school systems, teachers, and doctors consider themselves more qualified and better decisionmakers for a child to navigate gender dysphoria than the parents. School policies regarding gender dysphoria assume that psychological damage and even suicide will result if a gender-dysphoric child is not sexually affirmed. Therefore, if parents do not affirm the child's gender preference, the school has the right to encourage social transition and even hide it.

However, there is insufficient data to support the schools' claims. Studies show that gender identity disorders seem to go hand in hand with serious personality disorders (81.4%), and predominantly narcissistic personality disorders (57.1%). A 1991 study found that boys with 'gender identity disorder' invariably had mothers who had borderline personality disorder. Moreover, the authors of a study believe that:

> Crossgender identification in the majority of boys, but not in all, is a defensive solution to separation anxiety...It is believed that the father has as significant a role as the mother in contributing to his son's gender identity difficulties and that in future research on families of boys with Gender Identity Disorder (GID), both parents need to be studied. In this study, the clinical impression of the few fathers who have been

evaluated suggests that they too have difficulties with affect regulation and possibly with alcoholism.[72]

Sadly, in the name of inclusivity and affirmation, such studies on mental health are considered transphobic today, so parents are bullied into accepting the Woke dogma without hard scientific evidence.[73]

4

REPURPOSING GANDHI FOR MARXISM

The United Nations' Woke Outpost in India

The Mahatma Gandhi Institute of Education for Peace and Sustainable Development (MGIEP) based in New Delhi was set up as UNESCO's Category 1 research institute focused on transforming education towards the UN's Sustainable Development Goals 4.7. A Category 1 institute is defined as being institutionally and legally part of UNESCO and considered an integral part of its program. In other words, MGIEP is UNESCO itself operating in India, with Indian taxpayer money. It enjoys the full credibility and clout of the UN in the field of children's education.

The purpose of SDGs 4.7 is as follows:

> By 2030, ensure all learners acquire knowledge and skills needed to promote sustainable development, including among others through education for sustainable development and sustainable lifestyles, human rights, gender equality, promotion of a culture of peace and non-violence, global citizenship, and appreciation of cultural diversity and of culture's contribution to sustainable development.

This seems like a commendable goal nobody would disagree with. The detail we must note is that this education must be through Social Emotional Learning programs developed by a global network of organizations.

The MGIEP website describes its vision thus:

> *Building Kinder Brains*. We believe in Transforming Education with SEL for the Sustainable Development Goals (SDGs). At UNESCO MGIEP, we recognize the *urgent need for Social Emotional Learning (SEL) to be mainstreamed into education systems to transform education* and shape a future that is geared towards providing peace and human flourishing. SEL can be described as learning that allows all learners to identify and navigate emotions, practice mindful engagement, and exhibit prosocial behavior for human flourishing towards a peaceful and sustainable planet.[1]

Interestingly, MGIEP is quite open about turning child leaders into evangelists for its ideology:

> At UNESCO MGIEP, we work with youth organizations and young people worldwide by supporting their initiatives and *curating youth action* towards kindness and transforming education.[2]

All this sounds very impressive and uplifting, using Gandhi's name. However, few have drilled deeper to investigate the fact that its purpose is to urgently bring SEL into 'mainstream education systems'.

Interestingly, this was not MGIEP's original stated mission. When it came into being in the year 2009, its original mission was to 'research into education for peace and sustainable development', inspired by Gandhi's ideals. The founders of the institute 'envisaged work on curriculum and pedagogy and various disciplines of education (history, politics, economics and sociology, etc.) applied to problems of peace and sustainable development'.[3]

One must note that Gandhian ideas advocated going *away* from materialism and consumerism as the way to bring about sustainability, and his approach to peace was not through Marxist clashes between identities classified as oppressors and oppressed.

Neither would Gandhi have endorsed using behavioral science to rewire the brains of young children.

Post 2014, MGIEP took a drastic turn from its original mission. The new mission was to drive UNESCO's latest educational policy which is based on applying behavioral psychology and neuroscience to shape behavior for achieving SDGs.

As we discussed in the Introduction, *the neuroscience model of learning is reductionist*: It is a materialist model of the human being, and this undermines our notions of agency, autonomy, responsibility, and even human dignity.[4] It is aligned with a model of human psychology known as behaviorism according to which our thoughts are purely biological and can be modeled mechanically, and hence, can be manipulated externally.

This is contrary to our understanding of free will and agency. It becomes tougher to establish moral and ethical frameworks if the mind is considered nothing other than a mechanical biological computer. Critics also point out that this approach reduces the teacher to a kind of social stimulus acting upon regions of a student's brain and is 'an impoverished view of what really goes on in classrooms'.[5] This philosophy is diametrically opposite to Gandhi's ideals.[6]

True to its new mission, MGIEP has issued a 187-page guidebook advising textbook publishers and school systems on how to 'embed' SDGs goal into curricula, calling it Education for Sustainable Development (ESD). *The code word 'embed' requires certain specific ideologies in all subjects, even math and science.* We saw in an earlier chapter how a subject like math has been made political by preaching social justice as part of math education at the expense of teaching numerical problem-solving. The MGIEP also trains teachers on SEL and conducts global citizenship workshops.[7]

Unbeknownst to many, *the goal of school education has shifted 'from aiming to produce well-rounded workforce, which contributed primarily to the economic growth and its competitiveness, to becoming a catalyst of global citizenship, social justice and sustainability'*.[8] This new education is termed 'holistic' as it focuses on social, economic, political, and natural dimensions to achieve sustainability. Students' emotions are given importance and not learning outcomes. The MGIEP considers SEL and global citizenship education as twenty-first-century skills.

The programs of the MGIEP are essentially large-scale psychotherapy sessions to change behavior, imparted to all children without evaluating whether they require it or not. It is assumed that every child needs therapy in the form of Social Emotional Learning to meet the SDGs established by the UN. Group therapy aims to shape attitudes and compliance. The MGIEP is clear about its mission to produce activists through a curriculum that integrates,

> key sustainability standards into various subjects such as Math, Science, English and Social Sciences, this system would help transfer sustainability-related values to students who would act upon them and change their behavior. As a whole, ESD standards aim to cover the following areas: global citizenship, environmental awareness and stewardship, future thinking, social justice, as well as ethics and well-being.[9]

Some American school boards have begun rejecting Education for Sustainable Development, calling it fear-mongering: 'These catastrophists are using the CO_2 boogeyman and the threat of apocalypse to frighten people into submission'.[10] Such school boards have rejected textbook publishers pushing Woke agendas.

The MGIEP is driven by many of the issues we raised in our book, *Snakes in the Ganga*. Under the umbrella of Critical Race Theory, all kinds of identity warfare among groups are encouraged. For example, let us examine how MGIEP defines diversity:

> Diversity is defined as the factors that make social groups and individuals differ from the majority, or what is perceived as 'normal'. This chapter addresses race/ethnicity/language, religion, gender, sexuality, social class, disability and neurodiversity, as well as intersectionality among

> diversity types. It examines diversity, inequality (structural, institutionalized and historically embedded) and oppression (racism, sexism, heterosexism, classism, ableism, etc.), which hinder full human flourishing and social justice in pursuit of UN SDGs 4.5 and 4.7 (UN, 2015a).[11]

This is the Woke definition of diversity as empowering 'oppressed minorities'. Taking a page from Ibram X. Kendi, the American Woke guru, the MGIEP framework argues against merit-based education:

> The nature of 'merit' typically includes academic performance and/or personal qualities such as leadership and participation in extra-curricular activities but is often determined by the dominant group…Mainstream schools tend to provide curricula that reflect the dominant group's worldview, normalize it as universal, and advance the dominant group's interests while marginalizing minoritized groups.[12]

The MGIEP's policy paper for education also recommends getting rid of merit and credentials totally, revamping the curriculum to focus only on the SDGs: 'Implement the six domain curricula (environment, culture, society, technology, interpersonal, self) for a learning experience towards human flourishing'.[13]

The purpose of such an education is to make 'all students understand their own unconscious bias and mechanisms of oppression in schooling'.[14] The MGIEP calls this the 'whole brain learner' approach. The problem they want to counter is 'explicit gender and sexuality binaries in the curriculum, pedagogy and school culture'.[15] The MGIEP would like to direct the Ministry of Human Resource Development (MHRD) budget towards this Woke education to 'Re-organize education funding to ensure equitable and inclusive whole-brain learner-centric quality education for all learners at all stages of learning'.[16]

Creating a Generation of Breaking India Warriors

The goal of the MGIEP's flagship program is to brainwash children to become 'global citizens' by carrying the burden of the world's doomsday scenarios like climate crisis, world hunger, and poverty on their shoulders:

> UNESCO MGIEP's flagship project 'Global Citizenship' aims to achieve the goal of sustainable and peaceful societies, as outlined in SDG 4.7, through a digital curriculum on global citizenship education, with a focus on the development of key SEL skills. The curriculum has been specifically designed for adolescents in the age group of 12–14 years, utilizing understanding of the neuroscience and psychology of how an adolescent brain learns.[17]

The Finnish study on the correlation between Woke ideologies and heightened anxiety cited earlier, is also corroborated by MGIEP's research. The trauma being precipitated in young and impressionable minds serves the agenda to channel such disturbed and dysfunctional children into angry social justice warriors. The MGIEP admitted this in a paper acknowledging that SDGs are self-contradicting, causing cognitive dissonance that leads to fear and anxiety among children:

> The Sustainable Development Goals (SDGs) are not necessarily a set of consistent objectives but rather a series of potentially conflicting goals...For example, eradicating poverty—a societal objective—might entail (at least in the short term) working the self to the point of compromising personal well-being, another SDG...At the level of the individual and social collectives, these trade-offs in SDGs will be quite taxing because the conflicting goals are, in effect, inconsistent cognitions, generally referred to as cognitive dissonance or dissonance. According to dissonance theory—one of the most tried and tested theories in the behavioral sciences—inconsistent cognitions evoke aversive arousal state that leads to attitudes and behaviors

> aimed at reducing the arousal. Dissonance is constituted by two important social psychological processes: inconsistency among cognitions, a more rational phenomenon referred to as cognitive discrepancy, and the unpleasant emotional and motivational state that arises from holding two contradictory cognitions, referred to as dissonance.[18]

Thus, educators know in advance that the SDGs curriculum will create fear and anxiety by burdening a child with conflicting beliefs that cannot be reconciled. Having engineered this anxiety and dissonance, SEL comes to the rescue to build 'emotional resilience' by requiring children to accept Woke ideas like transgenderism, LGBTQIA+ rights, climateism, etc. After causing anxiety and dissonance, SEL steps in to help children 'regulate emotions, identify positive purpose, demonstrate empathy for others, take constructive action, and promote human flourishing'.[19]

The term 'resilience' has a specific technical meaning in Woke and is the opposite of 'fragility'.[20] The term 'fragility' refers to the defensiveness of oppressors when their oppressiveness is discussed. Those born into an oppressor community avoid the subject of their ancestors' oppression when it is raised, and this is called 'fragility'. Originally, it was defined to apply to white people who avoid discussing racism, but the Woke movement has expanded it to apply to all the oppressor identities. Thus, upper caste Indians, those opposed to Khalistan or Islamic radicalism, are being designated as 'white adjacent' and hence, oppressors, are 'fragile' when they refuse to apologize as oppressors.

The chain of events goes as follows:

Teach children to assume the role of 'global citizens' ➔ Traumatize them with catastrophic crises ➔ Cognitive dissonance, anxiety, fear ➔ Solution is 'emotional resilience' ➔ 'Regulating emotions' by channeling them into social justice activism

For example, MGIEP ran a workshop for youth titled, *Climate Change Anxiety Among Youth and How it Can Be Tackled Through*

SEL[21] that pressures young people to feel anxieties about climate change, and MGIEP offers SEL solutions to combat these anxieties. Another course that adults can get certified in is entitled *Climate Change: Understand, Reflect, Empathize, and Act.*[22]

The MGIEP promotes Social Emotional Learning as providing the competency to 'regulate emotions, identify positive purpose, demonstrate empathy for others, take constructive action, and promote human flourishing'.[23] But whose idea of 'positive purpose' is being promoted? For example, Indian children could be taught that their 'positive purpose' is to support Khalistan or Kashmir separatists or the Rohingya migrants because such causes require 'compassion' to help 'human flourishing'. Children might be taught that as 'global citizens' they should go out on the streets because it demonstrates empathy for others.

The SEL doctrine states that *emotional resilience is achieved by channeling unpleasant emotions into activism*. Children are thus taught to build 'emotional resilience' by directing their negative feelings into activism in support of SDGs' Woke ideas. 'Resilience' is the only escape mechanism available by accepting the oppressor-oppressed framework presented during the SEL 'struggle sessions' in Diversity, Equity, Inclusion training. These 'struggle sessions' are dramatized situations to traumatize children as oppressors until they confess to being racist, casteist, or homophobic.

As children begin to fall apart and get anxious about the impending doomsday scenarios, the pedagogy requires teachers to give even more 'SEL cycles', and thus the vicious cycle continues. It forces children to accept the personal sacrifices they must make, get them agitated about them, and channel the negative energy by becoming change agents. These cycles are also used to gather data that is used to refine the SEL strategies.[24]

The MGIEP has penetrated the Indian government's educational machinery successfully, using the very same educators who previously fought to bring Hindu ideas into education.

The brainwashing process may be summarized as follows:

1. Teach conflicting SDGs goal like climate change or world hunger.
2. Create cognitive dissonance using these conflicting goals to burden children with a choiceless, stressful situation.
3. These stressful circumstances create anxiety, anger, fear, and depression.
4. Infuse the curriculum with SEL behaviorism to help 'manage' the emotions, i.e. drive their behavior in a predefined manner.
5. Teach children to regulate emotions and be malleable by developing 'emotional resilience', which means accepting the Woke 'oppressor-oppressed' worldview.
6. This requires even more SEL cycles.

The figure that follows depicts the process.

While the MGIEP is predominantly funded by the Indian taxpayer, there is a systematic push to pave the way for tech companies to provide funding in exchange for board seats. Through sizeable donations, Microsoft, Dell, Samsung, and Hewlett Packard have seized the opportunity to shape the education system, while gaining access to enormous amounts of data collected from the MGIEP programs.[25]

These partnerships have coincided with a reorientation of MGIEP's mission towards an exclusive focus on 'harnessing the power of digital technologies to facilitate quality education for the 21st century Global Citizen' and the 'championing of digital learning, neuroscience and AI'.[26]

UNESCO is rolling out Social Emotional Learning on a large scale worldwide through MGIEP. This includes courses to train youth and educators globally:

> UNESCO-MGIEP has various capacity-building initiatives tailored specifically for learners, teachers, and youth which come in the form of online courses with *a crucial element of SEL* integrated into the content. The courses are multi-modal, interactive and self-paced, and are designed to build intellectual and emotional intelligence among learners.[27]

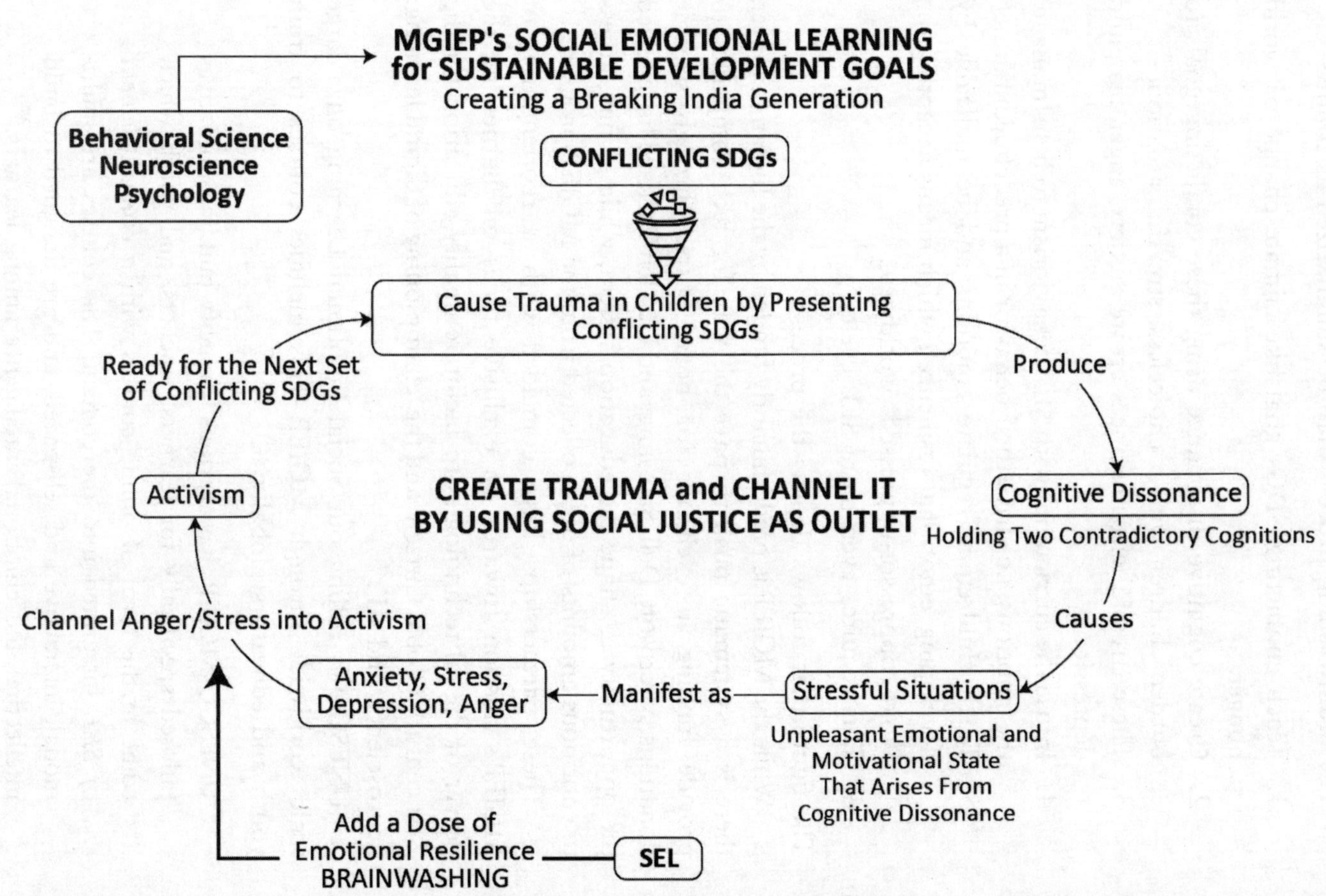
MGIEP's SOCIAL EMOTIONAL LEARNING
for SUSTAINABLE DEVELOPMENT GOALS
Creating a Breaking India Generation
Behavioral Science
Neuroscience
Psychology
CONFLICTING SDGs
Cause Trauma in Children by Presenting Conflicting SDGs
Produce
Cognitive Dissonance
Holding Two Contradictory Cognitions
Causes
Stressful Situations
Unpleasant Emotional and Motivational State That Arises From Cognitive Dissonance
Manifest as
Anxiety, Stress, Depression, Anger
CREATE TRAUMA and CHANNEL IT
BY USING SOCIAL JUSTICE AS OUTLET
Channel Anger/Stress into Activism
Activism
Ready for the Next Set of Conflicting SDGs
Add a Dose of Emotional Resilience
BRAINWASHING
SEL

Besides schools, MGIEP has also entered colleges, offering courses for credit on SEL. For example, it has courses on 'building SEL skills' and 'emotional resilience' for youth that were piloted at Chandigarh University.[28]

The MGIEP wants to weaponize young people as evangelists for the UNESCO ideology because, 'young people are often pushed to the periphery of the policymaking process in the areas of education, peace, sustainability, and global citizenship'.[29] It wants to turn the youth into 'compassionate disrupters' and train them in SDGs with courses that have college credit.

As a result of the success of the UNESCO-MGIEP, individual schools and teachers are rushing to get certifications in SEL because these certificates are seen as the path to advance oneself in the education field. For example:

- In 2022, MGIEP signed 'a key strategic agreement' with the National Council of Educational Research and Training (NCERT) to train and certify 8.4 million teachers in India on SEL.[30]
- The Directorate of Education, government of the National Capital Territory (NCT) of Delhi is training its staff in SEL for teachers, SEL for classrooms, and facilitator of SEL for schools.[31]
- The Delhi Skill and Entrepreneurship University (DSEU) has signed a Memorandum of Understanding (MOU) with MGIEP: 'With this partnership, we hope to positively impact our students' lives, enabling them to become responsible, empathetic, and engaged citizens of the world'.[32]
- The MGIEP, as a knowledge partner is developing the educational Centre of Excellence on Metaverse in collaboration with the state government of Karnataka, the Karnataka Digital Economy Mission (KDEM), the government of Karnataka and Excelsoft Technologies.[33]
- The Indian Institute of Technology Kanpur is collaborating with MGIEP on research in developing applications of cognitive science in the classroom.[34]

- The MGIEP signed an MOU with the National Institute of Technology (NIT) Meghalaya in 2024, to mandate SEL to students and faculty of the NIT and to also certify faculty in SEL education. According to this MOU, in true evangelical fashion, NIT will have to spread the 'good news' about SEL: 'NIT Meghalaya will actively promote the deployment of SEL courses through its key national and international events, fostering greater awareness and participation'.[35]

New MOUs are being signed at a frantic pace to roll out SEL and global citizenship agendas in India. The MGIEP has formed the Global Collective for SEL and Digital Learning, a group of governments, universities, and NGOs committed to mainstreaming SEL. For example, the Gandhi Smriti, the national memorial of Gandhi, and the Darshan Samiti, another Gandhian Institute, are part of this SEL collective. So too is the Educational Technology Interdisciplinary Programme at IIT Bombay. Tata Trusts funds an SEL project at TATA Institute of Social Sciences (another member of the global collective for SEL), which is working on a technology-enabled regional language initiative to service the SEL needs of students at the government secondary schools in Chhattisgarh, Mizoram, Rajasthan and Telangana and is available as Open Educational Resources (OERs).[36]

Finally, we would like to highlight that MGIEP's internal assessment acknowledges that despite two decades of promoting this theory on behavior psychology and neuroscience, there has not yet been a research validation of the premises on which their programs are based:

> Furthermore, over the last two decades, a rich body of information has been produced about how learning happens at the brain and behavioural levels, including individual differences and environmental influences on learning. The educational implications of claims derived from research from these various disciplines have yet to be evaluated in an integrated manner relative to the learning experiences and practices that exist.[37]

5

INTERNATIONAL PLANNED PARENTHOOD FEDERATION

The Dubious Origins of International Planned Parenthood Federation

In the early 1900s, the eugenics movement in the USA was advocating the selective breeding of human beings to limit the reproduction of 'undesirable' populations such as Blacks and the differently abled. *Margaret Sanger, who supported the eugenics movement in America, founded Planned Parenthood in 1916 to control the population by providing contraception and birth control.* Even today, the Planned Parenthood Federation of America is accused of targeting the Black community for abortions through their strategically located centers in predominantly Black neighborhoods:

> The National Right to Life Center estimates that by the end of 2021, 63.5 million abortions[1] had been performed in the United States since the Supreme Court's 1973 *Roe v. Wade* decision. Nearly 40% of women who seek abortions are African American, which is astounding, considering this demographic made up just 13.6%[2] of the population at the time of the 2020 census. This likely means that over 20 million black babies have been aborted during the past 50 years.[3]

Sanger then established IPPF in Bombay (now Mumbai) in 1952 'to promote Sexual and Reproductive Health and Rights for all'.[4]

However, population reduction still seems to be a major goal beneath the surface.[5]

Under heavy pressure, Planned Parenthood recently acknowledged its dark past. Only in 2020, Planned Parenthood of New York removed Margaret Sanger's name from its clinic, to 'reckon with its founder's harmful connections to the eugenics movement'.[6] Planned Parenthood was also accused of systemic racism by its Black employees the same year.[7] In 2015, Planned Parenthood was accused of removing fetal tissue and harvesting fetal body parts such as the heart and lungs from aborted babies to sell to research institutions.[8]

'Sexual Rights' of Minors Become Human Rights

Today, IPPF partners with the UN and other NGOs to get the legal definition of human rights changed to include 'sexual rights', and advocates for the following:

1. Establishing sexual rights as separate and independent from reproductive rights.
2. Blurring the line between adults and minors on the issue of sexual rights.
3. Making sexual rights a fundamental human right.
4. Comprehensive Sexuality Education to be a necessary part of education and health worldwide.

As part of their grand social engineering project to sexualize young children, IPPF argues that children are sexual beings from birth and *targets children as young as ten* to deliver pornographic sex education through SEL and CSE programs: 'Sexuality and sexual pleasure are important parts of being human for everyone – *no matter what age*'.[9]

The IPPF normalizes 'commercial sex work' or prostitution to children ages ten and under in its toolkit on CSE.[10] The following statements illustrate IPPF's subtle language in which they *give the right to minors to consent to sex*, all in the name of sexual rights:

> The rights and protections guaranteed to people under age eighteen differ from those of adults and must take into account the *evolving capacities of the individual child to exercise rights on his or her own behalf.*[11]
>
> IPPF begins from the premise that *persons under eighteen (18) are rights holders*, and that at different points within the spectrum of infancy, childhood, and adolescence, certain rights and protections will have greater or lesser relevance.[12]
>
> Societies must create environments in which children can achieve their optimal capacities and where greater respect is given to their potential for participation in, and responsibility for, decision-making in their own lives.[13]

According to IPPF, sexual rights in young people (age ten onward) entail:

- **Privacy:** parents need not be informed of their sexual rights including gender/sex change; this dismantles traditional parenthood.
- **Sexual health:** an umbrella term that includes abortion and puberty blockers.
- **Choose** sex and gender.
- **Sex/gender change:** surgery as well as hormone therapy paid for by the government or insurance.
- **Activism** including Cancel Culture to suppress opposing views.

This agenda is being slipped under the radar and is hidden deep in the language of various standards and laws. Following are some excerpts from IPPF's guidance document for the implementation of young people's sexual rights:[14]

- Laws that criminalize consensual sexual activity between adolescents can place adolescents at risk.
- Ensuring that all young people understand they are entitled

to sexual pleasure and the diverse forms in which pleasure is experienced is of primary importance for their health and well-being.

- Guarantee access to hormone treatment for transgender and intersex adolescents, with the proper care and guidance from medical providers and without the need for parental consent.
- Liberalize abortion legislation to enable all young women (including adolescents) to easily access safe abortion care, without parental or spousal consent requirements.
- Legislate for compulsory Comprehensive Sexuality Education from primary to preparatory schools, based on new global endorsements and standards.

The following diagram summarizes IPPF's guide on sex education starting at age ten.

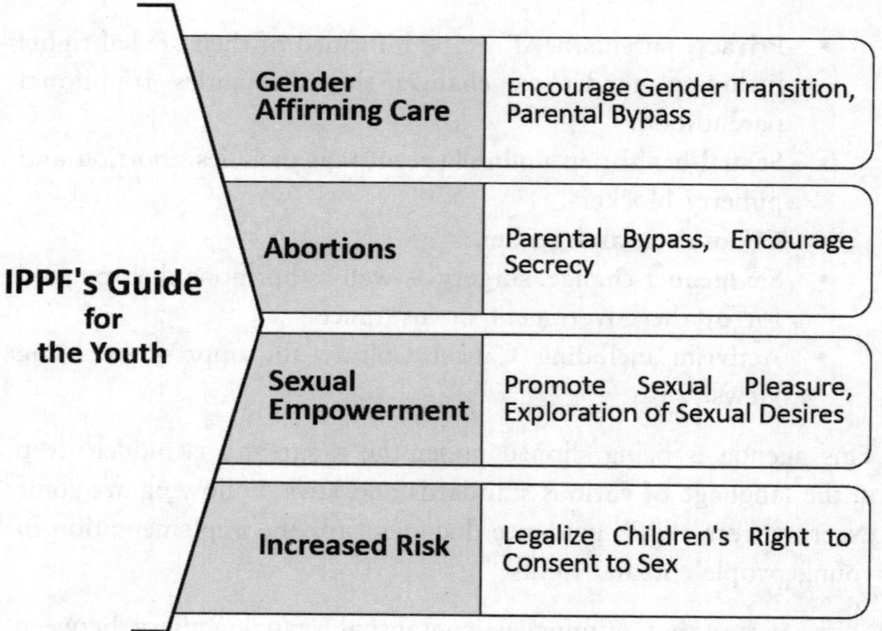

The bottom-line impact is to achieve IPPF's goals: get parents out of the way, lobby governments to pass bills that favor IPPF's mission, and open the floodgates to global nexuses and foreign ideologues to take control of Indian children's sexuality. This includes making abortions commonplace, introducing CSE to youth, and even normalizing, destigmatizing, and decriminalizing pedophilia. All this bypasses traditional values.

The recent rise in transgenderism by indoctrinating children presents a new frontier for IPPF.[15] Planned Parenthood in the USA has significantly expanded its gender-affirming care services with nearly all of its centers offering these services.[16] Instead of allowing puberty to play out naturally, the IPPF promotes medical intervention when a child has difficulty coping with changes associated with puberty. It evangelizes young children towards surgeries and hormones that deform the natural body. It offers puberty blockers under the pretense of providing compassionate, gender-affirming care. In effect, it creates trauma in the lives of young people by pressuring them away from nature and tradition and then offering 'solutions' that permanently distort them physically and mentally.

Therefore, the consequences of making sexual rights as fundamental human rights for minors creates a pipeline to pedophilia and enables pre-pubescent transgenderism.

Indoctrination to Activism

Through CSE programs, young people are encouraged to fight for sexual rights through protests against norms and structures. The IPPF has devised a new aggressive strategy known as 'Come Together' with sexual pleasure as the lubricant to drive agitations:

> Societal and legislative change for universal sexual and reproductive rights. To advance this goal, we will follow three critical pathways: ground advocacy, shift norms, and act with youth… through digital and social media platforms. And we know that to be effective, messaging about sexuality and safer sex should include pleasure.[17]

In its 2022 annual report, the IPPF reported that CSE was one of the main outcomes where sex education is all *about rights, pleasure, and mobilizing youth for activism*:

> IPPF MA [Member Associations] around the world are trailblazers in the provision of quality comprehensive sexuality education in and out of school: increasing young people's awareness of their rights, promoting gender equality, and empowering young people to make informed decisions about their health, relationships and sexuality.[18]

The IPPF leverages highly addictive social media platforms for 'education in and out of school' where sexual content takes priority over learning basic skills such as reading, science, and math.

Pornographic Curriculum

The CSE's sexualization curriculum emphasizes sexual exploration, pleasure, and rights to destigmatize and normalize transgenderism, gender fluidity, and pedophilia. To disguise this from critics, Planned Parenthood spun off CSE research and curriculum development into two separate institutes: Education, Training and Research (ETR) Associates, and the Guttmacher Institute.[19] Below is an example of ETR's guide to teachers titled *Making a Difference for teaching a twelve-year-old*:

> *What are some of the ways people express their sexual feelings to themselves or other people*? Elicit as many answers as you can. Answers may include: talking, hugging, holding hands, kissing, touching, saying 'I like you,' dancing, massage, *masturbation, caressing, cuddling, grinding, sexual fantasy, touching each other's genitals, oral sex, vaginal sex, anal sex*.[20]

The IPPF's *It's All One Curriculum* is a sex education framework 'to teach young people the critical thinking skills needed to build compassionate and just societies'.[21] Notice how social justice gets combined with sexuality. Following are a few topics *for children as young as ten*:

- 'Masturbation is not harmful; rather it is safe and a good way to learn about one's own body. One can masturbate frequently except when it gets in the way of other activities or if it disturbs or causes harm'.
- Guide to reaching orgasm using various methods. 'Women are more likely to have an orgasm if they (or their partner) stimulate the clitoris directly before, during, or after vaginal intercourse'.
- '*There is no right age to have sex.* Each person determines when he or she feels ready to have sex'.

Another IPPF guide published for young persons with HIV is titled *HEALTHY, HAPPY AND HOT.*[22] The guide explains that the internet is useful to learn about sex and pornography.[23] It makes clear that those who are HIV positive do not have to disclose their status to partners. It encourages youth with HIV to seek pleasure in sex, using sex toys and masturbation for exploration. It contains explicit language to describe oral, anal, and homosexual sex:

> Many people think sex is just about vaginal or anal intercourse... but sex can include kissing, touching, licking, tickling, sucking, and cuddling. Some people like to have aggressive sex, while others like to have soft and slow sex with their partners. There is no right or wrong way to have sex. Just have fun, explore and be yourself, as long as all parties agree! Improve your sex life by getting to know your own body. Play with yourself! Masturbation is a great way to find out more about your body and what you find sexually stimulating. You can also use sex toys to explore what you like, and what sensations feel best! Take time to explore your own and your partner's bodies. Your skin is the largest erogenous zone on your body, and your mind plays a big role in your desire for sex and sexual pleasure. Caress and lick your partner's skin. Explore your partner's body with your hands and mouth. Mix things up by using different kinds

of touch from very soft to hard. Talk about or act out your fantasies. Talk dirty to them. Tickle, tease and make them feel good. Do you know about people's hot spots? The clitoris, just above the vaginal opening where the labia meet, is the only organ in the human body to have the sole purpose of sexual pleasure. The penis is also sensitive to people's touch, especially the head. Some also find touching in and around the anus to be pleasurable, while some people enjoy prostate stimulation.[24]

Some people choose not to have safer sex. If this is something you and your partner agree to, then it is your choice…Use lubricant to reduce the chances of micro-tears in the vagina and anus. Limit the amount of body fluids like semen and vaginal secretions that you and your partner(s) share. Ejaculate (cum) outside, not inside. Get tested regularly for HIV and other STIs. Sometimes two people with penises (one HIV-positive and the other HIV-negative) sexually positioning themselves to reduce the risk of passing on HIV when having penetrative sex. This risk reduction strategy is often called "strategic positioning" which involves the HIV-negative partner taking on the insertive position (the 'top') because a penetrative partner is less likely to acquire HIV than a person who is taking the receptive position (the 'bottom').[25]

These IPPF guidelines present several issues:

- Graphic and excessive sexual instructions are provided.
- Sharing sexual content online does not communicate the serious risks involved such as legal, privacy violations, and cyberbullying.
- Pornography as a resource for learning about sex normalizes its use among youth. It presents a distorted view of sex that is unrealistic and often non-consensual.
- The internet and pornography are not appropriate educational tools.

Failure to Report Cases of Sexual Abuse

Another disturbing concern is that Planned Parenthood enables the child sex trafficking industry that uses its services. Much like the Catholic Church, Planned Parenthood has been under fire for not reporting underage rape and assault. For instance, a twelve-year-old girl in foster care was brought into Planned Parenthood for her second abortion within six months of the first, because the abuse was not reported to authorities.[26]

Global Players and the Impact on India

The IPPF hijacks the United Nations' machinery to spread its narrative using SEL/CSE programs. It uses its affiliates as branch offices to ensure the implementation on the ground. It has a joint venture with the UN and is also funded by the WHO, the Bill & Melinda Gates Foundation, George Soros' 437

, and the American government, among others.[27] Following are some of the highlights of IPPF funding:[28]

- $670.4 million in US government, corporations, and individuals in 2022, up from $633.4 million the previous year [2021].
- **$1.9 billion in total revenue,** up from $1.7 billion the previous year [2021].
- **$2.3 billion in net assets,** up from $2.1 billion the previous year [2021].
- $204.7 million in excess revenue; up from $133.7 million the previous year [2021].
- 727,000 active individual contributors, up from 590,000 the previous year [2021].[29]

The revenue for IPPF is increasing every year and is funded by the Woke global Left and its billionaire supporters. The SEL/CSE programs are being scaled worldwide because abortions and puberty blockers are a source of revenue.

The impact on India has been devastating because there is no pushback against these agendas. In fact, in its 2022 annual report, IPPF claimed success in lobbying and creating policy changes.[30]

The IPPF encourages abortions because it stands to gain financially, being the largest provider of this service. For instance, in one year alone a whopping 15.6 million abortions were performed in India.[31] The population of India is a big red flag that the UN and IPPF have been trying to reduce for a while. In her book *Unnatural Selection: Choosing Boys Over Girls, and the Consequences of a World Full of Men*, the American writer Mara Hvistendahl discusses how ultrasound machines were introduced in New Delhi, Haryana, and Bihar by NGOs, who also trained local doctors on abortions, leading to India's gender selection practice. The idea was to reduce the number of females in the Indian demographic, thus reducing the number of people who would get pregnant, contributing to population reduction.[32] The abortions of female fetuses were then blamed on Hinduism.

The strategy of IPPF along with UNFPA, UNESCO, UNICEF, The David and Lucile Packard Foundation, Bill & Melinda Gates Foundation, The Children's Investment Fund Foundation (CIFF), Ford Foundation, Rockefeller Foundation, and many others has been to somehow bring down the population of India by targeting women. The UN and foreign agencies use education as a Trojan horse to radicalize young girls through CSE and behavioral change.

The IPPF works in over 145 countries worldwide through its member associations. The Family Planning Association (FPA) is one such member association of the IPPF in India, and a later chapter exposes the complex dynamics and deception it uses to indoctrinate children in India.

6

A TALE OF TWO PROVINCES: JHARKHAND (INDIA) AND GANSU (CHINA)

The United Nations Targets Weak or Corrupt Governments

The UN targets countries that are the most vulnerable, such as Benin (West Africa), Indonesia, and Zambia to indoctrinate young minds with its CSE programs, in partnership with corrupt or weak governments supported by NGOs. In effect, the UN has put India on par with such countries as we describe next.[1]

To illustrate its easy exploitative entry into India, we will discuss how the UN is orchestrating the sexualization of minors in Jharkhand. In this predominantly rural and relatively poor Indian state, the state government has assigned itself the role of the obedient project manager. We will contrast this with a sex education program implemented in Gansu, an inland rural province in northwestern China, where the local government has taken a more direct executive role to safeguard its interests rather than the foreign agenda. Our analysis will focus on comparing the approaches of the sex education programs in these two regions.

The UN's CSE program finds its way into India through two main ministries: the Ministry of Human Resource Development and the Ministry of Health and Family Welfare.

In 2002, India launched the School AIDS Education Program (SAEP) aimed at preventing the spread of HIV/AIDS among youth. In

2006, this was expanded to prevent Sexually Transmitted Infections and substance abuse: the Adolescent Education Program (AEP), targeting individuals aged ten to nineteen.[2] However, due to its graphic depictions of the male and female anatomy, some of India's twenty-eight states—Gujarat, Madhya Pradesh, Maharashtra, Karnataka, and Rajasthan—decided to cancel this program.[3]

In 2009, as a workaround to this pushback, the Ministry of HRD in partnership with the United Nations Population Fund (UNFPA), introduced and re-branded the AEP under the banner of 'Life Skills Education' program (LSE), targeting young children.[4] The LSE program challenges binary gender and gender discrimination. The government misled Indian parents by introducing CSE content under the 'Life Skills Education' banner to avoid a backlash and sidestep controversy. This is acknowledged by an NGO affiliated with this program:

> While much of the information provided in the curriculum falls under the wide gamut of sexuality related information, the programme covers it under the title of 'life skills'. The programme itself is called *Adolescence Education Programme rather than Sexuality Education*. It is a moot point whether this is a strategic ploy (in order to avoid controversy of the kind that was raised in 2007), or whether it would have been better to call a spade a spade.[5]

However, this initiative was not strong enough for the UN and IPPF. With the support of prominent NGOs, they criticized the LSE program: 'The curriculum does not discuss various gender and sexual identities, sexual diversity, or pleasure; thereby inadvertently reinforcing the norms like sexual relationships between a man and a woman have sole legitimacy'.[6] The basis for criticism was that it lacked content on sexual relationships, consent, and pre-marital sex. They also felt that activism was missing because they wanted students to learn how to 'discuss relationships, negotiation and consent in the context of an intimate or sexual relationship' both outside and within the institution of marriage. They criticized the program for not teaching children to 'challenge and change cultural beliefs'.[7]

In a race to align with the UN's 2018 ITGSE standards (discussed earlier), developed through a collaborative process involving UN agencies such as UNESCO, UNAIDS, UNICEF, UN Women, and the WHO,[8] the Indian government changed the AEP/LSE program by bringing material that 'emphasizes adolescence as a time of possibilities, adventure, curiosity and learning'.[9] The government is taking steps to implement Sexual Orientation and Gender Identity and Expression (SOGIE) with enhanced *emphasis on rights, agency, and gender expression.*

The revisions incorporate some of the following topics:

1. Questions pertaining to masturbation.[10]
2. 'Young people experience sexual attraction and form romantic and sexual relationships'.[11]
3. 'Young people may often find their own values related to marriage in conflict with the values of the society and culture they reside in'.[12]
4. Same-sex relationships are taught in a workbook activity.[13]
5. A call to move away from a gender binary perspective.[14]

How India Sold Out Jharkhand's Marginalized Children to International Mandates

The following discussion about the UN's Comprehensive Sexuality Education's pilot project in Jharkhand illustrates how it works with local NGO partners at the grassroots level. The Jharkhand state government's sex education program has been outsourced to the NGO, C3, or the Centre for Catalyzing Change. In UN terms, these collaborating NGOs are called Civil Society Organizations (CSOs).

As noted previously, CSE's sexualization curriculum emphasizes sexual exploration, pleasure, and rights intending to destigmatize and normalize transgenderism, gender fluidity, and pedophilia. The C3 has a board member from Guttmacher Institute, the IPPF spin-off that ensures IPPF's influence. The following figure shows these connections.

The chair of C3, Suneeta Mukherjee, previously served as a UNFPA representative and is a former Indian Administrative Services officer, who is well positioned to exploit the government machinery for rolling out the controversial CSE programs in Jharkhand. The C3 also receives robust backing from Indian government bodies like the Ministry of Health and Family Welfare, the Department of Health, as well as the state governments of Delhi, Gujarat, Bihar, Chhattisgarh, Jharkhand, and Odisha.[15]

In addition, there are multiple Indian and Western corporates as funding sources:

- Corporates: Amazon, Microsoft, Merck, Thomson Reuters
- Indian NGOs: Azim Premji Foundation
- Foreign NGOs: The Bill & Melinda Gates Foundation, The Ford Foundation, The David and Lucile Packard Foundation
- Foreign/UN Agencies: WHO, UNESCO, UNFPA, UN Trust Fund, UK AID, US AID, Swedish International Development Cooperation Agency, International Finance Corporation (World Bank)

The partners of C3 include: IPPF and its India affiliate, the Family Planning Association of India (which is discussed in detail in a later chapter), the TATA group, and many more. These programs are designed to change the values of Indian youth and create a cultural disconnect from the previous generation. The C3 might be doing wonderful work in other areas, and even in sex education. We would commend them if their framework had been developed by Indians taking Indian values and culture into account without being dominated by the UN, IPPF, and other global interests.

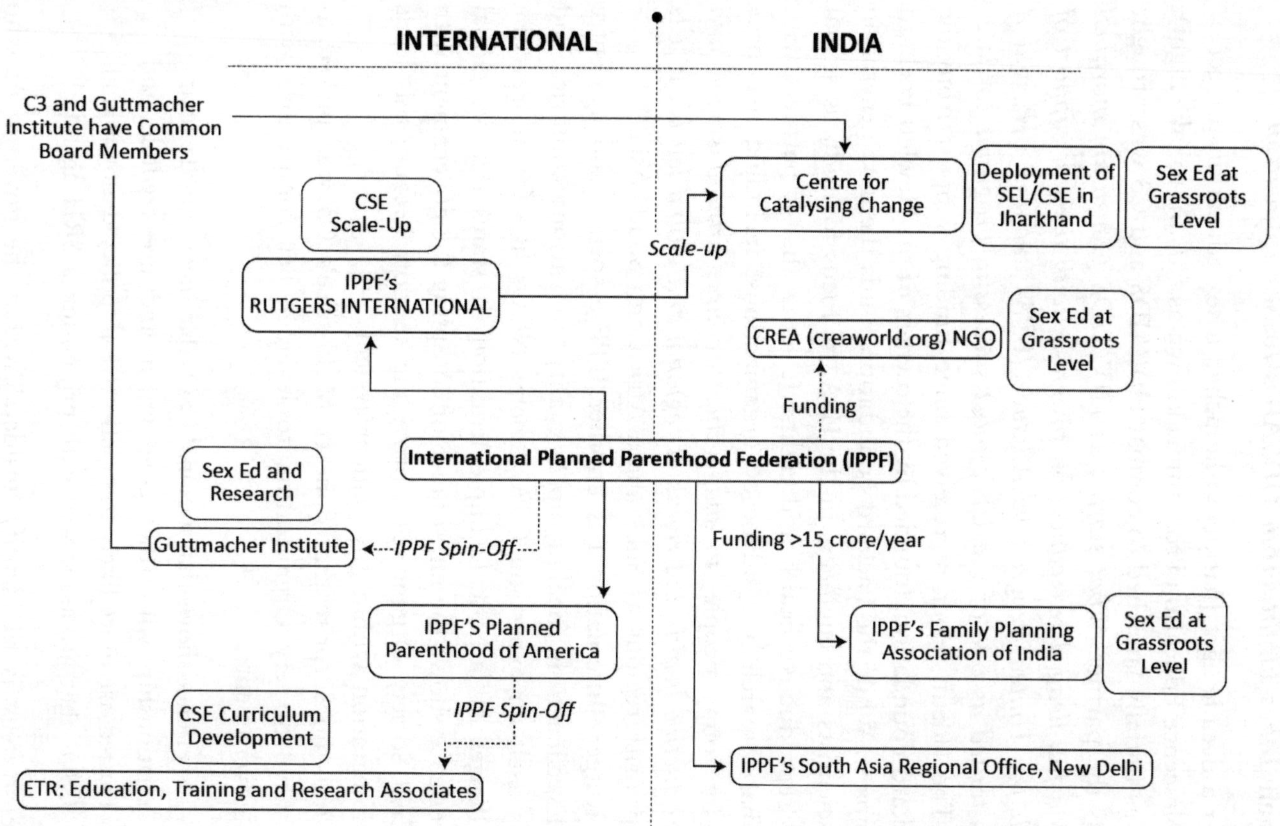
INTERNATIONAL
INDIA
C3 and Guttmacher Institute have Common Board Members
Centre for Catalysing Change
Deployment of SEL/CSE in Jharkhand
Sex Ed at Grassroots Level
CSE Scale-Up
IPPF's RUTGERS INTERNATIONAL
Scale-up
CREA (creaworld.org) NGO
Sex Ed at Grassroots Level
Funding
Sex Ed and Research
International Planned Parenthood Federation (IPPF)
Guttmacher Institute
IPPF Spin-Off
Funding >15 crore/year
IPPF'S Planned Parenthood of America
IPPF's Family Planning Association of India
Sex Ed at Grassroots Level
CSE Curriculum Development
IPPF Spin-Off
IPPF's South Asia Regional Office, New Delhi
ETR: Education, Training and Research Associates

Udaan *Takes Flight From HIV/AIDs to Sex Education*

Over a decade ago, Jharkhand launched a sex education project or Adolescence Education Programme known as *Udaan* (to take flight). It was initially launched to combat HIV/AIDS and C3 was brought in as the partner. *What started as HIV/AIDS prevention morphed into a full-fledged sex education program, with the full support of both the United Progressive Alliance (UPA) and the BJP, and it was touted as one of the UN's most successful programs to date.*

The Udaan program received huge funding support from the Packard Foundation, founded by the owners of the Hewlett Packard company. While the Packard Foundation funds the next generation of scientists and engineers in the USA, its focus for India is sexual and reproductive health and rights. It states that it partners with 'global research and advocacy organizations, including networks led by young people, *to shape the discourse around sexual and reproductive health and rights at regional and global levels*'. It lists its priority regions as Sub-Sahara Africa and South Asia.[16]

Rutgers International is another IPPF associate and a 'Centre of Excellence' in 'Scaling up Sexuality' in various countries and calls itself an expert on CSE. It helps NGOs like C3 address the challenges of large-scale implementation. It states that its global experience shows the importance of co-opting the government with a Civil Society Organization providing support because this leads to 'integration within government systems'.[17]

It is no surprise that Suneeta Mukherjee's C3 was picked as the Civil Society Organization to leverage her connections with the government:

> Experience shows that national CSOs that have a good existing relationship with (the) government and are credible and trusted are more likely to be effective in policy dialogue than CSOs that are associated with promoting a SRH agenda.[18]

The strategy is to identify 'insiders' within the government who can be coached:

> *Requests for CSO technical assistance should ideally be initiated by (the) government; effective partnerships are based on trust, and engaging with (the) government is easier for established national CSOs with a track record and existing relationships*; CSOs must have something to offer (the) government – in this case, skills, expertise and funding for technical assistance provided by the Packard Foundation.[19]

Rutgers' toolkit for scaling up proudly notes that the Jharkhand Udaan project was a huge success, because *C3 and the Jharkhand government disguised Comprehensive Sexuality Education as empowerment, life skills, and health to fool the community to gain acceptability*. It explains how it has learned to engage the local communities skillfully and tactfully:

> In most states in India, including Jharkhand, *there are social and cultural taboos about discussing SRH and explicit reference to CSE is problematic*, so SE is framed in terms of life skills, adolescent health or adolescent empowerment. C3 took steps to identify what was culturally acceptable, through formative research, to inform engagement with the community.[20]

A 2019 article claims Udaan is a program for empowerment, life skills, and health:

> Udaan, a school-based adolescence education programme, implemented by the Department of School Education and Literacy (DSEL), Government of Jharkhand, aims to influence and empower the adolescent boys and girls with age-appropriate knowledge on life skills and reproductive health and prepare them for a healthy transition to adulthood. The Udaan curriculum is part of the academic calendar and is transacted by teachers in State Government-run schools with technical assistance from Centre for Catalysing Change (C3).[21]

Reproductive health education is traditionally under the jurisdiction of the health department. To introduce CSE into the curriculum, the government had to make reproductive health education a part of the education department, thereby bringing in sex education in the guise of promoting health. This involves:

> Embedding programme management, supervision and monitoring within government staff responsibilities at all levels and developing a school-based management information system. The programme is mainstreamed into government systems – plans, budgets, monthly meetings, supervision, monitoring – is managed by government staff, and is delivered by teachers in government schools who have been trained by a cadre of master trainers selected from within the education system.[22]

The poor and vulnerable state of Jharkhand was also lobbied to transform AIDS education into sex education, and this was funded from its already strained budget. All this is being seen with gratitude towards C3 and Packard Foundation:

> The programme was already partially included in the state government budget, based on the budget allocation for the pre-existing AIDS education programme. Government has been responsible for funding programme management and implementation, as this is done by government staff and public-school teachers and has funded the costs of training teachers and of producing and distributing teaching and learning materials. C3, the state government's CSO partner, has been able to provide long-term technical assistance because the Packard Foundation has been willing to fund this support over an extended timeframe.[23]

Naturally, such a program attracted a backlash from the community, something the Jharkhand state government and C3 had anticipated. They deployed a media blast about the benefits of such a program and leveraged C3's connections:

> When there was a backlash against SE [sex education] in India, the programme was prepared and responded quickly –

> the *Secretary of the Education Department led on defending the programme, including in the State Legislative Assembly*, in responding to the media, and in engaging with community leaders.[24]

The state of Jharkhand came into being in the year 2000 with a young demographic and no established educational and health policies. This open-mindedness was exploited when Jharkhand *mandated* a sex education policy for all its schools. The IPPF's affiliate, Rutgers, brags about its success in this infiltration:

> State government buy in, together with a supportive national and state policy environment, provided a window of *opportunity and a mandate to introduce sexuality education in schools.*[25]

Despite all this success, Rutgers has further ambitions and is concerned about the 'prioritisation of the academic school curriculum, resulting in some Udaan curriculum sessions not being delivered'.[26] In other words, it sees academic courses on math, reading, etc., as obstacles because they divert resources and students' energies away from sexualization. The report presented to Packard Foundation for funding states that Udaan achieved less influence on the students' knowledge of topics like masturbation because academic priorities of the school curriculum came in the way.[27]

Another finding in the report is that the Nodal Teachers or NTs were uncomfortable handling the CSE curriculum, which resulted in 'selective teaching, due to NT discomfort with certain curriculum topics'.[28] What this means is the local teachers who resisted such sex education material are being seen as a roadblock and are to be managed by sidelining or buying their loyalty. The UN and its affiliates know that many adult teachers disapprove of its CSE content. This is why the strategy to bypass adults was implemented through the Rashtriya Kishor Swasthya Karyakram's (RKSK) program launched in 2014, which is discussed in a later chapter.

The CSE experts were also troubled that though their sex

education increased children's knowledge about sexual pleasure and masturbation, they lamented 'sadly' that it did not impact their behavior sufficiently. They write about this under the heading *Challenges*.[29]

A UNESCO report analyzing the success of Udaan gives accolades to the Jharkhand government, which is known to have been corrupt under the chief minister, Hemant Soren. *The UN looks for corrupt state governments* who will grant it full access and support to integrate its CSE curriculum into the entire academic curriculum:

> In the State of Jharkhand, *local government commitment, as well as a strong government NGO partnership, has been key to scaling up sexuality education*. A curriculum has been integrated into the school textbooks and into the in-service and pre-service education of teachers.[30]

The UN has been instituting its CSE and scaling it quietly in India in a clear effort to sexualize the innocent tribals of Jharkhand and set them loose as activists. For over two decades, tribal children in Jharkhand have been indoctrinated with 'pleasure and rights', framed within a broader 'comprehensive' educational approach.

The Udaan program has expanded significantly, reaching secondary, and even primary schools across the state. *Between 2015 and 2017, during the tenure of the BJP government, CSE was introduced to upper primary students throughout Jharkhand.*

The program has had a massive impact. It has reached over 900,000 students in more than 1,700 schools and 203 residential schools. Its training program has created a vast infrastructure by training 135 master trainers, 2,154 nodal teachers, and 24 district-level gender coordinators. This machinery is remote-controlled by the international agencies that have brought their ideology, agendas, funding, prestige, and overall support.

The Impact of Udaan on Tribal Children

Jharkhand has very low literacy rates—seventy-nine percent among males and fifty-six percent among females. The important question is: How did this redirection of resources on sex education affect the literacy and numeracy of the children of Jharkhand?

We plotted the results from Annual Status of Education Report (ASER) surveys and the results are abysmal.[31] Since 2007, when Udaan was started, numeracy and literacy have steadily plummeted year over year. In 2006, 60.1% of children in Standard V could read at Standard II level; this reading ability fell to 34.4% in 2014. Math ability similarly fell almost by fifty percent. In 2007, 41.7% of children in Standard V could divide. In 2014, that number plummeted to 21.1%, thanks to CSE.

One would think that the UN would be working on literacy, math, and other skill development of the tribal populations of Jharkhand to alleviate poverty. However, the UN and Jharkhand state administrators believe what the youth need most is sex education, with a focus on rights and pleasure, sprinkled with lessons on masturbation.

Meanwhile, the Piramal Foundation, which is a NITI Aayog partner for education, is also promoting SEL in districts across Jharkhand to embed SEL principles into education and community programs.[32]

Instead of fixing this abysmal academic record, the state of Jharkhand has partnered with UNICEF supported by the NITI Aayog, in promoting SDGs to tribals:

> The Department of School Education and Literacy, Government of Jharkhand (the nodal department for Goal 4) has taken steps to create awareness among all stakeholders, viz. teachers, parents, block and district officials on the present status and SDGs to be achieved...Besides, a number of capacity building initiatives are being planned to be undertaken by the government in different sectors.[33]

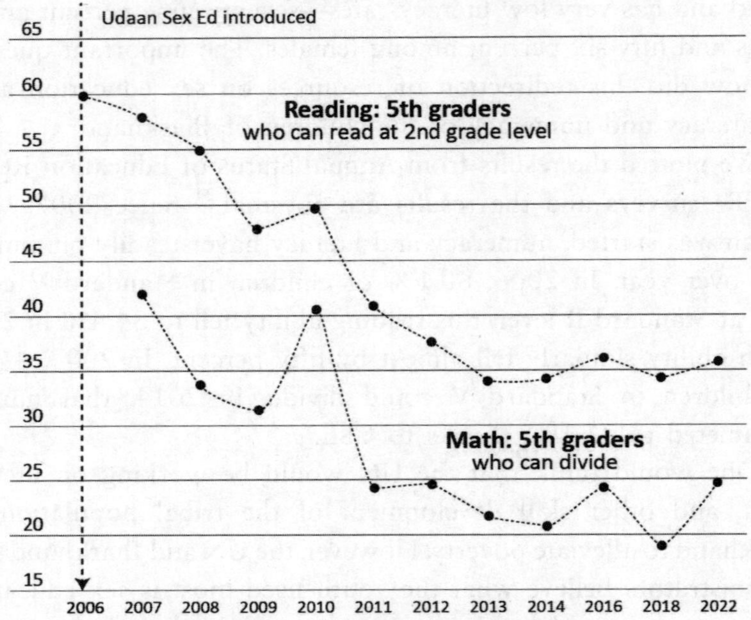
Jharkhand: Percentage of 5th graders
who can perform at 2nd grade level
Udaan Sex Ed introduced
Reading: 5th graders
who can read at 2nd grade level
Math: 5th graders
who can divide
65
60
55
50
45
40
35
30
25
20
15
2006
2007
2008
2009
2010
2011
2012
2013
2014
2016
2018
2022
Data Source: ASER 2022, ASER 2014, Trends over time

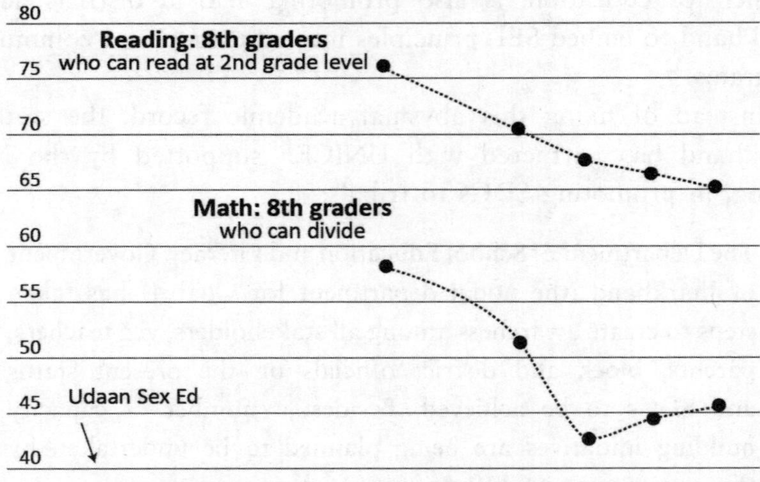
Jharkhand: Percentage of 8th graders
who can perform at 2nd grade level
Reading: 8th graders
who can read at 2nd grade level
Math: 8th graders
who can divide
Udaan Sex Ed
80
75
70
65
60
55
50
45
40
2008
2009
2010
2011
2012
2013
2014
2016
2018
2022
Data Source: ASER 2014, 2022 Trends over time

Evaluations of the program credit its success 'to a fortuitous combination of factors, the most important has been political commitment from the start'.[34] Strategic media has been crucial in sustaining Udaan's goals. Other states had successfully resisted these CSE programs: 'While this was happening in Jharkhand, AEPs in other states of the country were either halted because of opposition or slowly ran into the ground'.[35]

Jharkhand's approach to CSE is now being analyzed by various NGOs and international bodies, including the UN, to understand the elements of its success. These insights are intended to replicate Jharkhand's strategies in other parts of India and other poor places globally.

How Gansu (China) Asserts its Values

Unlike India, China does not let the global nexuses judge its success and dictate how to run its education and health institutions. While India's National Education Policy 2020 gives lip service to discipline as a guiding principle, it is prioritizing sexual rights, equity, and other Woke social justice ideas. China has a different approach, one that can *teach the world to prioritize one's national interest.*

While UNESCO guidelines on SEL/CSE apply to all signatories of the SDGs 2030, *each country may tailor these guidelines to comply with their local laws*. China quickly amended its child protection laws, adding sixty new articles, thus making it impossible to exploit its children in the name of SEL and CSE.

Gansu is a rural, undeveloped, and economically backward province, much like Jharkhand. China too, embarked on a sex education program in its rural areas, but with a much clearer focus:

1. For its rural communities, it moved to an internet platform for sex education, to deliver remotely and reached 700,000 students in 2,487 schools, across 29 provinces, with more than 40% of the students from rural areas.[36]
2. A teacher-facilitated platform titled 'You and Me' was created

and supported by the NGO 'Marie Stopes China'. *However, the entire content was developed by Chinese experts in sexual and reproductive health, with no outside intervention from UNESCO or other NGOs.*[37]

3. *The sex education content is standalone and not integrated into, and through, all subjects*. Their approach to sex education is practical with an apparent goal to teach protection of children from sexual harassment, STIs, and unwanted pregnancies.[38]
4. The content is sensitive about age appropriateness and the internet platform is designed only for middle schoolers between the ages of twelve-fourteen.
5. The middle school sex education package can also be used for high school students with no changes.

UNESCO and IPPF advocate the curriculum including sexual pleasure, desire, and details on erotic sexual activity. In contrast, the Chinese programs are practical, useful, scalable, and cost-effective given the mode of delivery. *This means that China made a clear decision on what is best for its youth and then developed a sex education framework accordingly*. The Indian government can certainly study its features and the results of such a program. Apart from establishing the framework and pedagogy to train teachers in sex education, the Chinese government has standardized the content to ensure that no one can meddle with it.

Importantly, the Chinese program does not brainwash children to have attitudes that are opposed to their parents or seek to sexualize children. Instead, a study finds that the program has a 'preventive impact' due to children 'seeking help when adverse outcomes happen'.[39]

It appears that the sex education package can further prevent adverse health outcomes caused by unsafe abortions or exacerbation of STIs in participants.[40] As an indicator of Chinese students' behavior, the study states: 'Due to the low prevalence of sexual behaviors among the participants, we could not assess the package's effects on influencing adolescents' sexual behaviors and other related sexual risks such as STIs'.[41]

The authors state that China's sex education program *did not* foster 'liberal attitudes among adolescents toward gender equity, gender-based violence, and homosexuality'. Foreign scholars interpret the above outcome as 'limitations of the program', but quite clearly, the program in China is working.

Sex education is mandated but it is based on what China deems appropriate for its schools. Other features of the amendments include limiting screen time and making service providers responsible for the welfare of minors. Laws to report sexual harassment in schools and prevention of bullying are also included.[42]

A law was enacted to promote a strong new generation, as laid out in Article 1:

> **Of protecting** the physical and mental health of minors, safeguarding their lawful rights and interests, promoting their all-around development – moral, intellectual, physical, aesthetic and hard-working spirit development, training them to be builders of and successors to the socialist cause with lofty ideals, sound morality, better education and a good sense of discipline, and fostering them to be a new generation to undertake the task of national rejuvenation.[43]

Article 3 of the law states the rights of minors. Noticeably, *missing from the list are the Woke ideas of sexual rights, and the expression of gender and sexuality rights*: 'The State shall guarantee minors' right to life, the right to development, the right to being protected and the right to participation'.[44] Article 4 states that the law is in the best interest of minors and that in matters related to minors, the requirement of 'combining protection with education will be fulfilled'.[45]

China is also constantly evaluating the costs and benefits of such sex education programs by its researchers from Tsinghua University in Beijing, and not relying on UNESCO to give them a report on the effectiveness of such programs.

Not surprisingly, UNESCO is not pleased with the Chinese taking aggressive steps by amending child protection laws that go against radical CSE programs. While UNESCO commends other Asian countries mandating CSE, it is disappointed by how the Chinese have enacted these airtight laws to protect its young generation:

> In Asia, the majority of countries have a national law, policy or strategy that refers to the provision of sexuality education, and in the Pacific approximately half the countries have policies in place…However, in a recent development in China, an amendment to the law on the protection of minors was passed in October 2020, declaring that schools, including kindergartens, should conduct 'age-appropriate sex education for minors'.[46]

Unable to push the Chinese on its CSE policies, a helpless UNESCO stands on the sidelines, pacifying the Chinese by stating:

> Innovative approaches to teacher training have been developed, such as the online *You & Me* education platform in China, which provides free-of-charge support to interested educators with basic teaching skills to conduct sexuality education, as well as access to a range of resources.[47]

China effectively strategizes proactively to protect its children, society, and cultural values. On the other hand, India is scaling at a rapid pace and doing just the opposite by selling out its future generation.

Sex Education in Singapore

The example of China implementing the SDGs in a culturally sensitive manner might seem like a powerful country asserting itself. Therefore, we also cite the example of Singapore doing the same despite being a small country.

Sex education in Singapore is rather archaic, with an emphasis on abstinence and awareness of Sexually Transmitted Diseases. It is also about 'character [building] and citizenship education'.[48] Students are taught to abstain from sex until marriage and the devastating consequences of pornography and teenage sexual activity. They learn the importance of respecting the boundaries of self and others in sexual relationships. What is glaringly missing is the trendy topic of gender fluidity. Singapore wants to build a robust future society and is not getting swayed by Western Woke ideas.

Here is the Singapore Ministry of Education's approach to sex education:

> Our Sexuality Education curriculum is anchored on Singapore's prevailing family values and social norms…Marriage is defined as being a union between a man and a woman…the importance of respect for self and others, both online and offline, and respecting personal boundaries for healthy relationships and safety... promotes abstinence before marriage, and teaches facts about contraception, consequences of casual sex, prevention of diseases, and how to say 'no' to sexual advances. This also helps to reduce the incidence of sexually transmitted diseases or teenage pregnancies. Sexuality Education teaches students what homosexuality is and the importance of mutual understanding, respect and empathy for everyone.[49]

Who Controls India's Education?

In the next section of this book, we highlight the interconnectedness of money, power, and influence in shaping agendas related to education in India. It seems India has already sold itself to unelected globalists who are making decisions for its citizens' education.

India's tech billionaires are the new oligarchs controlling governments through private and public partnerships to amass even greater wealth and gain power. They operate through a large network of NGOs and consultants that draft policies, conduct research, and run institutes while claiming to be 'evidence-backed'. These third-party organizations develop strategy documents, guidelines, standards, implementation plans, and progress reports—all this to turn the billionaires' visions into action plans. They also influence the government both directly and through the UN, WEF, and other international agencies. The UN and its agencies are in lockstep with these organizations. They speak the same terminology, use the same frameworks, and evangelize the same discourse.

The UN is a powerful entity capable of exerting influence on a global scale. It has the authority to impose sanctions on countries and pass resolutions that mandate policies and actions. It has the power to make international laws. For example, as we mentioned earlier, the UN is working with the International Commission of Jurists to make sexual rights a fundamental human right without age being a consideration, and even opening the door to potentially decriminalizing pedophilia. The UN also has the power to direct funding for large projects through the World Bank and the International Monetary Fund (IMF).

India's own HCLFoundation and the Tata Group are among the domestic players channeling philanthropy to sexualize Indian children. This vast and powerful network of foreign players in collaboration with India's government and oligarchs has launched many Woke initiatives in Indian education. If they genuinely cared for the children of India, they would support educational initiatives for skill development, reading, and math which are essential components of a quality education.

Our concern is with the funding that focuses mainly on sexualizing children with a CSE package being scaled up across India. We will also examine the way these giant entities lobby the government to change policies and bring in SEL with Woke components that are ill-suited for Indian culture. Unfortunately, each of India's policies and frameworks in education has been made in alignment with the mandates of the global nexuses.

In the next part of the book, we will drill deep and systematically explore the following diagram.

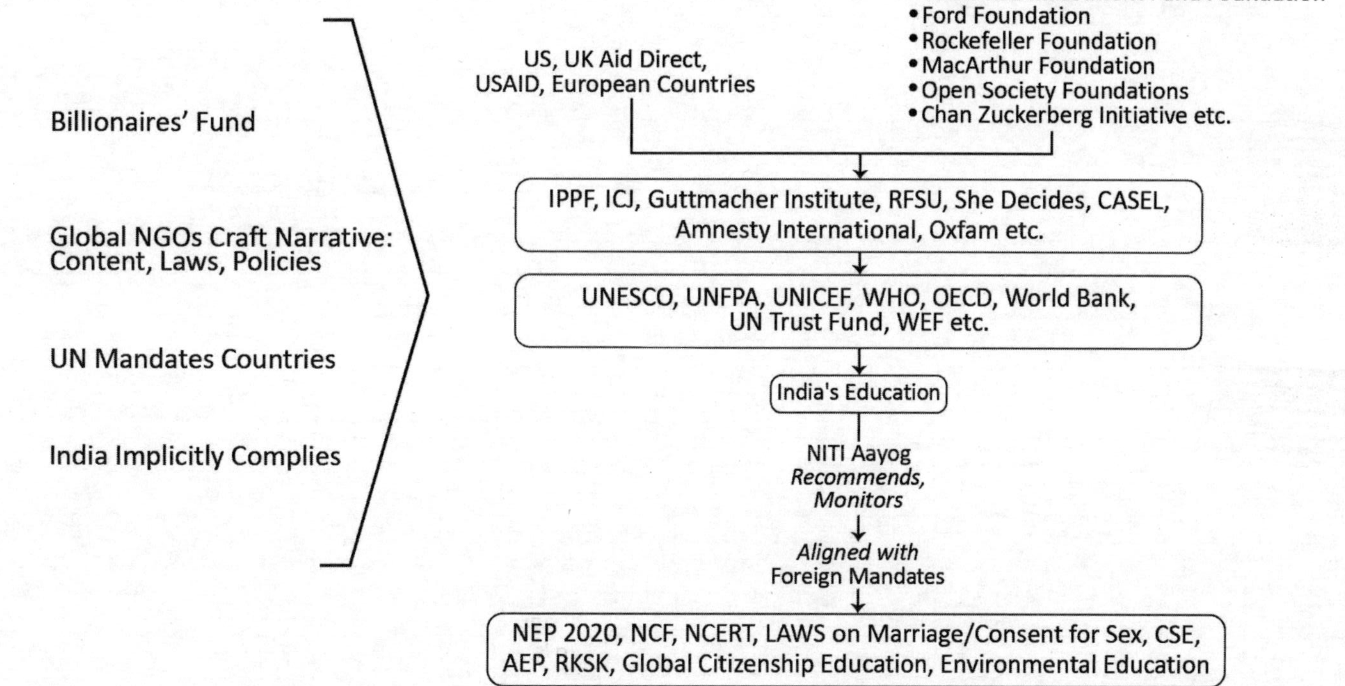
Who Calls the Shots on Education?
Billionaires' Fund
Global NGOs Craft Narrative: Content, Laws, Policies
UN Mandates Countries
India Implicitly Complies
US, UK Aid Direct, USAID, European Countries
• Bill & Melinda Gates Foundation
• David and Lucile Packard Foundation
• Children's Investment Fund Foundation
• Ford Foundation
• Rockefeller Foundation
• MacArthur Foundation
• Open Society Foundations
• Chan Zuckerberg Initiative etc.
IPPF, ICJ, Guttmacher Institute, RFSU, She Decides, CASEL, Amnesty International, Oxfam etc.
UNESCO, UNFPA, UNICEF, WHO, OECD, World Bank, UN Trust Fund, WEF etc.
India's Education
NITI Aayog Recommends, Monitors
Aligned with Foreign Mandates
NEP 2020, NCF, NCERT, LAWS on Marriage/Consent for Sex, CSE, AEP, RKSK, Global Citizenship Education, Environmental Education

PART 2

BREEDING A TROUBLED GENERATION

7

CHALLENGES FACING INDIAN EDUCATORS

We earlier discussed problems with Woke-based American education, how it corrupts children, and the network of global players pushing this. We argued that it is irresponsible to give very young, gullible, and impressionable children the right to consent to sex, especially when the curriculum promotes exploration, piques curiosity, and the pursuit of sexual desires. If minors are not protected, their inability to make informed decisions leaves them vulnerable to exploitation by adults who could justify their actions claiming the child consented. This is why it is dangerous for schools to teach children about sexual pleasure, masturbation, and sexual desire, and to normalize the use of pornography and social media platforms as resources for sex education. It is especially irresponsible if this is done by circumventing parental supervision.

We also discussed the globalists whose agenda is served by dismantling nation-states or weakening the sovereignty of nation-states. The weaker the nation-states become, the greater the power of globalists given their enormous wealth and technologies like Artificial Intelligence. We explained the vast network of globalists comprising oligarchs, Western institutions including liberal academic centers and think tanks, NGOs, and international bodies like the UN and the World Economic Forum.

We now turn our attention to India as the proverbial sitting duck. A major problem is that, unlike China, India did not develop national policies that could serve as the foundation and provide guardrails when importing foreign standards. The floodgates have been opened to welcome foreign norms, as well as foreign experts. The Indians trained under foreign experts and with foreign affiliations have become the new *adhikaris*. They have penetrated the Ministry of HRD and the Ministry of Health and Family Welfare to implement CSE. State-level initiatives are also underway with Gujarat, Bihar, and Odisha implementing CSE programs. For example, Gujarat plans to implement Jharkhand's CSE model, Udaan, which we discussed earlier.[1]

The landscape of sex education in India is marked by ongoing legal, cultural, and ideological battles in which the globalists have the upper hand. India's young demographic, especially its adolescent population between the ages of ten and twenty-four, is being targeted for sex education through Social Emotional Learning and Comprehensive Sexuality Education. These programs are not focused on empowering children to fend off sexual abuse, report violations without stigma, instill a zero-tolerance policy on bullying and harassment, and teach the risks of Sexually Transmitted Diseases. On the contrary, the impact of the latest genre of sex education is just the opposite: making children more vulnerable.

Furthermore, parents are being denied the right to have their children opt out of these CSE programs because they are not stand-alone modules, instead are integrated within the entire curriculum. We believe that all sex education programs should involve parents, and they must be transparent on content and delivery. The highest priority in formulating policies must be given to protect India's four hundred-plus million youth from sexual predators, violence, abuse, and disease.

Some state governments like Maharashtra are now mandating public universities to waive their entire tuition fees for transgender students.[2] For its part, the Ministry of Social Justice and Empowerment is handing out scholarships to trans students from the ninth standard onwards, a cost that is eventually borne by the Indian taxpayer. The National Education Policy 2020, though claiming to promote Indian

Knowledge Systems, is in fact, designed to align Indian education with global standards like the UN's Sustainable Development Goals.

Comprehensive Sexuality Education is being introduced through a murky web of government and private sector partnerships, drawing controversy for its focus on sexual rights and social justice causes aligned with Western ideologies, in conflict with traditional Indian values. Social Emotional Learning is being integrated into the curriculum, ostensibly to promote emotional health, but it is also a conduit for introducing broader socio-political agendas.

Proposed changes in societal norms such as lowering the age of consent for having sex to sixteen, are being slipped into the programs to 'empower women' and 'reduce infant mortality'. These changes are elements of a larger social engineering agenda that is undermining traditional family values and compromising national identity.

We will now explain how the Indian government's education policy has evolved to become increasingly subordinate to these global mandates. Part 2 provides detailed evidence to support our claims. Readers who prefer to skip the details can proceed directly to Part 3.

A History of Sex Education in India

Right to Education Act

In contradiction to the claim of being secular, many of India's laws discriminate based on religion. Typically, the Hindu majority is put at a disadvantage to help the minorities. One of the most discriminative laws is the 'Right to Education Act' (RTE) enacted in 2009 which applies *only* to Hindu-run schools, exempting religious minority institutions. This selective application discriminates against Hindu institutions: Only Hindu institutions are required to adhere to government-imposed curricula that include controversial Comprehensive Sexuality Education topics.

Its adverse effects have already begun unraveling over the past decade and will have even more devastating effects as the structural and pedagogical changes to the national curricular framework get implemented. See Appendix B for details on the legal changes.

The history of RTE begins in 2002 with an amendment to the Constitution, making education a Fundamental Right requiring states to provide free and compulsory education from the first to the eighth standard (ages six to fourteen).[3] The RTE mandates that twenty-five percent of the seats be reserved for marginalized groups in government schools and in *only* those private schools that are run by Hindus.[4]

Furthermore, non-Hindu institutions have the freedom to teach what they want while Hindu institutions are burdened by all sorts of government mandates.

The RTE also imposes strict standards of infrastructure that many schools struggle to meet, standards that apply only to Hindu schools and not those run by minorities. These demanding criteria have forced many Hindu schools providing basic education to shut down. A study found that less than thirteen percent of schools across India are compliant with RTE.[5] The government-run schools that fail to comply with the RTE are given time to remedy, whereas the Hindu schools not complying are declared rogue and shut down.[6] The National Independent Schools Alliance reported the 'closure of 7,659 schools in 2015-2016, and another 7,898 schools received notices to close'.[7] In Punjab alone, '1,170 private schools had been closed for non-compliance with the RTE norms'.[8]

A 2021 study by the National Commission for Protection of Child Rights (NCPCR) analyzed the state of minority-run schools based on 23,487 minority schools. The objective was to ascertain how the rights guaranteed to minorities for the preservation of their language, scriptures, and culture, conflicted with the fundamental right of their children to basic education. The findings showed the negative impacts of exempting minority schools from the RTE, with Christian schools becoming elitist cocoons and Muslim schools becoming 'ghettoes of underprivileged students'.[9]

SEL and CSE are Mandated Only for Hindu Children

In the USA, many Christian schools reject SEL and CSE because they do not agree with the values of sexuality. The same is true of Indian Christian schools. For example, one of the 'challenges' that the IPPF affiliate Rutgers International saw in Jharkhand's Udaan CSE project was the rejection by Catholic schools:

> Despite the overall success in scaling up and sustaining Udaan in Jharkhand, the programme has faced and still faces a number of challenges...The programme does not cover students in private schools – in Jharkhand many of these are Catholic mission schools and these are often less receptive to CSE.[10]

Likewise, madrassas in India are *not* jumping on to the SEL and CSE bandwagon. Under the freedoms afforded by the RTE, these minority institutions can reject the SEL/CSE curriculum, but there is no escape for Hindu children being forced into the SEL/CSE curriculum. Hence, the RTE becomes the weapon to selectively poison the minds of Hindu children with Woke education while exempting minority children.

National Education Policy 2020

Given the euphoria of NEP 2020, we would like to acknowledge the numerous independent initiatives in education, such as the Mid-Day Meal Scheme, that have been successfully implemented to increase nourishment and enrollment of children. Other initiatives such as *Beti Bachao Beti Padhao* (Save Daughter Educate Daughter) have increased awareness for educating girls. We also acknowledge that many educationists are designing curricula and content that are NEP-compliant and yet aligned with Indian civilization.

However, the impact of NEP has been more complex. The NEP 2020 was sold to the public as a way to get the young generation ready for India's ascent on the global stage. The reality is very different: *NEP 2020 was an effort to align India with SDGs 2030 and make Indian education adhere to Woke standards set by foreign institutions. The mandates and targets of SDGs 2030 are built into NEP 2020.*[11] The NEP explicitly:

> Proposes the revision and revamping of all aspects of the education structure, including its regulation and governance, to create a new system that is aligned with the aspirational goals of 21st century education, including SDGs 4, while building upon India's traditions and value systems.[12]

The principle of 'building upon India's traditions and value systems' is mentioned in the previous quote from the National Education Policy, but this principle is in direct conflict with the SDGs. For example:

- The central principle of 'equity' is an overriding theme of the SDGs, but it is the Woke idea of diversity based on Marxist oppressor-oppressed identities. In contrast, the Indian value system views all humanity as variegated and celebrates differences in attributes and qualities as part of the natural order.
- The CSE is not compatible with Indian values on sex education for young children.
- Allowing schools to bypass parents is incompatible with Indian values.
- Indian values teach responsibility in the form of dharma and prescribe improving one's lot through good karma, not victimhood.

The NEP is also moving away from meritocracy-based assessments towards Competency-Based Education to achieve education equity. This is discussed in a later chapter.

State Vernacular Languages and the National Education Policy 2020

Research shows that countries that take pride in their languages and receive STEM education in their mother tongues display better progress than countries that teach in foreign languages, a system followed from colonial times. The NEP was lauded for claiming to promote multilingual education. We also applaud the efforts to translate NCERT textbooks into regional languages and train teachers in regional language instruction, which is an enormous task in and of itself.

However, the ground reality is that many state governments are pushing English-medium education. For example, in 2019, the Andhra Pradesh government moved to English-medium for all classes starting from the first grade.[13] Jharkhand is also moving towards English-medium education in K-12 schools.[14] All across India, Indian language schools are shutting down. For example, in Punjab, there are hardly any Gurmukhi-medium schools. The lure of the English-medium school continues.

A common argument justifying English is that it gives access to better job opportunities and is the passport to higher social status and self-esteem. Indian courts also operate in English as the medium. This is why the NEP should have proposed incentives to employers for hiring non-English speaking and non-English educated candidates who are otherwise qualified. Such a system would boost vernacular language as the medium of education.

Those educated in non-English-medium should be declared *linguistically disadvantaged*, and a quota should be assigned for them to get jobs in the government and private sectors. There is no reason for ignoring an identity for the linguistically oppressed and classifying the English-educated as their oppressors. This would be consistent with Marxist and Woke framing of oppressors/oppressed.

Hiding Behind the Jargon

The NEP 2020 is full of vague, impressive-sounding jargon like 'holistic', 'multidisciplinary approach', eliminating 'harmful hierarchies among, and silos between different areas of learning', and 'multidisciplinary world to ensure the unity and integrity of all knowledge'.[15] Such superficial terms are entry points to inject a Woke curriculum without raising suspicion.

The NEP 2020 does not explicitly mention SEL, but uses benign SEL terms like compassion, empathy, emotional, and mental health, to produce an 'equitable and inclusive' society. These statements enable NGOs to slip in their SEL curriculum developed outside India.

The NEP also allows the exploitation of students by data collection of their sensitive private information—all under the pretext of being 'holistic'.[16] While analyzing the data can be useful, it can also violate privacy and be used to manipulate. A good example of such concerns was discussed in an earlier chapter to show how the Chan Zuckerburg Initiative partners with the government to implement free assessment systems and thereby gains access to data on hundreds of millions of children across the USA.

The National Curriculum Framework

The National Curriculum Framework for School Education (NCF) was drafted in 2023 in keeping with the vision of NEP 2020. It is the educational framework for ages three to eighteen and introduces social-emotional aspects and environmentalism into its framework. These topics seem desirable, but the goal is to make children activists for these global causes, taking away precious time from career-oriented learning or learning of Indian Knowledge Systems. We need to worry that literacy and numeracy rates have steadily dropped in India since 2008, and the global crises taught using SEL are a huge distraction.

The following criticism of the way the SDGs are implemented in American schools should be a warning to India:

> Hammering K–12 school children nonstop about the dangers of climate change in every class, even math, art, and gym, is child abuse...Barely one-third of fourth graders can read or do math at grade level, according to the latest national scores, but climate activists are demanding that kids hear about global warming in every class...Climate change is the left's religion. The messaging is as heavy-handed as catechism in a religious school.... It's also scary. Children are being told that global warming is killing their favorite animals. At

> Slackwood Elementary School in New Jersey, first graders are taught that transportation, heating, and raising livestock are 'making Earth feel unwell'.[17]

Young children are unable to comprehend the complex trade-offs of moving to zero carbon immediately. A first grader cannot evaluate the fact that her mother can't afford an electric vehicle. In the USA, social justice topics have permeated all subjects, not even sparing kindergarteners who are being asked to champion these causes as activists.[18] In Australia too, climate education has faced similar criticism. 'An Australian Liberal senator has accused the education department of pushing children into experiencing 'climate change anxiety', claiming there is a 'strong left-wing bend' across the school system'.[19]

The US State Department is funding a 'climate action podcast' to encourage India's commitment to fighting climate change. The USA cites an example of a 'successful U.S. Mission podcast' that it wants India to emulate, including *What's a Man? Masculinity in India*, a show that interviews Indian 'boys as young as seven years old and men across the LGBTQIA+ spectrum' to discuss perceived issues with the 'male-female binary'.[20] The USA has ambitious plans for India's activists, with a goal that 'the podcast in its first six months should reach at least half a million listeners across various podcast streaming platforms', and that at least ten percent of them 'should engage in a dialogue on social media through a dedicated hashtag committing to a sustainable lifestyle'.[21]

Vedic values include teaching children to appreciate the environment, understand the Divine presence, and protect it. However, the NCF is based on Western concepts of the environment as a material resource for human benefit, along with some social justice and human rights mixed in.

> Environmental Education critically addresses both social and natural concerns. Social concerns *include issues of gender and marginalization, equity, justice and respect for human dignity and rights*...Environmental values include but are not

limited to aesthetic appreciation of beauty of surroundings including diversity of physical and socio-cultural environment; sensitivity towards social, political, economic, cultural, and natural environment and phenomena; ability and motivation to identify and raise questions related to *human dignity, justice, and rights.*[22]

The NCF uses Sanskrit terms such as *annamaya kosha*, *pranamaya kosha*, and *manomaya kosha* for emotional and spiritual development, but it does not use the Vedic framework of the *koshas* as the structure to build the actual curriculum. It is misleading to use Sanskrit terms to promote the Western framework.[23]

Although the Right to Education Act mandates reducing the student-to-teacher ratio, the report card on Indian education continues to decline from bad to worse. According to the data in the Annual Status of Education Report 2022, *more than half of India's fifth graders cannot read at grade two levels, and only a quarter can do second grade division problems in mathematics.*

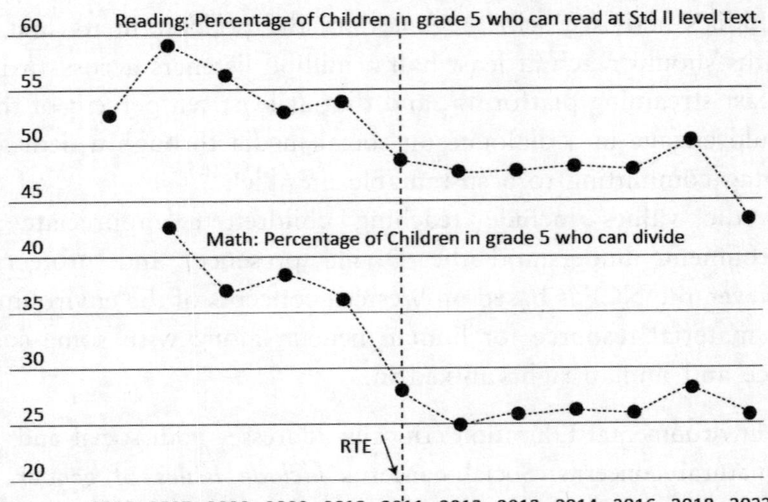

The case with eighth graders is similarly disturbing, with almost a third being functionally illiterate (i.e. cannot read at second-grade levels) and over fifty percent unable to do second-grade arithmetic.

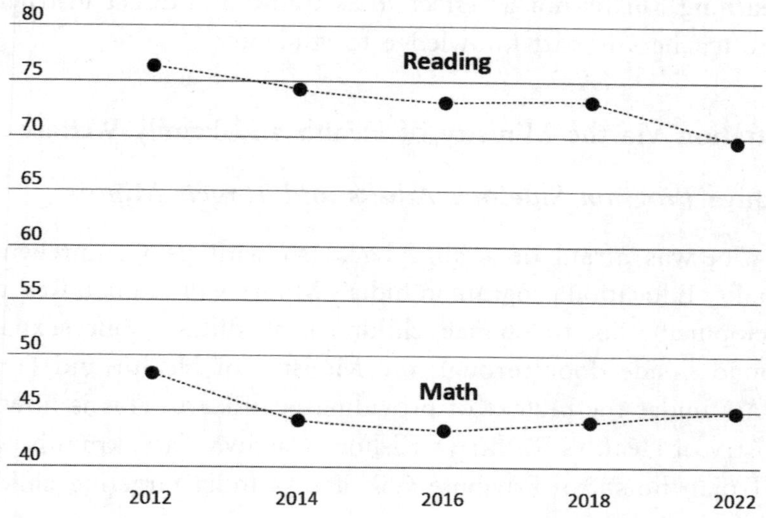

The NEP 2020 and RTE are clearly failing, and India's next generation is likely to be marginally literate. With such low basic literacy and math skills, the government should purge the education system of subjects that distract from basic learning. The teachers are already overburdened, yet they are being forced to get trained and certified with priority given to the UN mandates.

Furthermore, the Western ideas of demanding 'rights' have entered Indian classrooms, while the traditional Indian education system's values of discipline, duties, and responsibilities have been sidelined. Children need to learn clear boundaries and such an approach only blurs the boundaries. This includes eliminating detention and eliminating exams as the criteria for promotion to the next grade. Parents should reject the American 'soft parenting' style that is proving to be a disaster in the USA.

The NEP 2020 also talks about child-centered instruction, which means that teachers facilitate discovery and guide students but do not 'teach' anything. The West is learning that in the early stages of learning, this is not as effective as traditional direct instruction where teachers impart knowledge to students.

Infiltration Via the Ministry of Health and Family Welfare

Saathiya *Program Sidelines Adults and Targets Minors*

The UN was afraid of a huge backlash with its Comprehensive Sexuality Education program in India's Ministry of Human Resource Development. So, to change children's attitudes about sexuality, it found a side door through the Ministry of Health and Family Welfare under the pretext of providing healthcare. This is how the Ministry of Health's Rashtriya Kishor Swasthya Karyakram became the Trojan horse to distribute CSE across India targeting children aged ten to nineteen.

The RKSK was launched in 2014 under the banner of rights and well-being of adolescents including sexual and reproductive health in addition to nutrition, mental health, gender-based violence, and substance misuse. That is good. However, the globalists are managing the RKSK with NGOs playing a major role in directing the implementation of the program on behalf of the Ministry of Health and Family Welfare.

The RKSK was founded to improve nutrition, and mental health and prevent injuries and violence. In 2017, with the help of content from the Population Foundation of India, a Tata NGO, and the UNFPA, this program was repurposed to bring CSE content via the *RKSK Saathiya Program*. It contains three components: *Saathiya Sex Ed Kit* (training), *Saathiya Salah* (mobile App) and *Saathiya* (teenage peer educators).[24] The Population Foundation of India was founded by the India country director of the MacArthur Foundation and J.R.D. Tata, and had luminaries such as the late Ratan Tata on its governing board.

In effect, the UNFPA is shouldering the role of sex education on behalf of the Government of India in the name of promoting sexual health for youth. Having relinquished its role to safeguard the country's youth, the Indian health ministry praised the program as 'an ambitious program-apart from health we are talking about behavioral change and change in thinking'.[25] In 2022, the UNFPA spent almost ten million dollars in India.[26]

The strategy is to provide sex education using stealth approaches—hooking children onto mobile Apps with no content oversight, forming youth groups, and most importantly, training other children to act as peer educators.

The Saathiya Salah mobile App is designed to target and lure young people who are tech-savvy and enjoy digital platforms that are 'cool'. The strategy is to get children as young as ten hooked on the App, trusting it for sexual advice. These Apps are available 24/7 and are an effective means to reach the youth outside the classroom and without the scrutiny of elders. *This is how the UN can bypass parental and educator oversight on information presented to preteens and teenagers*. This opens the door to sexual exploration, sexual pleasure, masturbation, and sexual rights. The content on these Apps may not yet embrace the UN's full-blown vision for sexualizing children, but it is a step in that direction. Once the platform is established and becomes the 'go to' place for teen sexual advice, desire-driven sex education can be ratcheted up:

> The peer educators will be trained across the country in a phased manner, ensuring optimum use of the resource kit, which is a ready source of a range of communication material specially designed to help them to be recognized and respected as 'Saathiya', a good friend for the adolescents.[27]

The *saathiya* are typically a boy and girl pair being trained as advisors for a single village or community. Those who do not wish to approach their peer educators directly can access the App for advice. These 'peer educators' are also attached to Adolescent Friendly Health Clinics that 'Enable all adolescents to realize their full potential by making informed decisions concerning their health, by accessing the services and support to implement their decisions'.[28]

Many NGOs are feverishly working on making policy recommendations to the MHRD and the Ministry of Health and Family Welfare based on the gold standard set by ITGSE for Sexual and Reproductive Health and Rights (SRHR): 'The MHRD should integrate the elements of gender, sexual rights and sexual citizenship, pleasure, diversity and relationships...to make it comprehensive'.[29] They also recommend that *CSE should begin early, in primary school* 'to develop body and sex positive attitudes, to address gender discriminatory practices that begin before puberty'.[30] They have policy recommendations for the Ministry of Health and Family Welfare to 'invest in the training and mentorship of peer educators to effectively collectivize young people to impart CSE' and train the 'Adolescent Friendly Health Clinics' staff on abortion laws and the *RKSK Saathiya Program.*

The UNFPA states that it plans to spend sixty million dollars from 2023-7 on priority goals such as:

a. Sexual rights-based reproductive services across India targeting Scheduled Caste (SC)/Scheduled Tribes (ST).
b. Teach girls about bodily autonomy.
c. Accelerate CSE education to state governments based on global standards.
d. Use the Smart Cities Mission to access young people in slums.[31]

All this is done with the approval, support, and blessings of the government.

The RKSK is applauded by the UNFPA for the launch of Saathiya Salah App to spread CSE across India,

> [The RKSK] comprises facility based and community-based activities with a focus on adolescent participation, peer education and youth leadership. NGOs play a key role in supporting implementation of the Strategy, working with the Ministry of Health and Family Welfare.[32]

Many NGOs cite that schools are limited by time and capacity and use this to promote that, 'Therefore, out-of-school approaches such as RKSK could offer more flexibility in how information on CSE can be integrated and understood in the community itself'.[33] This has mixed effects. There are benefits, such as the provision of subsidized sanitary napkins to adolescent girls in rural areas. However, the same programs also allow the NGOs to piggyback and deliver sex education to adolescents using government resources.

The RKSK gives NGOs more flexibility to implement CSE, as one explains:

> The *Saathiya Salah* toolkit [of RKSK] makes an important deviation from the government's usual approach to CSE by providing an *unbiased platform* for young people to access information…It is significant because it highlights the importance of consent and acknowledges desire as normal across and between genders.[34]

Other NGOs in the sex education space praise Saathiya's success in normalizing sexual desire among adolescents:

> It [Saathiya] additionally makes significant strides in acknowledging desire as 'normal' across and between different genders… a welcome step in public health programming.[35]

Another bypass strategy acknowledged by UNFPA is to actively promote IPPF.[36] There is a revolving door of leaders moving between UNFPA and the IPPF. For example, the Comprehensive Sexuality

Education program director of IPPF in Africa is now a director at the UNFPA and she praised the RKSK saying,

> And India has done well in terms of prioritizing adolescents' health. In the last few years, the Indian government has initiated large scale national adolescent health programmes such as Rashtriya Kishore (sic) Swasthya Karyakaram and School Health and Wellness programme which have put its youth population front and center of development.[37]

She went on to promote the CSE doctrine, especially to girls as the antidote to all social evils:

> Likewise, it is crucial that we build agency and bodily autonomy for adolescent girls and young women which is vital to ensure positive health outcomes throughout the life course. This calls for a multipronged approach including safeguarding access to comprehensive sexuality education in our communities, schools, and vocational training institutions. This will empower adolescent girls and young women to make informed choices and decisions about their sexual and reproductive health and well-being.[38]

In 2019, two Lok Sabha (the lower House of the Indian Parliament) members pressed the minister for health and family welfare, Harsh Vardhan, for answers regarding the implementation of CSE across India: Was India going to meet its obligation as a signatory to the International Conference on Population and Development (ICPD) Programme of Action 1994, to provide free and compulsory Comprehensive Sexuality Education? In response, the health minister quickly issued a memo titled *Comprehensive Sexuality Education*.[39] This was misleading because this memo did not discuss CSE and only discussed vague issues like 'empowerment', 'life skills', and HIV/AIDS prevention.[40] It mentioned two programs by the government:

> A sixteen-hour module developed by NCERT, in coordination with state governments, targeting children inside and

outside of the school system. It used the vague language of 'empowerment' and invoked the fear of HIV/AIDS. This program is from the Ministry of HRD.[41]

A twenty-four-hour module with 'emphasis on preventive and promotive activities' to be rolled out under Rashtriya Kishor Swasthya Karyakram, under which: 'Two school teachers will be identified and trained as Health & Wellness Ambassadors in every school'. This bypasses adult teachers and instead uses peer advisors, toolkits, and mobile Apps without parents' knowledge as discussed.

School Health Ambassador Initiative

In 2020, the MHRD and the Ministry of Health and Family Welfare jointly launched the *School Health Ambassador Initiative* to roll out CSE throughout India based on Jharkhand's Udaan as a blueprint.[42] Every government school will train two teachers who will serve as 'Health and Wellness Ambassadors' and become CSE trainers. The Indian government spends heavily on training CSE ambassadors even though, as noted earlier, the standards are abysmal for basic education that would qualify a young person for a career. Such is the pressure to comply with UN mandates despite facing severe constraints in its education budget.

The Indian government spends less than three percent of its Gross Domestic Product on education and hence, many states have outsourced the training of these 'wellness ambassadors' to NGOs that have deep connections with foreign foundations and implement their agenda. Such NGOs play a dual role: On the one hand, they work closely with the NITI Aayog and other ministries to bring policy change for education; on the other, they have programs and toolkits ready for deployment once these policies are implemented. Essentially, the government is a puppet in the hands of NGOs that are controlled by global institutions. These NGOs are excited about RKSK, because:

1. RKSK mandates that two teachers as Health and Wellness Ambassadors must be dedicated to CSE. The NGOs train

these CSE experts on behalf of the government.

2. RKSK uses young people as peers because they are more open to pleasure-oriented and positive attitudes towards sexuality than traditional teachers.
3. RKSK also provides Adolescent Friendly Health Clinics where NGOs can freely train peer counselors with the content they have developed and supply abortion services.
4. RKSK enables NGOs to use technology: NGOs receive huge sums for scale-up of CSE.

UNICEF and the Ministry of Human Resource Development

Another UN agency that is pushing its agenda through the government is UNICEF, officially designated as the knowledge partner of the MHRD. Its tentacles have spread deep into India, including the following projects:

1. UNICEF is a partner in developing the International Technical Guidance for Sexuality Education standards and guidelines for CSE along with WHO, UNFPA, UNESCO, and RFSU (IPPF). We showed earlier that the ITGSE standard claims that children are sexual beings and that CSE should be focused on sexual rights and sexual pleasure. These ITGSE guidelines are relentlessly promoted in India as the standards that NGOs follow to create CSE content and integrate it into the government's RKSK.
2. Because Jharkhand's tribals were successfully targeted for the Udaan sex education project, UNICEF is working to bring Sustainable Development Goals to them.
3. UNICEF funds the two main NGOs advocating CSE in India: IPPF's Family Planning Association of India and Population Foundation of India. These will be discussed in later chapters.
4. UNICEF lobbied the Indian government to lower the age of consent for sexual activity. A government agency has accused UNICEF of using false data to make its case. UNICEF was

quick to distance itself from the report it co-authored and its NGO partner which UNICEF had funded.

5. As per its reports, UNICEF claims to leverage digital media to promote CSE to 'positively impact' children as young as ten.[43]
6. UNICEF endorses several sex vloggers including: 'Laci Green who hosts a vulgar blog called 'A Naked Notion' with 1.5 million subscribers'.[44] Green gives teens 'tips for hook ups' and lessons on 'pansexuality'...which means an 'attraction to all genders'.[45] UNICEF applauds Laci Green's videos because they take a positive and inclusive approach to sex and masturbation.[46]

Given this scandalous background, *UNICEF should be banned from working in India*, but sadly, the situation is just the opposite. UNICEF works closely with the MHRD and Indian state governments 'to develop an action plan for girls' education and out-of-school children'. This will be integrated into the education curriculum and pedagogy from age three to nineteen in all states.[47]

While there may be worthy projects in sexual hygiene and the prevention of child marriage, the agenda to sexualize youth through integrated curricula and digital applications remains a serious concern.

Development Initiative Supporting Healthy Adolescents

Like the RKSK Saathiya Programme, the Development Initiative on Supporting Healthy Adolescents is another government program being used as a vehicle to train peer sex educators for tribal youth. Funded by The David and Lucile Packard Foundation and under the guise of targeting states 'characterized by high fertility rates and poor reproductive health outcomes, MOUs have been signed with the state governments of Bihar and Jharkhand'.[48] Besides training peer sex educators, the focus of this program is to serve 'as peer pressure groups for change in their communities'.[49] The David and Lucile Packard Foundation also funds numerous other programs on sex education in India apart from this.[50]

New Influencers, Startups and Accolades

New players are being invited to promote directly to youngsters through social media using messages of sexual pleasure, masturbation, and rights. Leeza Mangaldas is one such influencer with over 2.5 million followers on social media.[51] Mangaldas champions coming out as a bisexual and promotes masturbation, sending a message to youth about 'a world where all sexual relationships are consensual, safe and pleasurable', with an entire section on orgasms. Some of her graphic content has been banned under obscenity laws:

> However, with increased moderation of media and censorship, creators are having their content removed by the platforms, which is, in turn, hurting their followers and their brand partnerships. Mangaldas attributes this to the fact that regulatory processes fail to differentiate between 'nudity, sexual solicitation, pornography, art and educational content'.[52]

ThatMate, a Pune-based tech company has rolled out their SEL program to over '100,000 students so far through partnerships with local schools'. UNICEF and the state of Jharkhand have partnered with ThatMate to provide Social Emotional Learning to six lakh students. This venture has support from NITI Aayog's Atal Incubation Centre and funding from the Ministry of Electronics and Information Technology (MeitY) as part of its TIDE 2.0 scheme.[53] Other funders include USAID, UNICEF, Ambuja Cements, and Tech Mahindra Foundation.

StandWeSpeak is a tech startup that promotes 'sex positive' CSE content, also funded by the NITI Aayog's Atal Incubation Centre. Working with many state governments, the website features an Artificial Intelligence bot that delves into gender fluidity, rights, and pleasure. They work with experts that include lawyers and 'intimacy coaches'. Not surprisingly, the chief executive officer of IPPF's Family Planning Association of India, Kalpana Apte, is a mentor for this startup along with others working in women's rights and sex education.[54] International accolades have been pouring in for Apte. She was 'invited to promote social and gender equality at the World Bank Group Youth Summit 2022 and won the Diana Award 2022'. The startup was also awarded prestigious accolades by the World Bank and the UNDP.[55]

The following diagram shows the infiltration happening under the radar.

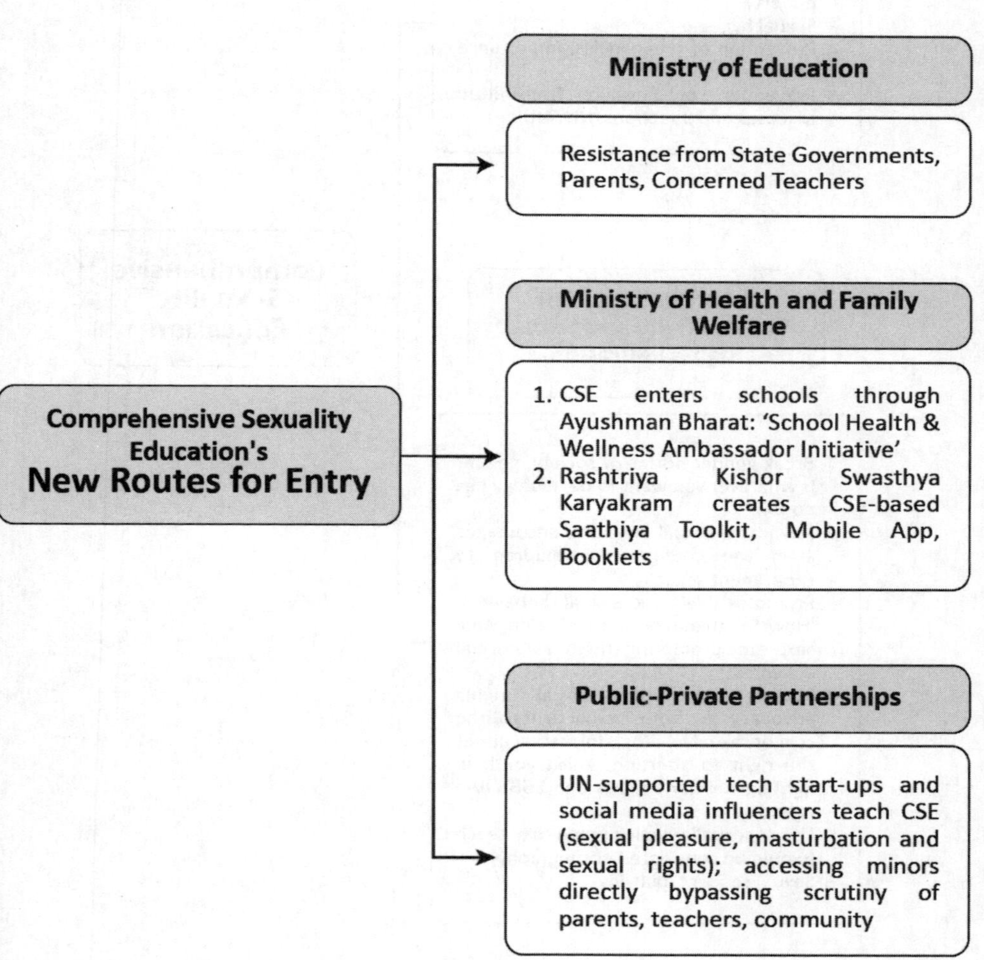

A VERY DILUTED VERSION of Regular Sex Education

1. Basic knowledge of male and female anatomy
2. Awareness of bodily changes during puberty
3. Sexual hygiene
4. Prevention of pregnancies, importance of abstinence
5. Prevention of Sexually Transmitted Diseases and Infections, HIV/AIDS

A DOUBLE DOSE of Sex Positivity and Sexual Rights Education

1. Break gender norms of society: gender is whatever you want to be; biology has no role
2. Advocates sexual pleasure; encourages even the youngest of children to experiment sexually
3. Promotes high-risk sexual behaviors: 'How to' guides on masturbation, anal sex, etc. promoting them as normal activities
4. Sexual Citizenship: sexual rights advocacy; promotes sexual rights at the cost of sexual health; information about the right to abortion, enlist youth in fighting for trans rights and LGBTQIA+ agenda
5. Use of sexually explicit graphics to teach (would be considered pornography)
6. Sexual consent, bullying

→ **Comprehensive Sexuality Education**

Legalizing the Woke Agenda in India

The Danger of Lowering the Age of Consent Laws

The old systems that were used to protect children from sexual predators are being dismantled with 'queering' which aims to blur the boundaries between adult and child, normative and outlandish. Once the traditional guardrails are dismantled, a whole new system, completely alien to Indian culture is being introduced. This new system threatens the safety and innocence of children.

The parallel infrastructure being built to queer Indian children uses devices like attractive CSE Apps, changing age of consent laws so young people can sexually engage with adults without stigma or criminality, and normalizing 'abortions' as a common lifestyle. The figure below shows how *queering the children of India is making them useful idiots for the Marxist project of dismantling society, family, and country*.

The purpose of queering is to destroy all limits and boundaries. We discussed at length the movement in the West to defend pedophiles, with scholars like the American anthropologist Gayle Rubin rebuking the age of consent laws that are meant to protect children from sexual predators. The strategy is to use sex between minors as the entry point to eventually abolish the laws against pedophilia. Guarding the boundaries is severely criticized as a culture that 'denies and punishes erotic interest and activity by anyone under the local age of consent'.[56] The high priestess of Queer Theory, Rubin says:

> These laws make no distinction between the most brutal rape and the most gentle romance...Nor are minors permitted access to 'adult' sexuality in other forms. They are forbidden to see books, movies, or television in which sexuality is 'too' graphically portrayed. It is legal for young people to see hideous depictions of violence, but not to see explicit pictures of genitalia. Sexually active young people are frequently incarcerated in juvenile homes, or otherwise punished for their 'precocity'.[57]

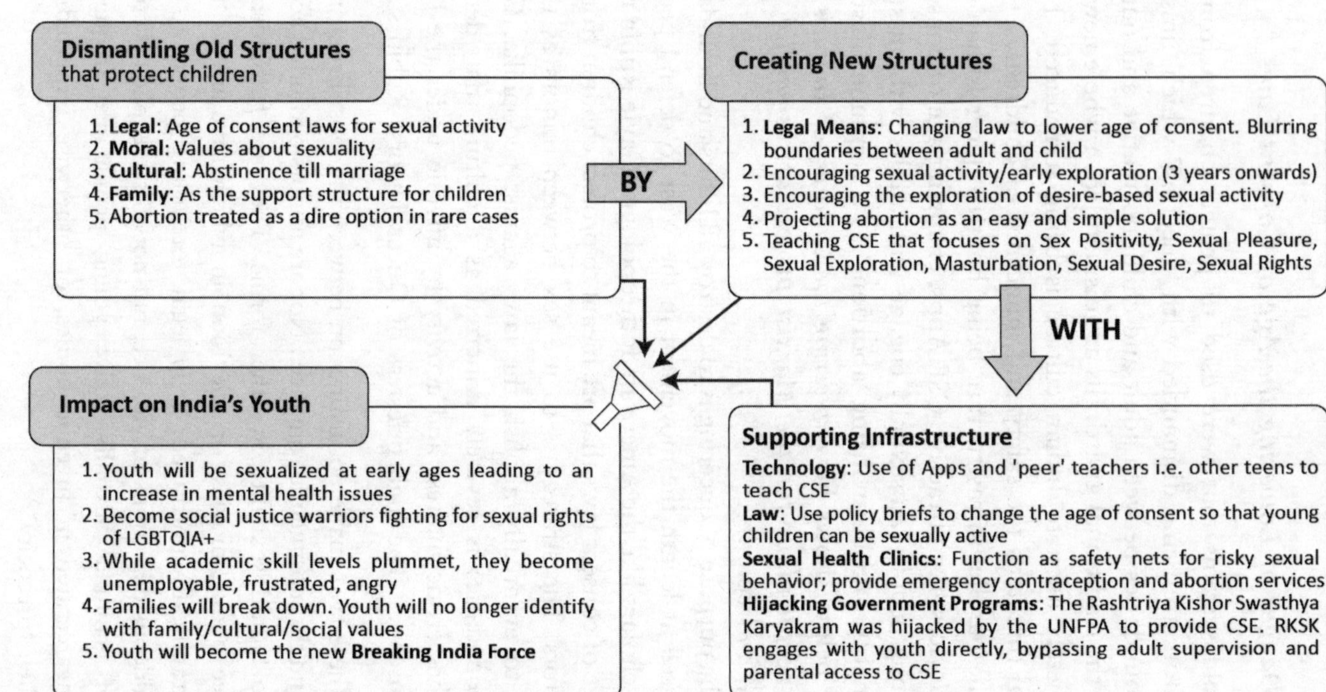
Dismantling Old Structures
that protect children
1. Legal: Age of consent laws for sexual activity
2. Moral: Values about sexuality
3. Cultural: Abstinence till marriage
4. Family: As the support structure for children
5. Abortion treated as a dire option in rare cases
BY
Creating New Structures
1. Legal Means: Changing law to lower age of consent. Blurring boundaries between adult and child
2. Encouraging sexual activity/early exploration (3 years onwards)
3. Encouraging the exploration of desire-based sexual activity
4. Projecting abortion as an easy and simple solution
5. Teaching CSE that focuses on Sex Positivity, Sexual Pleasure, Sexual Exploration, Masturbation, Sexual Desire, Sexual Rights
WITH
Supporting Infrastructure
Technology: Use of Apps and 'peer' teachers i.e. other teens to teach CSE
Law: Use policy briefs to change the age of consent so that young children can be sexually active
Sexual Health Clinics: Function as safety nets for risky sexual behavior; provide emergency contraception and abortion services
Hijacking Government Programs: The Rashtriya Kishor Swasthya Karyakram was hijacked by the UNFPA to provide CSE. RKSK engages with youth directly, bypassing adult supervision and parental access to CSE
Impact on India's Youth
1. Youth will be sexualized at early ages leading to an increase in mental health issues
2. Become social justice warriors fighting for sexual rights of LGBTQIA+
3. While academic skill levels plummet, they become unemployable, frustrated, angry
4. Families will break down. Youth will no longer identify with family/cultural/social values
5. Youth will become the new Breaking India Force

Thus, the first step to decriminalize pedophilia is to attack the age of consent. The goal is to 'queer' the age of consent and thereby decriminalize pedophilia as a transgression of boundaries. The second step is to sexualize children through CSE education, which is about encouraging and even pressuring them for sexual exploration, sexual rights, and pleasure. Both are done parallelly, one dismantles the guardrails that have protected children traditionally and the other introduces new trends through peer pressure and celebration of deviance.

The result will be a society of young people who will seek out such relationships that break child-adult boundaries. The goal is to make the legal system conducive to such behaviors. Lowering or abolishing the age of consent laws impacts children at an even younger age.

This tactic used in the West is being replicated in India. By showing false evidence of a few teenagers who were heavily penalized for sexual relationships, it highlights the absurdity of the law and lobbies for its removal. This is the first step in opening the floodgates to decriminalizing and destigmatizing pedophilia.

There are many forces involved in lowering the age of consent in India. The following figure shows the agencies and their mandates to push legal reform.

The Protection of Children from Sexual Offences Act (POCSO), established in 2012 is a child-centered act to protect children from sexual assault, harassment, and pornography. The law is concerned with minors who are coerced into sexual activity. The age of consent for sexual activity has been increasing steadily for over a century. The spirit is to prevent abuse and preserve childhood innocence, which, in our view, is a fundamental human right.

The Act defines a child as a person under the age of eighteen. Adolescents indulging in consensual sexual activity who are below eighteen, when faced with criminal charges for sexual activity, have different courts that handle their cases. If the legal system is confronted with cases such as these, they are held in special courts where the law can be applied using nuances given the situation on a case-by-case basis.

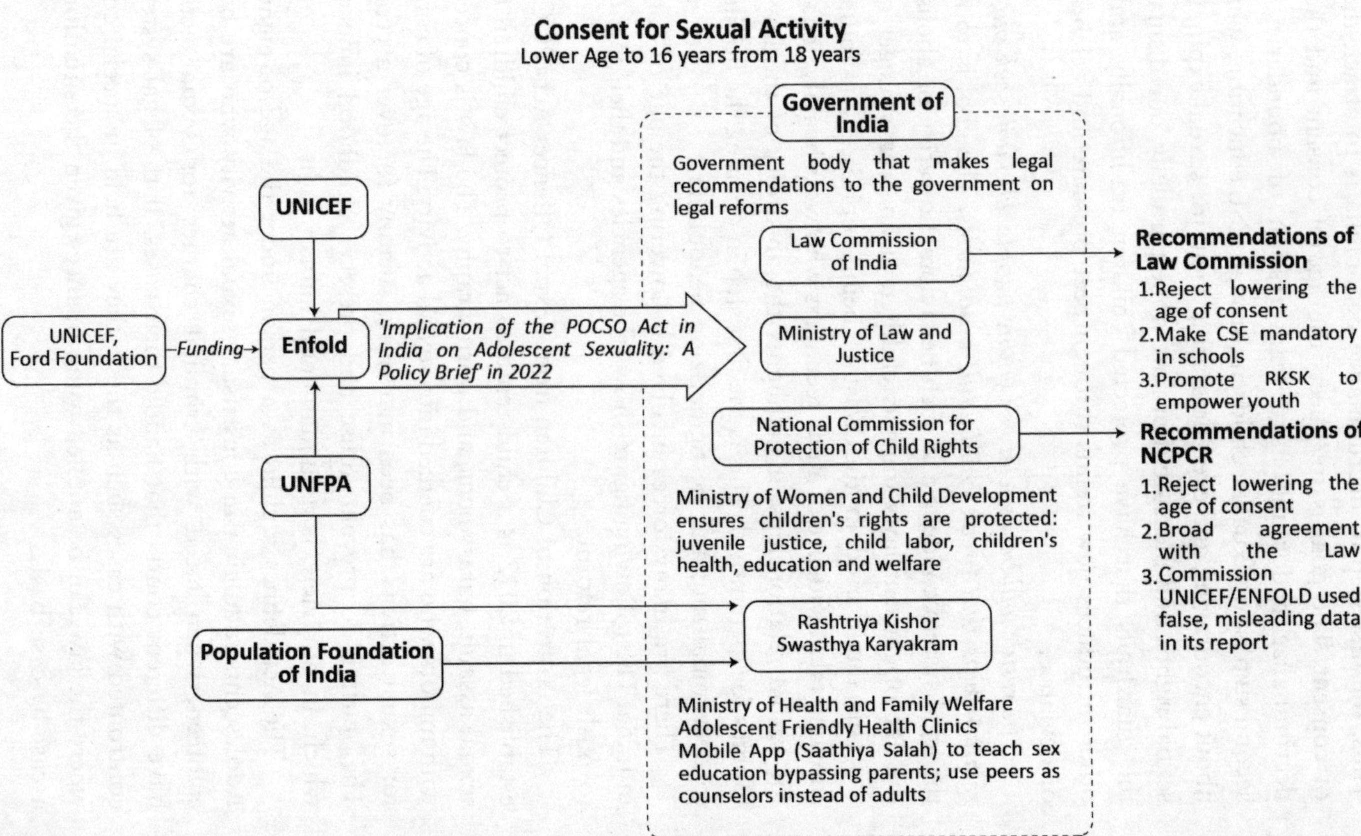
Consent for Sexual Activity
Lower Age to 16 years from 18 years
UNICEF, Ford Foundation
Funding
UNICEF
Enfold
UNFPA
Population Foundation of India
'Implication of the POCSO Act in India on Adolescent Sexuality: A Policy Brief' in 2022
Government of India
Government body that makes legal recommendations to the government on legal reforms
Law Commission of India
Ministry of Law and Justice
National Commission for Protection of Child Rights
Ministry of Women and Child Development ensures children's rights are protected: juvenile justice, child labor, children's health, education and welfare
Rashtriya Kishor Swasthya Karyakram
Ministry of Health and Family Welfare Adolescent Friendly Health Clinics Mobile App (Saathiya Salah) to teach sex education bypassing parents; use peers as counselors instead of adults
Recommendations of Law Commission
1. Reject lowering the age of consent
2. Make CSE mandatory in schools
3. Promote RKSK to empower youth
Recommendations of NCPCR
1. Reject lowering the age of consent
2. Broad agreement with the Law Commission
3. UNICEF/ENFOLD used false, misleading data in its report

The United Nations wants to change this law and bring down the age of consent from eighteen to sixteen years, accelerating adulthood and short-circuiting childhood. The other player is an NGO called Enfold, which works closely with UNICEF. Enfold runs DEI programs for corporations like Infosys, schools, and governments in Karnataka, Telangana, New Delhi, Jharkhand, Manipur, Madhya Pradesh and West Bengal.

Enfold also works with the Karnataka government to promote gender equity and SEL-related topics in school textbooks and the college curriculum. It receives significant funding from the Ford Foundation, UNICEF, NASSCOM, The UK Online Giving Foundation, the NoVo Foundation (operated by Warren Buffett's son, Peter), Indians for Collective Action, and the Zátiší Catering Group from the Czech Republic.

The UNFPA and UNESCO along with Enfold produced a report in 2022 citing rare, exceptional cases to make sweeping generalizations. This document was officially 'withdrawn' due to the backlash it received. Following is a summary:

1. The report cites that around twenty percent of the cases in five states are adolescents in romantic relationships. (The National Commission for Protection of Child Rights accused the UN and Enfold that this was false and misleading data).
2. The report cites the Madras High Court as having stated that these offenses stemmed from natural attraction and are thus not criminal offenses. It then made the leap to state that 'High courts have questioned whether the POCSO Act was enacted with the intention of regulating adolescent sexuality'.
3. The report then puts forth the UN's policy guideline on the age of consent:

> With respect to the minimum age of consent for sexual intercourse, the UN Committee on the Rights of the Child (CRC) in General Comment No. 20 on the implementation of the rights of the child during adolescence, has urged States to strike a balance between protection of children from

sexual exploitation and abuse and respect for their evolving autonomy.[58]

4. The report moves into the domain of sexual rights for adolescents, invoking the international human rights law framework asking to strike a balance between child protection and adolescent sexual rights.

Here are the recommendations made in the report:

A. CSE is good for teaching children about sexual rights:

> Concerns that adolescents are predisposed to making impulsive and poor decisions can be effectively mitigated through the provision of age-appropriate, evidence-informed, comprehensive, and rights-based sexuality education. Contrary to the belief that such education will trigger sexual behavior among minors, evidence supports that it delays sexual activity and promotes responsible sexual behavior.[59]

B. Government is 'obligated' to 'inculcate gender sensitivity and gender equality under the POCSO Act and Rules' and the mandatory school curriculum should foster 'positive and progressive attitudes' towards sexuality.[60]
C. Concerted efforts are needed 'to monitor its implementation in schools across India and ensure that the content pertaining to sexual and reproductive health is *comprehensive and rights-based*, and also include appropriate inputs on the legal framework'.[61]
D. The UNFPA, which co-authored this report with Enfold gets its 'sexualizing the RKSK' agenda into the report by putting further pressure on the government.[62] It supports that Adolescent Friendly Health Clinics perform abortion services and seeks exemption from the POCSO act in reporting minors and seeks legal reforms:

> 'Suitable legal reforms have to be initiated to ensure that service providers are not constrained and adolescents' access to such *information and services is confidential and unrestricted*. An amendment may also be required for the operationalization

of the clarification given by the Supreme Court on *mandatory reporting in the context of termination of pregnancies in consensual cases.*[63]

E. The Justice Verma Committee and the Madras High Court recommended lowering the age of consent under the POCSO Act to sixteen years citing examples from Bhutan, Sri Lanka, and Bangladesh:

> An amendment to the POCSO Act and the IPC is needed to decriminalize consensual acts involving adolescents above 16 years, while also ensuring that those above 16 years and below 18 years are protected against non-consensual acts under the POCSO Act.[64]

So, they recommend that the *age of consent should be lowered for all adolescents* and cite international human rights law standards that India should abide by.

The Law Commission of India did not buy into the Enfold recommendation and advised the Union Government that the age of consent should remain eighteen and that the government should not tinker with the POCSO Act, citing dangers of child abuse, trafficking, and prostitution.[65] While the Law Commission made a commendable decision in rejecting Enfold's recommendation, it also made a problematic one. The commission recommended that CSE be made mandatory in schools and suggested using RKSK to 'empower' youth. This is even more dangerous than lowering the age of consent and a huge win for the UN and its agencies. The end game is to radicalize and sexualize an entire generation and disconnect them from their civilizational roots.

The NCPCR also rejected the UNFPA-Enfold recommendation to reduce the age of consent and concurred with the Law Commission. Also, the NCPCR claimed that Enfold, UNICEF, and UNFPA used false data to make their claims:

> Our only objection is whatever data has been used by the UNICEF and Enfold was incorrect because they have not

> used Indian government data sources, specially NCRB, and they have been forced to withdraw the report.[66]

Because of this accusation of using false data to mislead the Indian government, UNICEF became nervous and immediately withdrew the report, stating: 'UNICEF does not endorse any representation or portrayal of the conclusions of the brief as the official UNICEF position'. Having *co-authored* the policy paper and funded Enfold, UNICEF then distanced itself:

> We are pleased to confirm that the paper is not UNICEF's policy position on the complex issue of the age of consent, and the conclusions are not endorsed by UNICEF India as policy recommendations. UNICEF does not endorse any representation or portrayal of the conclusions of the brief as the official UNICEF position.[67]

Other Social Engineering Efforts

In 2021, based on a recommendation by a NITI Aayog task force, the government proposed raising the legal age of marriage for girls to twenty-one, with the claim that this would decrease infant mortality, improve nutrition, and reduce issues related to early pregnancies. No objective study was mentioned to back the case for a higher marriage age, although the task force's recommendation was based on the feedback, they 'received [from] young adults is that the age of marriage should be 22-23 years'.[68] The task force promptly recommended 'that sex education be formalised and introduced in the school curriculum'.[69] Even in the most progressive Western countries such a law would be considered draconian. For example, in the USA, while most states have set a minimum age for marriage at eighteen for both boys and girls, ten states have a minimum age of seventeen years, twenty-three states have set the age at sixteen, two states at the age of fifteen, and five states do not have a set minimum age. California, which is one of the most progressive states has no minimum age for marriage, relying on approval from parents or guardians.[70]

Normalizing abortions to a point where the message to the

youth is to seek pleasure without worrying about consequences is dangerous. Abortion services are essential for the healthcare of women in certain situations, but policies should nudge people away from those situations in the first place. Instead, the policies are the exact opposite: nudging them, especially girls, towards risky sexual behavior. Also, gestational limits in abortions have not been debated from an ethical perspective of aborting a viable fetus.

India passed the Medical Termination of Pregnancy (MTP) Amendment Act, 2021 allowing for abortions from the previous upper limit of twenty weeks to twenty-four weeks. In common parlance, abortions performed in the late second trimester of pregnancy, between week twenty-one and week twenty-four of gestation (nearly six months into pregnancy) are considered 'late-term' abortions, given that *the fetus could be viable at this stage*. In the USA, even third trimester abortions known as late-term abortions are allowed in certain states,[71] and this is the direction in which the IPPF and other pro-abortion advocacy groups are taking the discourse.

The following government policies are being promoted or are already implemented:

1. Decrease the age of consent for sexual activity—advocated in the name of decriminalizing youth who engage in sexual activity.
2. Increase the age of marriage—advocated in the name of empowering women, decreasing infant mortality, and improving nutrition.
3. Formalize and mandate CSE across all schools and embed it in the core curriculum in a manner that barely mentions abstinence and focuses on pleasure-based sex, sex positivity, and sexual rights.
4. Make CSE ubiquitous through Apps and digital platforms that bypass parents and other gatekeepers who might object.
5. Open the doors to NGOs that freely provide contraception and abortion services, and make abortions look like a casual part of one's lifestyle. Abortion is treated so trivially that

fifteen million abortions are carried out in India annually.[72] This number is only likely to increase with these policies.

6. Train children to become activists for sexual rights and social justice causes as defined by Woke.
7. Degrade and humiliate the institutions of marriage, traditional values, and family.

Stringing the above laws and policies together paints a grim picture. It is a massive effort in social engineering as shown in the following figure.

Globalist Takeover of India's Education

As predicted in our earlier book, *Snakes in the Ganga*, we see increasing influence/control of global institutions and NGOs. They,

1. Are keen to change the course of India's education policy.
2. Fund content and pedagogy to fill the new curricular standards set by them.
3. Work with the Government of India as 'Knowledge Partners'.
4. Have shifted the goals of education from basic numeracy and literacy into a social justice agenda under the umbrella of achieving UN SDGs which are often against individual, family, or national goals.
5. Have started the social engineering project to usher in a new demographic of youth who will identify as 'trans' and start taking cross-sex hormones and/or resort to surgery.
6. Are on a mission to create a Breaking India Force of young Indians who will be indoctrinated through K-12 education.

The two main programs being feverishly implemented in India are SEL and CSE. Both these programs sound well-meaning, but as we have already shown, they are based on leftist ideology, rooted in Critical Race Theory, Queer Theory, social justice, global citizenship, and climateism, which is more to do with anti-meritocracy and social justice than the environment.

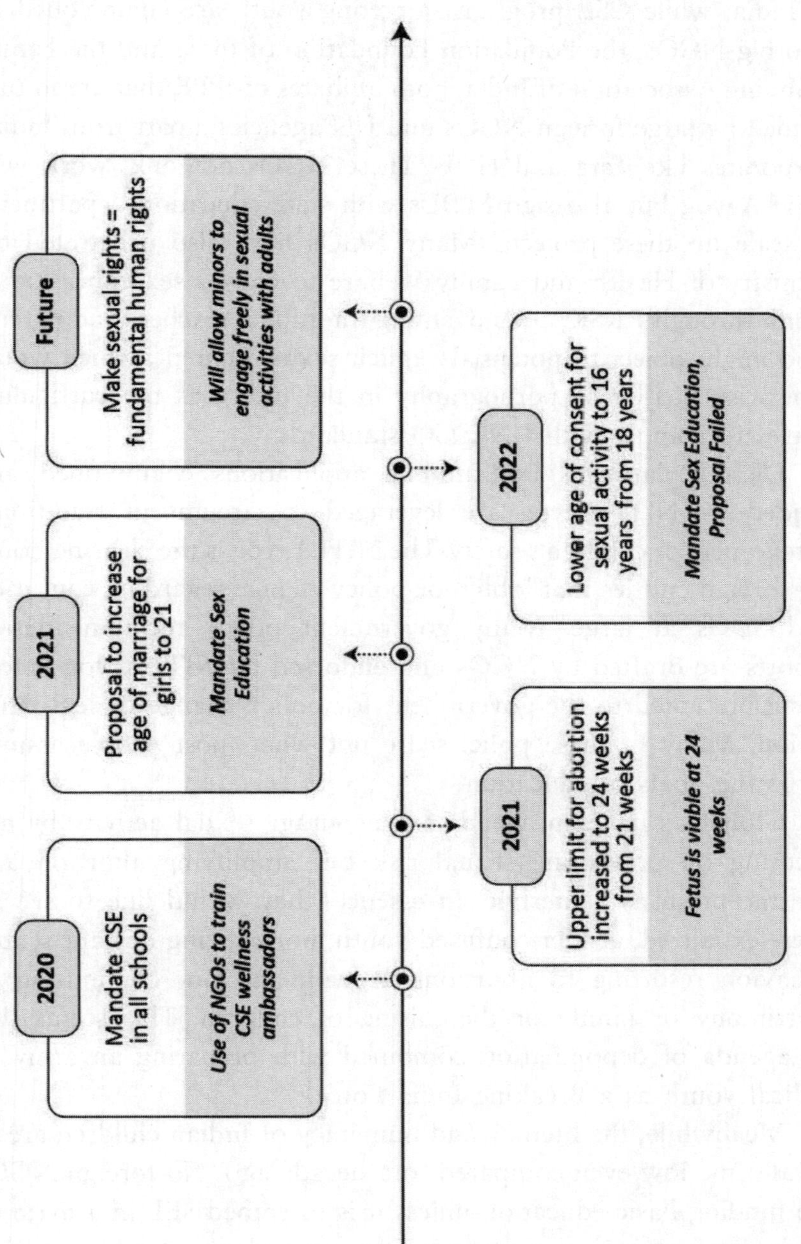
2020
Mandate CSE in all schools
Use of NGOs to train CSE wellness ambassadors
2021
Upper limit for abortion increased to 24 weeks from 21 weeks
Fetus is viable at 24 weeks
2021
Proposal to increase age of marriage for girls to 21
Mandate Sex Education
2022
Lower age of consent for sexual activity to 16 years from 18 years
Mandate Sex Education, Proposal Failed
Future
Make sexual rights = fundamental human rights
Will allow minors to engage freely in sexual activities with adults

We showed that the MGIEP is focused on scaling up SEL education in India, while CSE programs targeting youth are championed by two big NGOs, the Population Foundation of India and the Family Planning Association of India, both affiliates of IPPF, that are in turn funded by large foreign NGOs and UN agencies, apart from Indian corporates like Tata and HCL. These NGOs not only work with NITI Aayog but also sign MOUs with state education departments to scale up these projects. Many NGOs have also penetrated the Ministry of Health and Family Welfare to deliver sex education to youth through RKSK, circumventing traditional teachers and parents who might object to potential explicit sexual content, which would otherwise qualify as pornography in the future as the curriculum strives to comply with UNESCO standards.

Digital platforms and mobile applications championed and funded by NITI Aayog are leveraged to circumvent traditional gatekeepers of children's safety. The NITI Aayog is the clearing house for foreign entities that lobby for policy change regarding education and SDGs at large. Many government policy recommendation reports are drafted by NGOs and endorsed by NITI Aayog before being presented to the government for policy change or legislative action. Many of these policies are not what most people assume to be the goals of education.

Globalists have an agenda to encourage sexual activity by not focusing on preventing sexual risk but amplifying abortion and contraception as a lifestyle. In essence, they would like to see an over-sexualized, gender-confused youth, normalizing deviant sexual behavior, resorting to abortions at will, and not committing to matrimony or family or the raising of children. This seems like an agenda of depopulation combined with preparing an army of radical youth as a Breaking India Force.

Meanwhile, the literacy and numeracy of Indian children are at an all-time low even compared to a decade ago. No foreign NGOs are funding basic education unless it is to embed SEL in a math or reading curriculum in tune with Freirean pedagogy. India is giving

UN-mandated Global Citizenship Education and environmental education more importance than reading, writing, and arithmetic.

Marxists are notorious for language manipulation. The words 'fair', inclusive', and 'equitable' are being used to mean something entirely different than what the layperson assumes. Similarly, SEL is being used for brainwashing children to be aligned with these SDGs agendas. The NEP 2020 and the National Curriculum Framework were legislated to align with the global agendas of SDGs and hence, it is not surprising to see very little effort to bring Indian Knowledge Systems into schooling.

The Right to Education Act, which exempts minority institutions from the NEP 2020 provides an escape for Christian and Muslim children but does not give Hindu institutions a choice to 'opt out' of SEL and CSE programs. We therefore see no point in discussing the NCERT books in any detail, since they are based on a policy (NEP) and a curricular framework that are orthogonal to India's civilizational needs. We are interested in assessing the root of the problem, instead of merely assessing the symptoms.

An entire machinery is operating through legal, educational, and social channels for sexualizing Indian children. This did not happen overnight. It was meticulously carried out by foreign agents working with the Indian government for decades and accelerated since 2014. Appendix C shows the milestones impacting India's Sex Education Policy.

8

INDIA'S PUBLIC-PRIVATE PARTNERSHIPS FOR COMPREHENSIVE SEXUALITY EDUCATION AND SOCIAL EMOTIONAL LEARNING

Many of the government's sexual health schemes, policies, and strategies discussed here are beneficial for the youth. However, our concern is that they are being quietly used by international agencies to piggyback their interventions in India. *The playbook of NGOs is to establish the infrastructure initially with relatively benign sex education content to gain acceptance, avoid resistance from responsible adults, and gain traction as the 'go to' platform for youth. Once this is accomplished, the content can be switched to comply with 'global' standards of 'comprehensive' sexuality education as defined by the UN as previously discussed. This bait-and-switch approach is the hallmark of Marxists' praxis.*

This chapter discusses the principal NGOs that play a vital role in spreading CSE-based sex education and SEL programs in India. We will also cover other smaller players in the sex education space towards the end of this chapter.

India has signed agreements with UN agencies to enact policies supporting CSE as part of sexual and reproductive health and rights. While these foreign agencies and their affiliated NGOs applaud India's policies, they are unhappy with the level of progress in implementing them. A European Union (EU)-sponsored study in 2017 concluded that religious leaders and some politicians reject

CSE because of their 'fundamentalist attitudes':

> Only religious leaders and politicians with fundamentalist attitudes are against the introduction of sexuality education and use arbitrary notions of culture and norms to thwart that.[1]

Similarly, the UNFPA blamed India's slow progress on 'overarching socio-cultural factors'.[2]

IPE Global, Children's Investment Fund Foundation, and International Planned Parenthood Foundation

The SDGs 2030 agenda has created a market worth billions of dollars for consulting services to help governments and businesses comply with the UN. IPE (IPEGLOBAL.com) is one such consulting company that helps governments and businesses achieve SDGs:

> We are a Group that partners with governments, businesses, and leaders to deliver scalable and sustainable solutions. Focusing *on Human Development, Inclusive Growth & Resilience, and Good Governance*, we create value for our clients and communities to achieve economic growth & social equity.[3]

IPE Global lobbies NITI Aayog on behalf of its foreign partner, the Children's Investment Fund Foundation.[4] Apart from other projects in India, CIFF is particularly interested in funding CSE projects across India such as:

1. CSE Udaan Rajasthan.
2. The scaling up of CSE by funding the Population Foundation of India is discussed in the next chapter.
3. Dasra Adolescents Collaborative (DAC), which educates teenagers on sexuality.

IPE is a consulting company headed by Sunil Mitra, a retired Indian Administrative Services officer, who started the Udaan project in Rajasthan, similar to the one in Jharkhand discussed earlier.

This Udaan program is funded by the usual cabal of foreign NGOs mentioned often in this book, and 'ensures government scholarships to get and retain 43,000 girls in secondary school across 15 districts in Rajasthan by 2022'.[5] However, CIFF's Indian partner (IPE) is deceptive in reporting that the program is about 'preventing adolescent pregnancies'[6] and has three implementation strategies:

1. Keeping girls in secondary school.
2. Strengthening knowledge, attitudes, and practice on sexual health/reproduction.
3. Expansion of contraception methods and expanding contraception choices.

However, the retention of girls in school was a ploy to provide sexual know-how, training on sexual practices, and changing attitudes towards sexuality and reproduction.

Rajasthan: Udaan CSE

Bait and Switch

Stated Goal by Foreign NGOs

Scholarships to get and retain 43,000 girls in secondary schools across 15 districts

Actual Program by Indian Partner

Keeping girls in school by training them in CSE; teaching sexual practices; increasing sexual knowledge; changing attitudes about sexuality etc.

The Rajasthan Udaan program has provided sex education to over 350,000 girls and trained almost 5,000 teachers. IPE hired C.K. Mishra on its board, who was previously the Union health secretary and helped UNFPA launch sex education programs via the health ministry. Mishra is aware of RKSK and its mobile Applications to scale up sex education for adolescents in India; he also launched the Saathiya Salah mobile App. He is clear that he wants to change thoughts, behaviors, and lifestyles of youth through CSE, and he does so by circumventing responsible adults and parents:

> It is not an easy job as we are talking about 26 crore adolescent population in the country. This is a critical mass of asset which is available to the country and if we can drive this asset in the right direction, this is going to be the biggest dividend in terms of contribution to economy, Mishra said. He said that one of the best ways to reach out to the adolescents was to reach out to the community and therefore a system of peer education was designed. ... This is a very ambitious programme because apart from health, we are also talking about behavioural change. It is not about Health Ministry approaching adolescents with health messages, it's about changing thought, behaviour and lifestyle in adolescent(s), he said.[7]

HCL Champions Comprehensive Sexuality Education

Another good example of private industry involvement is Hindustan Computers Limited (HCL). Its billionaire founder Shiv Nadar runs Shiv Nadar Foundation, a pioneer in sexualizing Indian children through the CSE curriculum. We earlier discussed the Population Foundation of India and its task to scale up CSE throughout India to sexualize children. Serving on the board of PFI was a cofounder of HCL, Ajai Chowdhry, who is also a NITI Aayog 'distinguished fellow'.[8] Under Chowdhry's term on the board, PFI had a tie-up with HCL Foundation to scale up the 'ARSH (Adolescent Reproductive and Sexual Health) For You' sex education teacher training course on HCL platforms along with aggressive promotion on social media.[9] HCL Foundation is keen to scale up CSE teacher training while foreign NGOs fund the Population Foundation of India to scale the CSE curriculum and evangelize on the ground.

The diagram shows the connections.

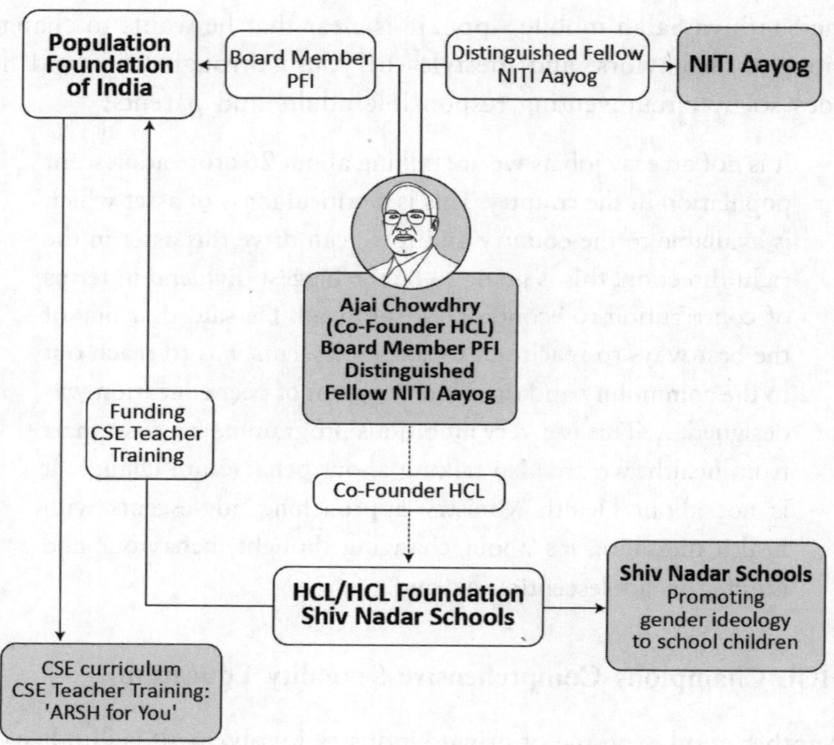

Recently, parents were caught off guard at Shiv Nadar schools (HCL Foundation's schools) when they saw a survey for children with an option to identify as 'nonbinary'. This caused anxiety among the parents:[10]

> I think the decision about what the children should learn about such sensitive and politically charged subjects should be left to the parents. The school can't enforce their own woke ideology on the students and their parents…Most parents

> don't speak up because they fear the repercussions the child might face, but this was simply not expected. We don't want such fantasy being fed to our children.[11]

HCL also funds the notorious IPPF's affiliate Family Planning Association of India, which claims that 'incorporating CSE lies at the heart of our youth-oriented initiatives', and conducted a program called 'My Choice My Right' to train a few thousand adolescents on CSE.[12]

Population Foundation of India: Sex Rights and Pleasure

The PFI is an epicenter for producing and distributing a CSE curriculum that promotes 'a rights-based and pleasure-affirming approach' to teaching sex education.[13] It uses very attractive and attention-inducing online Apps that bypass parental supervision. It also relies on youth peer sex educators to discuss sensitive topics with fellow teens that adults might consider inappropriate. The PFI plays a pivotal role in replacing the Indian government's sex education programs that are culturally sensitive and focused on preventing risky behavior.

The PFI is supported by some of the most prestigious philanthropists and is becoming a role model for other foundations, both Indian and foreign, making it trendy to sexualize Indian children. It has invested heavily in creating attractive online content and behavioral science to change youth attitudes toward sexuality by expanding CSE in India.[14] It is the hub of sexual education and health-related NGO activities and was the one that opened the floodgates to bring in foreign programs and the NGOs that develop them. It hosts the secretariat of Advocating Reproductive Choices (ARC), which is a network of 113 organizations working on sexual and reproductive health across India. The ARC performs lobbying and advocacy functions with the government and Civil Society Organizations, leveraging its network of NGOs to advocate sex education under the banner of family planning and sexual health.

The previous host of the secretariat of ARC was the International Planned Parenthood's Family Planning Association of India.

Apps and Artificial Intelligence Parenting the Children

UNICEF has funded PFI to develop an AI-driven chatbot, SnehAI that engages youth directly, circumventing parents and playing the role of their confidant. The Bill & Melinda Gates Foundation and the UNPF are also funders.[15] The free App uses both Hindi and English, rich graphics, video content, and a mascot from a popular Indian television drama.[16] It is marketed as 'a safe, non-judgmental, and trusted space for adolescents to seek out information and resources on their sexual and reproductive health and rights'.[17] It has become very successful as a trusted friend, adviser, and mentor for youth across India.

In 2020, the PFI launched Educately, a platform that hosts ARSH for You, a benign-sounding teacher training program to scale-up CSE online for free. The PFI proclaims that their CSE curriculum 'follows a rights-based and pleasure-affirming approach as outlined in the UNESCO Guidelines (2018) and the IPPF Framework (2010) for Comprehensive Sexuality Education' to gain legitimacy. ARSH for You is designed to train teachers in adolescent 'reproductive and sexual health and rights'.[18,19]

ARSH for You is gaining traction, with HCL Foundation funding PFI and using the program on the HCL academy platform to train its teachers on Comprehensive Sexuality Education. Rajasthan, Bihar, Uttar Pradesh, and Manipur are among some of the states signing MOUs with PFI, to implement ARSH for You, unsuspecting of what its sex education really means. The PFI ran the ARSH for You program in partnership with the Bihar government training,

> 956 teachers covering 163 schools. The pilot had a completion rate of 95%, with over 500 teachers successfully completing the programme..[20]

The diagram on the facing page shows the strategy to bypass parents and spread CSE in India.

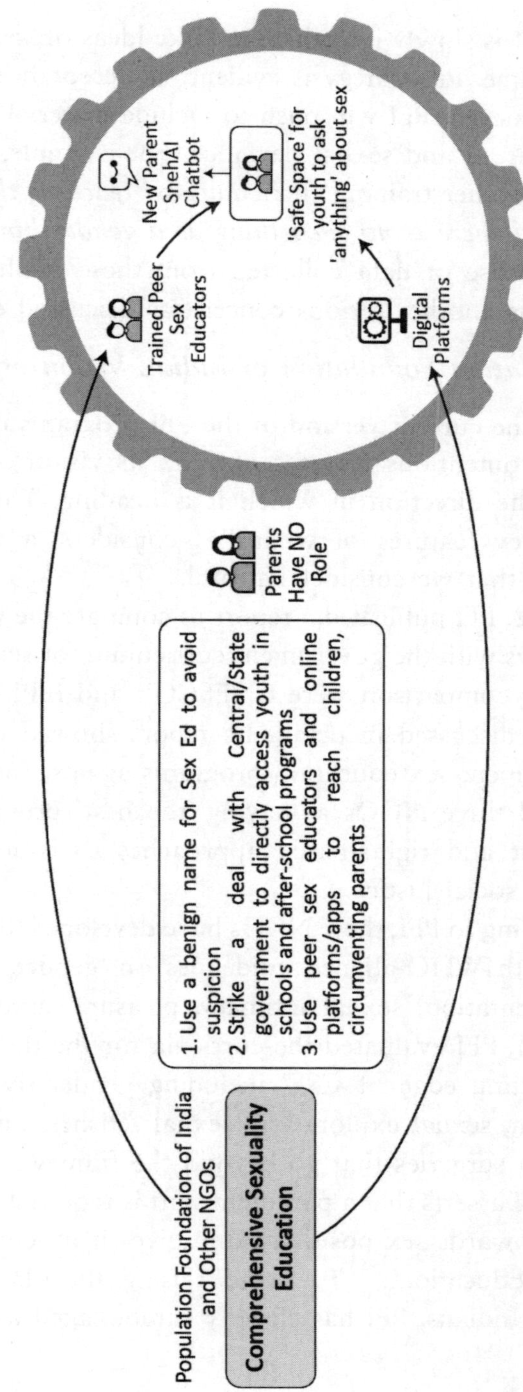
Strategy for Scale-up
and Delivery of Comprehensive Sexuality Education
Population Foundation of India and Other NGOs
Comprehensive Sexuality Education
1. Use a benign name for Sex Ed to avoid suspicion
2. Strike a deal with Central/State government to directly access youth in schools and after-school programs
3. Use peer sex educators and online platforms/apps to reach children, circumventing parents
Parents Have NO Role
Trained Peer Sex Educators
New Parent SnehAI Chatbot
'Safe Space' for youth to ask 'anything' about sex
Digital Platforms

The PFI is slowly introducing Woke ideas of sex education, one step at a time. Its strategy is evident: as acceptance of these initial ideas is achieved, PFI will push to include material that normalizes sexual pleasure and sexual deviance. For example, ARSH for You starts the teacher training curriculum by *teaching them that gender is fluid and there is no such thing as a gender binary.*

The misuse of data collected from these Artificial Intelligence platforms is another serious concern as discussed earlier.

The Population Foundation of India's Vision of CSE

Although the current version of the PFI programs does not include the most contentious features of CSE, its vision of sex education indicates the direction in which it is heading. Therefore, we will examine key features of what PFI considers 'a world class sex education' that we consider harmful.

In 2022, PFI published a report to compare the CSE curricula of three NGOs with the government curriculum for sex education. The criteria for comparison were UNESCO's and IPPF's frameworks,[21] previously discussed in detail. Its report showed the shortfalls of the government sex education programs against these standards. It highlighted three NGOs as having 'the best' programs that focus on feminist and rights-based approaches to issues like sexuality rights and social justice.

According to PFI, these NGOs have developed 'holistic' curricula aligned with WHO-aligned guidelines on 'gender, gender identity, sexual orientation, sexual intimacy, pleasure' among other areas. In addition, PFI evaluated the curricula for the themes it considers at the 'cutting edge of CSE' including gender dysphoria, erectile dysfunction, sexual exploration, sexual fetishes, kinks, and gender affirmation surgeries that go beyond the framework.[22]

The PFI asserts that a paradigm shift is required in sex education which is towards sex positivity, and gives it a new name: 'Holistic Sexuality Education'.[23] To avoid raising the alarm bells among concerned Indians, PFI has cleverly camouflaged its CSE programs under the categories of 'wellbeing' and 'empowerment' such as 'Safety and Wellbeing of Adolescents and Youth' (SWAY) and 'Feminist Adolescent and Youth-Led Action' (FAYA).[24]

Some of the contentious points in the PFI report are summarized below:[25]

- CSE should focus on sexual pleasure to solve the problems of early marriages, Dalits facing marginalization, women facing violence, and transgenders being marginalized.
- The solution to violence and discrimination against women is 'through the delivery of rights affirming CSE' which it says is internationally recognized.
- Advocates sexual 'skill-building as an integral part of programming' and 'meaningful youth engagement and strategies for advocacy, including community sensitization'. Online methods and peer sex evangelists need to be incentivized—in ways that bypass parents. It wants to 'use targeted approaches for gatekeepers and parents of young people'.[26]
- Avoids public resistance by cleverly using broad terms like 'adolescence education' minus the word 'sex', while at the same time wanting to use direct language to 'normalize' these concepts. It emphasizes using stealth techniques to sneak these ideas into children's lives without raising too much suspicion and *then* normalizing the concepts.
- NGOs should be asked to cover 'topics such as gender transgression, gender dysphoria, and gender affirmation surgeries that are rarely, if at all, covered...Therefore, it is evident that even current NGO-led curricula are not comprehensively inclusive of Sexual Orientation Gender Identity, Gender Expression and Sex Characteristics'.[27]
- *Non-transparency is a core strategy in the entire program.* The PFI's strategy is clearly explained:

While naming the AEP, the term 'sex education' was considered limited and instead 'adolescence education', was counterintuitively identified as a term that is more 'comprehensive', which leads to its unanimous acceptance and adoption. Using a broader banner of health or life-skills indeed does raise less suspicion and backlash and may even require less political manoeuvring, and while naming programmes is easily compromised due to these very reasons, *normalising sex and sexuality is a long-term process* that takes place by increasing comfort with these very terms and their related content. Therefore, working towards ensuring that curricula remain comprehensive and are not subject to political climates and the perceived readiness of communities to take on these topics without using the actual words themselves may be counterproductive.[28]

- The PFI would like to normalize LGBTQIA+ and other non-traditional, deviant sexual practices for Indian youth:

  Meaningfully engage young people with diverse realities and identities in the design and development of CSE programming…Apply an intersectional lens while designing content for a CSE curriculum so that it is inclusive of diverse realities of adolescents and young people and use rights-based and contextually relevant language and terminology.[29]

- The PFI considers Indian government sex education programs too narrow in scope because they only deal with nutrition, substance use, menstruation, and HIV/AIDS. Put simply, the programs are not Woke enough. Its main criticisms of the government programs were:
  - 'Much of the language in the content of both the AEP and SHP curricula is limited to the gender binary – man and woman'.

- o NCERT program discusses gender-based discrimination and violence mostly focused on the experiences of all women and not specifically trans women.
- o 'The content of both curricula function within a heteronormative framework and any acknowledgment of trans persons or queer people is limited to single line mentions'.[30]

The PFI harshly criticizes the government's guidelines for being based on biological facts, risk reduction, and avoidance of reckless sexual behavior, whereas the international guidelines are pleasure-based:

> Addressing sexual and reproductive health from a biomedical perspective has also resulted in the curricula not addressing emotional social and psychological aspects of SRH that are extremely crucial in enabling an individual to make informed decisions about their own body. This includes important discussions around the concepts of 'virginity', and reproductive self-determination, both within and outside of marital relationships. It should also be noted that while the ITGSE guidelines promote a more holistic understanding of health, at present the guidance on SRH [i.e., government] end up implicitly framing sexual health in relation to negative outcomes i.e. unplanned pregnancies and disease, which is counter-productive to the objective of helping adolescents develop a positive view of sex and sexuality.[31]

- The PFI asserts that a pleasure-based approach is critical because it contributes 'towards normalizing giving and receiving pleasure in sexual experiences'.[32] It cites a scholar saying, 'sexuality education should affirm the importance of negotiation in sexual practices in order to maximize opportunities for pleasure'.[33] It further complains: 'no factual information related to masturbation is provided as part of the content of the AEP curriculum…In IPPF's framework for CSE, pleasure was specifically mentioned as critical in all curricula'.[34] The PFI seems unconcerned about the prevention of Sexually Transmitted Diseases and instead considers sexual pleasure as the main focus because 'when only prevention of adverse health outcomes is focused on, sexual identity development takes a back seat, and the possibility of building the skills needed for effective communication of sexual needs and the expression of desires also suffers'.[35]

- Recognizing that Indian parents trust the government's official curriculum and teachers, PFI stresses the importance of penetrating the government's programs and 'motivating' teachers in its devious plan of sexualizing children. Undeniably, most teachers disapprove of CSE and the PFI fears that teachers may derail CSE education altogether:

> Teachers were not always comfortable in dealing with themes related to changes during adolescence, gender stereotypes, sexuality and sexual harassment and abuse…Considering that teachers are embedded in the larger culture of their school and community, and are influenced by social norms and their own experiences, their improper training can be extremely detrimental to school-based sexuality education programmes, and can lead to delivery of information that is inaccurate or assertive of values and attitudes that silence discussions of gender, sex, sexuality and rights.[36]

Under the PFI's influence, NGOs are bypassing the government and reaching the community with their own CSE curricula. This is advertised as partnering with civil society. The effect is that control of sex education passes on to unelected individuals and organizations that do not have the same accountability as the government does.[37] See Appendix D for a summary of the PFI's recommendations for

Indian children and our response from a dharmic civilizational perspective.

Many state governments are signing agreements with the PFI to implement ARSH for You and other PFI-run CSE programs 'to pilot models, in both in-school and out of school settings'.[38] Following are some concrete examples.

Rajasthan

The state government of Rajasthan has an agreement with the PFI to implement ARSH for You. Additionally, it also ran an after-school CSE known as Feminist Adolescent and Youth-Led Action in four districts using peer sex educators to 'advocate for [sexual] services and rights'.[39] The program was fashioned and packaged under the Rashtriya Kishor Swasthya Karyakram. 'A CSE curriculum was developed in consonance with the UNESCO technical guidelines for transacting with adolescents in intervention geographies'.[40]

This new sexualizing program of the PFI works like missionaries roaming the villages of India with a zeal to baptize kids into their sexual revolution. Young peer evangelists are recruited and trained to continuously pester youth to succumb:

> Initially, girls would make excuses like, we have work or our parents don't allow going out and refuse to talk to us. Nevertheless, we kept visiting them and there came a time when adolescents started inviting me to discuss some or the other topic. When working on the field, we make a group of 15-20 girls and talk about anything and everything they would shy away from – reproduction, internal organs, and sex, among others.[41]

Young girls succumbed to the FAYA program because they were shown some sexual bait, their curiosity was piqued, and they wanted to know more. Once indoctrinated, they learned to talk back to concerned elders:

> However, the conversations around sex did not go down well with the villagers. Recalling an incident, Yamuna said, 'Once I had gone to conduct a session on sex. A private school teacher from the village once overheard our discussion and said, 'You can't talk about these things openly as this will leave a bad impression on children'. It is then I told him that even school books have a chapter on reproduction but unfortunately, that is often skipped'.[42]

The PFI mocks Hindu practices in the name of myth-busting. It oversteps its boundaries when it comes to customs that discourage women from entering temples or worshipping during their menstrual cycle. The foundation would dare not correct Muslim or Christian religious practices or call them out for being superstitious and unscientific:

> This includes, not touching pickle while menstruating or not entering the temple. Yamuna said, 'Even I used to believe in these things until I joined PFI and we did practicums like holding the jar of pickle or touching holy basil plant.' We conduct practicums and use paintings and posters to educate the girls.[43]

In Rajasthan, besides the FAYA project, the PFI has secured commitments for its CSE from the Ministry of Health and Family Welfare, and Women and Child Development. The pledge, signed by four members of legislative assemblies and key bureaucrats, received significant media attention.[44]

Uttar Pradesh

The PFI is working closely with the government to draft a ten-year operational plan for incorporating ARSH for You and CSE into the population policy. The foundation took the lead, provided insights for all plans, and made proposals like promoting peer sex educators or 'wellness ambassadors'.[45]

ARSH for You has been used to train over eleven thousand Health and Wellness Ambassadors across five districts. The PFI provided an in-person orientation to the senior management and teachers at Delhi Public School in Lucknow, and the 'teachers will undergo its training'. It collaborated with The Bharat Scouts and Guides to indoctrinate adolescent scouts. With this MOU, ARSH for You will access many thousands of teachers and senior youth volunteers, and over three lakh youth volunteers. Additionally, 1,500 divisional and district-level scout officials will receive online training, and nearly one thousand technical coordinators from 75 districts have already received orientation.

Bihar

An MOU has been signed with the State Education Department to scale up CSE. The PFI conducted an ARSH for You pilot training session in Jehanabad district involving 493 educators. Additionally, eight hundred trainers from the District Institute of Education & Training (DIET) were trained, who further trained other educators in their districts. The PFI also trained fifty-six associate professors of *sehat kendras* (health centers), which are 'youth friendly spaces' that provide sexual health information.

Manipur

The ARSH for You CSE training will be implemented thanks to the approval from the National Service Scheme coordinator of Manipur. An orientation session was conducted with the head of the Department of Yoga at Manipur University. Another MOU has been signed with the state government to integrate CSE into the Child Care Institute and the Integrated Child Development Scheme, and its reach is saturating the rural adolescent population, particularly in resource-compromised areas with limited internet access.

The following diagram summarizes the PFI's work.

Founder: J.R.D. Tata
Board Member: Late Ratan Tata
≈60 Crore income
2020-22

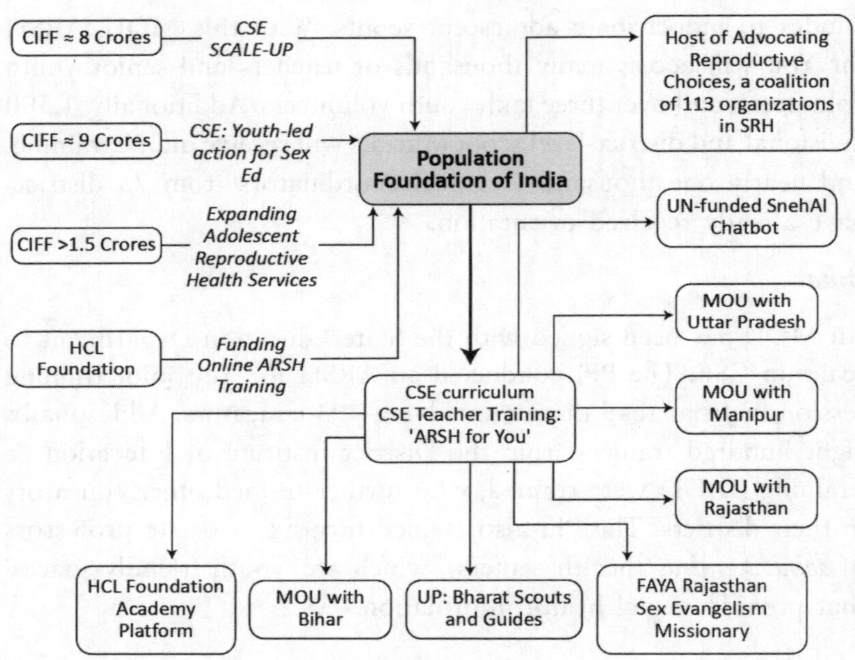

CSE: Comprehensive Sexuality Education focused on Teaching Sexual Rights and Sexual Pleasures
ARSH: Adolescent Reproductive and Sexual Health
CIFF: Children's Investment Fund Foundation (European NGO)

The Family Planning Association of India

Psychological Warfare and Deception

As discussed earlier, the Family Planning Association of India is one of the member associations of IPPF, a partner of the UN on Comprehensive Sexuality Education mandates. The FPAI, like its parent, IPPF, has nothing to do with planning a family as one would assume. Its agenda is quite the opposite, namely, to break up the

Indian family structure by sexualizing children from an early age with graphic sexual content and a sex-positivity framework.

We focus on how the FPAI is funded, the breadth and depth of its reach, and the deceptive tactics used as breaking forces for boots-on-the-ground activity. In contrast, we will show how China deals with the IPPF and how its version of NITI Aayog works for, and not against, the youth of China. Unlike the case of India, China's youth are taught to reject Western values that compromise national interests.

Once again, the TATA group is a big supporter. The prestigious TATA Mumbai Marathon raised funds for FPAI.[46] TATA Steel, TATA Motors, and TATA Trusts are all listed as supporters of FPAI along with HCL Foundation, Tech Mahindra Foundation, NASSCOM Foundation, the Bill & Melinda Gates Foundation, The David and Lucile Packard Foundation, UNICEF, UNFPA, and others on a lengthy list:

> FPAI has nurtured support from corporates and large private foundations to implement not only SRH services through CSR initiatives but also hosting sports and cultural events including the prestigious Tata Mumbai Marathon (TMM) ranked amongst the top 10 marathons in the world.[47]

The FPAI reaches more than thirty million annually, operates through forty-five branches/projects across eighteen states, supported by over three thousand community volunteers and over one thousand staff. Services are provided through 39 Reproductive Health and Family Planning Centres, 19 Urban Family Welfare Centres that are government-funded, 19 satellite clinics, 229 associated clinics, 56 outreach service units with support from 510 CBDs, 119 private physicians, and 33 other agencies. During the year 2020, its sexual health services were provided to 4.2 million clients, of which nearly 40% were young people below the age of 24.[48]

The FPAI has many programs and states, 'incorporating CSE lies at the heart of our youth-oriented initiatives'. Collectively, the branches have established approximately 2,114 youth groups and 3,882 new peer educators.[49]

It has launched a Scaling up Delivered and Enabled CSE project through its branch offices in cities across India: Each branch works with twenty schools/colleges and five NGOs to increase access to ninety thousand young people. The following table shows the reach of the operations:

Bidar:	'Formally entered agreements with 8 NGOs and established non-formal agreements with 6 NGOs to conduct health camps, CSE sessions and skill training'.[50]
Ahmedabad:	'Forged partnerships with Parivartan Foundation, SAATH Charitable Trust, Manav Sadhana and other youth groups and implemented specialized service sessions within the community'.[51]
Agra:	'Held a meeting with 12 NGOs/CBOs, offering CSE training to NGO staff members'.[52]
Pune:	Collaborated with NGOs such as Hope for the Children Foundation, Lila Poonawala Foundation, Rotary Club of Royals Pune, and Sevasarathi Foundation.'[53]
Mysuru:	'Bolstered ties with the University of Mysore, securing permission to establish a youth center within the campus. Collaborated with various entities to conduct reproductive health check-up camps for youth, women's groups, and men'.[54]
Murhu Project:	'Teamed up with the Jharkhand Tribal Development Scheme (JTDS) and TEJESWINI'.[55]
Kalchini:	'Formalized agreements with 7 NGOs and conducted 14 sensitization programs to enhance network connections'.[56]
Lucknow:	'Collaborated with 14 NGOs and formalized MOUs with 4, including Humsafar, Vigyan Foundation, Pt. G.B. Pant Institute and Saarthi Foundation'.[57]

Like other NGOs, FPAI has penetrated the government's RKSK platform to deliver CSE. It is also tech savvy and engages with youth through Zoom, WhatsApp, Skype, Google Meet, and YouTube.[58] The IPPF is also sponsoring 'The Youth Social Venture Fund' which is a global initiative to be hosted by FPAI to foster tech-driven innovations 'schemes [that address] the challenges young people face in accessing sexual and reproductive healthcare and information'.[59]

India comes under IPPF's South Asia Regional Office or SARO, headquartered in New Delhi. It also works with member associations in Afghanistan, Bangladesh, Bhutan, Maldives, Nepal, and Sri Lanka.[60] This reach is possible because many deceptive tactics are used to access youth and raise money:

> 'Services' are counted by 'discreet clinical interactions,' not by the number of individual patients. If one patient [is given] a free condom, a pregnancy test, a sexually transmitted infection test, and an abortion over the course of a year, that would count as four different services. This is how it downplays how central abortion is to its business: It muddies the math by giving an abortion procedure the same weight as providing a simple pregnancy test or free condom—they are all counted as one 'service'.[61]

Using the tactics of an evangelist, it mixes CSE interventions with STEM education for young schoolgirls, to attract students and get parental consent.[62] Similarly, it invents an excuse to indoctrinate girls in government schools in Nagaland: 'On the occasion of Menstrual Hygiene Day, a combined Adolescent Education Programme and CSE session was conducted'.[63] In yet another program ostensibly to help underprivileged girls, FPAI admits to sneaking in CSE along with STEM education: 'Comprehensive STEM education and CSE interventions are presently extended to young schoolgirls, including dropouts from grades 8 to 10, with the aim of boosting their academic achievements across our select branches'.[64]

The Family Planning Association of India employs manipulative marketing strategies[65] that exploit the vulnerabilities of young people. Framing their initiatives as essential educational opportunities, it obscures the underlying agenda of promoting specific ideologies. It uses persuasive narratives and emotional appeals to gain the trust of communities, making it challenging for the youth to recognize the coercive nature of the tactics. This approach not only compromises the autonomy of young people but also undermines the integrity of the educational programs. By embedding controversial content within seemingly benign educational activities, they ensure that their influence extends deeply and subtly into the lives of innocent children. This multifaceted strategy underscores the complexity and ethical concerns, highlighting the need for increased scrutiny and transparency in such initiatives.

Contrast with China

China's Relationship with the International Planned Parenthood Federation

The IPPF entered China in 1983 as a partner to implement abortions keeping in line with China's one-child policy. China's IPPF association, the China Family Planning Association (CFPA), is controlled by the Chinese Communist Party: 'CPFA is a national organization under the leadership of the party'.[66] It works in submission to the Chinese government's policies, and not the other way around: 'When CFPA was first created three years earlier, the official communique stated its purpose was to "implement government population control policies"'.[67]

Sex education in China is about health and wellness. China's Ministry of Education, National Health Commission, All-China Women's Federation, and China National Committee for the Care of Children all play a role in deciding the details of sex education for children at the central government level.[68] *They do not leave CSE curriculum to be filled in by foreign-funded NGOs as does India.*

From studies coming out of China, we are certain that IPPF's China Family Planning Association programs do not sexualize children. In 2023, a paper published on why CSE is not catching on in China revealed that CSE in China is 'neither comprehensive nor well-integrated' according to UNESCO and UNFPA.[69]

The Chinese health system focuses on AIDS, STI prevention, and sexual harassment, whereas the education system introduces modules in biology to help students understand bodily changes during puberty:

> However, topics related to sexuality, especially physiology and sexual intercourse, have always been a cultural taboo in China...some Chinese teachers continue to avoid mentioning this concept and are unwilling to take the initiative to help students understand relevant...With the continuous change in China's population structure afterwards, family planning policy has also changed. Under this pretext, the contents of publicity and education related to family planning have gradually disappeared, but the knowledge of reproductive and sexual health remains in the curriculum, which has now become an important part of sex education policy.[70]

The Chinese use the services of its high-ranking retired civil servants to direct sex education for youth as opposed to using peer educators like in India. *China does not succumb to international pressure to adhere to Western standards of sex education which does not fit its culture*. China's government, wielding considerable strength, often maintains its stance on various issues despite international pressure:

> In recent years, the Chinese government has been highly cautious of the spread of 'Western values' and sex education, especially when connected to human rights, e.g., LGBTQ rights. The Chinese delegation sent to these international conferences is usually combined with diplomats from the Ministry of Foreign Affairs and professionals from competent ministries and agencies. They are responsible for sharing the opinions of the Chinese government and providing policy suggestions to the leadership on how to respond (to) international trends.[71]

China's Equivalent of NITI Aayog

The Department of International Organizations is China's equivalent of NITI Aayog; it communicates with international players and ministries within the Chinese government. International organizations seek to influence Chinese policymaking through high-level meetings, but Chinese ministries are risk averse. When it comes to foreign programs, they exercise caution in initiating unconventional programs and do their internal political decision-making and evaluation.[72]

In 2016, China passed laws to clamp down on NGOs citing national security risk calling them 'hostile foreign forces'[73] that work to 'destabilize the government'.[74] Hence, NGOs were required to register with the police and work with an officially approved Chinese partner.[75] International agencies have a difficult time accessing local Chinese officials to buy into CSE programs. For example, the Education Bureau of Hong Kong, as part of teaching materials for secondary school students, advocates sexual abstinence to prevent pregnancy and the emotional distress that may follow. The bureau's suggestion to teenagers is to 'play badminton' when experiencing sexual impulses.[76] The bureau encourages students to sign a 'commitment form' to abstain from sex and pornography and show self-control as part of the sex education teaching on citizenship, economics, and society for schoolchildren.[77] Meanwhile, in Mainland China, the school system is teaching boys to be more masculine[78] and learn practical skills for survival.

When international agencies try to sneak in using their reputation of being from the 'United Nations', to jointly work on CSE projects at the local level, they find it difficult to break the chain of command:

> The attitude of local governments toward cooperation with international organizations varies and the brand of the United Nations is a double-edged sword. On the one hand, the international reputation makes it more convenient for any UN agencies to communicate with the local governments which are willing to cooperate with international organizations. On

> the other hand, some government officials are prudent and cautious of the potential political and diplomatic risks, so they tend to obtain direct and clear instructions from the upper-level government.[79]

China has inoculated its youth against Woke ideas, sees them as narcissistic, and even mocks them with the coined term, 'White Left':

> The influence of nationalism also takes shape in the anti-West sentiment in Mainland. Since the establishment of the People's Republic of China, and particularly after a series of nationwide political events in 1989, the government of Mainland has been highly cautious of 'Western values', especially those related to human rights. Unfortunately, the efforts made by the EU to promote the abolishment of the death penalty make abolishment a more 'Western idea', which can arouse nationalistic sentiments among some Mainland Chinese. In fact, the term 'White Left (Baizuo)', coined in 2010, has been widely adopted in recent years by the youth in Mainland (Qu 2017). The word refers to the Western leftist elites, who only advocate for so-called 'universal values' to satisfy their own feelings of moral superiority and evade 'real problems'. The abolishment of the death penalty, as a 'Western idea', is considered to be part of 'White Left' ideology because it focuses on the right of offenders, rather than that of victims. In fact, less than half the people in Mainland thought the government should follow the UN proposal of applying the death sentence only to the most serious crimes (Oberwittler and Qi 2009). The popularity of the term 'White Left' might reflect the development of China's digital nationalism (Schneider 2018), which tends to reject any 'Western ideologies'.[80]

China donates over one million dollars annually to the IPPF even though its affiliates have no chance of implementing their version of CSE in China. A CSE program for Chinese educators developed by an IPPF partner was shelved 'due to a lack of meaningful engagement between the government'.[81] Many European countries and the American government also fund the IPPF, yet India does not realize the war being facilitated and fought to radicalize its children.

Other Players in India's NGO Ecosystem

New NGOs are entering the lucrative fields of SEL and CSE with their innovative approaches. For example, the New Delhi-based Naz Foundation (India) Trust provides CSE combined with sports for adolescent girls. Girls Not Brides is another such foundation. Most of these are funded by the deep pockets of the same cabal of foreign NGOs supported by one or many of the UN agencies.[82] They share a common concern about India's population. Their impact is far-reaching, influencing government policies and educational programs.

The YP Foundation Starts Very Young

The YP Foundation's (TYPF) involvement in RKSK and Ayushman Bharat Yojana shapes the national health initiatives. It is a significant force in advocating sexual pleasure and rights-based CSE in India. Funded by organizations like PFI, IPPF, American Jewish World Service, WHO, Rohini Nilekani Foundation, and The David and Lucile Packard Foundation, it operates across eighteen Indian states. It targets rural children as young as nine with ideas derived from Queer Theory, proudly claiming: 'We prioritize engagement with young people from economically or socially marginalized and vulnerable communities and contexts'.[83]

They criticize the existing curriculum for its 'non-inclusive' understanding of gender and advocate a sex-positive CSE approach that includes discussions on masturbation and sexual intimacy outside of marriage.[84] They blame patriarchal attitudes for the lack of school education on sexual pleasures outside of marriage. Its policy brief for the Indian government states:

> Sexual and reproductive health, diversity, SOGIESC (Sexual Orientation, Gender Identity, and Expression, and Sex Characteristics), and pleasure are critical components of

> any CSE framework. … It is especially important for a CSE curriculum to adopt a sex-positive approach that discusses masturbation and different forms of sexual intimacy outside the framework of marriage and childbearing. *Given our patriarchal culture that restricts women's mobility and choices right from adolescence as a preventative measure against sexual assault, a CSE programme is a powerful tool that enables young people to develop ownership of their bodies and their rights.*[85]
>
> A majority of campaigns and subsequent curricula reinforce a heteronormative understanding of families and relationships, which automatically exclude young people who do not identify within the same.[86]

The YP Foundation is proud to claim its influence on government programs such as the RKSK and the Ayushman Bharat Yojana.[87] The foundation has copied Woke slogans like 'My Body, My Choice' from the USA and implemented the *Shareer Apna, Adhikaar Apne* (My Body, My Rights) program in Uttar Pradesh. It uses peer sex educators to radicalize young girls, causing conflicts with parents and families by its own admission:

> It was tricky to navigate and dialogue with their families about the outcomes of the programme. Not all families responded positively to peer educators articulating their beliefs or standing up for their rights. The perception was that the content made girls 'too independent' and 'difficult to control'.[88]

Dasra

Dasra is an organization founded by a Harvard Fellow, and partners with other nonprofits, government, and civil society. It collaborates with the Indian government and international bodies to integrate 'sexual rights' and align with the SDGs 2030 agenda.

It serves as a resource for anyone interested in identifying Indian actors that are championed by globalist agendas in education. Its 10 to 19 Community Initiative uses the banner of promoting adolescent health and hygiene to push its sex education for girls as young as nine.[89] Dasra's initiatives focus on girls' sexual and reproductive health rights. It collaborates with the government, NGOs, and other unelected bodies like WHO and UNICEF. The funders include the Bill & Melinda Gates Foundation, Bank of America, USAID, VIP Industries, Kiawah Trust, Children's Investment Fund Foundation, Chanel Foundation, The David and Lucile Packard Foundation, DSP BlackRock, and Tata Trust.[90]

Dasra's program called Dasra Adolescents Collaborative has contradictory goals: It wants girls to complete secondary school but also focuses on teaching sex prematurely in ways that distract one away from education.[91] It is popularizing condoms, sexual rights, and sexual pleasure as an integral part of adolescent life, and these are harming the students' fundamental education. Exposing ten-year-olds to experiment with sex is irresponsible because they are too immature to choose the right partners and understand the consequences of poor choices, including the risk of Sexually Transmitted Diseases and pregnancies.

Youth from all over the country are being trained as 'adolescent champions' to influence other adolescents.[92] The tactic is that adolescents are more comfortable talking to peers who make them feel empowered to make decisions about their bodies.[93] These peers collect data, conduct webinars, events, and publish reports and/or articles.[94] The Youth Advisory Group comprises young leaders as advisors to bring change and facilitate access to contraceptives. They put social pressure on adolescents to normalize having sex at a young age. The goal is to educate fifteen million adolescents.[95]

The Dasra Adolescents Collaborative also supports the government in implementing RKSK in ten districts within India spanning three states.[96] It also supports the Child in Need Institute which offers a counseling service called 'Teenline' for mental, sexual, and reproductive health. Funds are also allocated to C3, Quest Alliance, and Aangan Trust to implement their program in Chhattisgarh, Assam, and Jharkhand.

Ab Meri Baari (My Turn Now) is a key initiative to increase the reach of sex education by using online resources.[97] It has coached three hundred girls to understand the social issues around sexual and reproductive health and rights and to suggest improvements.[98]

The Dasra Collaborative also partners with the government of Jharkhand to meet the United Nations' SDGs for gender inequality in Jharkhand by focusing on sex education for girls.[99] It collaborates with India's first digital platform to disseminate information on love, sex, and relationships called Love Matters India, and has coached nearly sixty youth in Jharkhand in mobile journalism to increase awareness about Sexual and Reproductive Health and Rights. Another program called Mobikaar Citizens Journalism teaches adolescents to produce videos about SRHR.

Dasra Adolescents Collaborative hosted a conversation with the Ministry of Health and Family Welfare where it explains how it disguises sex education in schools:

> *We do not call it sex education per se, but it is called life skills education and is part of Health and Wellness Program.* Children are shown videos which is followed by a class discussion. The freedom is given to the children to discuss with openness.... There are no right or wrong answers.... Lot of efforts have gone into having it spread over several modules.[100]

The Nazariya Foundation

The New Delhi-based Nazariya Foundation identifies itself as a Queer Feminist Resource group and is funded by the Azim Premji Philanthropic Initiatives and Livguard Energy Technologies.[101] It conducts training on gender and sexuality, including the use of controversial content. Their seminars have drawn attention for their provocative materials aimed at dismantling traditional gender norms: 'Nazariya became infamous for advertising a coloring book for students with nude women wearing dildos and masturbating and proudly lists the benefits of its CSE program for children on its website'.[102] At the Tagore International School, a seminar on sex education included a picture of a hirsute male with enlarged breasts, breastfeeding a baby—a common stunt of shock value used by queer pedagogy to dismantle society and rob children of childhood innocence.[103]

The Teacher Foundation

The Teacher Foundation is a teacher training non-profit of the Shraddha Trust and has devised SEL standards based on CASEL, WHO, and other foreign frameworks. Its Indian Social Emotional Learning framework is a national program developed for Indian children aged six to eighteen. This is freely available online in multiple languages for educators and schools, and the government plans to distribute it through platforms like DIKSHA and NISHTHA.[104]

Sangath

Sangath, or 'togetherness' and 'consensus', a mental health NGO, has integrated CSE into the School Health Promotion and Empowerment (SHAPE) program in Goa using school health counselors as its gateway. The insights gained from this were adapted to fit into the existing practices of the state's Department of Education and led to another program called SEHER in partnership with the London School of Hygiene, the Public Health Foundation of India, and the State Council of Educational Research and Training. This has been funded by UNFPA and the MacArthur Foundation. The program delivers sixteen hours of classroom sessions through the government's TARANG life-skills program and conducts separate training for teachers and school counselors.[105]

Labhya Foundation

The Labhya Foundation focuses on developing scalable SEL programs for young students collaborating with state governments to create initiatives like learning Apps.[106] Its CEO, Richa Gupta is a UN leader for SDGs, an equity and inclusion Fellow at Harvard

University, and with many accolades from international agencies. She is also on the advisory board of Generation Unlimited and UNICEF India, and the steering committee of Karanga: The Global Alliance for Social Emotional Learning and Life Skills.[107]

TARSHI—Talking About Reproductive and Sexual Health Issues

TARSHI is an influential NGO working to sexualize children by breaking heteronormative ideas of family, marriage, and sexual relationships.[108] It produces courses and conducts workshops on CSE and other issues apart from advocacy. Its funders include The David and Lucile Packard Foundation and American Jewish World Service, IWHC, the Human Capability Foundation, the John D. and Catherine T. MacArthur Foundation, The Ford Foundation, Deakin University, Hivos, Astraea LESBIAN FOUNDATION FOR JUSTICE, Mama Cash; RFSU, an IPPF affiliate, and the Sexuality Information and Educational Council of the United States (SIECUS).

The SIECUS, also funded by The David and Lucile Packard Foundation, is a major player in setting sexual standards in the USA, not sparing even elementary school children. It is said to:

> Rake in millions of dollars each year from the federal government and abortion-focused charities. State and local education departments from Nebraska to New York have adopted the curriculum, but parents, doctors, and government officials are starting to push back against lesson plans that focus on hormone therapy, abortion, and gender transition... Dr Jeanne Stolzer, professor of child development at the University of Nebraska at Kearney, said that 'it is hard to know exactly what impact these standards will have because nothing this radical has ever been taught in schools before... It has the potential to really wreak havoc with kids socially, psychologically, emotionally'.[109]

9

INSTITUTIONALIZING TRANSGENDERISM

Weaponizing a New 'Victim'

The dharma traditions espouse respect for all humans as children of the Divine, regardless of the characteristics of their bodies. It is no surprise that in India, transgender individuals sometimes referred to as the 'third gender', have been an integral part of society since the earliest times mentioned in the texts. Also known as *hijras*, they have their *sampradaya* called 'kinnar' and have traditionally occupied distinct social roles in sacred rituals and ceremonies, especially during marriages.

However, our problem is with the recent Western transgender movement because of the following factors:

- Institutionalized Transgenderism: It manufactures artificial trans kids in an assembly line:

  > Medical experiments in gender medicine have gone [far], with discussions about surgeons performing 'nullification' and other extreme body modification procedures to create body types that *do not exist in nature*.[1]

- Politicization: Its divisive strategy claims that male/female are social constructs, and these social constructs were put in place by oppressors as part of their agenda to 'oppress' others. Hence, the transgenders have become coopted into the Marxist revolution where 'victims' are being united to overthrow the 'oppressors'. This has politicized transgenders and conflated their cause with unrelated Woke causes like sustainability, race, human rights, etc.

- Childhood interventions: It promotes transgenderism among children by actively soliciting them at very early ages to experiment with thoughts of changing their natural male/female bodies and emotions. It has infiltrated the education system and developed SEL and CSE curriculums, trained thousands of teachers, and created a vast ecosystem to normalize sexual and gender fluidity. This has devastated the lives of numerous children through irreversible sex change operations, hormone treatment, and psychological re-engineering.
- Anti-family: These interventions are bypassing the parents because the family is seen as the vehicle that transmits the false idea of binary sex and gender to the next generation.

In this chapter, we delve into the dark history of the World Professional Association for Transgender Health (WPATH), because the Indian Ministry of Health and Family Welfare along with the National AIDS Control Organization and others are implementing WPATH guidelines without a thorough analysis of the consequences.[2] We will present facts, leaked information from WPATH itself, and a medical report that 'transgender care' is more about activism than science. We will show how WPATH has infiltrated Indian academia, legislation, and Woke pop culture. Finally, we present its end game which is alarming and calls for immediate attention.

The first step in the grand scheme is to confuse children on gender by calling it a social construct, and then teaching them the pursuit of sexual pleasure and deviance in the name of 'queering' and introducing *Drag Queen Story Hour*. The idea is to instill an 'anything goes' attitude towards sex and thus progressively normalize and desensitize children with the help of CSE.

The second step is to encourage and direct gender-confused children into social transitioning with a change in name, pronouns, and clothing. Once on this psychological path, most children in the West move on to transition physically with the aid of puberty blockers, cross-sex hormones, and body mutilating surgeries (such as bilateral mastectomies performed on girls as young as thirteen).

Parents are manipulated into consenting with the emotional blackmail that their children face potential suicide, and are asked: 'Would you prefer a dead son or a living trans daughter?'

The Scandalous Origins of the World Professional Association for Transgender Health

WPATH creates the 'standards of care' for all transgenders, including children with 'gender dysphoria'.[3] It has a shoddy history, with its founders embracing a variety of unconventional lifestyles and behaviors, including drug use and fleeing from the US government. Here is the short version of the story of WPATH:

> WPATH — was a radical cult from the very beginning. The origin story traces back to a gender-confused, new-age, drug-addicted, lesbian rich kid named Rita Erickson, her prolific nudist friend, Zelda Suplee, and their Erickson Educational Foundation (EEF). After 'transitioning' from Rita to Reed, Erickson had 4 failed marriages, developed a drug addiction, and fled to Mexico to avoid drug charges. Her child had to take on a conservatorship of her estate due to her mental & physical decline. This didn't stop Erickson from using her EEF organization to fund the people & organizations that became WPATH — the who's who of unhinged doctors in the field of 'transsexualism' and 'transgenderism' including:
>
> - Dr. Harry Benjamin, who wrote 'The Transsexual Phenomenon.' In the book, he writes that he supported 'vaginoplasties' to create fake vaginas on

males, despite admitting that they're really 'wounds' which could degrade and become 'obliterated.'

- Dr. John Money, who directed twin boys, one of whom he was transitioning, to 'inspect one another's genitals & engage in behavior resembling sexual intercourse.' Ultimately, one shot himself and the other died of a drug overdose.
- Dr. Anne Lawrence, a man who admits to having autogynephilic, a paraphilia where he is aroused by thinking of himself as a woman, and said of his genital mutilation: 'For so many years I have longed to be penetrable, to be a vessel, a receptacle: and now I am.'
- Dr. Lawrence's writing appears to be from 1998, just a year after he resigned from a hospital after performing a non-consensual genital examination on an unconscious female patient, according to an incident report.[4]

As recently as 2023, the WPATH website openly and almost proudly recognized its origins with the Erickson Educational Foundation.[5] While WPATH publicly claims that its procedures are evidenced-based, its internal discussions indicate that members are engaging in experimental practices, particularly on young people to facilitate their widespread implementation.[6]

> We're explaining things to people who haven't even had biology in high school…It's like talking [about] diabetic complications with a 14-year-old. They don't care. They're not going to die. They're going to live forever, right? So I think when we're doing informed consent, that's still a big lacuna.[7]

A group known as Environmental Progress leaked internal documents called *WPATH Files*. It claims that these internal discussions among physicians will go down as one of the 'worst medical scandals in history':

> WPATH … has mistreated children for years while acknowledging that they can't possibly consent to these barbaric 'procedures.' It's time for the medical profession to do what it should have done long ago and shut down these con artists before they hurt anyone else.[8]

Below is a powerful expose on WPATH:

> Advocates of gender-affirming care say it's evidence-based. But now, newly released internal files from the WPATH prove that the practice of transgender medicine is neither scientific nor medical. American Medical Association, The Endocrine Society, the American Academy of Pediatrics, and thousands of doctors worldwide rely on WPATH. It is considered the leading global authority on gender medicine. And yet WPATH's internal files, which include written discussions and a video, reveal that its members know they are creating victims and not getting 'informed consent.' Victims include a 10-year-old girl, a 13-year-old developmentally delayed adolescent, and individuals suffering from schizophrenia and other serious mental illnesses. *The injuries described in the WPATH Files include sterilization, loss of sexual function, liver tumors, and death.* WPATH members indicate repeatedly that they know that many children and their parents don't understand the effects that puberty blockers, hormones, and surgeries will have on their bodies. And yet, they continue to perform and advocate for gender medicine. The WPATH Files prove that gender medicine is comprised of (sic) unregulated and pseudoscientific experiments on children, adolescents, and vulnerable adults.[9]

The following examples expose the vulnerability of teenagers when they make these life-changing decisions without being fully aware of the implications and consequences of their decisions. Some also express regret for transitioning as these procedures leave them either sterile, unable to enjoy sexual activity, or family life, and resulting in cancer or death:

> The problem is that drugs can cause tumors, even, apparently, in people as young as 16 years old...Many young patients experiencing gender distress do not appear to understand that they may suffer serious consequences from long-term hormone use and genital surgery...Despite the widespread and growing expression of concern within the WPATH Files over the negative side effects of gender medicine, WPATH members urge that irreversible surgeries take place when adolescents are just 16 or 17 years old.
>
> 'Oh, the dog isn't doing it for you?' Many gender medicine victims are filled with regret that they were sterilized. Nobody knows this more than the doctors who mistreated them. At times, their response to such regret appears callous. 'I follow a lot of kids into their mid-twenties, I'm always like, 'Oh, the dog isn't doing it for you, right?' They're like, 'No, I just found this wonderful partner and now we want kids. So you know, it doesn't surprise me.'
>
> For some gender medicine patients, there are fates worse than both sterility and loss of sexual function: 'After 8-10 years of [testosterone, they] developed hepatocarcinoma... died a couple of months after'.[10]

Globally, the decisions and judgments about transgender issues are being deferred to WPATH without sufficient scientific basis. Environmental Progress' report on WPATH raises key arguments:

- *Focus on Cosmetic Outcomes*: The report argues that transgender activists are overly focused on cosmetic changes rather than the deeper aspects of sexual health and functionality. For instance, it highlights concerns about the effects of puberty blockers on height while neglecting aspects like libido and orgasm.
- *Activist vs. Scientific Organization*: Environmental Progress claims that WPATH operates more as an activist organization than a scientific group. They argue that WPATH lacks the scientific rigor typically expected from medical entities

yet have positioned themselves as the leading experts on transgender health issues globally.

- *Scientific Basis and Decision Making*: The report suggests that worldwide decisions regarding transgender health are heavily influenced by WPATH without sufficient scientific backing. This includes concerns about the ethical implications of medical treatments promoted by WPATH, particularly those involving minors.
- *Ethical Concerns in Medical Practices*: The report contends that WPATH's guidelines lead to unethical medical practices, particularly concerning minors undergoing gender-affirming treatments. It asserts that these practices amount to experimental procedures without detailed studies of their long-term effects. It states that activist members of WPATH are aware that the so-called 'gender-affirming care' they provide can lead to lifelong complications, including sterility, and that patients often do not fully grasp the consequences, such as the loss of sexual function and the ability to experience orgasm. The leaked documents offer substantial evidence showing that WPATH professionals are conscious of the fact that they are not obtaining proper consent from children, adolescents, vulnerable adults, or their caregivers.[11]

The *Cass Review*

In recent years, England's National Health Service (NHS) has been grappling with a notable surge in the number of children seeking care for gender identity issues. Hilary Cass conducted an extensive examination of the field concerning gender-affirming treatments and produced a comprehensive report, the *Cass Review* (popularly known as *The Independent Review for Gender Identity Services for Children and Young People*) challenging the common activist narratives. This report presents its findings after systematic analyses of the evidence, making it clear that gender-affirming care is more about activism than science.[12] Here are some highlights:[13]

- Puberty blockers do not just pause puberty like flipping an on/off switch, as is often explained to patients. They come with severe side effects, and the *Cass Review* highlights concerns about the lack of solid evidence supporting these widely used treatments. The report also questions the safety and effectiveness of these treatments.
- Concerns of legal implications (lawsuits) related to conversion therapy (counseling practices aimed at changing an individual's identity confusion) create anxiety among clinicians, impacting their ability to provide care.
- The *Review* emphasizes the lack of substantial evidence regarding the long-term outcomes of interventions for gender-related distress.
- The *Review* advocates for a personalized care plan that addresses the complex needs of each child, including psychological and social factors, rather than rushing into medical interventions.
- The document indicates that children and adolescents referred to gender identity services often present with a range of associated psychological conditions. There is a significant prevalence of neurodevelopmental conditions (autism, ADHD). Incidences of depression and anxiety are higher in this population compared to the general population. Specifically, approximately thirty-eight percent of children and young people referred to gender clinics have been reported to experience depression.
- There is no evidence to suggest that puberty blockers are beneficial outweighing the risks, or that they prevent suicides.
- The *Review* squarely refutes the idea that gender-affirming care as practiced in the West today is 'evidence-based'.
- The *Review* challenges the prevailing practice in clinics across the USA, which prioritize immediate affirmation of an adolescent's stated gender without extensive psychological assessments.

The Endocrine Society and WPATH released guidelines in 2009 and 2012 respectively, recommending medical transitioning for youth. These guidelines influenced later recommendations despite concerns about their lack of evidence and rigor. Hilary Cass's *Review* pointed out close ties between WPATH and the Endocrine Society, implying collusion to give their guidelines undue credibility:[14]

> The corruption persisted in the formulation of national and regional guidelines by prominent organizations such as the American Psychological Association, the American Academy of Child and Adolescent Psychiatry, the American Academy of Pediatrics, and the Society for Adolescent Health and Medicine. It also extended to international guidelines from countries like Australia, Spain, Italy, and regions including Asia and the Pacific. Rather than grounding their recommendations in robust evidence, these guidelines deferred to the endorsements from the initial guidelines of WPATH and ES. Years later, when WPATH and ES updated their guidelines, they referenced the same national and regional guidelines that had initially drawn from their recommendations. This perpetuated a cycle in which each iteration reinforced the others, each time without sufficient evidence to support the recommendations... Additionally, it demonstrates how these subsequent guidelines cite and rely on each other, and how the latest Endocrine Society (2017) and WPATH (2022) guidelines have cited and drawn on the national and regional guidelines.[15]

Hilary Cass underscored the close relationship between WPATH and the Endocrine Society, pointing out their co-sponsorship and involvement in each other's drafts. The *Cass Review* reveals misleading practices within medical organizations endorsing youth transitioning. Instead of basing their recommendations on solid evidence, they simply echo each other's guidelines. The problematic nature of this circular referencing was highlighted.[16]

WPATH, which runs the *International Journal of Transgender Health* was quick to rubbish the *Cass Review* without any objective scientific criticisms, merely by bringing in Woke-based language of 'oppressor-oppressed' to refute the *Cass Review*:

> Cis-supremacy calls attention to the axes and forces of cis-power that actively dominate and oppress trans people, with cis-supremacy particularly harmful in cis-dominant institutions or processes that lack trans accountability. The Cass Review is an exemplar of cis-supremacy, and more specifically, of cis institutional dominance.[17]

Meanwhile, the American College of Pediatricians put out a statement calling WPATH and other organizations to stop using current protocols for gender dysphoria:

> As physicians, together with nurses, psychotherapists and behavioral health clinicians, other health professionals, scientists, researchers, and public health and policy professionals, we have serious concerns about the physical and mental health effects of the current protocols promoted for the care of children and adolescents in the United States who express discomfort with their biological sex.
>
> Therefore, given the recent research and the revelations of the harmful approach advocated by WPATH and its followers in the United States, we, the undersigned, call upon the medical professional organizations of the United States, including the American Academy of Pediatrics, the Endocrine Society, the Pediatric Endocrine Society, American Medical Association, the American Psychological Association, and the American Academy of Child and Adolescent Psychiatry to follow the science and their European professional colleagues and immediately stop the promotion of social affirmation, puberty blockers, cross-sex hormones and surgeries for children and adolescents who experience distress over their biological sex.
>
> Instead, these organizations should recommend comprehensive evaluations and therapies aimed at identifying and addressing underlying psychological co-morbidities and

neurodiversity that often predispose to and accompany gender dysphoria.

We also encourage the physicians who are members of these professional organizations to contact their leadership and urge them to adhere to the evidence-based research now available.[18]

The WPATH's Success in India's Laws and Academia

In April 2014, India's Supreme Court ruled that transgenders and gender variants (nonbinary, genderqueer, genderfluid, agender, two-spirit) had the right to self-determination of gender identity under the Indian Constitution. Following this judgment, the Transgender Persons (Protection of Rights) Act, 2019 was passed.

The Act aims to tackle discrimination in healthcare services and ensures that medical facilities cater to the needs of transgender individuals, including gender-affirmative procedures. It requires the government to *provide gender-affirmative surgeries, hormonal therapy, and counseling, following WPATH guidelines*.[19] Moreover, the Act advocates for enduring measures such as the evaluation of medical curricula and re-training of healthcare professionals for transgender care.

Since 2016, a push to make WPATH the standard of care for transgenders was aggressively advocated by transgender groups such as Nirangal, a 'human rights' NGO, Telangana Hijra Intersex Transgender Samiti (THITS), and Sampoorna Working Group, a network of trans and intersex individuals globally.

These groups want to mandate gender-affirming procedures and hormone therapy as in the West. They also use the same rationale as the West that suicide risk is real among trans people if their gender is not affirmed. However, there is no evidence of many suicides among trans people over hundreds of years across the world, long before these new political movements.

The Indian Standards of Care released in November 2020 is based on the guidelines from WPATH and even includes a parents' support group section to guide parents of their transgender children.[20] A small sample of new findings that counter the prevailing view is listed below from statsforgender.org:[21]

1. Gender-related distress goes away for around 80% of pre-teen children once they become teenagers. Adolescent Gender Dysphoria is a temporary diagnosis for most teens.
2. In one study, almost 9 out of 10 young people questioning their gender were under social influence to do so.
3. Trans-identified youth are disproportionately likely to suffer from eating disorders.
4. Puberty blockers potentially have a negative impact on neuropsychological functioning.
5. Gender-affirming hormonal therapy induces a gender-concordant fecal metagenome transition in transgender individuals.
6. Gender-nonconforming play is linked to increased behavioral difficulties in both boys and girls. Masculine play in girls is associated with autistic traits, while feminine play in boys is tied to peer relationship issues.
7. Testosterone use in trans-identifying females may increase inflammation, potentially worsening gum disease progression.
8. Trans-identifying adolescents spend 4.5 more hours per day on recreational screen time than their peers.
9. Puberty blockers are more than a 'pause button': roughly 98% of children who take them go on to take cross-sex hormones.
10. Intestinal vaginoplasty in patients with stunted penile growth from puberty blockers can lead to bowel inflammation, excessive discharge, persistent foul odors, and fecal leakage.
11. Trans identities are more strongly associated with the perpetration of bullying than subjection to bullying.

Meanwhile, huge budgets of taxpayer money are set aside by the government for the trans/queer community. They include:

12. Under the Ayushman Bharat Yojana, the Indian government allots Rs 5 lakh to cover gender-affirming care per transgender beneficiary per annum.[22] Across Tamil Nadu, gender transition

surgeries are offered for free by the state government.[23] Private NGOs have also sprung up to fund gender transition surgeries.

13. These incentives often impact the social behavior of young people as seen in the UK where 1,397 people sought legal gender changes in 2023-4, with 1,088 receiving approvals. This represents a threefold jump from 466 in 2020-1. The surge led by Millennials and Gen Z, was encouraged by a fee reduction from £140 to just £5.[24]
14. Ration cards for couples in 'queer' relationships to be treated as a household by the Department of Food & Public Distribution.
15. Free mental health programs for queers are being developed by the Ministry of Health and Family Welfare.
16. The Health Ministry has issued letters to stakeholders to:
    a. Ensure LGBTQIA+ health care rights
    b. Plan awareness activities
    c. Provide access to sex reassignment surgery
    d. Update curricula on LGBTQIA+ issues
    e. Offer tele-consultation services and sensitize & train health care staff
    f. Allow claiming bodies if no next of kin available.[25]
17. The Ministry of Social Justice and Empowerment is handing out scholarships specifically to trans students from the ninth standard onwards.

The Indian Academy of Pediatrics (IAP), formed a task force of pediatricians on 'transgender care' that studied guidelines given by WHO, UN, UNICEF, WPATH as well as the American Academy of Pediatrics, and the Association of Transgender Health in India.[26] The Indian Academy of Pediatrics accepted the WPATH guideline with one main difference, namely, that cross-sex hormone therapy and body mutilating surgeries can be done only after the child reaches the age of consent.

The IAP recommendations are in lockstep with Woke ideology:[27]

- Gender is not a binary concept but a spectrum of genders between the male and female poles with many blends.

- Education about gender fluidity should be incorporated into the school curriculum to develop a system where non-binary is normal.
- Transgender people are prone to face stigma, discrimination, victimization and abuse, which can cause significant physical and mental health issues leading to a high risk of substance abuse and suicide.
- Schools, work- and public-places should have gender-neutral restrooms and other facilities for gender-non-conforming individuals.
- The spectrum of gender identity variation and incongruence should be included as a part of medical education to promote training in gender-affirmative practice.
- Pediatricians dealing with a transgender child should not presume the gender identity or sexual orientation but should enquire about the client's description of self.
- Gender incongruence requires a multi-disciplinary team approach to deliver affirmative care including a pediatrician, child and adolescent psychiatrist, clinical psychologist, pediatric endocrinologist, gender-affirming surgeon, and speech therapist.
- Every trans child must get individualized care, honoring preferred names and pronouns, and informed choices about medical gender-affirmative care.
- Medical intervention should only follow the informed assent of adolescents and the consent of their primary caretaker.
- Gender-affirmative hormonal intervention and genital surgery can be done only after the legal age of consent i.e. 18 years.

The Association for Transgender Health in India is the local lobby of WPATH. It runs a soup-to-nuts transgender clinic, which we applaud for its useful health services for the transgender community, but we are concerned about WPATH's history of misleading adolescents with untested gender-affirming care.[28]

ATHI is aggressively advocating a change in healthcare policies.

It has introduced a new birth certificate that prevents specifying gender at birth. Collaborating with the Government of India, ATHI is developing culturally relevant guidelines for transgender health and establishing India's first LGBTQIA+ Health Center of Excellence at the All India Institute of Medical Sciences (AIIMS). Along with other groups, it has been organizing webinars to encourage gender-affirmative care, starting a whole new industry.[29]

The Ministry of Health and Family Welfare, Government of India along with the National AIDS Control Organization have developed a White Paper based on WPATH guidelines with the help of ATHI.[30] The paper recommends providing gender-affirming care 'to trans gender and gender-diverse individuals *beginning from early childhood through adolescence* to adulthood'.[31] The Government of India's White Paper is moving towards adopting the WPATH standard:

> The treatment in terms of gender affirmation has a range of models that are being used in the country. It is the need of the hour to ensure that there is a standardized document defining the 'Indian Standard of Care', *possibly adapting the global standards of care to the Indian context*. One such global standards of care is the WPATH guidelines, which is mentioned in the 2014 Supreme Court (NALSA) judgement.[32]

AIIMS has been co-opted to be a Center of Excellence in transgender health the WPATH way:

> For imparting education and skill training in this multispecialty, multidisciplinary, relatively young, and evolving field of healthcare. Its autonomous status and international repute will give transgender health its due importance and catalyse the much-needed reforms in medical education. The trained human resource shall not only provide the role models but shall also set the template for delivery of holistic gender-friendly healthcare in the country.[33]

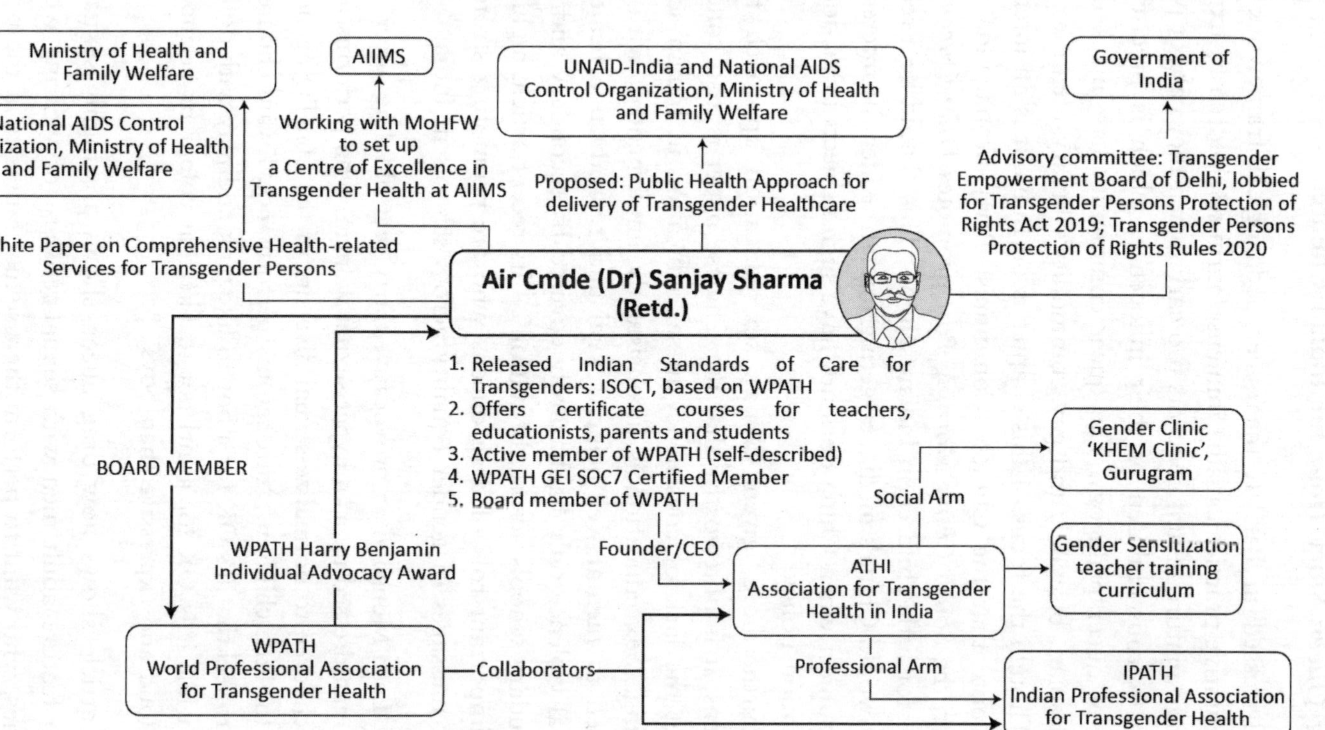

Source: https://www.wpath.org/media/cms/Documents/History/Awards/2022/2022%20Award%20Eblast.pdf?_1-1658500633

Drag Queen Story Hour for Indian Children

As discussed in Part 1, the queer pedagogical framework is an exploitative practice causing immense harm to children by exposing them to mature sexual concepts too early when they cannot process them. It robs children of their innocence, which is precisely the goal of queer pedagogy. The queer community has hijacked even the lesbian, bisexual, and gay community's binary identities.

Though the focus of this chapter is on India, it is an interesting side note that the Chinese Communist Party propaganda media outlet, the *South China Morning Post* promotes *Drag Queen Story Hour* for little children in Indian schools. This should be a red flag: Why would China's media, targeting foreign readers be interested in this subject when China does not have such subjects in its domestic education policy?

Furthermore, given China's sex education approach for its citizens, it is noteworthy that the Chinese paper is also concerned about the lack of consistency in sex education in Indian schools, writing: 'Sex education is inconsistently implemented, with issues related to mental well-being, sexual and reproductive health and sexual violence only haphazardly covered by secondary and senior secondary schools across the nation'.[34] Its recent article highlighted the important role of drag queens who are promoting strong and clear messages of gender equality across schools in India:[35]

> 'Lush Monsoon', a provocative thirty year old drag queen (a man dressed up as a hyper sexual woman) who performs for children to normalize sexual diversity of the LGBTQ agenda for little children…'through my performance, I want children to feel that it's OK for a boy to like pink and play with dolls, while it is OK for a girl not to like that colour or be more loud and expressive than boys'.[36]

The article shows how drag queen shows are highly sexual, and often feature adult men with sexual fetishes for wearing women's clothes, who want to perform their sexual fantasies in the presence of little children. Their stage names are sexually suggestive as in the case of 'Lush Monsoon', or 'Lil Miss Hot Mess'. Labeling them as 'drag artists' attempts to normalize and classify their fetishes as 'art', creating a grey area. However, the goal is to exploit children's curiosity with colorful drama, and groom them into sexual deviance:

> When drag artist Patruni Chidanand Sastry, 31, stepped on to the open-air stage at an elite school in the southern Indian city of Hyderabad – dressed in an embroidered blouse and skirt, a multicoloured wig and a mask made of sawdust and tamarind seed paste – children sitting in the front row looked at him in awe…Sastry takes his act to schools across Hyderabad as more learning institutes in India open their doors to drag artists, hoping to raise awareness among children on issues ranging from gender identity to safe sex…When they sing, dance and tell stories about gender-neutral fictional characters to children, drag artists say it creates awareness about equality that encourages kids to be curious about the lives of transgender people and to ask about pride marches, same-sex marriages and LGBTQ rights.[37]

The obvious reason is that China considers such disruptions of early childhood education a good way to destroy society and wants to export this psychological poison to its enemies while protecting its children.

The Keshav Suri Foundation

The Keshav Suri Foundation, run by the scion of the Lalit Suri Hospitality Group, targets children as young as three, and organizes *Drag Queen Story Hour* sessions 'to raise awareness about the rights of the queer community'.[38] Its benign-sounding Elphie book series, with an elephant donned in rainbow colors, focuses on teaching children to have 'unfettered acceptance'. The website states: 'Drag Queen Story Hour has truly been a project that has sailed through with care, love and nurture. We are thankful to some of the most amazing drag queens who took the leap of faith and helped us turn this dream into reality'.[39]

The drag queens at one such session talked to children about bringing fantasy to real life:

> As a drag queen, it makes me so happy to introduce kids to the idea of drag and read them stories of inclusivity and positivity. The message of drag is to not take identity and labels too seriously and just have fun, which immediately resonates with children. Children are drawn to the colourful personas of drag queens; we are the embodiment of fantasy in real life. They come up to ask us all kinds of curious questions and that's what we are encouraging.[40]

Queer youth are groomed to become social justice warriors, offering a 'Queer Youth Leadership course', 'designed to empower members of the queer community to become social leaders of change. Support the change that is necessary, help the members of the Queer community emerge as leaders'.[41]

As with aggressive Western NGOs that hand out report cards on trans friendliness to corporations affecting their ESG score, the Keshav Suri Foundation has also embarked on a rating system that it controls to rate Indian companies on trans inclusivity. It is a way to arm-twist corporations into promoting the Woke agenda and thus improve their ESG rating.

The Keshav Suri Foundation, in collaboration with the diversity and inclusion advisory consultancy, Pride Circle, and also Stonewall, has established 'the India Workplace Equality Index'. It serves to punish corporations in India that do not promote its Woke agenda, calling it a 'comprehensive benchmarking tool, empowering organizations to assess their advancements in LGBTQIA+ inclusion within the Indian landscape'.[42] Already, companies are clamoring for good ratings. Uber India won the Silver Standard Award for its workplace policies and practices. WIPRO was named a gold employer.[43]

ScoutMe, a football scouting platform, plans to expand to other sports in partnership with the Keshav Suri Foundation and the Bhaichung Bhutia Football Schools to launch transgender-inclusive sports across India. The Keshav Suri Foundation is queering football, by creating a football league without male/female binaries. This initiative called 'Kicking Gender Boundaries', was created in association with ScoutMe and the Rajasthan Football Association.[44] Schools like the Jayshree Periwal International School in Jaipur are queering sports, which will obliterate sports for women by making women compete with transgenders who are biological men. The school proclaimed: 'Kicking Gender Boundaries Jayshree Periwal International School hosted India's first and historic, all gender inclusive football match organized by Keshav Suri Foundation in association with Rajasthan Football Association and ScoutMe'.[45]

The Keshav Suri Foundation promotes the use of personal pronouns among school children, asserting that anyone can claim to be a woman and use female pronouns. This claim on womanhood is not meant to be just a superficial name and clothing change but must include all rights afforded to women by the law: ranging from access to female-only spaces to competing in women's sports. Eventually, the goal is to pass hate speech laws against 'mis-gendering' someone.

We believe that transgender individuals should not face bullying or harassment, just as other vulnerable or marginalized groups should be protected from such mistreatment. However, we contend that women-only spaces like restrooms are now being encroached upon with policies that permit men who simply identify as women. Women's prisons are being invaded by men identifying as women, often resulting in assault and rape of female inmates.

We also reject the sexualizing of children in the name of teaching diversity. Adolescents often go through body image issues, even when they are secure in their male or female identity, but the trendy discourse promoting trans might influence them to doubt their own gender identity. Without parental guidance and with strong pressure and bullying against heterosexuals in schools, they succumb and end up taking puberty blockers, cross-sex hormones, or even undergoing surgeries to transition. These teens sometimes de-transition a few years later only to find themselves sterile with missing or altered body parts from surgery, with irreversible problems.

The End Game

The laws are being systematically curated to push India surreptitiously on this social engineering project. A major strategy of this movement is to change the age of consent laws. Once this barrier is broken, we will see an increase in the following:

1. CSE and SEL education will openly teach children to pursue sexual pleasure, advocate for sexual rights in the name of liberation, and claim their sexual rights.
2. CSE will further indoctrinate girls by denigrating the family structure, and marriage.
3. Abortions are promoted as an easy tool to deal with the consequences of promiscuity.
4. Contraceptives are touted as safe with no side effects. Recent studies out of Denmark have shown that hormonal contraceptive use doubled the risk of suicide attempts and tripled the risk of suicide.[46] Studies also show that long-term use of oral contraceptives causes depression, behavioral changes, and weight gain. Women who use contraceptive pills as teenagers are 130% more likely to be depressed when adults.[47] A University of California, Los Angeles study also showed that contraceptive users process stress differently than non-contraceptive users.[48] Hair loss also seems to be a side effect of birth control pills.
5. Sexual rights will become fundamental human rights.
6. Pedophilia will be decriminalized if it can be shown as initiated by a minor.
7. The social engineering project confusing children on

gender will result in more young people identifying as transgender.

8. With the age of consent laws disappearing, the 'WPATH standards' will be pushed to transition children at early ages resulting in permanent damage and life-long dependence on pharmaceuticals.
9. Doctors will run successful practices in gender-affirming, raking in enormous profits for themselves and allied industries like pharmaceuticals.

10

NITI AAYOG AS THE GATEKEEPER

Many Indians are frustrated with the National Council of Educational Research and Training for not modifying textbooks to accurately reflect the history and civilization of Bharat. Instead, new 'Woke' content is surfacing in schools. India's institutions have been invaded unbeknownst to many. Many of India's top bureaucrats have post-retirement lucrative careers with international agencies as we saw with the Udaan projects in Jharkhand and Rajasthan. Hence, it is important to understand what drives the education policy and legislative changes.

Our diagnosis is that the root cause is India's blind commitment to the Sustainable Development Goals that shape its policies which trickle down to the National Education Policy 2020, National Curriculum Framework, and NCERT. The SDGs' unwavering commitment to Comprehensive Sexuality Education, Social Emotional Learning, Global Citizenship Education, and environmentalism is reflected in the NEP, NCF, and the NCERT. The SDGs would like an individual to think as a global citizen instead of prioritizing nation, culture, or family.

For example, if one applies this thinking to the Rohingya migration, an SDGs-based global citizen's stance on the issue would be diametrically opposite to the stance taken by a regular Indian citizen who sees national interest as the top priority. The SDGs thus create trade-offs in decision-making, which causes stress in children by forcing them to navigate challenging situations. Our concern is about the way the SDGs result in ideological and political agendas becoming embedded within SEL/CSE/GCE and resulting in a program of indoctrination for all children in the Indian school system.

Sadly, many of India's top bureaucrats work for foreign-funded NGOs and help them hack into the government apparatus. Indirectly, India is already being run by foreign agencies that lobby to make new rules, lay out the plan, monitor the implementation, suggest ways to fill in the gaps, and then evaluate the progress.

The Inside Job

The responsibility for assessing and overseeing the implementation of SDGs in India lies with NITI Aayog. This is why NITI Aayog has been infiltrated by foreign-controlled NGOs right from framing the curriculum to filling in the content. For example:

- The Population Foundation of India has a cozy relationship with NITI Aayog in making critical policy recommendations. In 2019, NITI Aayog organized a meeting with PFI to discuss strengthening India's population policy and family planning 'to realize its SDGs'.[1] PFI's recommendations such as 'addressing existing socio-cultural barriers towards contraception by investing extensively in innovative behavior-change communication strategies' guided NITI Aayog on attaining population stabilization.[2]
- PFI engages with the 'highest levels' of NITI Aayog as an expert by collaborating with NITI Aayog to prioritize adolescents' sexual health needs in policies and programs. As a partner of NITI Aayog, PFI lobbies the government for coordination among key ministries such as Health and Family Welfare, Women and Child Development, Youth Affairs and Sports, Education, and Skills Development and Entrepreneurship, along with domain experts. Additionally, they were invited by the Parliamentary Standing Committee

on Empowerment of Women to present on sexual and reproductive health.[3]

- During an event organized by NITI Aayog, the Institute of Applied Manpower Research, 3ie, UN Women, OXFAM, and other organizations evaluated progress in India.'[4]

Thus, *NITI Aayog evaluates India's progress across different dimensions using the criteria set by foreign institutions. Often, it uses foreign-funded NGOs as consultants to draft policies thereby outsourcing the government's job to foreign entities. The NGOs, backed by huge foreign funding, play a crucial role in attaining SDGs 2030's educational targets by being a bridge between global institutions and local countries.*

Further downstream, foreign NGOs are working closely with Civil Society Organizations (i.e. domestic NGOs) bringing the content and training modules in compliance with the new policies they successfully lobbied for. The foreign NGOs praise NITI Aayog for acknowledging 'the important role played by civil society organizations (CSOs) that work from the national level to the grassroots level on SDG-related issues'.[5] We discussed in detail the workings of Jharkhand's state-wide CSE and SDGs programs in previous chapters. These strategic projects are not in sync with India's civilizational orientation or sovereignty.

As an example, a foreign agency has developed a toolkit for domestic CSOs to monitor India's progress on SDGs. It states that India needs a 'holistic' approach to education and *not get fixated on numeracy and literacy*:

> The new NEP 2020 fails to adopt a holistic approach that is provided for in the RTE Act. Rather than focussing (sic) on the narrow definition of the purpose of education, i.e. the knowledge of literacy and numeracy, as highlighted as the learning crisis in NEP, the focus should be on adopting a holistic approach, provided in RTE Act.[6]

Hence, prioritizing SEL/CSE/GCE over reading and math is something the foreign nexus has decided and NITI Aayog is obediently following. Because NITI Aayog is complicit, India is following in the USA's footsteps: SEL sneaks its way using the attractive catch-all framework—'Whole School, Whole Community, Whole Child Framework'. As explained earlier, one must exercise caution when encountering recommendations like 'holistic', 'comprehensive', 'sustainable', and 'equitable', since imported jargon uses them differently than the average Indian understands. For example, 'holistic' often means the inclusion of CSE as a 'life skill education'. And the oft used 'holistic criteria' for college admissions applications simply means non-merit admissions based on race, gender, and sexuality.

American parents worry about SEL turning into unlicensed gender therapy, which is having dire consequences for children. People are also concerned about data privacy and the enormous leverage digital platforms have over youth. Unfortunately, India lacks similar watchdogs, and authorized but compromised entities like NITI Aayog have opened the floodgates to import radical American programs.

Circumventing the Gatekeepers of Society

The government essentially has three different programs to distribute CSE and SEL using public-private partnerships that go unnoticed by parents. The Indian government has outsourced these programs to private actors, who bypass the scrutiny of parents and other gatekeepers of children. They use digital platforms and mobile applications, peer educators replacing traditional teachers to spread sex positivity and pleasure-based sex education. Three programs are discussed across different sections in the book (see the following figure). Here, we summarize these programs to show how parents are being kept out of the CSE/SEL education loop while targeting their children on a large scale:

1. The RKSK targets in-school and out-of-school youth, with a mobile application and peer educators to teach CSE. The RKSK is under the aegis of the Ministry of Health and Family Welfare, and thus misses the scrutiny of educators. RKSK also has Adolescent Health Friendly Clinics where CSE can be delivered with the help of peer educators and a mobile application. This was described in an earlier chapter.
2. NITI Aayog has funded two technological startups, one for distributing SEL, and the other for CSE. These programs are aimed at training youth and providing CSE/SEL material on digital platforms.
3. NGOs such as the well-funded Population Foundation of India are scaling up teacher training in all government schools on pleasure-based CSE.

All these programs access children without the involvement of parents.

The following figures provide a consolidated view of these government and private initiatives brought into India. They all use untraditional channels for distribution, completely bypassing sincere teachers and concerned parents who would most certainly object to these programs.

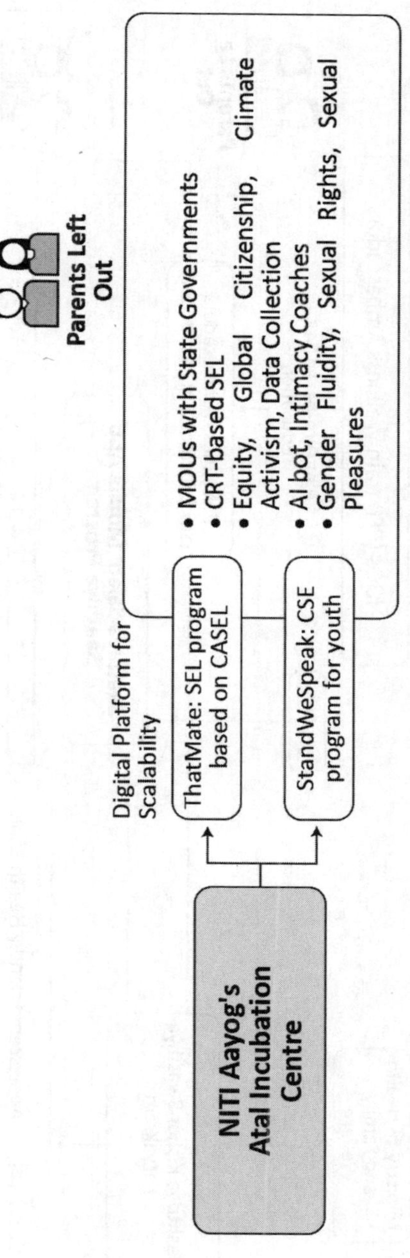
Leaving Parents out of
Comprehensive Sexuality Education and
Social Emotional Learning
Parents Left Out
NITI Aayog's Atal Incubation Centre
Digital Platform for Scalability
ThatMate: SEL program based on CASEL
StandWeSpeak: CSE program for youth
• MOUs with State Governments
• CRT-based SEL
• Equity, Global Citizenship, Climate Activism, Data Collection
• AI bot, Intimacy Coaches
• Gender Fluidity, Sexual Rights, Sexual Pleasures

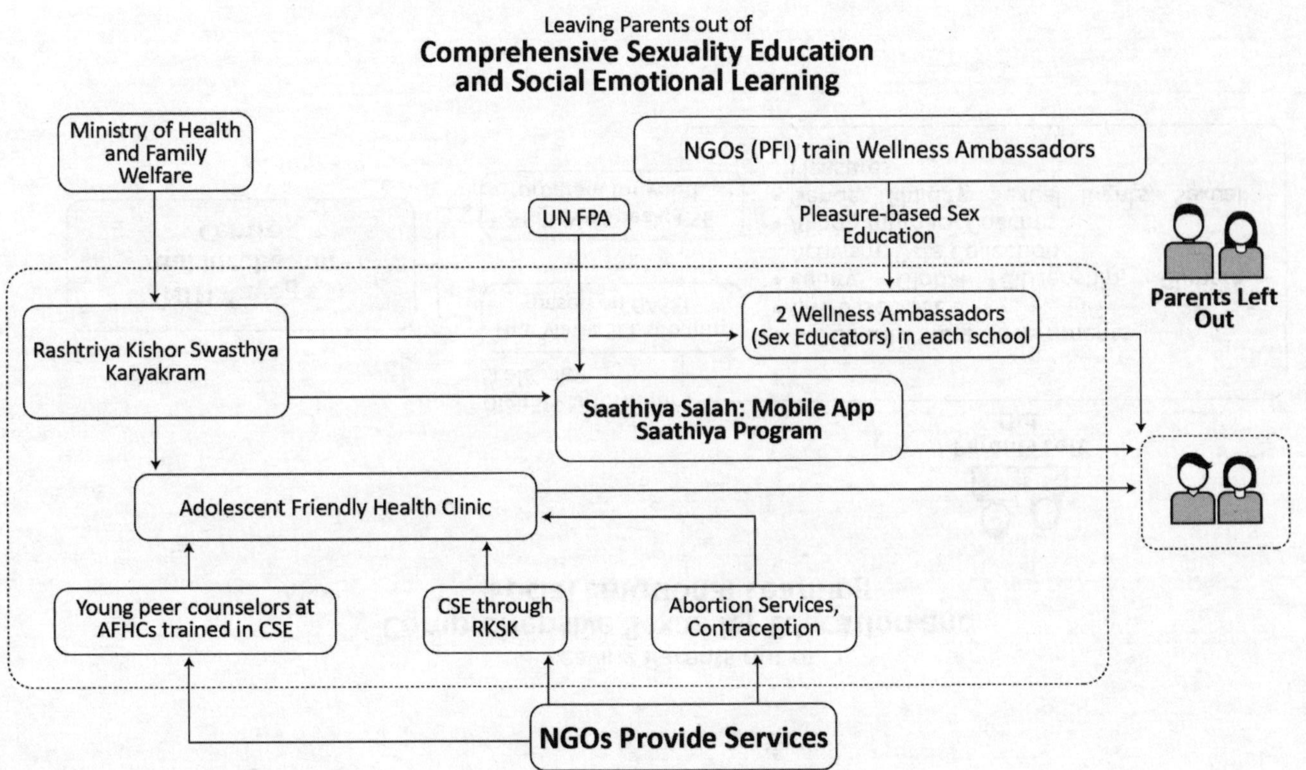
Leaving Parents out of
Comprehensive Sexuality Education
and Social Emotional Learning
Ministry of Health and Family Welfare
UN FPA
NGOs (PFI) train Wellness Ambassadors
Pleasure-based Sex Education
Parents Left Out
Rashtriya Kishor Swasthya Karyakram
2 Wellness Ambassadors (Sex Educators) in each school
Saathiya Salah: Mobile App Saathiya Program
Adolescent Friendly Health Clinic
Young peer counselors at AFHCs trained in CSE
CSE through RKSK
Abortion Services, Contraception
NGOs Provide Services

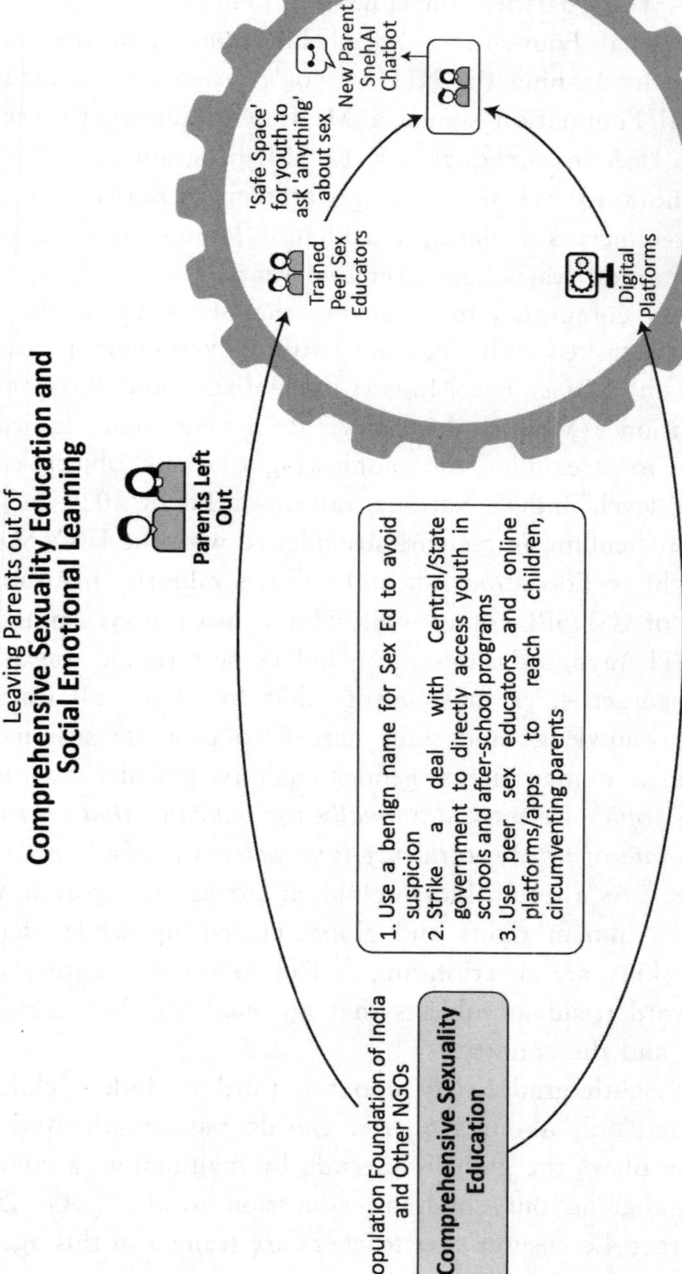
Leaving Parents out of
Comprehensive Sexuality Education and
Social Emotional Learning
Parents Left Out
Population Foundation of India and Other NGOs
Comprehensive Sexuality Education
1. Use a benign name for Sex Ed to avoid suspicion
2. Strike a deal with Central/State government to directly access youth in schools and after-school programs
3. Use peer sex educators and online platforms/apps to reach children, circumventing parents
Trained Peer Sex Educators
'Safe Space' for youth to ask 'anything' about sex
New Parent SnehAI Chatbot
Digital Platforms

Priorities Are All Wrong

The NITI Aayog's partners for education include the World Bank and the Piramal Foundation. Social Emotional Learning takes center stage in defining the NITI Aayog's vision for education.[7] The Piramal Foundation signed a MOU with Emory University in Georgia, USA to introduce a K-12 SEL program to distribute the curriculum to five thousand government schools with five lakh children across Gujarat, Jharkhand, Jammu and Kashmir, Maharashtra, and Rajasthan, over two years.[8]

India has committed to achieving the SDGs by 2030. The NITI Aayog is tasked with aligning Central Government-sponsored schemes to the SDGs. The Ministry of Statistics and Programme Implementation (MoSPI) has devised a National Indicator Framework to streamline the monitoring of these objectives at the national level.[9] India's National Education Policy 2020 and the National Curriculum Framework are aligned with the UN's SDGs, but the Right to Education Act 2009 allows minority institutions to opt out of CSE/SEL topics while Hindu institutions cannot.

The NITI Aayog's dashboard on India's performance on SDGs states that target 4.7.1 must ensure that by 2030, 'all learners acquire the knowledge and skills needed to promote sustainable development… human rights, gender equality, global citizenship'. *While these topics are tracked annually, the indicator that measures the literacy rate of fifteen to twenty-four years is tracked only once in ten years.*[10] As a result, Indian children are advancing quite well in areas like human rights and global citizenship while literacy and math skills are deteriorating.[11] The following figure shows the downward trend in subjects that are vital for the success of individuals and the country.

By the eighth grade, only about a third of Indian children can read, and only about a quarter can do basic math. And yet, NITI Aayog obeys the globalist agenda by maintaining a colorful dashboard aligning our children's education to the SDGs 2030 agenda. Target 4.c ensures that teachers are trained in this agenda through international cooperation for teacher training to ensure Indian teachers understand Woke principles.

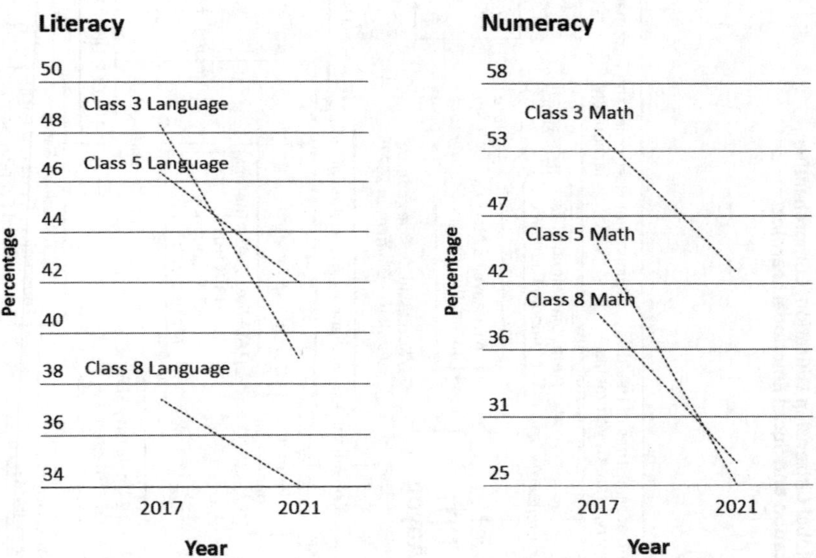

Percentage of students in grades 3, 5, and 8 achieving at least a minimum proficiency level in terms of nationally defined learning outcomes to be attained by pupils at the end of each of the above grades.

Data from: NITI Aayog's SUSTAINABLE DEVELOPMENT GOALS NATIONAL INDICATOR FRAMEWORK, PROGRESS REPORT 2023

As explained in previous chapters, many Indian teachers have taken issue with CSE and SEL programs. To circumvent this, NITI Aayog has funded two tech startups to do the dirty job of sexualizing Indian children as per the SDGs obligations.

The following figure shows NITI Aayog as the vehicle for NGOs to lobby the government; its role to ensure India complies with the UN and other international institutions, and in making education policy and legislative recommendations.

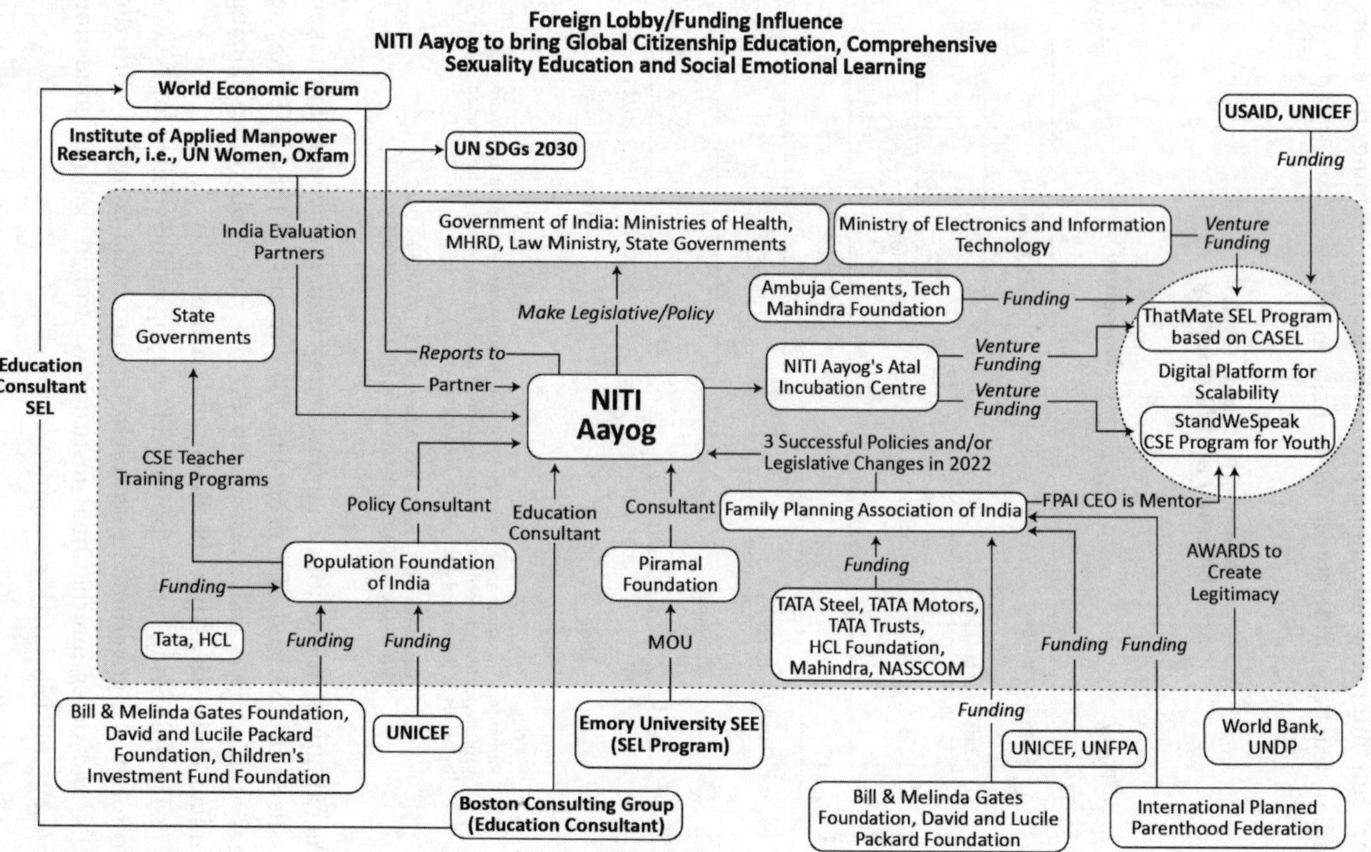
Foreign Lobby/Funding Influence
NITI Aayog to bring Global Citizenship Education, Comprehensive Sexuality Education and Social Emotional Learning
World Economic Forum
Institute of Applied Manpower Research, i.e., UN Women, Oxfam
UN SDGs 2030
USAID, UNICEF
Funding
India Evaluation Partners
Government of India: Ministries of Health, MHRD, Law Ministry, State Governments
Ministry of Electronics and Information Technology
Venture Funding
State Governments
Make Legislative/Policy
Ambuja Cements, Tech Mahindra Foundation
Funding
ThatMate SEL Program based on CASEL
Digital Platform for Scalability
StandWeSpeak CSE Program for Youth
Reports to
Partner
NITI Aayog
NITI Aayog's Atal Incubation Centre
Venture Funding
Venture Funding
Education Consultant SEL
CSE Teacher Training Programs
3 Successful Policies and/or Legislative Changes in 2022
Policy Consultant
Education Consultant
Consultant
Family Planning Association of India
FPAI CEO is Mentor
AWARDS to Create Legitimacy
Population Foundation of India
Funding
Piramal Foundation
Funding
TATA Steel, TATA Motors, TATA Trusts, HCL Foundation, Mahindra, NASSCOM
Tata, HCL
Funding
Funding
MOU
Funding
Funding
Bill & Melinda Gates Foundation, David and Lucile Packard Foundation, Children's Investment Fund Foundation
UNICEF
Emory University SEE (SEL Program)
Funding
UNICEF, UNFPA
World Bank, UNDP
Boston Consulting Group (Education Consultant)
Bill & Melinda Gates Foundation, David and Lucile Packard Foundation
International Planned Parenthood Federation

Failure To Do Due Diligence

India has much to learn from the USA's integration of Woke ideology in the form of Critical Race Theory and Comprehensive Sexuality Education across its institutions over the past decade. Unfortunately, NITI Aayog and others neither read the studies on American failures of Woke education nor use discrimination in deciding what is best for the youth of India. Simply duplicating the West without any understanding seems to be a bureaucrat's path to becoming an 'honorary white'.

Based on the following American outcomes, India must consider whether it wants to import these problems:

1. Young people are rewarded and celebrated for Woke advocacy and for coming out as transgenders.
2. Nearly a third of Gen Z, (those born between the mid- and late-1990s to the early 2010s) identify as LGBTQIA+ and it is a common way to gain attention on social media.
3. In the name of gender affirmation, children are:
   a. Socially transitioned with alternate names.
   b. Given puberty blockers and cross-sex hormones.
   c. Given irreversible hysterectomy and bilateral mastectomy surgeries. These mutilated bodies are sterile for life.
4. Critical Race Theory has produced a demand for reparations for the oppressed by the oppressors. In 2024, Black social justice leaders demanded fifteen billion dollars from the Boston government.[12]
5. The global citizenship mandate in the UN's SDGs 2030 is creating 'sanctuary cities' where illegal migrants are welcomed, overwhelming the budgets and capacities of the cities to deliver basic facilities. As a result, crime and human trafficking have also increased. Looting and rioting are commonplace in big cities.
6. Misgendering is now considered hate speech with severe consequences such as losing one's job.

7. Youth are experiencing mental health issues at unprecedented levels.
8. Youth are reluctant to hold stable jobs, buy homes, marry, and raise children.
9. Due to this polarization, there is an unprecedented clash within American society resulting in a fear of civil war.

India is adopting these very practices in a frenzied manner. The UN and its NGO partners strongly advocate for CSE, offering plans through the ministries, NITI Aayog, and state governments. Careful and systematic due diligence should have been undertaken by NITI Aayog, the Ministry of Health and Family Welfare, and the Ministry of Human Resource Development.

Following are some obvious red flags based on the experience in the West that ought to have been investigated by Indian authorities before blindly importing Comprehensive Sexuality Education disguised as a part of worthy movements like sustainability and climate change:

1. <u>Gender Fluidity and Identity Issues</u>: CSE is explicit about its agenda of stressing gender fluidity. Its psychological impact includes increased anxiety and confusion about sexual orientation and identity.
2. <u>Sexual Promiscuity</u>: CSE encourages sexual rights, pleasure, and experimentation by adolescents, which can lead to risky behaviors and increased rates of Sexually Transmitted Diseases and teenage pregnancies.
3. <u>Cultural and Social Breakdown</u>: CSE has faced significant backlash in several Western countries, with parents and communities expressing concerns about the erosion of traditional values and the inappropriate and damaging exposure of young children to sexual content.

Given the way India is blindly following the Western globalists' mandates, it is highly likely that India could face even worse outcomes due to the lack of robust systems to manage the potential disruptions caused by CSE. Therefore, indoctrinating India's children risks societal stability, and this should be seen as a Breaking India Force.

11

A CRITIQUE OF INDIA'S WOKE EDUCATION

This chapter summarizes our critique of India's policies on education that mirror Western models both in content and distribution. Content is the information taught to impart skills, values, and narrative, including facts, concepts, procedures, and principles in various subject areas based on a worldview. Distribution refers to the way the educational content is delivered to students. This can include the methods of classroom instruction, online learning platforms, multimedia resources, and more. We have concerns with both: *what* is being taught in Indian schools, and *how* it is being delivered.

Previous chapters discussed at length how the current curriculum is detrimental for students, and how the use of technology and NGO funding to support the delivery of education is amplifying the problem.

Problems With Trends In Indian Education

The content on CSE, SEL, environmental education, global citizenship, etc., has become a billion-dollar industry supporting consultants and 'experts' who are richly rewarded by global mandates and standards. Our issues with the content and values being taught are summarized.

Global Citizenship Education

The Global Citizenship Education agenda is driving the globalists' worldview that subverts nation-states. This is being promoted in the name of 'multiculturalism', which seems wonderful at face value. However, the actual content is about teaching young people to reject national identity and embrace various new trendy identities. In effect, new 'global *jatis*' are being artificially constructed and pushed down everyone's throat. Pride in one's nation is now considered a narrow view of identity, while global citizenship is being sold as the broad, open-minded perspective.

This approach to multiculturalism is designed to teach students to erase any idea of national sovereignty that grounds an individual. This has the effect of undermining the weaker nations while protecting the powerful ones. The weaker nations would turn into colonies and be exploited even more. A world system that favors global citizenship and frowns upon patriotism would put the globalists in control of shaping a 'post-nation' World Order. We cannot hand over the protection of all nations to the World Economic Forum and globalists like Bill Gates. In the case of India, it is the job of the Kshatriyas to protect the *rashtra*.

Though it is a noble idea to advance humanity beyond the geographically defined boundaries of nation-states, the root problem must be addressed first: As long as the individual ego craves greed, the accumulation of objects, sensory delights, impressing others, etc., *people will continue to form groups to gain a collective advantage over other groups*. This is why group identities are competing for resources with each other. As long as this is the condition of the human ego, the need for collective group identities will remain.

By dissolving the national identities of weak nations, the vacuum of collective identity will be filled by other dominant and aggressive groups like radical Islam, evangelists, Wokeism, Chinese supremacy, Western globalists, and so forth.

To transcend beyond group identities like nations, the prerequisite is spiritual advancement: We must work on diluting the harmful qualities of the ego. Only then can humanity evolve beyond identity boundaries.

This requires a bottom-up approach at the level of individuals, not a top-down approach to replace one set of egotist identities with another. Unfortunately, globalists have no understanding or strategies to help humankind evolve beyond the limitations of individual selfish egos.

The new global citizenship movement has done nothing to spiritually upgrade egos at the grassroots. It has suddenly caused borders to become open, resulting in a migration crisis as we see in Europe and the USA. This has resulted in tensions between native and foreign populations, each driven by selfish egos in different identity camps.

Under these circumstances, the UN's Sustainable Development Goals are a brainwashing program causing cognitive dissonance in children and coercing them to become foot soldiers of the globalists. The UN calls this activism 'Civic Engagement' to enhance the popular appeal of activism among young people.

Misuse of Environmentalism

The Vedic tradition has the most profound respect for nature and the environment, seeing it as sacred, and not merely as the ego's 'property' to be protected for human interests. Nature has her own rights.

Unfortunately, the 'climate change' industry today has become a catchphrase for all sorts of social justice. More than respecting the environment itself, the climate change movement has become an umbrella to promote corporate ESG, DEI, the trans movement, sex education, and other fearmongering in the education system. This has turned it into a cult-like movement that identifies many kinds of victims and conflates all kinds of social problems with climate change. The discourse includes topics like the effect of the climate crisis on the transgender community or some minorities.[1]

The climate change agenda is being used to instill fear to control people. Children are being traumatized by the fear of an impending apocalypse making them extremely anxious about their future.

Social Emotional Learning

Social Emotional Learning programs are Trojan horses being used to develop a Marxist consciousness that sees the abuse of power in every situation, relationship, structure, and institution. In *Snakes in the Ganga*, we show that they use pedagogy to produce equity (i.e. equality of outcome) rather than equality of opportunities. We reject this form of SEL because it is an untested and risky approach to mental health intervention that is being imposed regardless of whether a given student needs it or not.

Earlier chapters showed that the Western model of SEL is a product of Theosophy, a digested and distorted knowledge system initially created from dharmic traditions. We discussed that the digestion of yoga, meditation, and Vedanta into Theosophy was the initial foundation of SEL. Although the early Theosophists were not Woke, they pioneered this idea of bringing a dharma-friendly vocabulary to the West but distorted the content and framework.

Later, the Woke critical pedagogy assimilated Theosophy resulting in a second digestion of these ideas into what is called 'transformative' SEL. With these digestions of dharma into theosophy,

- Dharmic values of universalism have been replaced by Marxist notions of equity.
- Mutual respect for diverse cultures and religious expressions was a cornerstone of dharmic traditions. However, respect for a variegated universe has vanished, and instead, Cancel Culture promotes intolerance for diversity of thought.
- Psychology and behavioral science are now used to control and manipulate instead of using dharmic practices for internal growth.
- SEL has become a cult-like religion that mandates conformity, which is the antithesis of dharma.

We saw that CASEL and other SEL programs have adapted some dharmic methods for shaping healthy minds and turned them into techniques to brainwash children with Wokeism. The influences of dharma are clear, but the idea of samskaras has been adapted into what they call the 'dispositions' of students associated with skills. CASEL refers to the negative samskaras in its programs as 'durable skills' because SEL skills 'remain evergreen, essential for youth to thrive in adulthood, both in their personal lives and the labor market'.[2]

The renaming of SEL as 'durable skills' may be due to the backlash from American parents who are fighting SEL. SEL is therefore being marketed as durable skills 'which are aligned under four groups—empowering, connecting, impacting, and thriving—and include SEL skills such as self-awareness, the ability to communicate, showing empathy and respect, and resilience'.[3] The importance of a student's academic competency gets lost in this word salad of attractive terms.

By the end of K-12 education, brainwashing with negative samskaras transforms children from within. These programs are replacing the focus on reading and mathematics as evidenced by the poor performance in basic literacy and numeracy assessments.

Instead of following the Vedic system of samskaras to rebuild Bharat, India is adopting this large-scale Western brainwashing system that is educating a whole new Breaking India generation. While China prepares its students for excellence, India's adoption of American Woke education is crippling an already struggling education system that has neglected India's rich civilizational resources. This is further perpetuating the colonized mindset.

Neglecting Gifted Children

Most major intellectual breakthroughs in history have been initiated by a small number of ultra-gifted pioneers. India needs to focus on merit to foster a generation of leaders, scientists, and thinkers who can address the complex challenges of the future. However, India's obsessive focus on equity has neglected the value of its gifted students. This is why many of them run away to foreign countries where their advancement is easier because of meritocracy.

These gifted students possess the potential to become innovators and pathbreakers who should be driving future progress and development. By not providing adequate resources, support, and specialized programs tailored to their advanced abilities, the country risks stifling their potential, which will hinder India's ability to compete globally.

Comprehensive Sexuality Education and Social Emotional Learning

The Vedic system does not oppose desires but aligns them with the cosmic processes, the goal being to achieve *freedom from* desires. Desires are channeled to gradually transform the person to rise above the body, senses, and ego, constantly evolving through the social structures of varna and ashrama.

Dharmic traditions believe that the senses should not drive a person. On the contrary, the person must be in control of them and should drive the sense organs to achieve his *purusharthas* or goals. Control of the sense organs, known as *indriya nigraha*, has been a cornerstone of Vedic Mind Sciences like yoga. The *brahmacharya* ashrama teaches students to delay gratification and not be overcome by the fickleness of sense organs seeking pleasures. The CSE programs, on the other hand, goad children to pursue sexual desires and masturbation, claiming them to be fundamental 'rights'.

Practices like conscious witnessing and other meditation practices are designed to quieten and control the mind. The idea is to get freedom from the ego's conditioning that creates social injustices in the first place.

On the other hand, the Western goal of a corrupted ego being mobilized to fight injustice is counterproductive. These Woke programs are dedicated to expanding the lower realms of human experience by amplifying animal instincts and further entangling the individual in bondage rather than genuinely liberating them.

Over-Sexualization of Children

American childhood education's emphasis is becoming heavily oriented toward the active pursuit of sexual desires and pleasure, empowerment, and rights. These are ill-suited for India and potentially ill-suited for the world at large. We remind the reader that the Vedic ecosystem has a robust means and place for the fulfillment of desires, as explained earlier.

Our critique has been that Western education has an explicit goal to instill negative samskaras that teach children certain attitudes about sexuality and sexual desires while advocating the sexual 'rights' of the child to fulfill those desires. Besides the negative impact of over-sexualizing at an early age, this focus steals time away from instilling positive samskaras and important building blocks such as literacy and numeracy.

We have shown that many international agencies funded by billionaires have successfully implemented an agenda to sexualize children, normalize abortions, and encourage sexual desires—all in the name of children's right to sexuality. Under the guise of promoting inclusivity, children are indoctrinated into the trans agenda, and socially and/or medically transitioned oftentimes unbeknownst to parents. Known as 'gender-affirming care', this can lead to a loss of sexual function in adult life and produce adverse psychological consequences.

We showed that society is becoming de-sensitized to the sexualization of children, and in some cases, pedophilia too is being normalized. Children have been traditionally protected by certain laws precisely because of their inability to safely consent to sex, and yet these agencies and NGOs advocate giving children the right to consent to sexual activity.

As a result, young people at an early age are

- discouraged from marriage by portraying it as something binding.
- educated that sexual pleasure is a 'right', hence, liberating.

- encouraged to resort to abortions as an easy fix for sexual promiscuity.
- brainwashed into thinking that gender is a social construct, and hence, they can easily change their gender on a whim.
- told to avoid parental involvement in their sexual choices.

For example, we discussed that the IPPF's HIV guideline promoted by the United Nations advises youth infected with HIV that they may keep their HIV positivity secret from their sexual partner. Such ideas are systematically introduced and drilled in from very early ages.

The Vedic View of Transgenderism

At the outset, we point out that dharmic societies have traditionally not persecuted the trans community:

> Hundreds of years ago, under traditional Hindu culture, hijras enjoyed a certain degree of respect. But Victorian England changed that. When the British colonized India in the mid-19th century, they brought a strict sense of judgment to sexual mores, criminalizing "carnal intercourse against the order of nature." That was the beginning, scholars say, of a mainstream discomfort in India with homosexuality, transgender people and hijras.[4]

The Vedic view is to be aligned with the cosmic yajna. Diversity in all its forms and capabilities is the fabric of creation. Cosmic principles have produced a certain physical and mental body for everyone, human and nonhuman. To tamper with it using synthetic hormones or gender reassignment surgeries go against the yajna of alignment with the cosmos; it is an act of 'fixing' the cosmos by overriding its biological processes.

Every individual must enact using the cards they are dealt with as a result of past karma, and Vedic traditions help everyone evolve and reach higher goals. A healthy education system must help every kind of individual cope with and transcend their bodily conditioning.

Given this, do we have the right to re-engineer a person born in one sex, to another sex? Should we provide systematic brainwashing and medical interventions that mutilate the body, program the mind, and manipulate the emotions?

SEL and CSE operate against nature's biological processes, hence, they are anti-yajna. They will result in a generation of individuals turned into zombies controlled by technology Apps operated by globalists.

Instead of samskaras and yajnas to guide them toward the evolution of higher consciousness, these educational philosophies are recklessly pushing them into bondage. The dharmic tradition guides individuals from *samsara* (life within the confines of mental causation) to liberation from mental causation, whereas Western models of education will lead individuals into greater bondage and suffering on a scale never witnessed before.

Problems with Education Delivery

Two means are being used today to deliver education. One is scaling up with the use of technological platforms, online learning, and digital content. These delivery systems are being funded by international NGOs, UN agencies, and Corporate Social Responsibility resources. In achieving this scale-up, they bypass parents and dilute the role of traditional teachers.

Another distribution strategy discussed throughout the book is by using nice-sounding but deceptive vocabulary. This is a 'bait-and-switch' strategy. A friendly vocabulary that seemingly embraces universal values is deployed as a ploy to ensure the buy-in from parents. It uses wonderful terms like global citizenship, Social Emotional Learning, equity, civic engagement (for activism), and even democracy (for equity). Few parents understand the real implications and hence go with the flow of popular opinion.

The Competency-Based Education model sounds like an attractive student-centered model. On the surface, it resembles the Indian gurukulam system as a customized student-centric approach.

No wonder that CBE has become the rage in Indian education circles. However, CBE is entirely different in its goals, implementation, content, and intention.

The Indian government's much-touted National Education Policy 2020 introduced Competency-Based or skill-based learning as a student-centered approach, moving away from rote memorization and traditional exams. In 2024, Dharmendra Pradhan, the Union minister of education said that one of his educational priorities and the thrust of NEP is 'prioritizing a culture of competency-based education'.[5] This has incorporated the CBE assessment approach and changed the exam format with multiple-choice questions replacing long-form questions. However, long-form answers are a good way to assess the depth of understanding and demonstrate the ability to formulate arguments backed by reasoning. It is difficult for a student to hide his superficial understanding in this kind of assessment.

At first glance, the Competency-Based Education model seems benign, even making sense for the education of the masses because its self-paced learning seems ideal from a student's standpoint. However, it focuses primarily on the underperforming and struggling students and slows down the gifted ones. While undoubtedly, we must provide equal access to learning for India's poor, it is equally important to nurture those children with extraordinary talent and aptitude, as they have the potential to effect intellectual breakthroughs.

Adaptive Testing

The Scholastic Achievement Test (SAT) in the USA was once considered the barometer for aptitude and college readiness of high school students. The exam is now moving to a digital platform with a new 'multi-stage adaptive' approach to testing. Based on the student's performance on an initial module of questions, the exam will dynamically adapt the next batch of questions, increasing or decreasing the difficulty of the questions. While adaptive testing should quickly find each student's scoring level more efficiently and quickly, many worry that it is a ploy to achieve equity in student achievement by punishing the high-performing students. When questions are crafted by changing the level of difficulty based on student ability, it means that every student will not take the same test, making the test subjective. Standards are also being diluted by the permissibility of calculators throughout the test, the shortening of reading comprehension passages, and the simplification of the overall test structure.[6] At this rate, students might soon be allowed to use ChatGPT to answer questions. Educators might even wonder whether education is necessary given that a person can always get answers from generative AI.

Competency-Based Education is a Pipeline Feeding Anti-meritocracy, ESG, DEI, and Social Credit

Competency-Based Education is an educational approach where students advance based on their ability to demonstrate mastery of specific skills or competencies, rather than the traditional standardized content-based education that requires a student to spend specific amounts of time on certain topics.

CBE uses constant assessments to ensure that students do not fall through the cracks because it promptly addresses the accumulation of skill deficits. It is supposed to personalize the learning, giving the student flexibility to work at one's own pace, instead of a standardized pace for all. Its theoretical goal is to ensure that students acquire the essential knowledge, skills, and abilities necessary to gain mastery of the subject.

All this sounds perfect, but in reality, CBE is also about behavior manipulation towards specific motivations, attitudes, self-reflection, and self-perceptions of the student. The hidden problem is that the ultra-leftist cabal has defined the ideologies based on which the goals are established.

For instance, unlike the gurukulams' goal to emphasize excellence and inspire each student to achieve the best, CBE is designed to achieve education *equity* at the expense of the gifted children who are held back. The CBE assessment is more like a pass/fail measure, and hence, meritocracy and ranking are avoided to achieve equity or equal outcomes. Moreover, the focus on project work, communication, and group dynamics, while all important skills, are having the effect of blurring the individual's mastery of the subject that traditional exams measure.

In the USA, the curriculum in CBE programs incorporates SEL activities such as collaborative projects, group discussions, and conflict resolution training. Personalized learning in CBE often means personalized SEL goals. Students define SEL objectives that are tailored to their individual needs and contexts.

Social Emotional Learning is also a vehicle to sneak in Woke criteria of competencies—like global citizenship, SEL, CSE, and environmental competencies. Woke educators are systematizing victimhood and emphasizing identity politics by establishing what is called Trauma Informed Education (TIE).[7]

Trauma Informed Education is the latest buzzword added to the education framework. It essentially means that kids with Adverse Childhood Experiences or ACE need special consideration because bias can be explicit, implicit, and systematic. And micro aggressions and oppressed identities (i.e. race, caste, fatness, gender, LGBTQIA+, etc.) need special protection from 'oppressors'.[8] The ACE scoring system quantifies childhood trauma into a number and assigns ACE scores to students. When a student with a high ACE score ignores boundaries and fails to fulfill academic responsibilities, they do not face the same disciplinary actions as regular students.

Such 'Woke competencies' are incorporated in the name of building positive attitudes of students towards learning. Most CBE frameworks in the USA have eroded academic rigor by bringing competencies alongside academic skills. Student data is collected constantly for making assessments, turning this into a social credit system of education. SEL competencies are assessed using a variety of methods such as self-assessments, peer reviews, teacher observations, and reflective activities.

While we advocate providing every poor and marginalized child with the same opportunities available to the privileged, we also believe that society must nurture its talents to strive for excellence, because that produces breakthroughs for the benefit of society. As we well know, some students will certainly out-perform simply because they are by nature, more gifted. Variation in performance also arises based on the student's effort, aptitude, interest level, and attitude toward a given subject matter at hand. However, the architects of CBE downplay the importance of a 'gifted' or 'exceptionally talented' student.

Thus, CBE aims to provide education to produce equal outcomes, and this is possible only by lowering the performance of gifted students. Equity is being achieved by bringing everyone down for the sake of equalizing. The pass/fail assessments of CBE remove meritocracy-based ranking, providing no way to identify extraordinarily skilled students. While CBE can help each student achieve their personal best, it cannot completely equalize innate differences in ability and aptitude.

In summary,

1. CBE does not assess a student's comprehensive understanding of the subject matter. Hence, it cannot identify gifted students and nurture them to their maximum potential. Essentially, it betrays gifted children.
2. CBE is a tool designed for equity, designed to achieve equal outcomes in education by rigging the system.
3. The rigging is done by classifying certain communities as 'oppressed' and flattening the outcomes for all, and by incorporating other 'competencies' such as ACE at the expense of academic competencies. Although CBE is sometimes promoted to raise academic competencies initially, often the classic 'bait-and-switch strategy is employed to switch' to non-academic competencies.
4. CBE's thrust is designed to make SEL competencies the major focus of education.

Unfortunately, India has blindly adopted the American educational philosophy without evaluating the effects of these models implemented within American schools. Due to this lack of due diligence on the part of India's education policymakers, it has not understood the failure of American liberal arts programs, DEI policies, SEL, and CSE curricula. It has not recognized the anti-meritocracy political ideology that is destroying education.

Competency-Based Education in the USA is also using SEL as a pipeline for feeding into the corrupt college admissions process and thereafter for social justice activism. It is slowly turning into a social credit system for children and youth, who will effortlessly adapt by agreeing and complying with competencies of global citizenship, environmentalism, equity, and SEL. The pipeline is designed to give students credit for compliance with ESGs of the corporates, which are also based on DEI and environmentalism rather than technological and other innovations that benefit society.

It is also worth noting that these competencies and ESG criteria can be changed overnight by the elites, rendering earned credits valueless as people scramble to earn new credits based on the new criteria of a new SEL or ESG. Such a system becomes a totalitarian tool to control people through non-merit-based criteria, raising questions on freedom, fundamental rights, and liberty. Social exclusion, limited mobility, and unplugging from the system await those who do not comply.

Parents Replaced by Philanthropists, the State, Big Tech

In the highly polarized landscape, parents in the USA want to influence the values taught to their children. However, NGOs play a crucial role in advancing Competency-Based Education in school boards by focusing on the values and competencies that they consider essential. While NGOs can play a supportive role in the educational ecosystem, entrusting them with the primary responsibility of teaching values is often driven by political or ideological biases that might not align with the values parents wish to impart to their children.

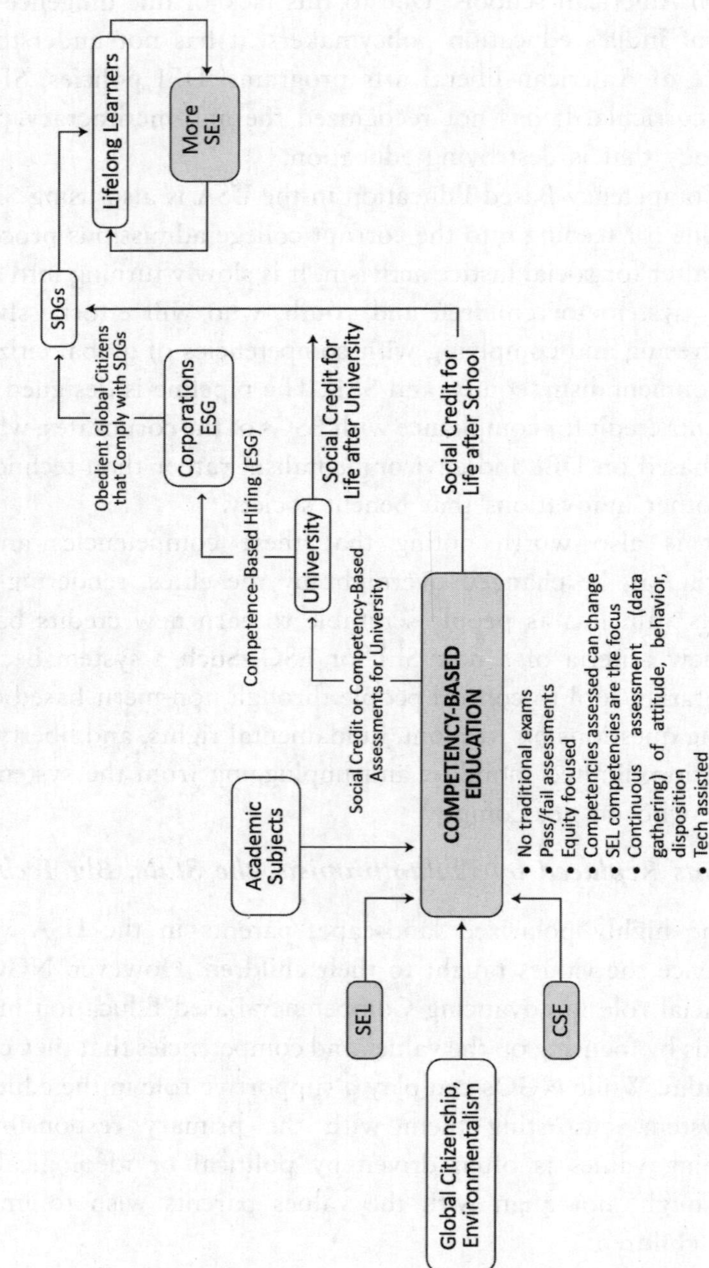
Prepping the Next Generation for
Sustainable Development Goals
Global Citizenship, Environmentalism
SEL
CSE
Academic Subjects
COMPETENCY-BASED EDUCATION
• No traditional exams
• Pass/fail assessments
• Equity focused
• Competencies assessed can change
• SEL competencies are the focus
• Continuous assessment (data gathering) of attitude, behavior, disposition
• Tech assisted
Social Credit or Competency-Based Assessments for University
University
Competence-Based Hiring (ESG)
Corporations ESG
Obedient Global Citizens that Comply with SDGs
SDGs
Lifelong Learners
More SEL
Social Credit for Life after University
Social Credit for Life after School

The Bill & Melinda Gates Foundation is a major funder of organizations like KnowledgeWorks and Battelle for Kids that are in the business of working with state governments in the USA to implement CBE systems.[9] KnowledgeWorks provides a comprehensive framework and customized technical solutions for CBE.[10] According to this enterprise, traditional forms of exams and grading are considered inherently racist and oppressive and need to be replaced: 'personalized, competency-based learning is ideally suited to become tracking's replacement infrastructure and thereby function as an equity and anti-racist catalyst'.[11]

KnowledgeWorks does not believe in meritocracy:

> Gifted and Talented Education (GATE), Talented and Gifted (TAG), Career and Technical Education (CTE), Advanced Placement (AP), International Baccalaureate (IB), honors, ... These are just some of the names we invent to separate students based on perceived ability. We say perceived ability because the criteria used to determine that ability (typically: teacher selection and standardized tests) are lacking in scientific merit and frequently biased. And yet the practice endures.[12]

The bait-and-switch strategy is alarmingly common in educational models hiding their Marxist frameworks. Many educational frameworks promise one thing to gain initial support, only to shift their mission and goals once they have secured the buy-in.

Moreover, educational models often employ misleading jargon, using terms that have a different meaning than what is assumed by a layman. This deceptive language combined with a colonized mindset can be disastrous in India, where due diligence is shallow. Indian policymakers ought to be nurturing their own traditions' experts instead of depending on NGOs and management consultants for key policy issues of national interest.

Here are a few examples of terms that are misused in the CBE framework:

- Competency starts as academic competency but then swiftly switches to SEL competencies. However, these competencies and evaluations are defined by SDGs and the globalists' agenda which includes social, emotional, and behavioral dimensions aimed at promoting sustainability, inclusiveness, equity, and global citizenship.
- Lifelong learning means that SEL skills must be constantly upgraded to maintain one's social credit scores, which can be changed by the globalists.
- Accountability is used as an excuse to collect all kinds of data on children who are to be surveyed continuously. This is a privacy issue. The data is used to model their psychological behavior and control them using sophisticated behavioral management algorithms.
- Meaningful assessment is a phrase used to dumb down the academic component of CBE. Conventional testing using problems and long-form questions are to be replaced by project-based or work-based learning. This evaluates relative progress rather than objective progress.[13] The issue is who decides what is 'meaningful' and how the assessments are conducted.

India Jumping on the American Bandwagon

Many organizations in India are jumping onto the CBE bandwagon. Simple Education Foundation (SEF) is a Delhi-based NGO that works closely with governments (Delhi, Uttarakhand, Punjab, Jammu & Kashmir), and SCERTs. Funded by BCG, WIPRO foundation, Max Foundation, and foreign FCRA donors,[14] it also works with many partners like Peoples Archive of Rural India (PARI), founded by Neville Roy Singham who is known for his connections with the Chinese Communist Party, to bring in content. The ownership and use of student data has been left ambiguous.

The Simple Education Foundation is working to implement CBE in government schools and touts the benefits of social and emotional skills without providing evidence. Partnering with Teach For India, they have begun to roll out CBE modules in several states.[15] ACER India[16] is another NGO that has been training teachers on Competency-Based Education for the Delhi and Punjab school systems.[17]

The state boards and the NCERT should not hand over teacher training and content creation to NGOs that are mainly funded by foreign entities. It is common to see NGOs doing the work of the government (content creation, training, and assessment) in schools across India.

India's Ministry of Education has begun to roll out CBE-based assessments across various states[18.] It is not uncommon to see new announcements by the MHRD about CBE in everything from medical education to the National Skill Training Institute for Women.[19] Even the Institute of Chartered Accountants of India has released a CBE called the New Scheme of Education and Training.[20]

Despite several advantages to CBE, it opens the floodgates to lowering standards in the name of equity and teaching harmful competencies that brainwash children.

PART 3

LEARNING FROM INDIA'S PAST EDUCATION SYSTEM

12

THE VEDIC PHILOSOPHY OF EDUCATION

Who is Being Educated?

Before discussing our approach to education, we must pose the pertinent question: *Who* is the individual being educated? An educational system must be designed based on a clear understanding of the student as an individual self, his/her purpose in life, and how the individual participates in society. It is individual selves that experience the world, and the goal of education should be to help optimize the aspirations of individuals.

The desired outcomes of education are partly internal to the individual, for which we must understand the inner psychological domain; and partly external, for which it is mandatory to understand the individual's relationships with society, nature, and the cosmos at large. A theory of the individual self and society is an important starting point.

However, there are multiple worldviews with disparate theories. Therefore, we first need to select a clear framework of the individual self and the collective self, their inter-relationships, and their goals. From that foundation, we can strategize the goals of an education system and develop the criteria for evaluating it.

Our position is built on the Vedic worldview, a worldview that is profound, comprehensive, ancient, yet futuristic. Most importantly, the Vedic worldview is constantly renewed being flexible with time, place, and the individual's dispositions.

We forewarn the reader of the glaring problem with India's imported education system: It does not begin with a discussion on the nature of *who* is to be educated and what the purpose of life is. Therefore, Indian educators have unconsciously imported an education system built on Western cosmology and its notion of the ego, its relationship with society, and its purpose.

As a result, the Western model of education increases the conditioning of the ego with more desires, aversions, selfishness, avarice, fear, various harmful habits, and addictions. Therefore, it is no surprise that many Indians express discontent with the outcomes that stem from these foreign models.

The Vedic worldview posits that Ultimate Reality comprises two realms: paramarthika and vyavaharika. And these realms are integrally unified and not separate.

- Vyavaharika comprises the entire cosmos that we can know through our senses, and this corresponds to the empirical realm as understood by conventional science.
- Paramarthika is the transcendent realm that is beyond our senses and hence, beyond scientific empiricism. Its existence is denied by materialism, but some version of it is found in all spiritual faiths.

In the Vedic system, vyavaharika is dependent on paramarthika, but the converse is not true: paramarthika is independent of vyavaharika and not influenced by it.

A fundamental tenet is that every human has the potential to transcend beyond the limits of vyavaharika and this is the ultimate purpose of human life. Vyavaharika is the realm in which we presently exist, and in which this discussion is taking place.

Vyavaharika, though not the Ultimate Reality, is the mental bubble in which the unenlightened person spends his entire life, trapped in its hierarchies, rules, duties, and responsibilities. The enlightened person lives in the paramarthika realm where these structures blur or disappear altogether. An audacious claim of this system is that every individual has the innate potential to achieve a cognitive shift from vyavaharika to paramarthika while living in this body. In other words, one can achieve a state of enlightenment in the human body—as distinct from having to die and then go to some place like heaven to experience a higher realm of existence.

The Vedic tradition offers profound and detailed explanations of the ego as the central character driving the individual's life. This individual ego is the entity that experiences the world and acts in it. All Indian traditions have evolved from this framework in which the individual ego is the central entity to be understood, and its life must be managed according to this understanding.

The ego is the nexus of experiencing the world through the body. The body is a complex entity with physical, mental, and spiritual layers fed by the senses, and the mind-intellect that makes the choices. Its organs are the means to perform its actions. This mental-physical complex is heavily conditioned as a byproduct of its prior choices (i.e. karma), and this conditioning influences its cognition and ability to make choices. Many practices, including chanting, rituals, yoga, pranayama, and meditation are recommended to nurture and cultivate the body-mind-sense complex by deconditioning the ego.

The eventual goal of all Indian spiritual traditions is to liberate the self from this condition, which amounts to freedom from the ego. Ancient rishis discovered a multitude of paths and processes that can lead us toward 'freedom from' compulsions and programmed behavior. (Later in this chapter we will elaborate on the important principle known as 'freedom from'.) This ultimate liberation is called *moksha* or nirvana. However, there is a long journey for the ego before the self attains such liberation, and the purpose of a dharmic lifestyle is to embark on such a journey and become closer to eventual liberation.

Vedic First Principles

Vedic cosmology is a vast subject that requires a lifetime of study to understand in depth. For the ease of the reader, we will summarize the fundamental concepts from which the rest of our thinking about education follows.

The following elements, though far from being a comprehensive discussion of Vedic metaphysics, suffice as the first principles needed for our discussion on the philosophy of education.

- The Vedas refer to *rtam* as the eternal deep structures and patterns that become manifest as the entire cosmos. These patterns show the cosmos in perpetual dynamic equilibrium with its multiple parts and levels interacting in complex ways.
- As part of this dynamic cosmic equilibrium, humans must perform their role; this human effort is called yajna. There are several levels of yajna: managing one's well-being, serving one's family including ancestors, and serving humanity, nature, and deities (cosmic intelligences).
- Karma is a system of causation that operates the cosmos. It includes all the causation at the material level known to physics, which we call the 'laws of nature'. However, the theory of karma goes beyond the physics of the material level and includes agencies that are outside the scope of physics such as deities, for instance. Furthermore, it also includes effects called *samskaras* which are seeds that manifest *later*.
- Human pursuits are referred to as the *purusharthas*, and these have been organized into the categories of *artha* (material prosperity), *kama* (desires), dharma (responsibilities as part of one's yajna), and moksha (final liberation from the limits of causation).
- Each person is free to formulate his/her portfolio of pursuits by mixing and matching these goals. This is called one's *sva*-dharma, a dharma that is tailored to an individual. However, to be aligned with the cosmos and perform one's

yajna, the Vedic system recommends having a sva-dharma in which artha and kama are pursued within the framework of dharma, and not disconnected from it.

- The social system known as varna-ashrama was developed to optimize individual and collective pursuits in keeping with the above principles. It is designed to help individuals by recommending many kinds of lifestyles suitable for the diverse spectrum of egos, yet in harmony with the cosmos.

In the following pages, we briefly explain these concepts and then apply them to argue our philosophy of education.

Rtam

Rtam refers to the patterns residing in the cosmic womb, as the potentials from where the cosmos emanates and becomes all the phenomena we call time, space, causation, and matter, all the *devatas* (gods) and living creatures, and in fact, all reality. The universe is the expression of rtam, the latent patterns whereby the unmanifest cosmos becomes manifested. *Rtam is the grammar of the cosmos.*

Rtam is not separate from the creation that emerges from it. The relationship between rtam and creation is unlike the relationship between an object and its design because the design stays outside the object itself, whereas rtam enters and pervades the cosmos at every level and in every component. So, the blueprint enters every particle, every moment, every law of causation, and every abstract concept and principle.

The universe functions in keeping with rtam at every level. All the domains of knowledge—including physics, biology, mathematics, astronomy, arts, medicine, etc., are based on rtam as the underlying principle that gets expressed in many ways.

To understand how rtam is encoded within each aspect and part of the cosmos, one may use the analogy of DNA: The DNA of a creature is encoded in every cell of the body, even though each organ is very different from the other. Similarly, the same rtam manifests as all the diversity in the cosmos. The rtam in the galaxy is the same rtam in a flower, in a human, and in every electron.

The Vedic understanding of diversity is based on this principle of rtam: There is harmony across such diverse entities in the cosmos precisely because all the forces and processes comprising the cosmos are regulated, ordered, and harmonized by rtam. This is like saying that all organs of a healthy body function in harmony because the same DNA regulates them and yet there is diversity across different types of tissues and processes in the body.

This fundamental unity is captured by the Sanskrit word *purna*, which has a deep meaning in dharma. It is often interpreted as 'completeness' or 'infinity'. One of the greatest sages of all times, Sri Aurobindo translates it as 'integral'.

Rtam manifests as cyclic cosmic processes. The universe comes into being and eventually passes away, reverting to an unmanifest state, then lies dormant until it emerges again at the commencement of another cycle. This pattern is as natural as inhalation and exhalation and is repeated throughout eternity. Everything—all matter, spirit, humanity, down to the tiniest particle, every moment in time, and every unit of space – is ever-changing.

The Human Condition: 'Freedom To' and 'Freedom From'

The idea of freedom in the Vedic system is radically different from the idea of freedom in the Western worldview. The book, *Being Different: An Indian Challenge to Western Universalism* by Rajiv Malhotra, describes the former as 'freedom from' and the latter as 'freedom to'. We will now explain these different approaches to freedom.

Most humans are heavily controlled by things external to them. They are like blind bats sending sonar signals and using the echoes to determine their location in space. They send signals to other people and use their responses as reference points to define themselves, their identity, trajectory, values, and purpose. This habit is a lifelong system of mental and psychological training by external forces leading to the voluntary slavery of external people, places, and things.

This is a form of social portfolio management. The typical individual has a dynamic portfolio comprising his/her relationships with external entities; each of these relationships has a certain valuation (weightage) assigned at a given point in time. The value assigned to each entity changes according to the latest circumstances. Hence, the portfolio consists of many moving parts, and one's entire life is spent trying to optimize this portfolio of relationships.

The Buddha's Second Noble Truth declares that it is impossible to achieve a resilient (endurable) state of blissful equilibrium by pursuing this approach. In fact, it declares this as the cause of all *dukkha* (suffering, pain, sorrow, distress, anxiety, grief, and misery). People need psychological equilibrium/resilience which they hope to achieve through clever portfolio management as discussed above. However, such a pursuit is futile and merely leads to further addictive behavior. The portfolio of external dependencies is always fragile, and this is the cause of the psychological state of dukkha.

Most people are trapped in this web and define their goals in terms of maximizing their abilities to take actions—like the ability to buy material things, travel, speak their mind, and participate in whatever the ego desires. This is the pursuit of 'freedom to' in which the criterion for valuing something is based on how it contributes to one's power and capacity 'to' perform. A person with greater freedom to do such things is considered more successful than one with less ability. However, this pursuit is a slavery that cannot succeed in its goal because of the fragile nature of any temporary success it accomplishes and its dependence on relationships with external entities that are always changing.

True freedom is entirely different. It is the 'freedom from' this condition of dukkha. Freedom 'from' is an internal and not an external state. It is a state without the compulsions, habits, and conditioning that compel one to perform externally. A person lacking this freedom 'from' is living a programmed life chasing the social rat race in competition with all the other rats. The deluded ego is perpetually fighting its misery by trying to outrun the misery. The entire life of chasing 'freedom to' is like that of an addict chasing one temporary relief after another, ultimately getting exhausted and ending up in crisis.

There is a plethora of proven spiritual practices that gradually lead one to become less concerned about other people's approval—like being invited to a gathering or not, getting complimented or not, and so forth. This does not mean one should become anti-social or replace attachment with revulsion. Rather, it means a posture of freedom with respect to others, while seeing them with love and harmony.

Only after one has attained freedom from all these games being played by the ego can one be truly free 'to' enjoy external actions and relationships. In other words, a person's 'freedom to' is a fake sense of freedom because it is bondage to his conditioned ego chasing endless and unachievable pursuits. And upon attaining a state of 'freedom from' this bondage, one enjoys a life of *ananda*/bliss.

Upon enjoying 'freedom from', one can engage in an active external lifestyle including the pursuit of kama and artha without being in bondage. The Vedic system's goal is to help every individual attain this state of 'freedom'. This includes the freedom to enjoy all kinds of desires, including sexual desires.

The Vedic path out of this miserable condition is by re-aligning the ego and this is where yajna comes in. Western models are centered around 'freedom to', with new social justice movements and causes emerging continually to satisfy the ego.

Yajna

The cosmic drama of creation, sustenance, and dissolution is maintained by the principles of reciprocity and harmony between various *levels* of reality. Yajna is the human re-enactment of this drama, and it aligns us with the fundamental interconnectivity and interdependency across all entities in the cosmos. Specifically, yajna is our act of giving towards harmony within oneself, with other humans, with nature, between the micro and macro levels, between humans and divinity, etc.

Yajna differs from ordinary transactions that we perform because yajna advances us toward a higher level. In other words, *ordinary karma comprises transactions within the same level of reality, whereas in yajna we perform actions that will take us to a higher level.*

Yajna shifts the human drama by orienting the ego towards harmony with the cosmos. It realigns our goals by balancing them with responsibilities towards all other entities including humans, animals, nature, and the cosmos at large. Dharma is based on the principles of yajna.

The principle of yajna is what differentiates Indian social ethics from Western social systems. The West has placed great emphasis on human 'rights', but not enough on human 'responsibilities'. The result has been the flareups of major battles between rival groups, each clamoring for more rights relative to the other. However, dharma focuses on our responsibility towards oneself, family, local community, the rashtra (nation), humanity at large, and all nature seen as a person. Yajna emphasizes one's responsibilities by sacrificing the selfish benefits of the individual ego and working selflessly towards a higher cause. Rights naturally follow when responsibilities are fulfilled. Rights must be earned through meeting obligations not simply being granted based on identity activism.

The yajna system assigns responsibilities towards each of the following interconnected aspects of the cosmos: managing one's well-being, serving family including one's ancestors, and serving humanity, nature, and deities.

To manage one's well-being, it is better to follow one's sva-dharma rather than chasing someone else's. This entails evaluating one's inherent traits, desires, skills, and aptitude, and living accordingly. Be non-attached to the rewards and focus on the virtuous goal. Be clear, and do not let emotions influence you. Accept the present condition as the right situation resulting from past karma, and do not judge the situation. Be in the present moment, patient, relaxed, stress-free, and alert. Practice witnessing one's mental processes as a detached observer, distancing oneself from the doer of actions.

Gradually, this leads beyond the ego's habitual state. That is when one can examine one's psychological processes, like a scientist making empirical observations using a clean instrument with a disinterested posture. The next step is to integrate this state of detachment into one's daily life, coming back full circle but with a more evolved outlook.

As a result of such practices, one manages the ego as a vehicle to travel through life rather than being controlled and driven by it. Choices become spontaneous, selfless, and virtuous.

From such a state of freedom, one can pursue yajna towards other people and society at large. Seeing everyone as comprising the integral unity, one can respect everyone's role, place and capabilities with humility and free from judgment.

Such a state of freedom also allows for a yajna entailing destruction of adharma with violence if needed, to preserve harmony.

It is advisable to not push your sva-dharma on others. Encourage them to discover their sva-*bhava* (innate qualities) and formulate it accordingly. Everyone is different, yet equal—this is the Vedic notion of diversity and mutual respect.

The cosmos is living and has personality. One's yajna with nature and the cosmos is based on seeing everything as part of integral unity. Hence, one must feel responsible for the well-being of nature and appreciate the mutual co-dependence of everything. It becomes natural to feel the needs of all sentient beings in making decisions, and not be selfish. Every action has a universal dimension, and nothing is in isolation from the rest.

By contrast, the Western sustainability models are driven by human selfishness because nature is seen as man's property that is to be protected as such, and nature does not have its rights.

Disentanglement from Karma

Vedic cosmology posits a universe governed by impartial laws, some that can be comprehended by the human mind, and others not. Karma is one such law that is only partially visible for direct perception. It is a system of causation—everything in the empirical realm is the effect of some karma as the cause. The outcomes produced by karma are *phala*, the fruit or result of wilful action.

The cosmic system of karma is more complex than physical causation and goes beyond what modern physics recognizes. Whatever physics terms the 'laws of nature' is included in karma as a subset, but the converse is not true: There are concepts in karma theory that are beyond the scope of physics. For instance, an action has a side effect or samskara/imprint; this functions like a seed that influences future causation. Therefore, if we harm someone but escape the consequences, the samskara will produce a future phala. Also, there are agencies of causation that live beyond the realm of our senses—other realms beyond space-time where deities reside (*deva-loka*).

The principle of ahimsa occupies a special place in the pursuit of all goals. It can be loosely translated as the minimization of collective harm, or the maximization of collective good/harmony. Ahimsa does *not* mean abstaining from violence altogether. In fact, in many contexts, ahimsa *requires* engaging in war and destruction to protect and optimize collective harmony. This is the lesson taught in the *Mahabharata*.

As a person's level of consciousness evolves, his relationship with karma changes. One can broadly consider three stages or levels at which individuals operate regarding karma:

A. <u>Gamifying ordinary causation</u>: The typical ego knows only the direct causation that his senses can detect. Hence, he is blind to the implications beyond the directly observable consequences of his actions. Ergo, he lives his life gamifying his transactions with others, hoping to optimize the outcomes for his ego's benefit. However, this is a game that nobody can ultimately win—as we observed in the Buddha's Second Noble Truth. It might produce temporary delights, but it is fragile at best and not sustainable long-term.

B. Gamifying the karma system: The individual who is on a spiritual journey begins to understand the karma system. He knows there are consequences of his actions beyond the immediate outcomes, in the form of samskaras that will produce future outcomes. So, now he starts performing 'good' karma to receive phala/outcomes that are favorable. However, he is still operating from the ego trying to gamify the karma system for his selfish benefit. For instance, he prays to receive material benefits for himself and his family, in exchange for donations. This is transactional dharma, a form of gamification.

C. Transcending the ego: There are *sadhanas* (practices) designed to transcend sensory experiences. The practitioner moves from desire-driven actions to *nishkama* where actions are free from material gain and intended purely to become aligned with the cosmos. The guru initiates disciples into these practices customized for the individual after making sure they have the right attitude and predisposition. At some stage, the ego is purified enough and acts spontaneously without seeking any reward. This can be in the form of surrender to the divine. It can be a state where the person's body-mind complex has become a vehicle used by the cosmos to perform without the ego as the agency doing anything from its side. Now the actions are not transactional, seeking no reward whatsoever. One has advanced beyond the game. This is 'freedom from' the game of life.

Living a Wholesome Life

Individual Goals and Pursuits

The classification of universal pursuits of

- **Artha** (material well-being)
- **Kama** (desire)
- **Dharma** (righteous action in harmony with the cosmos)

- **Moksha** (liberation or freedom from causation)

applies to all human beings regardless of cultural, faith, or linguistic differences. Note that the system does not prohibit pursuits of material wealth and prosperity (artha) or desires (kama). It prescribes dharmic approaches that are aligned with the overall trajectory towards final liberation.

We must emphasize that contrary to popular views held by many, the Vedic system is not against the fulfillment of desires. In fact, it reveals a profound understanding of desires. It posits that:

- Desires are fundamental to the human condition.
- Desires cannot and should not be suppressed.
- However, desires must be pursued in a disciplined manner (with respect to time, place, and circumstances) and not without ethical guardrails.
- The pursuit of desires should move one towards *freedom from the desires, and away from increased dependence on them.*
- And thus, the Vedic system has developed a social architecture and infrastructure to fulfill desires by keeping dharma in context.
- This ultimately means that the goal is to fulfill desires in ways that maximize ahimsa toward oneself and others while performing yajna to the cosmos through responsibilities and obligations.

The Vedic system is designed to help a diverse society of individuals to pursue these goals by catering to their different temperaments, sensibilities, and competencies. It accommodates immense diversity while ensuring that society works in harmony with nature.

This is the reason why India has produced more diversity and sustainability for the longest period than any other civilization alive today. No other society comes even close. The secret is: not imposing one set of commandments or dogma on everyone, but rather, offering an open-architecture approach to society in which diverse individuals can advance in their distinct ways.

Because the cosmos is the Divine manifested in different forms, the respect for diversity is respect for the Divine. This is our sacred principle and our yajna must be aligned with it. This is the fundamental premise of the Vedic social structure.

The varna and ashrama *vyavastha* (system) comprising rights and obligations was developed to serve this purpose. It is an infrastructure that allows desires to be fulfilled alongside responsibilities in the form of a yajna.

Varna-and-Ashrama Infrastructure

The varna-ashrama system fosters interdependency among diverse individuals in ways that are aligned with the cosmic yajna. It advocates that society needs to be organized for the optimal performance of the yajnas to efficiently attain the fourfold pursuits as outcomes.

The varna-ashrama system was designed to optimize the distribution of resources, power, and responsibilities via two complementary systems working in tandem: the varna system (principles applicable to the decentralized distribution of occupations) and the ashrama system (principles applicable in specific stages in an individual's life). This is the basic infrastructure using which one can transact in society and attain the fourfold goals discussed earlier.

The varna system helps optimize an individual's *contributions to society*, while the ashrama system helps the individual optimize his or her *self-growth* in the pursuit of personal goals. The former is collective optimization, while the latter is individual optimization. Both systems complement and complete each other. They are designed to fulfill responsibilities and duties to self, family, community, and the cosmos.

The <u>varna</u> system prescribes four categories of vocations:

- **Brahmin:** responsible for intellectual pursuits, charged with knowledge generation, distribution, and preservation.
- **Kshatriya:** responsible for governance, charged with

protection and welfare of citizens, and preservation of law and order.
- **Vaishya:** responsible for economic welfare, wealth generation, and wealth preservation.
- **Shudra:** responsible for skill preservation, and as the labor force.

These are characterized by the following:

- Duties are based on vocation to be discharged in service of the collective society.
- Restrictions and boundaries of control and influence are designed to minimize conflicts in the use of scarce resources.
- Rewards are commensurate with risks.
- Restrictions on the accumulation of types of social capital are designed to prevent excess concentration of capital and power.

The <u>ashrama</u> system prescribes four stages in life: brahmacharya, *grihastha*, *vanaprastha*, and *sannyasa*.

- The **brahmacharya** or student stage of an individual is spent in the intellectual pursuit of specific knowledge. This knowledge is to be imparted free (to avoid corruption), allowing a student to live a frugal life free from consumerism.
- When brahmacharis of any varna enter the **grihastha** ashrama (the stage of marriage and family), they become the main producers and contributors to the economy.
- **Vanaprastha** is the stage when the individual begins to withdraw from society and focuses on social work.
- This culminates in total withdrawal in the final life stage of **sannyasa** where one can dedicate oneself solely to attain 'freedom from'.
- These ashramas are designed to channel individual lifestyles and help achieve their goals consistent with the broader interests of society. Following are some characteristics:

- Responsibilities differ for individuals through each of these different stages of life.
- The duration of time spent in each ashrama ensures a well-balanced life overall.
- The nature of custodianship of a certain type of capital changes in each stage.

The grihastha ashrama is the only period in an individual's life concerned with the accumulation and distribution of material resources. Even in this stage, the individual is perceived merely as a temporary custodian of society's resources and capital that are in his trusteeship.

Furthermore, within the grihastha ashrama, the allocation of resources and power is not equal: individuals and groups receive rewards commensurate with the risks undertaken. A Kshatriya, for instance, is allowed to enjoy the pleasures that come with being a member of royalty like recreational hunting because of the risky nature inherent in his duties in warfare. A Vaishya's enjoyments are limited to the realm of material wealth.

The idea in the final two stages of life is to minimize dependence on society thereby reducing one's transactions that cause further bondage. By minimizing one's participation in selfish causation, one's footprint in vyavaharika is reduced. Sannyasa is intended to take the individual 'off the grid' of societal causation altogether. The old karmic causation gradually depletes itself by playing out in one's life, and eventually one is free from causation altogether. That 'freedom from' is the path to paramarthika.

This system also gives every individual the choice to *live outside* the varna-ashrama social grid. Such a person is called a sannyasin. He is the ultimate environmentalist minimizing his footprint of transactions with society, his level of consumption, and his *himsa* (harm) to the environment. However, such an individual cannot cherry-pick benefits from society.

A modern-day approximation could be the Amish community in the USA that has chosen to exist completely outside of mainstream society. They are self-sustaining and unplugged from the established American society even to the extent of rejecting taxpayer-funded resources like electricity and water. A big difference between the Amish and the Vedic sannyasin is that the Amish lack anything equivalent to the sophisticated Vedic cosmology in which to embed their lifestyle. Hence, they lack the equivalent of the Vedic rishis as research exemplars.

The following figure illustrates this complex ecosystem: fourfold goals, fourfold varnas, fourfold ashramas, all harmonized to optimize the goal of transcending the limits of karmic causation, and thereby attaining the state of 'freedom from'.

It depicts each varna's occupational roles, levels of risks entailed, and whether the members are producers or consumers in each stage of life. This interdependency explains why varna cannot be surgically separated from the ashrama system and judged by Western norms.

One must appreciate the checks and balances that traditional Indian society imposed to ensure that all individuals, however diverse in skills, goals, and thought, could work towards their personal goals harmoniously, while being contributing members of society with domain-specific expertise and access to, and control of, domain-specific resources. Thus, the modern habit of cherry-picking one aspect of this structure and judging it based on modern societal norms is both, meaningless and reckless.

We claim that the varna-ashrama system has a lot to teach on how to structure society so that no one is left behind, and yet, individuals are granted the freedoms to excel within a certain domain.

It is important to point out that the varna-ashrama system championed individual contributions to society as evidenced by many folk stories and maxims. The idea was simply to provide a self-enforced varna-ashrama infrastructure (without any Church-like centralized authority) to ensure that human free will does not run amok and is instead channeled to maximize contribution toward cosmic harmony.

Four-Fold Goals of Life

Pursuit of *Artha*, *Kama, Dharma*				**Pursuit of *Moksha***	
***Vyavaharika* Realm/ in Causation**				**Toward *Paramarthika* Realm/Minimizing Causation**	
VARNA	**Domain-Specific Intellectual Pursuit/Study**	**Contribution to Society**	**Risk/ Reward**	**Slow withdrawal from society**	**Complete withdrawal from society**
Shudra	Metallurgy, Agriculture, Trade, Crafts	Wage Earner: Skilled Workers in Guilds	Low Risk/ Low Reward		
Vaishya	Business, Finance, Economics	Entrepreneur: Independent Business	Medium Risk/ Medium Reward		
Kshatriya	Art and Science of Warfare, Governance	Military Combat: Law and Order	High Risk/ High Reward		
Brahmana	Shastras, Indic Knowledge Systems	Alms/charity: Teaching, Rituals, Collective Well-being	Minimal Risk/ No Reward	Spiritual Pursuit	
ASHRAMA					
Brahmacharya		*Grihastha*		*Vanaprastha*	*Sannyasa*

Consumption   Contribution

The Vedic idea that everything is a manifestation of the Divine results in a collective yajna where everyone and everything is viewed as a contributing member of the collective, leaving no one relegated to the 'victim' status. The Marxist concept of victimhood is perhaps born out of the Christian idea of man being born a sinner. This is not applicable in the Vedic framework.

The Gurukulam System and the Integral Unity of all Grammars

India's traditional gurukulam system of education was not just about imparting knowledge; it was an immersive experience where students lived with the guru who served as the teacher and role model. This close arrangement allowed the guru to effortlessly impart samskaras—deep-rooted impressions and values—through daily interactions and activities. Education in the gurukulam was not confined to the *shastras* alone; learning occurred continuously in all aspects of life, simply by being in the presence of the guru and following the guru's example.

Students were not only taught hard skills but also soft skills through rituals and practices. For example, the rituals of *bhuta* yajna ingrained a profound appreciation for the sacredness of the environment. The belief that all elements of nature are divine and interconnected was a cornerstone of the students' lifestyle.

From dawn to dusk, rituals encompassing prayers were seamlessly woven into what could be considered a truly 'holistic' education through samskaras. This started at first light with ritualistic bathing and prayers to Surya Bhagavan (the Sun God) and the life forces.

An important Vedic principle is that the cosmos is integrally unified. *This is called the dance of Shiva.* This unity of all physical reality also applies to knowledge, and hence, all shastras in different domains are inherently interconnected. No shastra is considered a stand-alone subject. *The principles of integral unity in the cosmos are therefore reflected in every shastra.*

This insight is what led to the discovery of the periodic table in chemistry. One of the greatest achievements in the modern era, a crown jewel of human thought if you will, is the periodic table, said to be discovered by the Russian chemist, Dimitri Mendeleev. Mendeleev realized that periodicity was a fundamental law, governing the nature of all elements and created a theoretical structure to represent the elements in the universe. This structure also informed him about the missing elements yet to be discovered, and he confidently left empty slots for these undiscovered elements. He knew more about these undiscovered elements than those who discovered these very same elements later. He could predict all this because the structure he produced was robust and universal. This is how the 'grammar' of chemistry was born.

However, what inspired Dimitri Mendeleev to come up with such profound grammar for chemistry? Mendeleev happened to be a close friend of Otto von Böhtlingk, an Indologist and philologist in Saint Petersburg, a leading hub for classical Oriental language studies. The two collaborated on various projects and it is here that Mendeleev was exposed to Panini's grammar, *Ashtadhyayi*.[1] This opened a door that had no precedent in Western thought.

Besides providing grammar for human language, Sanskrit also has a *philosophy of the integrally unified order in the universe*. Just as all parts and levels of the physical cosmos are integrally unified, so also are all knowledge domains reflecting each other because of their common DNA-like deep structure. Panini's Sanskrit grammar can therefore serve as a structure that can be mapped to other domains including chemistry. Sanskrit grammar provides comprehensive rules for assembling the fundamental elements of language such as word roots, prefixes, and suffixes, enabling the construction of grammatically correct words and sentences just like chemistry has been a quest for discovering the elements as building blocks.

The genius of Mendeleev was that he got this philosophical insight into the integral unity of nature and was able to apply

Sanskrit grammar to the structure of elements in nature. This led to *Mendeleev's system by which he could generate all possible compounds made from element combinations, and yet leave out impossible or wrong combinations of elements.*

This is how Mendeleev 'borrowed' and applied very similar principles from the *Ashtadhyayi* to the domain of chemistry. He took the *Ashtadhyayi* as the template and developed an isomorphic grammar for chemistry.

A common principle of all Indian Knowledge Systems and hence, reflected in all shastras is that there exists a sound grammar that has well-defined units, or building blocks with tight definitions, rules, and precise meanings, and is put together in a robust framework—be it linguistics like the *Ashtadhyayi*, logic or *tarka* shastra, medicine or ayurveda, mathematics or *ganita* shastra, prosody or *chanda* shastra, the science of ornamentation also known as *alankara* shastra, and the shastra of music, dance and theatre known as the *natya* shastra.

Once mastery is gained over these fundamental building blocks of a shastra's grammar, the door opens to introduce creative aspects through improvisation in any domain of knowledge. Just like Mendeleev learned from the *Ashtadhyayi* that only certain combinations of basic units are stable and thus permissible in the periodic table, so too only harmonious components are permissible in keeping with the grammar of dance. This is the framework that great rishis like Bharata Muni and Maharishi Panini have handed down to humanity.

Let us apply this principle of the integral unity of various domains to appreciate how the shared grammatical structures work in harmony. When enjoying the classical forms of Indian dance, one should notice how *simultaneously*,

- the grammar of mathematics or ganitam in the dancer's footwork uses number theory and combinatorics to produce intricate rhythmic cycles.
- the grammar of linguistics guides the lyrics of the stories of love, devotion, valor, and sacrifice.

- the grammar of aesthetics or alankara shastra embellishes these lyrics.
- the grammar of prosody or chanda shastra ensures that the verses are in harmony following the meter.
- the grammar of music or *sangeeta* shastra polices the melody in the raga.
- the grammar of theatre, drama and dance or the natya shastra guides everything from spatial awareness to ensuring that movements are aesthetic, with tight definitions on intricate *mudras* or hand gestures, and *abhinaya* or facial expressions.

Performing a beautiful dance is like playing N-dimensional chess. It is a culmination of grammar applied in a multidimensional way. There is grammar of not just one subject in isolation but an ecosystem of many subjects, each with its specific grammar, all harmoniously working together to produce a spectacular show. This is the integral unity of the shastras. It is grammar of the shastras all the way, through and through!

Similarly, ganitam, which may be loosely translated as Indian mathematics, encompasses various disciplines such as arithmetic, trigonometry, algebra, geometry, poetry, prosody, and the principles of literary composition and ornamentation (alankara shastra). The importance of *rasa*—the aesthetics or emotional dimension that brings life to art—can also be vividly observed in ganitam texts. In traditional Indian Knowledge Systems, *rasa* is not just confined to the performing arts but extends to mathematical texts like Bhaskaracharya's *Lilavati*. The verses in these texts are crafted not only to convey mathematical concepts but also to evoke a certain emotional response.

The verses in *Lilavati* pose mathematical problems with practical applications and incorporate the aesthetic qualities of poetry. These verses are meaningful and even carry themes that glorify love or the environment. The integration of *rasa* ensures that the content is not just reductionist like Western systems. It is not a dry exposition of arithmetic or algebra but is enriched with poetic elements that resonate emotionally.

This approach of the infusing *rasa* reflects a holistic understanding of education, where the cultivation of intellect and emotion go hand in hand. They become a medium through which students can experience the joy of learning, the beauty of logical thought, and the deeper connection between mathematics and the broader cultural, environmental, and philosophical traditions of India. The goal is to nurture well-rounded individuals who appreciate the interconnectedness of all forms of knowledge. We thus observe how a grammatical framework, though seemingly rigid, offers enormous flexibility for creativity across disciplines, all within the framework of the shastra. The shastra system is inherently interdisciplinary because it reflects the inter-domain nature of integral unity.

A good example is Rajiv Malhotra's argument against the American scholar Sheldon Pollock. In *The Battle for Sanskrit: Is Sanskrit Political or Sacred, Oppressive or Liberating, Dead or Alive?* Malhotra responded to Pollock's thesis that the strict rules of *Ashtadhyayi*, which define the Sanskrit language, render it rigid and incapable of fostering creativity and evolution. Pollock's entire criticism of the Sanskrit tradition was based on the premise that observations from the empirical world should shape the theoretical framework rather than using a predefined structure, as seen in Sanskrit *vyakarana* (grammar).

However, this is a blind spot for Pollock and other Western scholars, as well as some Indians like Sanjeev Sanyal, an advisor to the Indian government. What they overlook is the foundational difference in perspective. The grammar of Sanskrit and hence, all shastras emerges from a framework of integral unity, a unity directly experienced at higher levels of consciousness. This is also why the grammars in our example of Indian dance all seamlessly fit together, allowing for creativity across domains through improvisation within the rules to maintain harmony.

Unlike the constantly changing vyavaharika realm, the paramarthika realm represents the domain of absolute truths, perceived from an elevated state of consciousness. This higher state, which Malhotra refers to as 'the rishi state', offers immense scope for creativity, one that transcends the limitations of the empirical and materialistic views common in Western traditions.

Therefore, while Pollock views Sanskrit grammar as a limiting structure, it is a profound and dynamic system that allows for endless creativity. This distinction between the empirical and the transcendent is crucial for understanding the true potential of Sanskrit and the broader shastra traditions, which is lacking in Western worldviews.

The implication of all this is that India's education policymakers must have foundational knowledge in:

1. Western social theories
2. Vedic cosmology based on integral unity
3. Vastness of ideas embedded in Indian Knowledge Systems
4. Value of adhyatma-vidya
5. Skills needed for the economy and nation-building
6. Knowledge production, distribution, and scaling-up

Samskaras as Education by Installing Long-Term Tendencies

We will now apply the ideas discussed above to the field of education. The fundamental question is: Given the varna-ashrama framework to facilitate the fulfillment of desires in alignment with yajna, how does society ensure that this infrastructure is implemented *and* used? That would enable us to create a society where individuals have an innate sense of dharma and awareness of integral unity with the cosmos.

To address this need, the rishis created a system of cultural practices known as samskaras. Each samskara is a procedure to install a tendency in the individual, a tendency that would spontaneously evolve the individual's free will to pursue desires (kama) and other goals (purusharthas) within the dharmic framework of optimization of ahimsa. The installation of such samskaras influences future outcomes. Whatever karma one accumulates, apart from the immediately visible effects (phala), the same karma or action *also* produces a samskara.

For example, the Vedic system encouraged the performance of *pancha maha* yajnas or five sacred obligations regardless of varna or ashrama, to be performed daily. These are *deva* yajna (for devatas), *pitru* yajna for ancestors, *bhuta* yajna for the ecosystem, *manushya* yajna for fellow human beings, and *brahma* yajna for the Vedic heritage.

The regular practice of the pancha maha yajnas serves as a constant reminder of the universe's interconnectedness. These sacred duties cultivate a deep sense of gratitude in the individual for the collective forces that sustain life in the cosmos. Modern science is now acknowledging the role of gratitude in treating anxiety and depressive disorders that are associated with nurturing negative thinking patterns.

These yajnas are to be integrated into one's daily life to achieve harmony. Living harmoniously mandates an understanding of our role within the broader context of the world. It also involves being mindful of ourselves, others, and the environment. A mature and sensitive person appreciates everything in creation and does not see nature as resources for exploitation to gratify the ego's game. Such a person understands the importance of using free will wisely, choosing actions based on what should be done rather than succumbing to programmed behavior.

The performance of the pancha maha yajnas teaches an individual to express gratitude to:

- the cosmic intelligence in the form of daily puja, or *isvara aradhana*
- one's ancestors in the form of *tarpanam* rituals and serving parents
- the rishis by being a custodian of shastras and the Vedic vision
- the creatures in the ecosystem, by feeding birds/animals, watering plants etc.
- fellow human beings by offering help to the less fortunate

These yajnas have a profound impact on how the individual sees himself/herself in the interconnected cosmos. They help the individual view creation as sacred, focusing the attention on individual responsibilities to the collective at all levels.

Education is a system of installing samskaras for the future benefit of the student. Besides individual samskaras in the form of subtle mental impressions within the person, there can also be collective samskaras like the deep memory of the cosmos, resulting from free-willed actions or karmas by people. The free will of humans is programming the cosmos and impacting its future outcomes both at the personal and collective levels. This is the Vedic theory of cosmic evolution.

A useful analogy is with machine learning used by Artificial Intelligence to train algorithms. That is the education system meant for robots. The equivalent of samskaras is in the form of giant tables, vector spaces, tokens, etc., all of which drive the learned behavior of algorithms. Likewise, a child's education is a samskara that trains and conditions his cognitive system, the way he processes experiences and thinks. This shapes the orientation of the mind, which will drive individual action in the future, leading to future outcomes. The karma system is the feedback loop by which the samskara is tested and choices are optimized for future results.

Samskaras that were created in one's prior life are carried forward to the present life in the form of innate capabilities within the person as well as the external circumstances one faces throughout life. A newborn excelling in some field is the result of a prior life's samskaras.

Vasanas

An individual's psychological traits are called *vasanas*, which last over the individual's lifetime and carry over to future births. A person's actions result in samskaras that collectively result in strong vasanas or orientation. This is karma theory depicted as follows:

Actions ➔ Samskaras ➔ Vasanas ➔ Future Personality and Choices (Desires)

Repeated samskaras or karmas of a certain kind develop the mind's proclivity in a particular direction or a vasana. The strength of the vasana depends on the strength of the mental impressions or samskaras arising from the repetition of certain kinds of karma (willful action). The vasanas become an integral part of the individual's personality, resulting in a mind with a set of likes and dislikes or orientations. This is how desires are shaped. These samskaras influence the individual's future choices.

Vasanas born out of positive samskaras draw the individual to constructive pursuits, both for the individual and society. Negative samskaras have the opposite effect, giving rise to corresponding vasanas that lead to self-destruction and the destruction of society.

Vasanas guide the use of free will, creating a positive ego. For example, yoga shastra guides a person using *yama* and *niyama* (dos and don'ts) to cultivate a positive ego. Thus, the dharmic system

1. ensures that the individual has developed a mental proclivity to perform righteous action (or good karma which is in harmony with the cosmos), which would yield favorable phala or result of action.
2. enables the optimization of karma-phala through samskaras.

This process allows the individual to ultimately move beyond the ego, to a state of 'freedom from' worldly constraints. The following figure shows the relationship between karma, samskara, and vasanas.

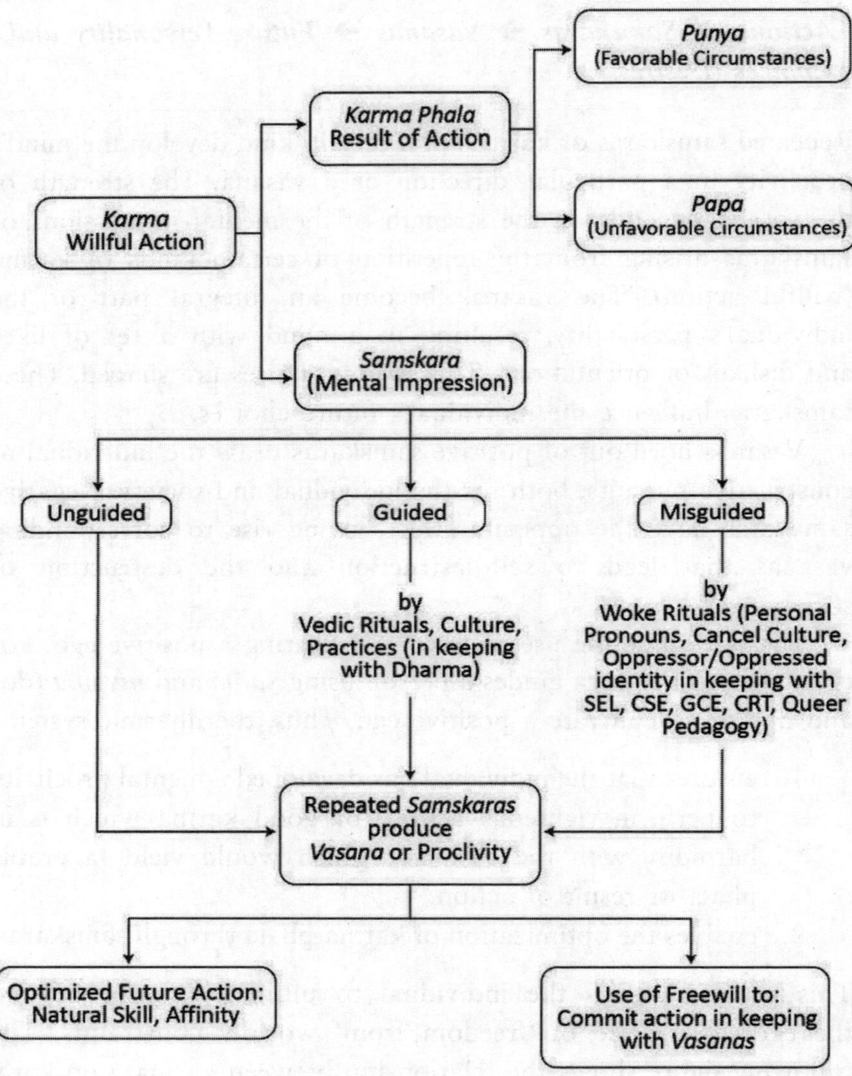

Samskaras can be classified as: guided, unguided, and misguided. These will be described next to prepare us to critique the American education system's obsession with sexuality in childhood education, which we will argue are misguided samskaras and produce negative vasanas and proclivities.

Vedic Guided Samskara: Towards 'Freedom From'

The Vedic rishis were masters in discovering samskaras for the welfare of diverse people in society and developing learning systems as training and installation of useful samskaras. The role of Vedic education is to install samskaras in the students as per the principles of dharma. The instillation of samskara or dispositions, attitudes, traits, and orientations is considered the main goal of education.

These samskaras are essentially pre-programmed packages of learning in the form of diverse processes including rituals. There is a deliberate installation of specific subtle mental impressions at certain times and places (i.e. *desha*, *kaala* specific). The goal is to influence the orientation and attitudes of the individual, starting at conception and continuing throughout life.

There are sixteen 'formal' Vedic samskaras corresponding to an individual's life stages, and these pre-programmed packages are designed to be suitable for specific milestones in the individual's journey. The aim is to develop the mind's tendencies to produce future actions consistent with the dharmic context, that will fulfill the individual's desires in harmony with the cosmos. Various cultural practices and daily rituals are also part of programming one's samskaras. These rituals are performed in the early years when the mind is pliable and thus create enduring habits in sync with the cosmos.

And thus, a dharmic *drushti* or cognitive lens is developed in the student as he sets out into the world. Traditional Indian education reinforces the samskaras repeatedly, so the proclivity of the mind veers in the right direction. The formations of such mental impressions or predispositions are reinforced through Vedic literature that extols positive role models in extreme circumstances. They are also reinforced through practices like chanting, yoga, *satsang* (true community), meditation, and rituals.

Desires are embraced and fulfilled while adhering to dharma, keeping in mind the impact of one's actions on others. Slowly, the individual's vasanas steer the individual to seek higher desires starting at artha and kama and eventually proceeding to dharma and finally, moksha. *The goal of instilling samskaras is to help the individual's desires evolve by shaping his mental orientation.*

Gradually, these positive samskaras help evolve the individual towards the state of 'freedom from' we discussed earlier.

Unguided Samskara: 'Freedom To' Driven by Peers and Rat Race

Unguided samskara is produced by letting the mind develop its orientation according to ad hoc circumstances. This would be the case for someone who did not receive formal education and is driven by external influences of all sorts, without guardrails. Such a mind is not developed systematically using structure to shape its algorithms.

Some such individuals might pursue certain fields, develop an affinity for them, and could become successful. However, others might develop proclivities leading to actions considered undesirable by society and harmful to themselves. In other words, the shaping of the mind is left to chance.

Misguided Samskara: 'Freedom To' Driven by Wokeism

The Western education system has understood the power of guided samskaras, unfortunately, with a Marxist agenda. Lately, behavioral science, psychology, and neuroscience have been incorporated into technology platforms that are installing Woke samskaras into young impressionable minds on an unprecedented scale. Comprehensive Sexuality Education programs are designed to instill samskaras to shape young minds to have desires of sexual exploration, deviance, masturbation and so on. This is damaging to societies, communities, and nations.

For example, we saw in earlier chapters how UNESCO's MGIEP uses behavioral science, neuroscience and psychology to design Social Emotional Learning courses that indoctrinate children to align with the SDGs. CSE, SEL, GCE, and environmentalism are all repeatedly hammered into children year after year starting from kindergarten, to create repeated samskaras leading to strong Woke vasanas. Activism for social justice, sexual rights, and environmental rights (which is the stated end goal of these programs) nurtures the ego centered on 'freedom to'.

We call these misguided samskaras because children's minds are meticulously sexualized and shaped for activism with their strong vasanas propelling them into action that will dismantle institutions, the family structure, and the very fabric of society.

Our goal in writing this book is to provide frameworks and insights for building an education system for India that will incorporate shastras and pedagogies relevant to a modern Bharat. We have discovered that we urgently need to focus specifically on the K-12 system to arrest the rot being imported into India, a rot that is accelerating the ruin of an already failed education system. Hence, the scope of this book is limited to urgent matters facing K-12.

It is amply clear that the imported Western education modules that specifically target very young children in their formative years will result in installing negative samskaras (psychological imprints) through carefully designed programs that turn them into social justice worriers.

Vedic Approach to Diversity, Identity, and Sustainability

A rich biodiversity comprises different interdependent species thriving in a dynamic equilibrium. Similarly, cultural health involves different types of people in dynamic exchange with each other. Just as the death of a species is unhealthy for the biological ecosystem, the death of religions, languages, and other cultural forms is grave for humankind's collective evolution. Like rich soil, a rich culture nurtures many kinds of cultural seeds as different types of potential.

This includes respecting diverse approaches to the Divine. Any religion that considers itself the exclusive truth is like a dangerous weed spreading at the expense of other life forms. Respect for the Divine also entails recognizing the divine presence in all beings. Cultures and religions should not end up in museums but encouraged to thrive in their respective native settings.

With this broad statement of the Vedic principle of diversity, let us examine the king's coronation in the *Mahabharata*, in which he is told:

> Be like a garland-maker, O king, and not like a charcoal burner. —*Mahabharata*, XII.72.20

The garland is a metaphor for diversity, comprising flowers of many hues and forms strung harmoniously for the most pleasing effect. It symbolizes social coherence combined with diversity. On the contrary, charcoal is a metaphor for reducing diversity into homogeneity by burning all the flowers into lifeless ashes. The garland-maker is facilitating and celebrating diversity, and the king, in taking the oath, is being asked to exemplify this role. He is to avoid being like the charcoal-burner who is a reductionist and burns everything down to charcoal.[2]

The decentralized, contextualized, and open architecture of the Vedic social framework is described in the garland metaphor. The varied nature of Indian culture is a coherence (garland) of distinct particulars (flowers), avoiding both extremes—incoherence with the chaotic scattering of flowers on the one hand, and reductionist, homogenized like charcoal, on the other.

There can be no reductionism or freezing of dharma. It is forever unfolding and assimilating. This is how India's quintessential context-sensitivity exemplifies plurality: *Equality is good but not at the expense of diversity*.

As explained in considerable detail in the book *Being Different*, a comfort with diversity has been built into Indian society—not like the top-down identity warfare being championed in modern democracies. India's diversity is multifaceted: different languages, food, styles of dressing, aesthetics, culture, deities and modes of worship, spiritual lineages, and so forth. This list is endless.

Instead of blindly adopting Western Universalism's approaches to diversity, educators need to take a step back and study the Vedic metaphysics and social structure that has directly resulted in such unparalleled diversity over millennia. This is not accidental. It is a civilization that has not just 'tolerated' diversity but celebrated it, seeing each form as a unique manifestation of the Divine.

On the other hand, Western movements often seek to homogenize and reduce everyone to the *same thinking*; and diversity is limited to race and sexual orientation. In earlier times, the homogeneity of thought was imposed by conquerors who sought the annihilation of their predecessors by the burning of old books in the name of one exclusive truth; the modern equivalent is Cancel Culture prevalent on American campuses and the public square. This is charcoal burning.

Charcoal burning is the reason that there has not been a harmonious coexistence among different civilizations (for example, the Native Americans and the European settlers), when they could have easily benefited by combining their resources constructively for mutual benefit.

Christianity has a history of stifling the diversity of the native peoples, pejoratively called pagans. Christianity put an end to diversity due to its centralized and monopolistic structure. The Protestant Reformation movement in the sixteenth century broke up the pan-European monopoly of the Church after excessive violence in Europe. However, what resulted were multiple warring Church monopolies in different countries. What is lacking in such systems (compared to India's diversity) is the diversity of thought that emanates from a variety of deities, rituals, and identities.

The Woke model of diversity is based on social theories that divide society into oppressors and oppressed, and hence, thrives on championing victimhood. Diversity is being weaponized by pitting identities against one another, whereas the Vedic approach to diversity is the interdependency among different entities; the goal is to optimize the total ecosystem. Woke diversity is superficial and synthetic.

The latest homogenization using Woke ideology is through standardized indexes like the index for Environmental, Social, and Governance, and the index for Diversity, Equity, and Inclusion. These shut out dissenting voices. The three or four American asset management firms (BlackRock, State Street, Vanguard, etc.) comprise a cartel that defines and enforces these indexes by which individuals, corporate entities, and governments are measured. Like the Spanish Inquisition of the fifteenth century, they function like apostles deciding the values by which society will operate. The ESG, DEI, and World Economic Forum are movements that impose a uniform canon of beliefs on society, and these beliefs have been defined by the high priests of Wokeism. These are the charcoal burners of today.

These Woke ideologies suffer from several issues: They undermine meritocracy, replace individual rights with identity politics, worsen divisiveness among groups, and thwart academic freedom and free speech by adopting Cancel Culture. The Western idea of diversity is about superficial differences in the color of skin and physical body types, but not mutual respect for diverse ideas, worldviews, aptitudes, and roles. This is the opposite of true diversity.

A root problem is the progressive politics of *equity* which is replacing the liberal ideal of *equality*. Equality means equal opportunities for all. Equity, however, means achieving equal outcomes artificially by imposing bias and allocating the resources required to force this. Equity celebrates victimhood and rewards it. Equity-based policies have created divisive societies pitting one group against another. This is against the way nature operates, which is closer to a meritocracy of entities in healthy competition.

Contrary to the Woke model built upon the glorification of victimhood, the Hindu American diaspora provides counterexamples of success through merit. Hindu immigrants are the most financially successful group in the USA at every level of education and other demographic variables, even though many of them were victims of ethnic cleansing like the Kashmiri Pandits in the northern Indian state of Jammu & Kashmir. Still more left their native homelands as refugees driven away during India's Partition in 1947, especially the Punjabis and Sindhis. Many came from modest backgrounds. Yet, we do not see victimhood clubs and camps in these groups.

Does dharma hold the secret sauce that makes Hindus successful? Does the dharma-based mindset teach people to optimize from the locus of their present circumstances, instead of wallowing in victimhood? Social scientists, however, do not seem to be interested in studying Hindu immigrants for their success.

Achieving and Maintaining Diversity Through Reinforcing Identity

Ashrama as Identity
Brahmacharya/Grihastha/Vanaprastha/Sannyasa

Varna-based identity
- Domain of Work/Livelihood (*Karma*)
- Language/Culture/Social Norms/Food
- Celebration of Festivals/*Tarpanam* (oblations to ancestors)
- Performance of Special Rituals
- Worship of
  - *Kuladevata*
  - *Gramadevata*
  - *Ishtadevata*

Other Identity Markers
- Role in Family, Workplace, Community
- Geography-based: Rashtra, Village
- Gender: *Stree* and *Purusha Dharma*

A society that strengthens and nurtures differences with mutual respect is a diverse society. Vedic society has a long history of hailing and nourishing individual differences, giving rise to several identities that keep the individual grounded. The 4x4 varna-ashrama matrix gives rise to sixteen identities. The individual's *kula devata* (family lineage deity), *grama devata* (local/village deity), *ishta devata* (personal choice of deity), and other personal customizations add additional dimensions to diversity.

Furthermore, gender, geography, and an individual's role in family, community, and country, each is a context that adds additional facets to diversity and identity. Many of these identities specialize in specific types of contributions to the collective good, and hence, the proliferation of identities helps to nurture and channel different kinds of talent in a society.

The variety of identities that Vedic metaphysics uses has been an obstacle for missionaries and Marxists. It is not accidental that the diversity of Indian identities is a target of Wokeism's dismantling mission. Its goal is to destroy the identity grid and render individuals vulnerable by bringing them under Woke control. This is apparent in the prevailing discourse on gender and sexuality with a campaign to confuse young people by attacking traditional and biological sexual and gender identities, the last remaining identities in the melting pot of the West.

The fact that India has remained so diverse demonstrates some profoundly resilient civilizational structures that have nurtured and preserved this diversity even through the turbulent periods of Islamic and European colonization. The absence of a central authority to dictate social policies has been an important factor.

Some of the differences between the contextual, non-normative Indian society and the normative Western society can be summarized as follows:

- Justice was administered in India using varna-specific contextualized *Dharmashastras*, whereas the Western system prefers normative codified laws.
- Varna and jati comprised a fluid and decentralized matrix of interdependence and self-governance, in contrast with the West's preference for centralized management.

- In India, there was simultaneous continuity and change through the sampradayas, whereas in the West there have been mutually exclusive and hostile stages of history: Premodern to Modern to Postmodern, etc.
- India's pluralistic faiths coexisted and interacted with mutual respect in contrast with Christianity's and Islam's exclusivity dogmas imposed through coercion.
- India's influence spread across much of Asia peacefully, whereas Western civilization spread violently through military subjugation and genocide.

Inspired by the West, India's progressives and secularists have imitated Western social theories. Sanskrit and local vernaculars have been subverted by English, and Western values have become the path to advancement. Progress is often *defined in opposition* to tradition, and those advocating tradition are often branded as fanatics or fundamentalists. Indian narratives are stereotyped as mythology.

An index of true diversity that could be measured objectively must include the following:

- <u>Language</u>: How many languages are spoken by at least one percent of the given population?
- <u>Diverse paths</u>: How many deities, lineages, independent forms of worship, and rituals exist in its mainstream?
- <u>Mutual respect among religions</u>: Do religious organizations interfere with other faiths through conversion that undermines diversity?
- <u>Culture</u>: How much diversity in food, social norms, and aesthetics is thriving?
- And so forth.

Sustainability is another much-touted buzzword by global organizations like UNESCO, WHO, WEF, and major corporations and liberal thinkers today. However, what exactly is meant by sustainability? In simple terms, any ecosystem is considered sustainable if it maintains balance, nourishes all living and non-living entities within, and is in harmony with the cosmos. This ideal is the very essence of dharma.

We must note that diversity is the bedrock of sustainability: for a system to be sustainable, it must be diverse. In a Vedic society, it is the varna-ashrama infrastructure that sustains such diversity. It helps with the fulfillment of human desires in ways that do not cause further dependence but ultimately transcend the desires. It decentralizes social capital by setting fluid boundaries among different kinds of capital—intellectual, political, financial, and human capital. It rewards risk-takers and yet ensures that excessive competition does not destroy diversity, all the while keeping the individual connected to the cosmos through his yajna. Thus, dharma is fundamentally a path to sustainability.

However, sustainability is presently being defined from the perspective of Western Universalism. This relies on 'diversity' as defined by Critical Race Theory and the Woke movement based on it, which seeks equal outcomes for all. The Brookings Institution explains how 'sustainability' has been expanded to include CRT ideas of social justice like the notion of 'equity':

> Sustainability is now understood to extend beyond the environment to incorporate equity, justice, and opportunity, to ensure the long-term viability of communities.[3]

The notion of equity is the very antithesis of how diversity manifests in nature. For instance, individual members of a given species differ in their qualities; only through cloning can one create an artificial system in which all individuals are the same. The Critical Race Theory mindset assumes that everyone is, or ought to be, the same in attitudes, intelligence, sensibilities, skills, interests, and luck. Differences are seen as the result of social bias and abuse. While no system is perfect, it is naïve to think that all humans are endowed with the same level of skills and other features. This is an artificial construct against nature, and thus not sustainable.

Force-fitting a CRT-based structure that is against nature and the cosmos is neither sustainable nor beneficial. The irony is that these CRT ideologies are being widely applied across businesses and institutions even though common sense tells us that they are artificial interventions against nature and cosmic harmony.

Dharma maintains that all nature is a manifestation of divinity. Divine personality is expressed through nature's diversity, and we must respect it as such. This leads to entirely different ideas of conservation between dharma and the Western approach. Conservation of nature in the Western system is motivated by the desire to protect natural resources as *human property*. Water should not be polluted because that would harm the fishing industry, and not because the fish are living beings with their rights. Western ethics and social thought are entirely obsessed with the premise that humans are the owners of nature. Experiencing nature as divinity has been dismissed (or even banned) as idolatry!

Vedic metaphysics asserts that *nature is a being with personhood and has rights*. Western Universalism's position is considerably different: that nature is human property and hence, sustainability is to protect industry and the consumerist society. The core principles of dharma like ahimsa, vegetarianism, and animal rights are not given adequate weightage in Western Universalism.

The Western sustainability model maximizes the fulfillment of human desire, a goal that mother nature simply cannot sustain. Such an approach has led to processes like creating artificial meat, and changing the DNA of animals, and the biology of cows so they do not emit methane, a greenhouse gas. The move to modify nature so that humans can indulge in their materialistic desires is the exact opposite of Vedic ideals.

The following quotes give some terrifying ideas proposed by the World Economic Forum in the name of sustainability:

> The WEF wants cows to start receiving Bovaer, a feed additive produced by Dutch company Royal DSM NV. Just a quarter of a teaspoon of Bovaer per day will cut methane burps by

a third for a dairy cow, claims the WEF. That should make agriculture climate-friendly but also economically dependent.[4]

Whenever you can play God, the WEF is on fire. Globalists are celebrating projects that specifically breed genetically modified starfish and corals in laboratories to 'stabilize' the ecosystem in the ocean.[5]

Now you can take sea urchins and use their innards as a delicacy to make sushi. Is that just a mirage? Because at the same time, WEF, Bill Gates & Co. are working on artificial meat that will one day feed the world. However, while waiting for our laboratory-created meat, we are encouraged to eat bugs.[6]

The following table summarizes some differences between Vedic and Western approaches.

	Vedic Civilization	Western Civilization
Track record	Only living civilization that still has enormous diversity in innumerable facets despite colonization.	A history of destruction of diversity the world over.
Diversity	True, unparalleled diversity achieved and sustained in every aspect of individual, society, and country.	Diversity only in name. No diversity of thought, worship, dress codes, or rituals.
Sustainability	Life lived in sync with nature.	Manipulation of nature as property.
Method	A life of yajna, transcending ego.	Egocentric, ego glorification.
Resource distribution	Minimization of competition; distribution of different types of capital across different groups; individual as custodian with limits.	Hyper competition; capital concentrated with a few; no limits.

Values	Mutual respect, focus on contribution, ahimsa, and cosmic harmony.	Tolerance at best, focus on consumption, Western Universalism, and equality of outcome.
Resource management	Reducing consumption with maturity and withdrawal.	Endless expansion of desires.

This discussion raises fundamental questions about *whose* values determine the criteria and goals for this Western concept of sustainability. The problem with the present sustainability movement is that it is a Western-dominated movement. In India's context, it needs to be defined in keeping with Vedic principles. It cannot be a mandate imposed by global elites.

We would like to take a turn on an optimistic note, offering readers a sense of hope. Despite the rot brought about by modern educational systems, we have gurus who remain steadfast in their commitment to the Bharatiya *paddati* (traditional Indian approach) and continue to innovate in how they transmit knowledge. Their efforts are a beacon of light, showing that the wisdom of Indian pedagogy is not only alive but evolving, producing new knowledge.

However, to fully appreciate this 'good news', it is essential to first understand the historical context—specifically, how Indian teaching systems were digested by European colonizers. By understanding this history, we can better appreciate the significance of those who are working to preserve and revitalize the true essence of Bharatiya education. These topics will be taken up in the following chapters.

13

INDIAN EDUCATION BEFORE THE BRITISH EMPIRE

British colonialists conducted surveys on traditional Indian education and their reports show that they were highly impressed. They documented how superior, pervasive, and deep the education was. It was based on the Vedic approaches to knowledge generation, distribution, and preservation.

The rishis of India had delved into many subjects that were unknown to the rest of the world. They also developed pedagogical frameworks for the efficient distribution of knowledge and codified knowledge in frameworks giving us the Vedic schools of thought. It is a widely known fact from the historian, Dharampal's (1922-2006) *The Beautiful Tree*, that society was educated, with functioning schools in every village, before the assault by the British model of Macaulay education.

After the decay of the Indian education system, the replacement British model was slow to gain traction. It left the masses of India uneducated or poorly educated. This is the rot that continues today and is poised to take a turn for the worse with the latest importation of America's Woke education.

Dharampal's work is a great source of reference that refutes many false claims being made by eminent historians. Contrary to popular belief, even Shudras and other communities from the low socio-economic strata had good access to Indian education before the British dismantling of traditional systems. Dharampal presents precise statistics using the British surveys on the indigenous education system of India. The table below summarizes Dharampal's findings of the Madras Presidency in 1825.

Community Profile of Boys Undergoing Instruction in Schools and at Home in the District of Madras, ca. 1825

	Brahmins	Vaisyas	Sudras	Other Castes	Hindus	Muslims	Total
Instructed in Schools	410	853	3,678	447	5,370	153	5,523
% of Total	7.42	15.12	66.59	8.09	97.23	2.77	
Instructed at Home	7,586	6,132	7,589	3,449	24,756	1,690	26,446
% of Total	28.68	23.19	28.70	13.04	93.61	6.39	
Total	7,996	6,967	11,267	3,896	30.126	1,843	31,969

Source: Dharampal, *The Beautiful Tree*

Similarly, he shows that girls were well-educated in family-based schools. Other foreign scholars in the early 1700s also found education to be widespread in India:

> In 1713, German missionaries stationed in Tranquebar/Tarangambadi informed their readers that 'one can find, in all towns, places and villages, schools in which the youth is informed in reading and writing.' These missionaries left vivid accounts of the schooling and pedagogy in eighteenth-century Tamil Nadu (Liebau 1998).[1]

Although education was decentralized, Indian Knowledge Systems formed the foundation of these schools in terms of content and pedagogy. For instance, Gurmukhi-medium schools of the Sikhs of Punjab are a great example of what was seen across other gurukuls of India with minor variations. In his book, *The Construction of*

Religious Boundaries: Culture, Identity, and Diversity in the Sikh Tradition, Harjot Oberoi describes accounts of well-established Sikh gurukuls run by Udasi and Nirmala sects of Sikhs in the early 1800s, which attracted students 'from a wide spectrum of social and denominational backgrounds'.[2] He recounts free Gurmukhi schools that were attached to *dharamsalas* or shelters, imparting instruction in languages, classics, scriptures, rhetoric, astrology, and medicine to students. The Udasis and Nirmalas were renowned for their quality of education in the nineteenth century. Other intellectual groups called Gianis and Bhais also ran educational institutions. The Bhais combined secular and religious education across all of Punjab in villages and towns by establishing Gurmukhi-medium schools.

Here are some highlights from Oberoi's book, dealing with Sikh education in Gurmukhi-medium schools in the nineteenth century for very small children:

- School started at age five for both boys and girls, and they attended the same school.
- Children were first taught to write on the ground and then on a wooden slab.
- Numbers, basic math, and measurements were taught.
- Religious and secular texts were taught.

A British survey in 1882 showed that there were 829 Gurmukhi-medium schools across Punjab. The survey shows that these schools also followed a similar curriculum as that of the rest of India, which was based primarily on Indian Knowledge Systems. For example, after primary education, students were taught specialized subjects like:

- *Vyakaran* (Grammar/Linguistics)
- *Granth Kavya* (Poetics)
- *Alankar* (Alankara shastra or rhetoric)
- *Pingal* (Chanda shastra or prosody)
- Literature

- History (*Itihasa*)
- *Niti* (Logic or *Tarka* shastra)
- Arithmetic
- Astronomy (*Jyotisha*)
- *Lilavati* (*Ganitam*)

In the pre-colonial era, schooling was decentralized and often funded by the teachers and the community. There are accounts of Thinnai schools of Tamil Nadu, Pyal schools of Orissa (now Odisha) and other places, and of course *paathshalas*. All these were village schools often managed by a single teacher, serving the educational needs of the local communities. Classes were conducted in a verandah of the teacher's house with pupils of varying abilities. Children could be seen writing on sand, which was a common practice across India.

The key to scaling education with a limited number of teachers was through the widespread use of students to teach each other in a controlled environment. Often, younger pupils in tiny groups were guided and monitored by an older pupil and thus the entire school could usually be run by a single teacher.

These Indian methods of effective knowledge transmission for scaling-up education to the masses were appreciated and digested by the West and led to tectonic changes in Western economies and societies.

The Steam Engine of Education: The Madras Monitorial System

While European digestion of Indian linguistics, mathematics, astronomy, metallurgy, etc., is well known, the digestion of successful pedagogical methods used in ancient India remains an untold story. On the one hand, the British brought the Macaulay system of education to India, but simultaneously there was a parallel effort in digesting Indian pedagogical methods into Europe and subsequently into America. The following is an important story about how Indian pedagogy was adopted by England and the USA.

It started in Egmore, a central district in Madras (now Chennai). In 1702, a dharamsala at a strategic location in Egmore, was repurposed for a British military fortification called the Egmore Redoubt.[3] Over time, after having served its military purpose, it began housing sick soldiers and was even briefly occupied by the French until it finally became the home of the Madras Male Asylum. This institution provided refuge for young, orphaned boys born to Indian mothers and British officers and soldiers who had abandoned their offspring after returning home to England.

The problem of these abandoned children was so severe that in 1787, the Scottish Anglican priest Andrew Bell, sailed to India to address the matter, after having spent some time as a private tutor in Virginia. Bell was given the task to 'superintend the education of children'[4] of the Madras Male Asylum. His mission was to indoctrinate the abandoned children of the asylum with Christian beliefs while offering them basic education and skills.

At that time, education in Europe was not for the masses because Europeans had not figured out a way to scale education; they found it economically unfeasible to educate the masses. Bell was all too familiar with the issues of education and knowledge transmission since he had spent most of his life as a tutor in Scotland and the newly independent United States of America.

Bell faced an unsurmountable task at Madras Male Asylum. The boys were unruly and poorly behaved, with no family to support them. His staff was minimal and badly trained. He struggled to educate the boys under these circumstances. The boys made little or no progress until one day, while on a walk, he closely observed a native Malabar school. Here, Bell saw children learning and teaching one another to write alphabets on sand. 'He hastened home, repeating to himself as he went "Eureka! I have discovered it". He gave immediate orders to the usher of the lowest classes to teach the alphabet in the same manner'.[5] Bell, it seems, had stumbled on to the discovery as to how India had achieved the education of its masses despite all the adversities the country had faced.

Bell stayed in India for ten years—learning, experimenting, and digesting the Indian pedagogical method used by traditional gurukulams. He called it the 'Madras system of Education'.

The key idea that Bell had discovered was that Indian schools used *mutual teaching by students*, which was efficient and helped with scaling-up education because every student was a teacher as well. Bell noticed that children made great peer teachers and enthusiastic learners in such a system. Teaching each other was a great success. He also copied the memorization techniques from Indian gurukulams using chanting in meter. The Indian schools ensured that mornings and evenings were spent on memorization. He also appreciated the importance of teaching every individual according to their merit rather than age:

> Arithmetic tables, for example, were memorized as follows: one boy wrote and at the same time rhythmically recited a number, and the others repeated it, the pupils taking turns acting as the precentor... In South India, the categories in which students were organized concerned not age but individual merit: 'a scholar rises from one [class] to the other according to his capacity and progress'.[6]

Bell closely observed these successful practices of the traditional gurukulam where children were learning in small groups, and he adopted these very same ideas to teach his students at the asylum. He was careful not to attribute the Indian gurukuls for his observation even though this eventually became a groundbreaking discovery for Britain. He compiled his observations in the book *The Madras School: Or Elements of Tuition: Comprising the Analysis of an Experiment in Education Made at the Male Asylum Madras*.[7] He appropriated a standard practice of gurukulams across India and presented it to his British peers as his discovery.

Bell had discovered that the gurukulams' methodology enabled a single instructor to effectively teach a large class of students within a single space simultaneously. India was known for a single village schoolmaster successfully educating the entire village. The instructor merely needed to impart knowledge to a group of the most proficient students, who would then educate and oversee their peers, a system used by thousands of village school teachers for centuries across India.

In private letters written to his friends in Europe, Bell, a life-long tutor who valued pedagogy, had stumbled upon a miracle. He relates the progress of his digested Indian education system enthusiastically:

> In the course of 2 years I have had boys talk (sic) to speak and write and spell English and to advance in Arithmetic. many of them route (sic) beautifully.......every boy is either a master or a scholar and generally both. He teaches one boy while another teaches him. The success has been rapid.[8]

In another letter, he writes:

> The progress of my pupils is beyond what you would believe in Europe. I have bound (sic) out a boy, a clark (sic) in a most respectable department, and for 5 years only who in little more than 12 months after he began to learn his A B C, wrote read and ciphered well. You would be astonished at the sight of my youngsters, of 6 7 and 8 years old.[9]

This method was also economical, he observed. Older boys who had greater proficiency in the subject, serving as teachers to the younger boys, removed the need for teachers with special subject matter expertise:

> Navigation, mensuration, trigonometry surveying and the branches of the mathematics connected with them cannot well be taught at any private school by any teacher of abilities but at a great expense. Whereas at this school, any of these branches of education can be introduced with very little or no addition to the present establishment of teachers.[10]

Although Bell's accounts reveal his enthusiasm for his discovery, the system was nothing new for India. Many Western scholars also are keenly aware that Bell merely copied the idea that was prevalent all over India, or as we would call a 'digested' Indian idea without credit:

> In 1814, the Court of Directors of the East India Company (EIC) opined that Bell's new mode of education was, basically, the 'mode of instruction that from time immemorial has been practised' under Indian village schoolmasters ... Andrew Bell had acted as a mediator who 'advocated the adoption' of the 'Indian system of teaching with the help of monitors' in England.[11]

The elegance of traditional Indian pedagogy had numerous benefits:

1. Large groups could be managed with very little teaching resources.
2. Peer teaching helped maintain discipline and it was easy to implement stringent discipline in the learning environment.
3. Students learned to learn and teach, and this system of mutually reinforced learning took place with very few resources.
4. Students who were eager to please the teacher willingly taught other students with enormous success.
5. A hierarchy of students based on merit was maintained and was continuously re-ranked as children gained subject matter competency. The system provided an environment of healthy competition among students.
6. Students strived to do well, because of the incentives of merit-based promotion within the hierarchy.

This system was successful in building character in students that Andrew Bell had never witnessed, not even through his Bible lessons on morality. He called it 'the steam engine of the moral world', and an 'intellectual engine' that 'has the seat of its power and operation in the human breast, is everywhere in action, and, by an infallible and irresistible impulse, in giving motion to the moral and intellectual'.[12]

After spending ten years in India, Bell returned to London and began to write about what he had learned in India, which he considered a fresh and much-needed approach to structuring education in Britain. It was much later that his writings gained notable attention. The National Society for the Education of the Poor founded in 1811 used the Indian method to teach the masses. Very soon it became the basis for elementary education in England, Scotland, and Ireland.[13] By 1832, there were over ten thousand schools in England and Scotland that were using the Madras system.[14]

The impact of the Indian system was so profound that 'It formed the basis for the most extravagant hopes for the improvement of mankind'.[15] The *Westminster Review* of January 1824, estimated the improvement made in the art of teaching as 'of more importance to the advancement of knowledge than any discovery that has been made since the invention of the alphabet itself'.[16]

So great was Bell's 'discovery' to Britain, that Westminster Abbey has a marble monument dedicated to Andrew Bell, showing him seated with his students in his successful attempt to copy the Indian school system. The inscription describing the monument reads:

> Sacred to the memory of Andrew Bell D.D. L.L.D. Prebendary of this Collegiate Church: the eminent founder of the Madras System of education, who discovered and reduced to successful practice the plan of mutual instruction; founded upon the multiplication of power, and the division of labour, in the moral and intellectual world, which has been adopted within the British Empire as the national system of education of the children of the poor. In the principles of the Established Church, Dr Bell was born in the city of St Andrew's N.B.27th of March 1753. Appointed minister of St Mary's church Madras 1789, Master of Sherburn Hospital 1809, Prebendary of Westminster 1810. Died 27th of January 1832...

In the mid-nineteenth century, Joseph Lancaster, a Quaker (those who belong to the Religious Society of Friends) educator in London, was on a mission to educate the masses and the underprivileged. Lancaster's classroom methods used ideas from the Madras Education System that Bell had developed in his school's practices and touted it as a successful blueprint for elementary education. Like Bell, Lancaster employed older students, whom he called 'monitors' to teach younger ones.

Lancaster soon experienced significant success in the United

Kingdom, particularly in London, where he began attracting large numbers of students and quickly gained popularity. King George III (1738-1820) supported his efforts financially and encouraged the spread of his educational model throughout England. His destitute upbringing did not prepare him for his financial success and Lancaster led a life of extravagance which resulted in debt and bankruptcy. He then emigrated to the USA.

Lancaster promoted his educational system to various educational societies in the USA, leading to the establishment of schools across eastern United States, particularly in urban areas like New York and Philadelphia. By 1810, Lancaster reported significant success, with many new schools opened and thousands of children educated in America.[17]

Bell accused Lancaster of plagiarism, claiming that he had copied his ideas without giving him due credit. He alleged that Lancaster 'stole the idea of employing student monitors from him'.[18]

After this 'second digestion' of the Indian system of education (the first digestion being that of Bell in Madras), the Bell and Lancaster systems gradually merged and evolved into a comprehensive model of elementary education. The system came to be known as *Joseph Lancaster's Monitorial System,* or *the Monitorial System,* or *the Lancaster System*, and was considered the main influence of nineteenth-century education in Europe and the USA.

This was a pivotal turn in the history of the Western education system when it adopted the Madras Monitorial System of education in schools. They had finally figured out a cost-effective and efficient way to educate their masses, which they could never have dreamt of accomplishing before. After Bell and Lancaster renamed and improvised the Indian system for the Western ecosystem, they promoted this system across the world.

It was the first time that the Europeans started theorizing and conceptualizing systems for the education of their masses, which had previously never been attempted. The Europeans spread this system widely wherever they had influence:

> Monitorial teaching soon became discussed internationally and widely adapted in France, Russia and the Ottoman Empire; in the United States and Spanish America, as well as West Africa and India. In a number of places, such as England, New York and Philadelphia, parts of Latin America and Eastern Europe as well as in colonial contexts, monitorial schools even became the nucleus of public elementary education.[19]

While Indians had freely educated the masses without fear in the entire spectrum of subjects, the new mass education system in Europe was limited to some basic education, namely, the study of the Bible, and some job skills. The vision was to keep the labor force 'in its place' and based on the fear of the risk of 'elevating' the minds of the masses.

> Lancaster's supporters and the BFSS put more emphasis on the enabling dimension and the communication of as much knowledge as possible, while Bell and the Church faction stressed the importance of maintaining social order and keeping the children of the poor in their place:
>
> It is not proposed that the children of the poor be educated in an expensive manner, or even taught to write and cypher. Utopian schemes, for the universal diffusion of general knowledge, would soon realize the fable of the belly and the other members of the body, and confound, that the distinction of ranks and classes of society, on which the general welfare hinges, and the happiness of the lower orders, no less than that of the higher, depends. Parents will always be found to educate, at their own expense, children enough to fill the stations, which require higher qualifications; and there is a risk of elevating, by an indiscriminate education, the minds of those doomed to the drudgery of daily labour, above their condition, and thereby rendering them discontented and unhappy in their lot. It may suffice to teach the generality,

> on an economical plan, to read their bible and understand the doctrines of the holy religion.[20]

By 1806, the Indian gurukulam system of education had reached New York, and it remained the mainstream method of education for the next fifty years and helped transform the USA into an economic powerhouse. The New York Free School was the first to be based on the Indian model run by one William Smith, who had been trained in England. The Indian gurukulam method was so successful that, 'in process of time, about three thousand children have been educated in schools in that city'.[21]

In the USA, this Indian gurukulam style of education was considered groundbreaking, as it was in England. The governor in his address to the New York Legislature in 1818

> drew a parallel between the establishment of the Lancasterian system and the introduction of labor-saving machinery… Lancaster had the good fortune to secure the patronage or arouse the interest of the powerful and learned of his time. Sydney Smith called George III's support of Lancaster the brightest passage in the history of his long reign. James Mill, Jeremy Bentham, the Duke of Bedford, Sydney Smith, De Witt Clinton, and Thomas Jefferson were advocates of the system.[22]

14

AN EXAMPLE FOR INDIAN EDUCATION TODAY

The knowledge delivery system that was digested by Bell and Lancaster remains alive in some parts of India, even though much of the country has adopted the Western factory-styled education model for both content and delivery. In this fashionable new model, content is curated to emphasize entertainment and indoctrination of a certain leftist narrative, while delivery is accomplished by children sitting in classrooms grouped by age, often instructed by a single teacher.

Many Indians who tout 'decolonizing' Indian education and promote Indian Knowledge Systems are recycling a nostalgic general discussion of the glorious history of education in India without having drilled deep enough into the subject.

We would like to present a homegrown success story of education that has been long forgotten and that urgently calls for revival. This case study is especially noteworthy because the model we present is comprehensive, including content, pedagogy, and knowledge transmission of the subject matter.

We will look at a specific gurukulam that specializes in teaching linguistics, which is not only foundational to Indic Knowledge Systems but has also been digested by the West to shape its understanding of languages. The methods employed in this gurukulam are the ones that revolutionized education in Europe and the USA transforming them into leading knowledge producers, as discussed in the previous chapter.

We will also connect the dots to showcase a system that works even today on a large scale and uses Indian Knowledge Systems as the content. We have divided the education process into three parts:

1. Content: Refers to the *moola shastra/moola grantha* or the primary shastra or content that needs to be taught.
2. Pedagogy: Refers to the methods or approaches used by the teacher to divide and present the content for instruction, to assess a student's understanding, and teach the content.
3. Class dynamics for knowledge transmission: Refers to the strategies in the learning ecosystem for approaching the student, keeping the student motivated, and involving and arranging the class for instruction keeping in mind the ability and level of competence of the student.

The content, pedagogy, and knowledge transmission approaches have an immense impact on the learning outcome. The content, especially if it is intellectually rigorous like the shastras, needs to be carefully broken down keeping the whole vision of the shastra in mind, to facilitate assimilation by the student. The architecture of this pedagogy is vital as we will see in this case study.

The class dynamics for knowledge transmission also has a huge impact on learning outcomes as we saw in the monitorial system that Westerners adopted from India. Class dynamics include arranging the students into groups for efficient learning, surprise spot quizzing, examinations, time of day and duration for various learning activities, methods for rote learning for efficient memorization, and providing an immersive learning environment that accommodates students of varying learning abilities and competence levels.

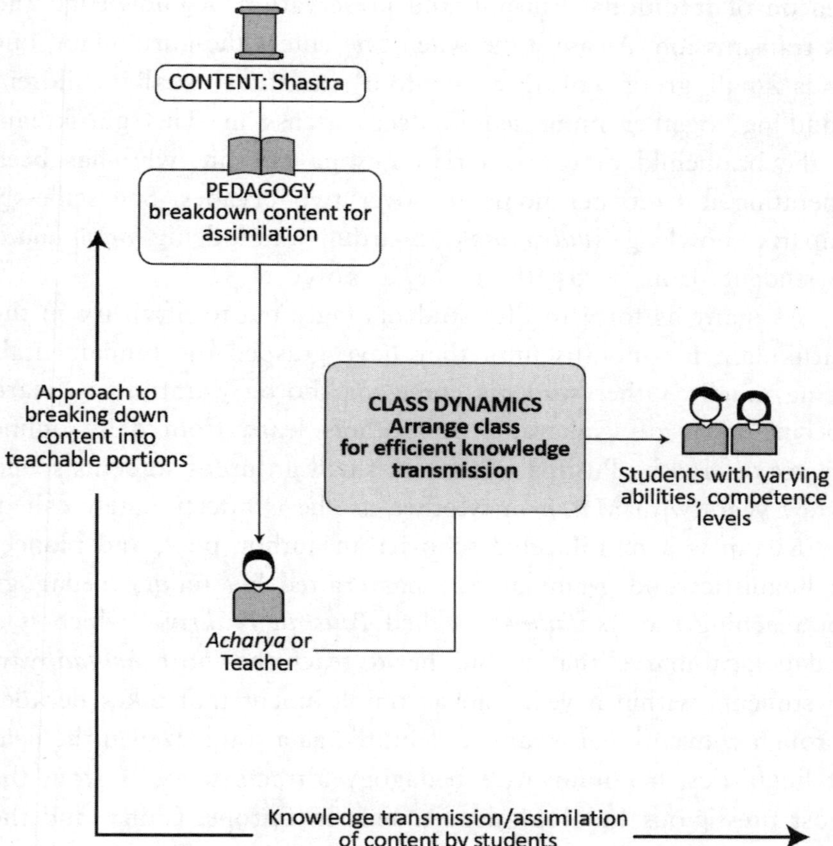

We present a case study of a traditional gurukulam where an Indian Knowledge System is being taught today, using ancient methods combined with innovations in pedagogy that have proven to have a measurable impact on learning outcomes. We shine the spotlight on the Panini Shodh Samsthanam to illustrate how content, pedagogy, and class dynamics (learning ecosystem) come together in producing scholars of Panini's *vyakarana* (grammar), which is the specialty of this gurukulam.

Nestled in the city of Bilaspur in the central Indian state of Chhattisgarh, the Panini Shodh Samsthanam stands as a beacon of traditional learning and preservation of knowledge and its transmission. At any time when one enters the gurukulam, one finds small groups of three or four students (usually children) huddling together immersed in deep discussion. This gurukulam is the brainchild of octogenarian Pushpa Dikshit, who has been operating it from her home for over two decades. She selflessly imparts knowledge (*vidya daan*), boarding and lodging (*anna daan*) to students from across the globe, at no cost.

As many as forty to fifty students (ages ten to fifty) live in the gurukulam for months until they have grasped the fundamentals being taught. Other students come for shorter durations to learn specific areas of vyakarana. Still others learn from daily online classes offered by Pushpa Dikshit. A small group of students spend a few years with *Mataji* or Mother, as she is affectionately called.

Mataji is a multifaceted scholar: an author, poet, and pioneer in linguistics and grammar. She has crafted her unique pedagogy for teaching the *Ashtadhyayi* called *Paushpi Prakriya,* which is a pedagogical marvel that enables her to teach the entire *Ashtadhyayi* to students within a year—an accomplishment that takes decades through conventional means. Celebrated as a trailblazer in the field of linguistics, her innovative pedagogy attracts scholars from the most prestigious Indology departments in Europe, China, and the USA. She has single-handedly revolutionized the study of vyakarana shastra and fundamentally transformed its pedagogical landscape. However, some background is required on the subject matter under consideration, to understand the innovations in this gurukulam's education.

Content

Maharshi Panini's vyakarana, also known as the *Ashtadhyayi*, stands out as an unmatched masterpiece of the human intellect. *Ashtadhyayi* is foundational not only for Sanskrit studies but also as the bedrock of modern Western linguistics. It presents the analysis of linguistic structures—phonology (the study of sound and sound patterns in language), morphology (the study of words, and the principles behind word formation), and syntax.

It has a compact set of four thousand rules for Sanskrit in eight chapters using an algorithmic approach to word formation that serves as a comprehensive framework for understanding the structure of all languages. It is a sophisticated language model where users can input the root, with an optional prefix, and a compulsory suffix to form any Sanskrit word, and *Ashtadhyayi*'s algorithmic engine churns out grammatically correct words as output by applying the correct rules of word creation.

The study of *Ashtadhyayi* is a prerequisite to understanding any shastra or Sanskrit-based knowledge system. However, learning *Ashtadhyayi* has been, and continues to be, a challenge for most students of Sanskrit.

Pedagogy

Historically, Panini's *Ashtadhyayi* has been within reach of only a few select dedicated students of high caliber. Those who could devote years to studying under a vyakarana guru were the ones who could attain a certain level of mastery. For everyone else, it remained shrouded in mystery and an impossible task given the sheer time and intellectual horsepower needed to unravel it.

Traditionally, following Panini's initial composition of *Ashtadhyayi* (authored in the fifth century BCE) students of grammar memorized the entire *Ashtadhyayi* in the sequence of sutras as presented by Panini. The disruption and consequent destruction of many sampradayas by Muslim and European colonizers led to the erosion of teaching methods and pedagogy. With the loss of these knowledge transmission systems, the brevity and coded meta-language of *Ashtadhyayi* poses a monumental challenge for many students, as they attempt to navigate through the labyrinth of its sutras with rules and meta rules.

Due to the complexity, the original approach of learning *Ashtadhyayi* was replaced with a *prakriya* approach, which was a method to pick out different sutras scattered across the eight chapters of the *Ashtadhyayi* to find the ingredients or individual operations (sutras) that can be used to derive certain *padas* or words (noun and verb forms). By the seventeenth century, *Vaiyakarana Siddhantakaumudi* commonly known as *Siddhanta Kaumudi* by Bhattoji Dikshita was the standard text in use, offering a pedagogy for navigating the *Ashtadhyayi* using the prakriya method (by function), which did not follow the sequence of Panini's *Ashtadhyayi*, but instead selected sutras across various chapters to construct certain word forms.

Even this became difficult for many students to master; hence, a simpler and more diluted *Laghu Siddhanta Kaumudi* was written by Bhattoji Dikshita's disciple, Varadaraja. Today, *Laghu Siddhanta Kaumudi* serves as a basic primer for teaching *Ashtadhyayi*, which also follows the prakriya method. Most post-graduate students struggle to fully grasp even the *Laghu Siddhanta Kaumudi*.

While the abridged *Laghu Siddhanta Kaumudi* gives a glimpse of Panini's genius in *Ashtadhyayi*, students who want to take a deeper dive, study *Siddhanta Kaumudi* which takes over ten years to complete, and sometimes takes decades to gain an understanding of *Ashtadhyayi*. And even after such a long study, students struggle to exhibit mastery of *Ashtadhyayi*. The Arya Samaj (a movement that believes in the *Vedas*) also has a rigorous pedagogy for Panini's *Ashtadhyayi*, starting with their Prathamavritti curriculum, but many students drop out because they are unable to survive the rigor and brute force approach of the Arya Samaj's pedagogy.

Pushpa Dikshit realized that Bhattoji Dikshita's method in his *Vaiyakarana Siddhanta Kaumudi*, the principal commentary on *Ashtadhyayi*, was not the ideal way to convey this ancient knowledge. Instead, she pointed out that Panini's approach was quite distinct from Bhattoji Dikshita's. She argued that if Panini's method were applied at the educational level, it would be much more effective than the complex strategy employed by Bhattoji Dikshita.

This goes to show that Indian Knowledge Systems need not be frozen in time and that innovation and continuous improvement are part of our tradition, which somehow has been forgotten by many Sanskrit scholars of today. With the Paushpa Prakriya, *Ashtadhyayi* becomes accessible and saves decades in a student's life. It re-organizes and re-classifies the material to impart knowledge using building blocks to help the student assimilate the knowledge.

What Mataji has achieved with Paniniya-vyakaranam may be unprecedented in the field's history. She implemented two key strategies: first, providing a systematic framework for organizing the *Ashtadhyayi*; and second, ensuring thorough practice of each functional module of this framework. By breaking down Paniniya-vyakaranam into its fundamental components, Mataji has aligned her pedagogy with Panini's logic, making *Ashtadhyayi* inherently intuitive when approached in line with Panini's methodology.

With the Paushpa Prakriya, students use the sutras to gain mastery of a specific algorithm that performs a specialized function as opposed to the traditional approach of figuring out the use of various algorithms to produce certain final forms of output, i.e. noun or a verb. Her approach is to gain mastery of individual functions through practice. This is different from the focus of the prakriya approach of Bhattoji Dikshita to create the final output of the noun or verb form. Once mastery is gained with individual functions, the student can assemble the functions to achieve the desired output. According to Pushpa Dikshit, this is aligned with Panini's vision.

Knowledge Transmission

The Panini Shodh Samsthanam gurukulam is also a living example of the Indian 'monitorial' system for knowledge transmission. It ensures that knowledge is transmitted efficiently, according to each learner's ability, with checks and balances. The gurukulam's students are extremely diverse and yet knowledge is transmitted efficiently by one octogenarian guru to forty to fifty young students. Her students vary in:

1. Age
2. Level of competency
3. Academic backgrounds: some are from traditional Veda paathshalas while others go to modern English medium schools. Still others are research scholars from foreign universities.
4. Locations: students from all over India, Nepal, Europe, China and the USA.
5. Language
6. Sex: both male and female students.

The Western education system's practice of organizing students into age-based classes is seldom questioned. It has been assumed that this is the optimal approach to learning. However, this approach diverges from the traditional gurukulam model which does not adhere to rigid age-based groupings. Instead, gurukulams embrace a mixed-age group with a hierarchy of roles based on merit, fostering an environment where students of different ages and even generations learn together.

In contrast to the compartmentalized nature of age-specific divisions, mixed-age groupings offer numerous advantages. They encourage collaboration and mutual learning among students with varying levels of experience and knowledge. Younger students with less subject competence benefit from the guidance and mentorship of older (and usually more knowledgeable) peers, while older students reinforce their understanding by teaching and assisting younger ones. The practice of mixed-age groupings based on merit and intergenerational learning is the bedrock of the Panini Shodh Samsthanam.

It not only enhances collaboration and community but also cultivates a profound sense of self-worth and purpose among older students who are looked upon as role models, and who recognize their value and contribution to the learning community.

Conversely, younger students benefit from the supportive and inclusive atmosphere created by mixed-age groupings. They feel more comfortable asking questions and seeking guidance from older peers, free from the fear of judgment or embarrassment. This open exchange encourages curiosity and critical thinking, as younger learners feel empowered to actively engage in the learning process and express their ideas without reservation.

This mixed-age learning environment can also transcend hierarchies of age and authority. There are instances where younger students, despite their age, possess advanced competence compared to others, and such youths take on the role of teaching and instructing older peers or even adults. For example, it is not uncommon to see a seven-year-old girl confidently teach a small group of adults in their twenties, captivating their attention with her depth of understanding and clarity of explanation. Such experiences not only validate the capabilities of younger learners but also instill a sense of pride and accomplishment. Witnessing their peers excel in teaching motivates other children to strive for excellence, fostering healthy competition and a spirit of achievement. This is how the mixed-age learning environment at the Panini Shodh Samsthanam promotes a culture of mutual support, continuously pushing the boundaries of the students' capabilities while transcending traditional notions of age, gender, and expertise. All this is done under the supervision and direction of Pushpa Dikshit.

Other features of the knowledge transmission process include:

1. A series of six volumes written by Pushpa Dikshit serves as the guideline and provides the learning pathway for the study of *Ashtadhyayi*.
2. Each day begins with chores around the gurukulam allocated to the students. At seven in the morning, students assemble in the hall to begin their studies. The day begins by reviewing the previous day's material and then delving into new teachings.

3. Students rely heavily on the guidance of other students in the gurukulam to catch up on their progress. Small groups of students can be seen teaching and learning, throughout Mataji's home like the Indian traditional 'monitorial' system that captivated Bell and Lancaster. It is an effective system for sclaing-up knowledge transmission and is beneficial to all participants.
4. Advanced students are allowed to teach under the guru's supervision.
5. Pushpa Dikshit reviews, conducts spot quizzes, and tests, and teaches as per her analyses of each student's progress.
6. Students learn efficient techniques to commit to memory various sutras and other materials. The science of committing to memory involves
   a. What: content (sutras, etc.).
   b. When: time of day is crucial for learning by heart.
   c. How: number of repetitions, mentally or saying it out aloud.
   d. How often: revisions.
   e. Specialized techniques for memorizing content in both metrical and non-metrical forms.
7. From time to time, students are exposed to the ideas of eminent visitors to the gurukulam.
8. Senior students are involved in editing books and other papers. They also conduct online classes for remote students of the gurukulam.
9. As Bell noticed, students' discipline, attitude, and responsibility are noticeably worthy of appreciation especially when compared with students of similar ages who attend Western-styled schools.

The adoption of mixed-age learning models that incorporate customized learning solutions on a large scale is the hallmark of traditional Bharatiya education. By studying and implementing these proven approaches, coupled with the strategic integration of technology, India holds the potential to revitalize its rich knowledge systems, pedagogies, and modes of knowledge transmission to educate its masses. This holistic approach not only aligns with India's cultural heritage but also addresses the pressing need for educational reform to meet the demands of the modern world.

The Ministry of Education has an opportunity to promote inclusive and personalized learning experiences that cater to the diverse needs and abilities of students across the country. By embracing the principles of collaboration and mentorship inherent in these models, India can foster a culture of lifelong learning and intellectual curiosity among its young citizens.

Since the eighteenth century, Europeans have been astonished by the high levels of mass literacy in India, a feat they could scarcely imagine achieving in their societies. Upon studying the Indian gurukulam and Thinnai schools, they swiftly adopted and implemented these pedagogical concepts in Europe and the USA. Simultaneously, they began imposing the Macaulay-inspired model of European education in India, aiming to sever India's deep-rooted cultural and civilizational connections as part of their colonization strategy.

This new Westernized education system deliberately excluded Indian languages, traditional knowledge systems, lineages (sampradayas), and ancient scriptures (shastras). Furthermore, they instituted classrooms based on age and not by subject for knowledge transmission, forcing a disruption of India's traditional system.

Immersive Learning

A gurukulam like the one discussed above where the students are steeped in study while living with the guru achieves an unparalleled depth in the subject matter. This facilitates rapid mastery of subjects through constant immersion in the knowledge system utilizing three key stages of *shravanam* (listening), *mananam* (reflection) and *nidhidhyasanam* (assimilation). This intensive method allows students to internalize complex concepts and achieve rapid proficiency.

Often misunderstood as overly specialized, the traditional

gurukulam system offers a unique approach to education that achieves both depth and breadth simultaneously. Like a hologram, where each fragment contains information of the whole, each shastra in the gurukulam system contains the essence of all knowledge. This integral unity of shastra allows students to gain a comprehensive understanding of the world through the intensive study of a single discipline. By delving deeply into one area, students gain insights that apply universally across disciplines. For example, all the shastras in the integrally unified system reflect the ultimate goal of moksha in the paramarthika realm. In vyakarna shastra it is said,

> व्याकरणाध्ययनात् धर्मविद्यां प्राप्नोति, धर्मविद्यया मोक्षमवाप्नोति
>
> (Through the study of grammar, one attains knowledge of righteousness, and through that knowledge, one attains mokṣha.)

Bharata Muni, author of the *Natyashastra* says:

> न तज्ज्ञानं न तच्छिल्पं न सा विद्या न सा कला ।
> नासौ योगो न तत्कर्म नाटेऽस्मिन् यन्न दृश्यते ।।
>
> (There is no wisdom, no learning, no art, nor craft nor action that is absent in natya.)

This comprehensive approach to education prepares a student for a profession, and more importantly, for life itself.

By replicating the gurukulam model of knowledge transmission, Europe and the USA were able to achieve literacy of the masses, which significantly contributed to their economic growth and helped propel them out of the Dark Ages. In exchange, India received Western content and teaching methodologies. Indian schools were restructured to mirror British schools, marking the beginning of what can be seen as the Dark Age of Indian education. India shifted away from its rich educational heritage towards a system that prioritized a colonized curriculum and models of schooling over the holistic and competency-based approaches of the past.

CONCLUSION: THE WAY FORWARD

In this book, we have offered a *purva-paksha* on the education system that India has adopted while simultaneously giving the reader a glimpse of what is possible. It is up to us as stakeholders to demand more from the government, look for alternate sources to educate our children, and feverishly resurrect the dying breed of civilizational knowledge to revive that *vidya*, or that knowledge which liberates—सा विद्या या विमुक्तवे!

The National Education Policy 2020 states some obvious purposes of education such as:

- providing a 'holistic' education
- securing good jobs and skill development to create human capital for a growing economy
- reliance on meaningless rote learning as opposed to developing thinking skills
- discovering a child's passion
- achieving equity, inclusion, and education for all
- teaching young people *how* to think rather than *what* to think
- imparting soft skills like social skills and not just pragmatic hard skills
- teaching children the love for learning
- making children the agents of social change

Our critique shows that India's NEP has failed in those areas that relate to civilization matters. The NEP represents a missed opportunity for India to address fundamental questions about the purpose of education.

Often, these 'feel-good' statements lack substance and depth and serve as superficial pathways to import Western paradigms.

The West has developed models to address educational issues based on its worldview along with globalist agendas. Sadly, India has blindly adopted these models wholesale, without a critical assessment to evaluate their effectiveness in the context of India's distinct civilizational values.

Furthermore, even a basic assessment of how these models have performed in the USA reveals significant shortcomings. The American education system has lost meritocracy, and it champions social divisiveness. Meanwhile, China has catapulted as the meritocratic leader on the world stage. China excels in knowledge generation and distribution. The American system

- instills victim orientation in a child's mind, and then
- glorifies the feeling of victimhood
- teaches children that feelings are indeed facts, and
- meritocracy and virtues like hard work, and punctuality are oppressive.

A critical evaluation or purva-paksha would have revealed the unsuitability and irrelevance of these models for India, as we have shown. Before crafting the NEP 2020 the education ministry should have conducted a thorough review of the Western education system, like the one offered in this book.

Moreover, India should address education based on Vedic frameworks: What is the Vedic view on environmentalism, equality, soft skills, citizenship, social justice etc.? That should have been discussed in position papers and policy statements by including inputs from a variety of scholars before developing NEP. The present NEP 2020 must be rewritten in certain areas that concern the issues addressed in this book, and this should be premised on an understanding of Vedic social sciences.

The Western social contract model depends on *agreement among egos*, but this cannot succeed in establishing sustainable equilibrium. Woke is a response to the ego's 'difference anxiety' turning it into reverse hatred or identity camps or canceling others. Because the ego is heavily burdened with toxic conditioning (samskaras), it changes its game at different life stages: one jumps around through different kinds of ambitions both individual and family, various forms of indulgence and pastimes, eventually ending up in old age without purpose. A precious lifetime is wasted fighting the latest fires and competing with others. The fight/flight response never produces any enduring contentment.

The Vedic approach sees difference as being inherent in every aspect of the cosmos. It is not a problem to be managed with blame, or the oppressor/oppressed dialectic. Differences should be not just tolerated but mutually respected, celebrated, and experienced as Bhagawan's *lila* or beauty. One must first gain insight into why such a life is meaningless, and transform oneself by cultivating a positive, healthy ego aligned with cosmic principles.

Unfortunately, the UN's Sustainable Development Goals do not begin with individual yoga to advance humankind's consciousness. They are entirely a top-down approach to social contracts and enforcing them using carrots and sticks approach.

To build a robust, national education policy rooted in Vedic civilization, India's policymakers, educators, parents, and others concerned must do the following:

1. Stop blindly complying with the UN's SDGs 2030 in matters related to education. Instead, it should follow China's example of paying lip service to SDGs while adapting them to fit into the nation's specific civilization matrix.
2. Stop SEL from MGIEP and other organizations, Global Citizenship Education, and CSE programs across the country pending a comprehensive reassessment of the underlying philosophy and its relationship with Vedic principles.
3. Focus on literacy and numeracy as a first step.
4. Do not allow NGOs to collect data on students.
5. Prohibit private actors from providing sex education or SEL, online or in-person, with their content.
6. Do not allow foreign-funded or influenced NGOs to train

teachers, provide content, or anything that is related to the core content and pedagogy in education.

7. While CBE programs can indeed improve access to education for the poor and the marginalized, these programs should be purely academic and merit-oriented, while being self-paced.
8. Develop specific programs to identify and groom the top ten percent of the country's talent in all fields.
9. Formulate strict policies to restrict children's use of social media.

Furthermore, the strategic integration of technology can enhance the reach and effectiveness of these educational initiatives, particularly in remote or underserved areas. Artificial Intelligence-based digital platforms can facilitate access to quality educational resources, connect students with expert mentors and educators, and enable collaborative learning experiences regardless of geographical constraints. However, this must be explicitly aligned with Indian civilization and not be allowed to run counter to it.

India's classical body of literature is renowned for its rich and diverse collection of poetry, prose, and aphorisms which spans several millennia and encompasses a variety of languages and styles. Sanskrit poetry and prose, epitomized by the works of Kalidasa, Maagha, Bhavabhuti, and Bhartrihari, is celebrated for its profound philosophical themes, intricate metaphors, and lyrical beauty. Tamil literature, with masterpieces like Sangam poetry and the epic *Silappadikaram,* offers vivid depictions of love, valor, and nature. Similarly, every region has contributed to the rich literary heritage of Bharat, embodying a timeless exploration of human emotions, philosophy, and the natural world. The Itihasa-Purana tradition is a cornerstone of India's classical literature, encompassing historical narratives that have profoundly influenced Indian civilizational thought, delving into complex themes of dharma and the human condition.

Teaching these Indian classics would benefit in the following ways:

1. Indian literature gives importance to *rasa* (essence). It addresses complex emotions head-on, presenting characters that navigate ethical dilemmas and overcome obstacles, offering timeless lessons in emotional resilience and personal growth. Indian literature is rich in stories of values and role models that children can look up to and emulate. It cultivates virtue and prepares the student for life, and not merely a job.
2. Studying Indian literature helps a child understand Bharat's rich history from its own value system. This is the best way to pass down India's civilizational wisdom to the next generation.
3. Many texts in Indian Knowledge Systems combine multiple fields and do not view subjects in isolation. For example, Bhaskaracharya's *Lilavati* is a text on ganita shastra (loosely translated as mathematics). Its sloka form is set to meter and has the following features:
   a. Concepts of arithmetic, algebra and geometry, number theory.
   b. Presents more than three methods for multiplication and over eight methods for addition.
   c. Work of beautiful poetry; rasa filled.
   d. Uses real-world application in its examples.
   e. Poetry is set to meter.
   f. Lyrical beauty and aesthetics.

The traditional education system comprising the sixty-four Vidyasthanani refers to the traditional Indian classification of sixty-four arts and sciences that were considered essential for a well-rounded education. These disciplines encompass a wide range of skills, knowledge, and artistic pursuits, reflecting the holistic approach to education. Appendix E provides the list of these arts and sciences. It is important to revive and teach some of these relevant knowledge systems.

Indian Knowledge Systems are designed to align humanity

in harmony with the planet, and such an alignment is inherently sustainable. This alignment is yajna. It is imperative to educate our young generation with this lens to guide the present world in crisis. India should offer leadership and guidance in this regard through the revival of the timeless wisdom of the rishis. This holistic approach has at its core, environmental sustainability, social harmony, and spiritual well-being. By tapping into the relevant principles of Indian Knowledge Systems, India can pave the way for innovative solutions that the world desperately needs.

This should be the path for India to reclaim its historic role as a vishvaguru, or world leader in education, knowledge production, and knowledge dissemination. However, this requires all stakeholders to re-evaluate the current policies that are dangerous to India's sovereignty, stability, and survival.

APPENDIX A: PETITIONED LETTER TO WHO OVER PANDEMIC TREATY

May 17, 2024
World Health Organization
H.E. Dr. Tedros Adhanom Ghebreyesus
Office of the Director General
Avenue Appia 20
1211 Geneva, Switzerland

Dear Dr., Tedros, Director-General of the World Health Organization,

We write to express profound concern over the WHO's handling of amendments to the International Health Regulations (IHR) and the drafting of the pandemic treaty.

As Director-General of the WHO, you represent the ideals of the United Nations, including "establish[ing] conditions under which justice and respect for [treaty obligations] and other sources of international law can be maintained." The global pursuit of peace and human rights is anchored in the rule of law and, indeed, without the rule of law, tyranny and oppression prevail. It is thus imperative that you honor existing treaties and international laws yourself.

Article 55(2) of the IHR mandates that the text of any proposed amendment be communicated at least four months before the Health Assembly where it will be considered. Claiming that the dissemination of an initial draft in February 2023 meets this requirement, despite ongoing negotiations, is absurd. Equally unreasonable is the assertion that this requirement applies only to the Director General and Member States, not the working group they appointed, when the Article makes no such distinction. Both arguments show a blatant disregard for both the spirit and the letter of the law.

The World Health Assembly (WHA) Rules of Procedure numbers 8, 10, 11, & 15 also prohibit rushing agreements without due diligence. Additionally, Rule 14's requirement for full disclosure of all obligations, including financial obligations, has been grossly violated, with crucial details deferred until some future time. This essentially forces Member States to sign a blank check.

Moreover, the hasty adoption of multiple instruments with overlapping technical, administrative, and financial requirements will inevitably lead to confusion and could seriously undermine global health efforts going forward. This underscores the critical need to adhere to the four-month minimum requirement.

Besides the concerns about timing and notification, the legitimacy of any agreement fundamentally relies on its adherence to the following fundamental principles of the rule of law:

1. **Valid Voting Process:** An authentic roll-call vote with a two-thirds majority present must be documented and available for verification. Without this proof any "agreement" is null and void.
2. **Clear and Final Wording:** The terms of any agreement must be explicitly defined within the document itself. It is unacceptable to use open-ended wording that defers crucial decisions to unaccountable committees.
3. **Member-Led Negotiations:** The bureau's role should be solely to facilitate discussions, not dictate outcomes. Negotiations must be transparent and inclusive, accommodating the capacities of all delegations, especially those from smaller countries. Ad-hoc, concurrent negotiations without proper notice or translation violate the principles of international law.

Using potential pandemics as a pretext to violate the principles of good governance erodes trust and undermines international cooperation when it is most needed. Proceeding with the adoption of new amendments to the IHR or the proposed pandemic treaty at the upcoming 77th World Health Assembly would be contrary to law. Should you proceed, any resulting agreement will immediately be null and void. Conversely, following these basic principles of good governance will demonstrate the WHO's commitment to global health and the rule of law.

Sincerely,
Christopher H. Smith, Chairman
House Foreign Affairs Subcommittee on Global Health, Global Human Rights, and International Organizations[1]

APPENDIX B: MILESTONES IN RTE ACT

Year	Law	What it says	Implications
2002	Added Article 21 A in 86th Amendment. Launch of Sarva Shiksha Abhiyan	Education is a fundamental right: free and compulsory education to all children between ages 6 to 14.	All children have a right to free education, and education is compulsory, i.e. mandated till age 14.
2005	Added clause 5 in Article 15, in 93rd Constitutional Amendment	Allowed special provisions by states, with respect to admission to educational institutions for backward classes, Scheduled Castes, Scheduled Tribes in all aided or unaided educational institutes, but NOT in minority educational institutes.	States are at liberty to mandate educational institutes to make provisions for affirmative action for minorities with respect to education; However, Christian, Muslim and other minority institutes are exempt from providing state-mandated reservations for SC/ST/backward groups
2009	RTE enacted Section 12(1)(c) of the Act	Free, mandatory, *inclusive* education for all. Also, it mandates unaided private schools to make 25% reservation of seats for children belonging to the economically weaker section and disadvantaged groups. but Article 30 of the Indian Constitution guarantees protection to linguistic and religious minority groups to establish and manage their institution.	*Inclusive* Education: mandate to include underprivileged children. Mainstream and Hindu schools must set aside 25% of seats under reservation for disadvantaged groups. This does NOT apply to Christian and Muslim-run institutions.

2012	Amendment to RTE	Minority education institutions are exempted from following the RTE Act.	RTE is applicable ONLY to government, private, and Hindu schools. Minority institutions do not have to follow stringent rules of RTE.
2014	Pramati judgment by Supreme court	The Supreme Court declared that the RTE Act is not applicable to schools run by religious minorities.	Gives minorities the freedom to run their institutions however they want, with little restriction, in the name of the rights of minorities. Hindus have no such free hand to administer their schools Results: financial burden because of compliance and 25% reservation; no free hand to administer schools; many schools shut down.

APPENDIX C: MILESTONES IN INDIA'S SEX EDUCATION POLICY

Sex Education Program Year	Program Design	Scope	Age	Nature of Program
School AIDS Education Program (SAEP) 2002	National AIDS Control Organisation (NACO)	Prevent the spread of HIV and AIDS among youth.	classes 9-11	Standalone Module
Adolescent Education Program (AEP) 2005	MHRD	Preventing STIs, HIV/AIDs **Scope Creep:** Substance abuse and basic sex education	10-19 years	Standalone Module
Life Skills Education Program (LSE) 2009	MHRD in partnership with **UNFPA**	Preventing STIs, HIV/AIDs, substance abuse, and basic sex education. **Scope Creep:** Teach 'positive relationships'; challenge gender norms and stereotypes; and address gender discrimination.	13-18 years	Standalone Module
Rashtriya Kishor Swasthya Karyakram (RKSK) Saathiya toolkit mobile app– January 2014; Sex Education Inclusion in 2017[2]	**Scope Creep**: New ministry penetrated Ministry of Health and Family Welfare with content help from **UNFPA, PFI**	Nutrition; mental health; NCDs; prevent injuries and violence; basic sexual health—reduce teenage pregnancies, preventing STIs, HIV/AIDs; substance abuse.[3] **Scope Creep**: Teaches that homosexuality is normal; teaches to change attitudes toward masculinity and femininity; teaches gender as a social construct.	10-19 years	**Scope Creep**: Increased scalability Bypass adult teachers and instead have peer advisors; toolkit; mobile app, Q&A booklet.

Udaan, Jharkhand, 2006, 2017	Jharkhand, UNESCO, C3			**Scope Creep**: A curriculum has been integrated into school textbooks and the in- and pre-service education of teachers.
School Health Program 2018	Ayushman Bharat: MHRD and MOHFW	Information about health; promoting healthy behaviors among children. **Scope Creep**: CSE through Wellness Ambassadors, trained by foreign-funded NGOs.	Starts at 14 years	**Scope Creep**: Wellness Ambassadors are trained by foreign- funded NGOs that promote CSE.
Ayushman Bharat's 'School Health Ambassador Initiative' 2020	Union HRD minister, Ramesh Pokhriyal and Union health minister, Harsh Vardhan	**Scope Creep** from Ayushman Bharat of 2018: A school-based health and wellness program: Will include CSE based on Udaan, and SEL. There are 11 themes under health which include SEL and CSE topics such as emotional and mental well-being, gender equality, interpersonal relationships, and reproductive health.	All schools	NCERT has prepared a curriculum to embed SEL and CSE; teacher training program also developed.
NITI Aayog helps tech startups (public-private partnerships) Post 2020	Online CSE accessible to all	Startups, social media influencers giving CSE education on sexual pleasure, rights, and other topics	All ages	Scale up via online; partnerships with state governments.

APPENDIX D: OUR RESPONSE TO RECOMMENDATIONS BY THE POPULATION FOUNDATION OF INDIA

Theme	PFI Recommendations (Selected)	Our Response
Gender & Sex	• Ensure that the curriculum clearly establishes gender as a social construct. • Avoid using terms like 'both genders', 'opposite gender', or 'third gender' that stem from a binary understanding of gender. • Use gender-neutral language across the curriculum. • Do not use gender identities (man and woman) and sex categories (male and female) interchangeably. • Clearly articulate the difference between a person's gender identity and gender expression. Avoid using vocabulary or tools that result in a conflated understanding of the two. • Do not use a binary definition for transgender people. Also talk about non-binary identities. • Include discussion around gender dysphoria, gender affirmative surgeries, and other transgender healthcare issues. • Include content around intersex categories and address misconceptions and stigma around intersex bodies. Clarify that a person being intersex does not mean they would identify as transgender and not all transgender people have intersex bodies.	• Respect for biological reality with terms like 'male' and 'female' that have longstanding meanings. • Replacing traditional terms with gender-neutral language could lead to confusion and undermine linguistic clarity. • Gender-neutral language culturally shifts us away from Indian values, potentially leading to ideological indoctrination in education. • Oppose including discussions on transgender and intersex issues in educational curricula as it could confuse and distress children and infringe on parental guidance. • Gender-neutral language policies infringe on parental rights to teach Indian and Hindu values. • Indian Hindus hold a spiritual view of life: we are a transmigrating soul that is genderless and without attributes. The aspiration is to transcend identities altogether and the mind-body complex. • We stand for freedom of speech without being compelled to use gender-neutral terms.

	• Address how biological experiences, gender, and cultural norms affect the way children and young people experience and navigate their sexuality. • Address transgression (rewards and punishments) power relations, inequalities, and discrimination.	• Hindu and Indian parents teach children about the importance of karma and dharma to improve life. We are skeptical and opposed to theories that emphasize power relations, inequalities, and discrimination as central to understanding gender and sexuality. Such theories can promote a victimhood mentality and undermine personal responsibility and accountability.
Relationships	• Do not enforce the idea that 'blood relatives' are the only family a person can have. Discuss non-heteronormative family structures as well. • Avoid messaging such as 'home is always a safe space', or 'your parents would never wish you harm or do anything to hurt you'. This might not be the reality for all participants particularly those living in abusive households.	• Children benefit from stable, traditional family structures where they can learn about healthy relationships and moral values. • In the Indian and Hindu view, stable, two-parent heterosexual households along with extended family and community provide the best environment for raising children, and normalizing alternative family structures could undermine family stability. Blood relatives as a source of support and stability for individuals, particularly children. • While instances of abuse are unacceptable and should be addressed, it is important to respect the role of parents in providing guidance and support to their children.
SRH	• Do not use terms like 'male hormone' or 'female hormone' as hormones are not sex-specific. • Use language like 'pregnant person', 'person seeking abortion', 'menstruator', or 'people with vaginas'	• We stress the importance of using terms like 'male hormone' and 'female hormone' to describe biological differences and oppose ambiguous language that could lead to misunderstandings in medical contexts.

	• instead of 'girl/woman' to reiterate the difference between gender identities and sex categories and to be inclusive of transgender and/or intersex individuals. • Provide information about different contraceptive methods and their effectiveness in avoiding early and unintended pregnancy. • Address the harmful notion that menstruation is the sole indicator that a person is ready to get pregnant or that 'pregnancy/childbirth completes a woman'. • Reinforce the concepts of bodily autonomy and reproductive self-determination. • Provide comprehensive and accurate information on abortion access and post-abortion care, address the fear, stigma, and misconceptions related to abortion. • Provide information about reliable local SRH service points. • Address the problematic notion of 'virginity' and various problematic cultural practices that stem from it. • Address reproductive processes such as erectile dysfunction, ejaculation (process, types, wet dreams, and myths).	• Terms like 'pregnant person' and 'menstruator' obscure the biological distinctions between male and female bodies and could lead to misunderstandings or miscommunication in medical contexts. • Biological sex is an objective reality. Replacing terms like 'girl' and 'woman' with more gender-neutral language erases and undermines women's rights and identity. This also disregards cultural traditions that have been in place for millennia. • Medicalization of gender identity, particularly involving minors, due to the irreversible nature of some medical interventions and long-term consequences. • The idea of virginity as a valuable virtue helps to counteract the negative influences of a hypersexualized culture and encourages young people to make responsible choices about their sexual behavior.
Sexual Citizenship	• Provide a comprehensive definition of sexuality and sexual identities according to WHO. • Clearly articulate the difference between sexual identity, sexual orientation, and sexual behaviors.	• We protect the sanctity of life from conception, opposing efforts to promote abortion access and post-abortion care as disregarding the rights of the unborn child.

	• Differentiate between romantic and sexual relationships. • Do not provide absolute definitions for various sexual orientations as conflation of gender and sex as well as sexual preferences might result in mislabeling an individual's sexual orientation. Therefore, the emphasis should be on self-determination rather than providing rigid labels for sexual orientations. • Address the stigma associated with people who identify as asexual or aromantic. • Reiterate that every person has the right to choose their partner(s) without having to label themselves. • Clarify the difference between a person's gender identity, gender expression, and sexual orientation. • Discuss the impact on a person's access to rights due to their sexuality. • Provide information about different laws and policies relevant for LGBTQIA+ individuals. • Address the stigma surrounding people who sell sex.	• Comprehensive information about abortion access in educational settings could undermine parental authority and values. • We uphold traditional moral values in matters of sexuality and view non-traditional sexual acts as leading to moral degradation and societal harm. • While sex work is often driven by complex factors such as economic necessity or exploitation, efforts should be directed toward addressing underlying issues such as poverty, addiction, or coercion.
Pleasure	• Include sex-positive messaging and center pleasure in discussions around sexuality. • Address stigma and misconceptions related to masturbation.	• Advocate for protecting children from exposure to inappropriate or harmful content related to sexuality, such as pornography and supporting parental involvement in sex education.

	• Address the notion that 'only boys masturbate'. • Discuss how different individuals experience arousal and orgasm differently. • Discuss the positive and negative effects of substance use and the risks associated with it. • Develop content around sexual exploration (self-love, experimentation, desire, fantasy, porn, sex toys) and destigmatize non-penile-vaginal sexual acts. • Include chemsex ('party and play' or 'wired play', sexual activity mostly between men under the influence of drugs), fetishes and kinks.	• We protect family values and the well-being of children and families and oppose the normalization of non-traditional sexual behaviors. • We promote abstinence of substance use as it degrades the mind. We are opposed to discussing 'positive effects' of substance use to normalize or glamorize it. • We caution against promoting messages that normalize or encourage behaviors that could undermine the institution of marriage or family values. • Sex positivity promotes moral relativism, where there are no absolute standards of right or wrong regarding sexual behavior. This lack of moral clarity leads to harmful consequences such as the breakdown of family cohesion and the objectification of individuals. • We view behaviors like chemsex, fetishes, and kink as morally problematic, potentially leading to physical and psychological harm, and contributing to the breakdown of traditional family values. • We are concerned that glamorizing these behaviors could increase experimentation and normalize risky sexual behaviors. • Excessive focus on sexual liberation can lead to the erosion of traditional family structures and moral standards. It promotes a culture of hedonism.

APPENDIX E: LIST OF EIGHTEEN VIDYAS AND SIXTY-FOUR KALAS[4]

Eighteen *Vidya Sthanani*

- Four *Vedas*
- Six *Vedangas*
- Four *Upangas*
- Four *Upavedas*

Four *Vedas*

- *Rigveda*
- *Samaveda*
- *Yajurveda*
- *Atharvaveda*

Six *Vedangas*

- *Shiksha* (Phonetics)
- *Kalpa* (Rituals)
- *Vyakarana* (Grammar)
- *Nirukta* (Etymology)
- *Chanda* (Metrics)
- *Jyotisha* (Astronomy)

4 *Upangas*

- *Nyaya*
- *Mimamsa*
- *Itihasa Purana*
- *Dharmashastra*

4 *Upavedas*

- *Dhanurveda* (Warfare)
- *Gandharvaveda* (Music)
- *Shilpaveda* (Architecture)
- Ayurveda (Medicine)

Sixty-four *Kalas*	***Chatushashti Kala* (Art Forms)**
• Singing • Instrumental music • Dancing • Painting • Forehead adornments • Making decorative floral and grain designs on the floor • Home and temple flower arranging • Personal grooming • Mosaic tiling • Bedroom arrangements • Creating music with water • Splashing and squirting with water • Secret mantras • Making flower garlands • Head adornments • Dressing • Costume decorations • Perfumery • Jewelery making • Magic and illusions • Ointments for charm and strength • Manual dexterity • Skills of cooking, eating and drinking • Beverage and dessert preparation • Sewing (making and mending garments) • Embroidery • Playing veena and drum • Riddles and rhymes • Poetry games • Tongue-twisters and difficult recitation • Literary recitation • Drama and storytelling	• Verse composition game • Furniture caning • Knowledge of the art of *Kama* • Crafting wooden furniture • Architecture and house construction • Distinguishing between ordinary and precious stones and metals • Metal-working • Gems and mining • Gardening and horticulture • Games of wager involving animals • Training parrots and mynas to speak • Hairdressing • Coding messages • Speaking in code • Knowledge of foreign languages and dialects • Making flower carriages • Spells, charms and omens • Making simple mechanical devices • Memory training • Game of reciting verses from hearing • Decoding messages • The meanings of words • Dictionary studies • Prosody and rhetoric • Impersonation • Artful dressing • Games of dice • The game of *akarsha* (a dice game played on a board) • Making dolls and toys for children • Personal etiquette and animal training • Knowledge of dharmic warfare and victory • Physical culture

APPENDIX F: GLOSSARY OF FREQUENTLY USED ACRONYMS

CSE	Comprehensive Sexuality Education	The latest import from the USA teaches children about sexual rights, masturbation, and sexual pleasure. Prevention of unwanted pregnancies, risks, and abstinence are not the focus. In the name of being comprehensive, sex education includes 'how to' guides on sexual activity, masturbation, use of sexual toys, and other sexual acts.
DQSH	Drag Queen Story Hour	DQSH is a sexualized performance and storytelling by drag queens, who are adult male transgenders dressed up as women in sparkly seductive clothing exhibiting raunchy salacious behaviour in the presence of little children. It is a brainwashing program in schools, that normalizes sexual deviance and queer lifestyle and teaches children to see traditional sex and gender roles as oppressive. The message to children is that changing gender and sexual deviance is casual and normal.
FPAI	Family Planning Association of India	IPPF's Member Association tasked with advocating and advancing the goals of IPPF.
GCE	Global Citizenship Education	Promoted by the UN as part of SDGs which indoctrinates children to identify as global citizens as opposed to citizens of their nation. The program views illegal migration positively, while diminishing the importance of national identity. Global citizenship places the responsibility of global issues on the shoulders of children at the expense of responsibility towards their own country.
IPPF	International Planned Parenthood Foundation	An international NGO that is not about planning for parenthood as its name suggests. It is a leading provider of abortion services, gender-affirming care, and other reproductive health services. It operates through its member associations such as the Family Planning Association of India. IPPF has its roots in the eugenics movement and is funded by Western nations and private donors. It works closely with the UN to promote CSE and lobbies nations to adopt Woke sex education policies.

ITGSE	International Technical Guidance on Sex Education	UNESCO's 2018 guidelines on CSE that include teaching elementary school children about gender identity, teaching five-year-olds to explore their sex and gender, and focussing on sexual pleasure and sexual rights for children. ITGSE was drafted in collaboration with the IPPF member associations.
RKSK	Rashtriya Kishor Swasthya Karyakram	Program of the Ministry of Health and Family Welfare originally launched to improve nutrition and mental health. Later, repurposed for the use of CSE delivery. Uses mobile app and youth sex educators.
S D G 2030	Sustainable Development Goals	UNs' goals for all countries are to be reached by 2030, which plans to transform every aspect of humanity. Includes many aspects of Woke ideology.
SEL	Social Emotional Learning	SEL is a program ostensibly designed to build emotional regulation, resilience, and more. In practice, it serves as a social engineering program to indoctrinate children to adopt the 'correct' Woke stance and turn them into social justice warriors. It: • encourages students to fixate on their personal feelings, promotes self-centeredness, victimhood, and narcissism. • causes cognitive dissonance and anxiety in children. • is a subtle brainwashing program in DEI, prepping young people for ESG compliance as they enter the workforce. • facilitates the collection of children's private data and behavioral profiling.

BIBLIOGRAPHY

10to19Community. 'Collaborative Practice'. Accessed November 15, 2024a. https://10to19community.in/collaborative-practice/.

10to19Community. 'Donors and Partners'. Accessed November 15, 2024b. https://10to19community.in/donors-and-partners/.

10to19Community. 'Transforming Adolescent Lives through a Bold and Collaborative Solution'. Accessed November 15, 2024c. https://10to19community.in/. 576

3ie. 'Population Foundation India'. International Initiative for Impact Evaluation (3ie), Accessed November 15, 2024. https://www.3ieimpact.org/about-us/members/population-foundation-india.

Ab Meri Baari. 'Building Effective and Replicable Solutions with Young People'. Accessed November 15, 2024. http://www.abmeribaari.in.

ACER India (@ACERorgINDIA). 'ACER India conducted a workshop for teachers on competency-based assessments for the Delhi Board of School Education (DBSE). Study shows improvement in teachers' assessment skills after workshop'. X, February 20, 2024. https://x.com/ACERorgINDIA/status/1759842830065799304.

ACER India (@ACERorgINDIA). 'Today is the first day of ACER's 2-day workshop on competency-based learning and assessment at the Punjab School Education Board (PSEB) for principals and teachers from Adarsh Senior Secondary Schools'. X, September 22, 2023. https://x.com/ACERorgINDIA/status/1705137389260214532

Ahuja, Aastha. *In Rajasthan, Adolescents Are Getting Out-Of-School Lessons On Comprehensive Sexuality Education*. *NDTV*, September 12, 2022. https://swachhindia.ndtv.com/in-rajasthan-adolescents-are-getting-out-of-school-lessons-on-comprehensive-sexuality-education-70940/.

AICTE. *National Education Policy, 2020*. 2020. Ministry of Human Resource Development, Government of India, Accessed November 15, 2024. https://www.aicte-india.org/sites/default/files/nep2020.pdf.

Allred, Lynn. '"Sexuality Education" Rejected From WHA Resolution!' UN Family Rights Caucus, May 2, 2022. https://unfamilyrightscaucus.org/sexuality-education-rejected-from-wha-resolution

Along. 'Creating Intentional Spaces for SEL in 2022'. Along, February 8, 2022. https://www.along.org/blog/creating-intentional-spaces-for-sel-in-2022/.

Along. 'Tools to Help You Create a Responsive Classroom Environment'. Along, Accessed November 15, 2024. https://www.along.org/features/.

Anderson, Collin. *Want to Inspire 'Changemakers' in India to Fight Climate Change? Biden Could Fund Your Podcast. The Washington Free Beacon*, May 27, 2023. https://freebeacon.com/biden-administration/want-to-inspire-changemakers-in-india-to-fight-climate-change-biden-could-fund-your-podcast/.

Andrews, Jack L., Louise Birrell, Cath Chapman, Maree Teesson, Nicola Newton, Steve Allsop, Nyanda McBride, et al. *Evaluating the Effectiveness of a Universal eHealth School-Based Prevention Programme for Depression and Anxiety, and the Moderating Role of Friendship Network Characteristics*. *Psychological Medicine* 53, no. 11 (2023): 5042–51. https://doi.org/10.1017/S0033291722002033.

Angad, Abhishek. *In Jharkhand, Thousands Sit for a Look-In at "Quality English Medium" Schooling – for Free*. *The Indian Express*, May 31, 2023. https://indianexpress.com/article/india/in-jharkhand-thousands-sit-for-a-look-in-at-quality-english-medium-schooling-for-free-8637690/.

ASER. Annual Status of Education Report 2022. 2022. https://asercentre.org/aser-2022/.

Aussie17. *Massive Rallies Break Out in Japan Against WHO's Pandemic Treaty*. PharmaFiles, April 13, 2024. https://www.aussie17.com/p/developing-massive-rallies-break.

Bagchi, Barnita, Eckhardt Fuchs, and Kate Rousmaniere, eds. *Connecting*

Histories of Education: Transnational and Cross-cultural Exchanges in (Post) Colonial Education. Berghahn Books, 2014.

Bahl, Deepika, Shalini Bassi, Subhanwita Manna, and Monika Arora. *Adolescent Friendly Health Clinics (AFHCS) in India and their Compliance with Government Benchmarks: A Scoping Review*. F1000Research 12 (2023).

Bailey, Nancy. *Nancy Bailey's Education Website: The Trouble with Social-Emotional Learning: Why Be Concerned? Here's Why!* NEPC, May 26, 2022. https://nepc.colorado.edu/blog/trouble-social-emotional.

Balasubramanian, P., Rajalakshmi Ram Prakash, and N. Srilakshmi. *Religious Fundamentalism and Comprehensive Sexuality Education (CSE) in South India*. Rural Women's Social Education Centre (RUWSEC), 2016. https://arrow.org.my/wp-content/uploads/2017/03/5.-India.pdf.

Barik, Priyanka. *ARSH for You: A Teacher Training Programme on Adolescent Health and Well-Being!* Noticebard, September 8, 2023. https://school.noticebard.com/teachers/teacher-training-programme/.

Barry, John. *Mindfulness, Mental Health, and Attitudes to Critical Social Justice: Interview with Psychologist Dr. Oskari Lahtinen*. Centre for Male Psychology, May 23, 2023. https://www.centreformalepsychology.com/male-psychology-magazine-listings/mindfulness-mental-health-and-attitudes-to-critical-social-justice-interview-with-psychologist-dr-oskari-lahtinen.

Bell, Andrew. The Madras School: Or, elements of tuition: comprising the analysis of an experiment in education, made at the male asylum, Madras; with its facts, proofs, and illustrations; to which are added, extracts of sermons preached at Lambeth; a sketch of a national institution for training up the children of the poor; and a specimen of the mode of religious instruction at the Royal Military Asylum, Chelsea. T. Bensley, 1808.

Bell, David, and Thi Thuy Van Dinh. 2024. *Pandemic Agreement: A Guide*. Brownstone Institute, March 22, 2024. https://brownstone.org/articles/the-who-pandemic-agreement-a-guide/.

Bhattacharya, Abhik. *Demographic Dividend and Sexual Health: Comprehensive Investment Necessary For Development, Says UNFPA Director Julitta Onabanjo. Outlook India*. July 11, 2023. https://www.outlookindia.com/national/demographic-dividend-and-sexual-health-comprehensive-investment-necessary-for-development-says-unfpa-director-julitta-onabanjo-news-301978.

Bhattacharjee, K., *Tagore International School Partners with Nazariya to Teach Gender Identity Politics to Children. OpIndia*. July 20, 2020b. https://www.opindia.com/2020/07/tagore-international-school-nazariya-gender-identity-politics-brainwashing-children/.

Bhuptani, Ankit (@CitizenAnkit). 'Advancing LGBTQI healthcare—The Health Ministry has issued letters to stakeholders to:...' X, September 2, 2024. https://x.com/CitizenAnkit/status/1830601313085735249.

Big Think. 'Berkeley professor explains gender theory|Judith Butler'. YouTube video. June 8, 2023. 00:13:24. https://www.youtube.com/watch?v=UD9IOllUR4k

Bill & Melinda Gates Foundation. 'KnowledgeWorks Foundation'. Bill & Melinda Gates Foundation, Accessed November 15, 2024. https://www.gatesfoundation.org/about/committed-grants/2018/10/inv-008761.

Biswakarma, Rina, Katherine Maslowski, Michael J. Reiss, and Joyce C. Harper. *Parenthood intentions of 16–18-year-olds in England: a survey of school students. Human Fertility* 27, no. 1 (2024): 2310639.

Boninger, Faith, and Alex Molnar. *Don't go 'Along' with corporate schemes to gather up student data*, Kappan, March 1, 2022. https://kappanonline.org/dont-go-along-with-corporate-schemes-to-gather-up-student-data.

Borenstein, Seth, Jamey Keaten, and *The Associated Press. Humanity Has Just 2 Years "to Save the World", UN Climate Chief Says. Fortune*, April 11, 2024. https://fortune.com/2024/04/10/united-nations-climate-chief-humanity-has-2-years-to-save-the-world/.

Bourn, Douglas. 'Global Citizenship Education and Paulo Freire's Pedagogy of Hope'. Global Citizenship Foundation, August 21, 2022. https://www.globalcitizenshipfoundation.org/article/global-citizenship-education-and-paulo-freires-pedagogy-of-hope

Brain, Julien (@julien_brain). '🏆 "Gold" employer: Another recognition of Wipro's commitment to LGBTQ+ inclusion in the workplace by the India Workplace Equality Index 2022, a partnership between Keshav Suri Foundation, Pride Circle, and Stonewall UK. 🏳 'At Wipro, we are committ....' X, December 8, 2022. https://twitter.com/julien_brain/status/1600821303488831488.

Browning, Webster E., *Joseph Lancaster, James Thomson, and the Lancasterian System of Mutual Instruction, with Special Reference to Hispanic America. Hispanic American Historical Review* (1921): 49-98.

Bryan, Audrey. *From 'the conscience of humanity' to the conscious human brain: UNESCO's embrace of social-emotional learning as a flag of convenience. Compare: A Journal of Comparative and International Education* 54, no. 5 (2024): 770-784.

Buckley, Chris. *Xi Jinping Thought Explained: A New Ideology for a New Era. The New York Times,* February 26, 2018. https://www.nytimes.com/2018/02/26/world/asia/xi-jinping-thought-explained-a-new-ideology-for-a-new-era.html.

Butler, J. (1990). *Gender trouble: Feminism and the Subversion of Identity*. Ann Arbor, MI: Routledge.

Buttons, Christina. *New Systematic Review Exposes Deceptive Practices Among Medical Organizations That Endorse Youth Transition*. Buttonslives.news, April 11, 2024a. https://www.buttonslives.news/p/new-systematic-review-exposes-deceptive.

Buttons, Christina (@buttonslives). 'The review found that clinical guidelines globally used to treat gender-questioning children and adolescents were crafted in violation of international standards for guideline development and recommended medical interventions for minors despite insufficient evidence'. X, April 12, 2024b. https://twitter.com/buttonslives/status/1778491543466152103.

Camp, Emma. *Bad Schools Aren't Always Underfunded. Reason*, February 15, 2023. https://reason.com/2023/02/15/bad-schools-arent-always-underfunded/.

Campbell, Matthew. *French Philosopher Michel Foucault 'Abused Boys in Tunisia. The Sunday Times,* March 28, 2021. https://www.thetimes.co.uk/article/french-philosopher-michel-foucault-abused-boys-in-tunisia-6t5sj7jvw.

Capital Projects. 'History'. University of Saint Andrews, Accessed November 15, 2024. https://capitalprojects.wp.st-andrews.ac.uk/new-college-development/history/.

Carter, Craig A., *Pedophilia Is No Joke. World,* July 14, 2023. https://wng.org/opinions/pedophilia-is-no-joke-1689295195.

CASEL and CIVIC. 'Portraits of a Graduate'. February 2, 2024. https://casel.org/portraits-of-a-graduate-2024/.

CASEL. 'What Is the CASEL Framework?' Accessed November 15, 2024. https://casel.org/fundamentals-of-sel/what-is-the-casel-framework/.

Centre for Catalyzing Change. 'Our Supporters'. Centre for Catalyzing Change, Accessed November 15, 2024. https://www.c3india.org/our_supporters.

Chan Zuckerberg Initiative. *Chan Zuckerberg Initiative and Gradient Learning Launch New Tool to Support Teacher-Student Relationships. PR Newswire.* June 28, 2021. https://www.prnewswire.com/news-releases/chan-zuckerberg-initiative-and-gradient-learning-launch-new-tool-to-support-teacher-student-relationships-301320945.html.

Chandra-Mouli, Venkatraman, Marina Plesons, Alka Barua, Aradhana Patnaik, Aparajita Gogoi, Manju Katoch, Mohammed Ziauddin, Rita Mishra, and Anand Sinha. *What Did It Take to Scale-Up and Sustain Udaan, a School-Based Adolescent Education Programme in Jharkhand, India?* David and Lucile Packard Foundation, May 2017. https://www.packard.org/wp-content/uploads/2017/05/Udaan-case-study.pdf.

Chandra-Mouli, Venkatraman, Marina Plesons, Alka Barua, Aparajita Gogoi, Manju Katoch, Mohammed Ziauddin, Rita Mishra, Vinita Nathani, and Anand Sinha. *What did it take to scale up and Sustain Udaan, a school-based adolescent education program in Jharkhand, India?, American Journal of Sexuality Education* 13, no. 2 (2018): 147-169.

Children's Investment Fund Foundation. India. Accessed November 15, 2024. https://ciff.org/regions/india/.

China Daily. Global Civilization Initiative Outlines the Way to Transcend Estrangement, Clashes and Superiority: China Daily editorial. March 16, 2023. https://global.chinadaily.com.cn/a/202303/16/WS641303a9a31057c47ebb4e73.html

China Development Brief. China Family Planning Association. Accessed November 15, 2024. https://chinadevelopmentbrief.org/ngos/china-family-planning-association/.

China SCIO. 'Full text of Xi Jinping's keynote address at the CPC in Dialogue with World Political Parties High-level Meeting'. The State Council Information Office: The People's Republic of China, March 16, 2023. http://english.scio.gov.cn/topnews/2023-03/16/content_85171478.htm

Christodoulou, J.A., Okano, K.H., Gove, A., McBride, C., Raihani, R., Strigel, C., Pérez, L.T., and Chakraborty, A. *Diversity and Social Justice in Education.* In *Reimagining Education: The International Science and Evidence Based Assessment*, ed. A.K. Duraiappah, N.M. van Atteveldt, G. Borst, S. Bugden, O. Ergas, T. Gilead, L. Gupta, J. Mercier, K. Pugh, N.C. Singh, and E.A. Vickers. New Delhi: UNESCO MGIEP, 2022.

Conron, Kerith J. *LGBT Youth Population in the United States*. UCLA School of Law: Williams Institute, September 2020. https://williamsinstitute.law.ucla.edu/wp-content/uploads/LGBT-Youth-US-Pop-Sep-2020.pdf.

Cornell University Library. 'The Feminist Sex Wars: A Retrospective by Gayle Rubin'. YouTube video, 1:48:29. June 1, 2022. https://www.youtube.com/watch?v=DWjqeAarm2I.

Crowder, Steven (@scrowder). 'BREAKING: Self-Described "Globalist" United Nations Legal Affairs Official Says He's "Not Sure Institution is Going to Survive" Second Trump Term; Reveals Colleagues "Terrified" of His Reelection; Admits U.N. is "95% useless" at Primary Function of International Peace & Security…' X, August 29, 2024. https://x.com/scrowder/status/1829161105677234637.

CSE. 'CSE Harmful Elements Analysis Tool'. Comprehensive Sexuality Education, Accessed November 15, 2024. https://www.comprehensivesexualityeducation.org/wp-content/uploads/15-Harmful-Elements-Making-A-Difference-5th-Ed-Final.pdf.

CZI. 'CZI and Gradient Learning Launch Along, A New Tool to Support Teacher-Student Relationships'. Chan Zuckerberg Initiative, June 28, 2021. https://chanzuckerberg.com/newsroom/czi-and-gradient-learning-launch-along-a-new-tool-to-support-teacher-student-relationships.

CZI. 'How We Support Education'. Chan Zuckerberg Initiative, accessed November 15, 2024. https://chanzuckerberg.com/education/well-being/gradient-learning/.

Dabrowski, Ted, and John Klingner. *Illinois Education 2022: Not a Single Student Can Do Math at Grade Level in 53 Schools. For Reading, It's 30 Schools. Wirepoints*, February 14, 2023. https://wirepoints.org/not-a-single-student-can-do-math-at-grade-level-in-53-illinois-schools-for-reading-its-30-schools-wirepoints/.

Das, Saptarishi. *Age of Consent Under Pocso Act: 'Law Panel Did Its Work, Govt Will Take Final Call'. The Hindustan Times*, October 8, 2023. https://www.hindustantimes.com/india-news/age-of-consent-under-pocso-act-law-panel-did-its-work-govt-will-take-final-call-101696706532331.html.

Dasra India. 'Youth Charcha: The importance of youth participation and partnership…'. YouTube video, 22:18. February 28, 2021. https://www.youtube.com/watch?v=1fE9gW9JX2I.

Dawkins, Richard (@RichardDawkins). 'This ridiculous article (shame on the once-great Scientific American) ignorantly misunderstands the nature of the sex binary…' X, January 31, 2024. https://twitter.com/RichardDawkins/status/1752403995174252724.

Deeksha, Johanna. *Lessons from Chhattisgarh's New English-Medium School Programme. Scroll.in*, November 30, 2022. https://scroll.in/article/1038558/lessons-from-chhattigarhs-new-english-medium-school-programme.

Dhaliwal, Sarbjit. *Pvt. Schools Not Following RTE Norms, Finds Study. The Tribune*, India, February 24, 2015. https://www.tribuneindia.com/news/archive/features/pvt-schools-not-following-rte-norms-finds-study.

Dig Watch. *China Makes Amendments in Laws to Protect Minors Online*. October 19, 2020. https://dig.watch/updates/china-makes-amendments-laws-protect-minors-online-0.

Diller, Rita. *Sex Ed Publisher ETR an Offshoot of Planned Parenthood Abortion Biz. Life News*, February 4, 2013. https://www.lifenews.com/2013/02/04/sex-ed-publisher-etr-an-offshoot-of-planned-parenthood-abortion-biz

Doherty, Erin. *The Number of LGBTQ-Identifying Adults Is Soaring. Axios*, February 17, 2022. https://www.axios.com/2022/02/17/lgbtq-generation-z-gallup.

Doing Sociology. 'Debates on Sexuality, State and Citizenship: An Interview with Pushpesh Kumar'. YouTube video. August 27, 2020. 00:44:21. https://www.youtube.com/watch?v=q_siITLIlnc

Dolan, Eric W., *Study: 'Woke' Attitudes Linked to Anxiety, Depression, and a Lack of Happiness. PsyPost*. March 17, 2024. https://www.psypost.org/study-woke-attitudes-linked-to-anxiety-depression-and-a-lack-of-happiness/.

Downey, Caroline. *Civil-Rights Complaint Filed over 'Black Excellence' Pledge by Denver School District. National Review*, February 21, 2024. https://www.nationalreview.com/news/civil-rights-complaint-filed-over-black-excellence-pledge-by-denver-school-district/.

Downey, Caroline. *Schools Push Radical Ideology under Guise of 'Social-Emotional Learning,' Parents Warn. National Review*, April 4, 2022. https://www.nationalreview.com/news/schools-push-radical-gender-ideology-under-guise-of-social-emotional-learning-parents-warn/.

Drabinski, Emily. *Queering the Catalog: Queer Theory and the Politics of Correction. The Library Quarterly* 83, no. 2 (2013): 94-111.

Duraiappah, Anantha, Nienke van Atteveldt, Stanley Asah, Gregoire Borst, Stephanie Bugden, J. Marieke Buil, Oren Ergas et al. *The international science and evidence-based education assessment*. npj *Science of Learning* 6, no. 1 (2021): 7.

Dutton, Edward, and Emil Kirkegaard. *Do conservatives really have an advantage in mental health? An examination of measurement invariance?*. *Scandinavian Journal of Psychology* (2024).

Eden, Max. 'Issues 2020: Public School Spending Is at an All-Time High'. Manhattan Institute, July 25, 2019. https://manhattan.institute/article/issues-2020-public-school-spending-is-at-an-all-time-high.

Eden, Max. 'The Trouble with Social Emotional Learning'. American Enterprise Institute, April 6, 2022. https://www.aei.org/research-products/testimony/the-trouble-with-social-emotional-learning/.

Educately. 'ARSH for You-A teacher training program on adolescent health and well-being'. YouTube video, 5:12. December 29, 2020. https://www.youtube.com/watch?v=8Wd2_d3FIeA.

Education21. 'UNESCO MGIEP to Train and Certify 8.4 Million Teachers in India in SEL and Digital Pedagogies'. Education21, December 12, 2022. https://education21.in/unesco-mgiep-to-train-and-certify-8-4-million-teachers-in-india-in-sel-and-digital-pedagogies/.

EduKitchen. 'Critical Pedagogy as an antidote to Neoliberal Fascism'. YouTube video, 1:06:15. November 10, 2022. https://www.youtube.com/watch?v=2Ewc1tE55ws.

efiletax (@efile_tax). 'The Institute of Chartered Accountants of India (ICAI) has released a set of Frequently Asked Questions (FAQs) on the New Scheme of Education and Training (NEST), offering detailed insights into its key features…' X, July 4, 2023. https://x.com/efile_tax/status/1676045894985330688

Elbertson, Nicole A., Marc A. Brackett, and Roger P. Weissberg. *School-based social and emotional learning (SEL) programming: Current perspectives*. Second International Handbook of Educational Change (2009): 1017-1032.

Ellis, R. Evan. *The Trouble With China's Global Civilization Initiative*. *The Diplomat*, June 1, 2023. https://thediplomat.com/2023/06/the-trouble-with-chinas-global-civilization-initiative

Emmerling, Robert. 'Daniel Goleman-Member Emotional Intelligence Consortium'. Consortium for Research on Emotional Intelligence in Organizations, Accessed November 15, 2024. https://www.eiconsortium.org/members/goleman.htm.

End Wokeness (@EndWokeness). 'Racial justice leaders are now demanding $15 billion from Boston and additional cash from "white churches"', X, March 25, 2024. https://twitter.com/EndWokeness/status/1771982203557192016.

Ericksen, Irene H., and Stan E. Weed. 'Re-examining the evidence for school-based comprehensive sex education: A global research review'. Issues L. & Med. 34 (2019): 161.

Family Watch. 12 Harmful Elements for Children in Proposed WHA Para. June 2, 2021a. https://familywatch.org/urgent-12-harmful-elements-for-children-in-proposed-wha-para/.

Family Watch. 'International Planned Parenthood Federation Exposed: A Seven-Part Webinar Series'. Family Watch. February 10, 2021b. https://familywatch.org/2021/02/10/ippfexposed/.

Family Watch. *Search Results for IPPF.* Family Watch. https://familywatch.org/?s=ippf. Accessed November 15, 2024.

Fetzer Institute. Our Founder. Accessed November 6, 2024. https://fetzer.org/about/founder.

FOX 5 Washington DC. 'Amid a rise in bad behavior, an Arlington middle school changes rules | FOX 5 DC'. YouTube video. April 4, 2022. 00:02:25. http://www.youtube.com/watch?v=QilJNWth_nM

FPAIndia. 'Tata Mumbai Marathon, 2023'. FPAIndia, Accessed November 15, 2024. https://fpaindia.org/events/tata-mumbai-marathon-2023.

FPAIndia. Annual Report 2022. Family Planning Association of India, 2022. https://fpaindia.org/pdf/Annual-Report-2022.pdf.

França, João. 'Henry Giroux: "Those Arguing That Education Should Be Neutral Are Really Arguing for a Version of Education in Which Nobody Is Accountable"'. CCCB LAB, July 2, 2019. https://lab.cccb.org/en/

henry-giroux-those-arguing-that-education-should-be-neutral-are-really-arguing-for-a-version-of-education-in-which-nobody-is-accountable/.

Gagnon, Laurie. 'Illustrating the Competency-Based Education Definition'. Aurora Institute, April 4, 2024. https://aurora-institute.org/cw_post/illustrating-the-competency-based-education-definition/.

Gambini, Bert. 'Chatbot Provides Safe Space to Learn About Sexual, Reproductive Health'. University at Buffalo, February 22, 2022. https://www.buffalo.edu/inclusion/UBInclusiveNews/AllStories.host.html/content/shared/university/news/ub-reporter-articles/stories/2022/02/wang-srh-chatbot.detail.html.

Genspect. 'Why Biological Sex Is Being Undermined-Dr. Colin Wright'. YouTube video, 35:19. January 19, 2024. https://www.youtube.com/watch?v=-4WV9xv62f4.

Gentleman, Amelia. *Sex Education Curriculum Angers Indian Conservatives*. *The New York Times*, May 24, 2007. https://www.nytimes.com/2007/05/24/world/asia/24iht-letter.1.5851113.html.

Gewertz, Catherine. 'Seattle Schools Lead Controversial Push to "Rehumanize" Math'. EdW, October 14, 2019. https://www.edweek.org/teaching-learning/seattle-schools-lead-controversial-push-to-rehumanize-math/2019/10.

Ghosal, Sharmistha. *Drag Queen Story Hour to Raise Awareness on Queer Rights in Kolkata*. *Indulge Express*, May 16, 2019. https://www.indulgexpress.com/msociety/2019/May/15/drag-queen-story-hour-to-raise-awareness-on-queer-rights-in-kolkata-14973.html.

Ghosh, Abhik, and Paul Kiparsky. *Did the Sanskrit Alphabet Influence Mendeleev's Periodic Table?* *American Scientist*, November 2019. https://www.americanscientist.org/article/the-grammar-of-the-elements.

Giami, Alain, and Erick Janssen. *25th Congress of the World Association for Sexual Health (WAS) and SASHA (South African Sexual Health Association)*. *International Journal of Sexual Health* 34, no. S1 (2022): 1-331.

Giordano, Alice. *Educator Sexual Misconduct Is On The Rise In US Public*

Schools. The Epoch Times, January 17, 2023. https://www.theepochtimes.com/us/educator-sexual-misconduct-is-on-the-rise-in-us-public-schools-report-4985345.

Girls Not Brides. "Member Directory." Girls Not Brides, Accessed November 15, 2024. https://www.girlsnotbrides.org/our-partnership/member-directory/.

Giroux, Henry A., *Remembering Paulo Freire as a Freedom Fighter. Policy and Practice: A Development Education Review* 33 (Autumn 2021): 114-118.

Give (@GiveIndia). ' Queer Youth Leadership course, by Keshav Suri Foundation, is designed to empower members of the queer community to become social leaders of change. Support the change that is necessary, help the members of the Queer community emerge as leaders. Donate now: http://bit.ly/NoPrideinPrejudice_T', X, November 26, 2019. https://twitter.com/GiveIndia/status/1199317564737769472.

Global Education Magazine. A Critical Interview with Henry Giroux, Global Education Magazine, January 13, 2013. https://globaleducationmagazine.com/critical-interview-henry-giroux.

Goldman, Robert P., *Transsexualism, Gender, and Aanxiety in Traditional India. The Journal of the American Oriental Society* 113, no. 3 (1993): 374-402.

Goleman, Daniel. 'About–Daniel Goleman'. Daniel Goleman, Accessed November 15, 2024. https://www.danielgoleman.info/speaking/.

Goleman, Daniel. *Meditation as meta-therapy: Hypotheses toward a proposed fifth state of consciousness. Journal of Transpersonal Psychology*, Vol. 3 (1971), pp. 1-25. (1971).

Goleman, Daniel. *Psychology, Reality and Consciousness*. In *Paths Beyond Ego*, ed. Roger Walsh and Frances Vaughan, 20. Los Angeles: Jeremy P. Tarcher, 1993.

González, Oriana, and Sabrina Moreno. *How Late in Pregnancy Each State Allows Abortions. Axios*, May 14, 2022. https://www.axios.com/2022/05/14/abortion-state-laws-bans-roe-supreme-court.

Goode, Sarah. *Studies on Adult Sexual Contact with Children. Paedophiles in Society: Reflecting on Sexuality, Abuse and Hope* (2011): 126-157.

Government of Assam, Biswanath District. Rashtriya Kishor Swasthya Karyakram (RKSK). Accessed November 15, 2024. https://biswanath.gov.in/portlet-sub-innerpage/rashtriya-kishore-swasthya-karyakram-rksk.

Government of India. *The Constitution (Ninety-Third Amendment) Act, 2005. No. 93 of 2005.* January 7, 2009. https://www.india.gov.in/sites/upload_files/npi/files/amend93.pdf.

Grady, Denise, and Nicholas St. Fleur. "Fetal Tissue From Abortions for Research Is Traded in a Gray Zone." *The New York Times,* July 28, 2015. https://www.nytimes.com/2015/07/28/health/fetal-tissue-from-abortions-for-research-is-traded-in-a-gray-zone.html.

Green, William. 'The Emotionally Intelligent Investor w/ Daniel Goleman'. The Investor's Podcast, July 23, 2022. https://www.theinvestorspodcast.com/richer-wiser-happier/the-emotionally-intelligent-investor-w-daniel-goleman/.

GSA Network. 'FAQ'. GSA Network, Accessed November 15, 2024. https://gsanetwork.org/faq/.

Gupta, R., Kaushik, N., Asokan, A., Gupta, R., Nair, M., and Kanjoor. R., 'Surgical care: surgical management of Gender Incongruence'. Indian Standards of Care for Persons with Gender Incongruence and People with differences in Sexual Development/Orientation version 1 (2020): 66-165.

Gutstein, E. (2005). *Reading and Writing the World with Mathematics: Toward a Pedagogy for Social Justice*. Oxford, UK: Routledge

Guttmacher Institute. 'National Estimate of Abortion in India Released'. Guttmacher Institute, December 11, 2017. https://www.guttmacher.org/news-release/2017/national-estimate-abortion-india-released.

Guttmacher Institute. 'Abortion and Unintended Pregnancy in Six Indian States: Findings and Implications for Policies and Programs'. Guttmacher Institute, November, 2018. https://www.guttmacher.org/report/abortion-unintended-pregnancy-six-states-india

Harris, Shane. 'New Variant of the "CRT-virus": "Social-Emotional

Learning"'. Amac, April 5, 2022. https://amac.us/amac-in-the-media/new-variant-of-the-crt-virus-social-emotional-learning/.

Harvey, Lauren J., Fiona A. White, Caroline Hunt, and Maree Abbott. *Investigating the efficacy of a Dialectical behaviour therapy-based universal intervention on adolescent social and emotional well-being outcomes. Behaviour Research and Therapy* 169 (2023): 104408.

Hauf, Patrick. *Meet the CDC-Backed Groups That Want to Teach Trans Ideology to Kindergartners. The Washington Free Beacon*, July 24, 2021. https://freebeacon.com/culture/meet-the-cdc-backed-groups-that-want-to-teach-trans-ideology-to-kindergartners/.

HCLFoundation. 'We are happy to bring the 3rd batch of 'ARSH for You' on #HCLFoundationAcademy!...' X, May 25, 2022. https://x.com/HCL_Foundation/status/1529397762663788544.

HCLFoundation. 'Academy by HCLFoundation invites you to join Batch IV of "ARSH for You" – a 6-week online Training of Trainers (ToT) course on Adolescent Reproductive and Sexual Health (ARSH)...' LinkedIn, 2024. https://www.linkedin.com/posts/hclfoundation_arsh-activity-7158701138882551808-PEJE/.

Hogan, David. *The market revolution and disciplinary power: Joseph Lancaster and the psychology of the early classroom system. History of Education Quarterly* 29, no. 3 (1989): 381-417.

Horowitz, David. *Dark Agenda: The War to Destroy Christian America.* 2019.

Horton, Cal. *The Cass Review: Cis-supremacy in the UK's approach to healthcare for trans children. International Journal of Transgender Health* (2024): 1-25.

Huang, Ling. 'Stanford Professor Jo Boaler's Math Revolution and War Against Algebra 2'. Nonpartisan Education Blog, October 20, 2020. https://nonpartisaneducation.org/blog1/2020/10/jo-boalers-reform-math-fallacy-outline/.

Huges, Mia. *The WPATH Files. Environmental Progress*, March 4, 2024. https://environmentalprogress.org/big-news/wpath-files.

Hylton, Sara, Jeffrey Gettleman, and Eve Lyons. *The peculiar position of India's third gender. The New York Times*, February 17, 2018. https://www.nytimes.com/2018/02/17/style/india-third-gender-hijras-transgender.htm.

ICJ. 'The 8 March Principles for a Human Rights-Based Approach to Criminal Law Proscribing Conduct Associated with Sex, Reproduction, Drug Use, HIV, Homelessness and Poverty'. *International Commission of Jurists*. March, 2023. https://www.icj.org/wp-content/uploads/2023/03/Principles-Report_English.pdf

Impact 500. 'Center for Social Impact: Impact 500 Organizations'. Impact 500, Accessed November 15, 2024. https://impact500.gced.in/?filter=Country-%3AIndia%3BFocusArea-%3ASocial%2520and%2520Emotional%2520Learning,Global%2520Citizenship%2520Education%3BDelivery-%3AK-12%2520Education.

India Today. *Ayushman Bharat PMJAY for Transgender: All You Need to Know. India Today*, August 28, 2022. https://www.indiatoday.in/information/story/ayushman-bharat-pmjay-for-transgender-all-you-need-to-know-1993316-2022-08-27.

IPE Global. 'Release of Policy: NITI SAMVAAD Nurturing a Vibrant Girl Capital in India'. *IPE Global*. September 25, 2023. https://www.ipeglobal.com/niti-samvad-nurturing-a-vibrant-girl-capital-in-india/.

IPE Global. 'About Us'. *IPE Global*. Accessed November 15, 2024. https://www.ipeglobal.com/about-us/.

IPPF. '2022 Annual Performance Report'. *International Planned Parenthood Federation*. June 6, 2023a. https://www.ippf.org/resource/2022-annual-performance-report.

IPPF. 'Exclaim! Young People's Guide to "Sexual Rights: An IPPF Declaration"'. *International Planned Parenthood Federation*. Accessed November 15, 2024a. https://www.ippf.org/resource/exclaim-young-peoples-guide-sexual-rights-ippf-declaration.

IPPF. DELIVER+ENABLE TOOLKIT: Scaling-up comprehensive sexuality education. (CSE). International Planned Parenthood Federation, 2018.

https://www.ippf.org/sites/default/files/2018-03/IPPF%20Deliver%20and%20Enable%20-%20CSE%20Toolkit.pdf

IPPF. Sexual Rights: An IPPF Declaration. International Planned Parenthood Federation, accessed November 15, 2024b. https://www.ippf.org/sites/default/files/sexualrightsippfdeclaration_1.pdf.

IPPF. 'Fulfil! Guidance Document for the Implementation of Young People's Sexual Rights (IPPF-WAS)'. *International Planned Parenthood Federation*. Accessed November 15, 2024c. https://www.ippf.org/resource/fulfil-guidance-document-implementation-young-peoples-sexual-rights-ippf-was.

IPPF. All One Curriculum: Guidelines and Activities for a Unified Approach to Sexuality, Gender, HIV, and Human Rights. International Planned Parenthood Federation, September 2020a, https://www.ippf.org/sites/default/files/2020-09/ItsAllOneCurriculum_English.pdf

IPPF. Health, Happy & Hot: A GUIDE TO YOUR RIGHTS, SEXUALITY & LIVING WITH HIV. International Planned Parenthood Federation, June 2020b, https://www.ippf.org/static/happyhealthyhot/Healthy_Happy_and_Hot_Guide.pdf

IPPF. Financial Statements 2021. *International Planned Parenthood Federation*. Accessed November 15, 2024d. https://www.ippf.org/resource/financial-statements-2021

IPPF. Family Planning Association of India. International Planned Parenthood Federation South Asia Regional Office (SARO), Accessed November 15, 2024e. https://sar.ippf.org/about-us/member-associations/family-planning-association-india.

IPPF. 'We're SARO-the South Asia Regional Office of IPPF'. International Planned Parenthood Federation South Asia Regional Office (SARO), Accessed November 15, 2024f. https://sar.ippf.org/about-us.

IPPF Centers & Funds. 'About Us'. *Accessed* November 15, 2024. https://bp.seippf.org/about_us.

Israel, Melanie. 'Planned Parenthood Taxpayer Funding Up; Abortion and "Transgender" Services High Priorities'. The Heritage Foundation, June

13, 2023. https://www.heritage.org/life/commentary/planned-parenthood-taxpayer-funding-abortion-and-transgender-services-high.

Israel, Melanie, Trey Boyd, and Macy Petty. 'Don't Defend Planned Parenthood's "Gender-Affirming Care." Defund It'. The Heritage Foundation, August 10, 2023. https://www.heritage.org/gender/commentary/dont-defend-planned-parenthoods-gender-affirming-care-defund-it.

Ivey-Stephenson, Asha Z., Zewditu Demissie, Alexander E. Crosby, Deborah M. Stone, Elizabeth Gaylor, Natalie Wilkins, Richard Lowry, and Margaret Brown. 'Suicidal Ideation and Behaviors Among High School Students—Youth Risk Behavior Survey, United States, 2019'. MMWR Suppl 69, no. Suppl-1 (August 21, 2020): 47–55. DOI: http://dx.doi.org/10.15585/mmwr.su6901a6.

Jain, Dipika. *Right to health and gender-affirmative procedure in the Transgender Persons Act 2019 in India. Indian Journal of Plastic Surgery* 55, no. 02 (2022): 205-210.

Jaiswal, Maahi. *Sex Education Initiatives in India Break Cultural Taboos. Mount Holyoke News*. November 17, 2023. https://www.mountholyokenews.com/global/2023/11/17/sex-education-initiatives-in-india-break-cultural-taboos.

Jamison, Peter, Laura Meckler, Prayag Gordy, Clara Ence Morse, and Chris Alcantara. *Home Schooling's Rise from Fringe to Fastest-Growing Form of Education. The Washington Post,* October 31, 2023. https://www.washingtonpost.com/education/interactive/2023/homeschooling-growth-data-by-district/.

Jin, Zhao, Fuyu Guo, Kai Wang, Hanxiyue Zhang, Wenzhen Cao, Jiayi Hee, Yuan Yuan, Minne Chen, and Kun Tang. 'Effects of an internet-based and teacher-facilitated sexuality education package: A cluster-randomized trial'. Children 8, no. 10 (2021): 885.

Johnson, Daniel. *Michel Foucault: The Prophet of Pederasty. The Critic*, April 2021. https://thecritic.co.uk/issues/april-2021/michel-foucault-the-prophet-of-pederasty/.

Joseph, Jithin T. *Comprehensive Sexuality Education in the Indian Context: Challenges and Opportunities. Indian Journal of Psychological Medicine* 45, no. 3 (2023): 292-296.

JPISchool (@JPISCHOOL). 'Kicking Gender Boundaries Jayshree Periwal International School hosted India's first and historic, all gender inclusive football match organised by Keshav Suri Foundation in association with Rajasthan Football Association and ScoutMe'. X, December 3, 2019. https://twitter.com/JPISCHOOL/status/1201726357543145473.

Kaushal, Ravi. *Abandon Plans for ITEP as It Takes Back Teachers to Colonial India, Say Eminent Educators. News Click*, May 26, 2023. https://www.newsclick.in/abandon-plans-itep-it-takes-back-teachers-colonial-india-say-eminent-educators.

Keenan, Harper, and Lil Miss Hot Mess. 'Drag pedagogy: The playful practice of queer imagination in early childhood'. Curriculum Inquiry 50, no. 5 (2020): 440-461.

Kerith J. Conron. LGBT Youth Population in the United States. UCLA School of Law: Williams Institute, September 2020. https://williamsinstitute.law.ucla.edu/wp-content/uploads/LGBT-Youth-US-Pop-Sep-2020.pdf.

Keshav Suri Foundation. 'Drag Queen Story Hour has truly been a project that has sailed through with care, love and nurture. We are thankful to some of the most amazing drag queens who took the leap of faith and helped us turn this dream into reality'. Facebook, October 13, 2020. https://www.facebook.com/KeshavSuriFoundation/posts/drag-queen-story-hour-has-truly-been-a-project-that-has-sailed-through-with-care/3784758208237524/.

KESHAV SURI FOUNDATION. 'KESHAV SURI FOUNDATION'. KESHAV SURI FOUNDATION, Accessed November 15, 2024. https://keshavsuri.foundation.

Kingkade, Tyler. *We're Coming For Your Children' Chant at NYC Drag March Elicits Outrage, but Activists Say It's Taken Out of Context. NBC News*, June 28, 2023. https://www.nbcnews.com/nbc-out/nbc-out-proud/re-coming-children-chant-nyc-drag-march-elicits-outrage-activists-say-rcna91341.

Kissu, Sagrika. *NCR's Shiv Nadar School Wades into 'Woke' Territory, Adds Non-Binary Gender Option in Forms. The Print*, February 21, 2024. https://theprint.in/india/education/ncrs-shiv-nadar-school-wades-into-woke-territory-adds-non-binary-gender-option-in-forms/1972801/.

KnowledgeWorks. 'Implementing Personalized, Competency-Based Learning'. KnowledgeWorks, Accessed November 15, 2024. https://knowledgeworks.org/work/implement-personalized-learning/.

KnowledgeWorks. 'Let's Face It: Tracking Is Intentional Systemic Inequity'. KnowledgeWorks, November 2, 2021. https://knowledgeworks.org/resources/tracking-is-intentional-systemic-inequity/.

LaChance, Mike. *Immigrant Parents from India Flee the United States After Elementary School Hides Gender Transition of Their Daughter. The Gateway Pundit*, January 30, 2024. https://www.thegatewaypundit.com/2024/01/immigrant-parents-india-flee-united-states-after-elementary/.

Lahtinen, Oskari. *Construction and validation of a scale for assessing critical social justice attitudes. Scandinavian Journal of Psychology* (2024).

Lancing, Logan, and James Lindsay. *The Queering of the American Child: How a New School Religious Cult Poisons the Minds and Bodies of Normal Kids. New Discourses*, 2024.

Law Commission of India. Age of Consent under the Protection of Children from Sexual Offences Act, 2012: Report No. 283. Government of India, September 2023. https://cdnbbsr.s3waas.gov.in/s3ca0daec69b5adc880fb464895726dbdf/uploads/2023/09/20230929466194485.pdf.

Laytner, Bill. *How Psychics, Ouija Boards Played into Tigers' World Series Wins. Detroit Free Press*, December 30, 2018. https://www.freep.com/story/sports/mlb/tigers/2018/12/30/john-fetzer-detroit-tigers-ouija-board/2135404002/.

Learning4Impact. '10to19 Adolescents Collaborative'. *Learning4Impact*. Accessed November 15, 2024. https://www.learning4impact.org/project/10to19-adolescents-collaborative.

Leavenworth, Stuart. *China Battles Foreign Influence with New NGO Law.*

The Christian Science Monitor, April 28, 2016. https://www.csmonitor.com/World/Asia-Pacific/2016/0428/China-battles-foreign-influence-with-new-NGO-law.

Legrenzi, Paolo, and Carlo Umiltà. *Neuromania: On the Limits of Brain Science*. Oxford University Press, USA, 2011.

Leite, Stephanie. 'Using the SDGs for Global Citizenship Education: Definitions, Challenges, and Opportunities'. Globalisation, Societies and Education 20, no. 3 (2022): 401-413. https://doi.org/10.1080/14767724.2021.1882957. https://osf.io/preprints/socarxiv/xp52e.

Lewis, Helen. *Britain Is Leaving the U.S. Gender-Medicine Debate Behind. The Atlantic*, April 12, 2024. https://www.theatlantic.com/ideas/archive/2024/04/cass-report-youth-gender-medicine/678031/.

Lindsay, James. *The American Library Association is Queering the Catalog. New Discourses*, July 31, 2023. https://newdiscourses.com/2023/07/american-library-association-is-queering-the-catalog/.

Lindsay, James. *The SEL Cycle. New Discourses*, March 1, 2023. https://newdiscourses.com/2023/03/the-sel-cycle/.

Lindsay, James. *The Marxification of Education: Paulo Freire's Critical Marxism and the Theft of Education. New Discourses*, 2022.

Littlejohn, Reggie. *International Planned Parenthood Working Hand in Hand with the Coercive Population Control Machine in China. Women's Rights Without Frontiers*, April 28, 2016. https://www.womensrightswithoutfrontiers.org/blog/international-planned-parenthood-working-hand-in-hand-with-the-coercive-population-control-machine-in-china.

Live Action. 'Sex Abuse Cover Up at Planned Parenthood-Overview'. YouTube video. May 30, 2018. 00:04:54. https://www.youtube.com/watch?v=6R8gtSP3Guk

Lo, Hoi-ying. *What Do Hong Kong Teens Think About Official Advice on Controlling Sexual Impulses? South China Morning Post*, August 31, 2024. https://www.scmp.com/news/hong-kong/education/article/3276648/what-do-hong-kong-teens-think-about-official-advice-controlling-sexual-impulses.

Macklem, Gayle L. Preventive Mental Health at School: Evidence-Based Services for Students. Springer, 2014.

Maher, Bill. *Real Time with Bill Maher*. Season 22, Episode 12. Aired April 19, 2024, on *HBO*.

Mantri, Geetika. *Only 13 pc Indian Schools RTE-Compliant: Why This May Not Reflect Education Quality. The News Minute*, January 17, 2019. https://www.thenewsminute.com/news/only-13-pc-indian-schools-rte-compliant-why-may-not-reflect-education-quality-95181.

Marantz, Sonia, and Susan Coates. *Mothers of boys with gender identity disorder: a comparison of matched controls. Journal of the American Academy of Child & Adolescent Psychiatry* 30, no. 2 (1991): 310-315.

Mathur, Sanyukta, and Sreela Das Gupta. Improving Adolescent Lives Through an Integrated Program: The DISHA Program in Bihar and Jharkhand, India. ICRW, September 2006. https://www.icrw.org/wp-content/uploads/2016/10/Improving-Adolescent-Lives-through-an-Integrated-Program-The-DISHA-Program-in-Bihar-and-Jharkhand-India.pdf.

McCaughey, Betsy. *Sex Ed Is Getting Too Extreme. The Epoch Times*, March 22, 2023. https://www.theepochtimes.com/opinion/sex-ed-is-getting-too-extreme-5141379.

Matthew, Elizabeth Grace. *The Predictable Failure of Restorative Justice in Schools. The Hill*, September 9, 2023. https://thehill.com/opinion/education/4181444-the-predictable-failure-of-restorative-justice-in-schools/.

Maughan, Shannon. *'It's Perfectly Normal' Turns 20. Publishers Weekly*. September 18, 2014. https://www.publishersweekly.com/pw/by-topic/childrens/childrens-book-news/article/64055-it-s-perfectly-normal-turns-20.html.

May, Tiffany, and Amy Qin. *The High School Course Beijing Accuses of Radicalizing Hong Kong. The New York Times,* September 1, 2019. https://www.nytimes.com/2019/09/01/world/asia/hong-kong-protests-education-china.html.

McBride, James, Noah Berman, and Andrew Chatzky. 'China's Massive Belt and Road Initiative'. Council on Foreign Relations, February 2, 2023. https://www.cfr.org/backgrounder/chinas-massive-belt-and-road-initiative.

McCaughey, Betsy. *Sex Ed Is Getting Too Extreme. The Epoch Times*, March 22, 2023a. https://www.theepochtimes.com/opinion/sex-ed-is-getting-too-extreme-5141379.

McCaughey, Betsy. *Climate Crazies Want to Use Schools to Brainwash Your Kids With This Radical Agenda. Fox News*, September 8, 2023b. https://www.foxnews.com/opinion/climate-crazies-want-schools-brainwash-your-kids-radical-agenda.

McKenna, Thomas. *Randi Weingarten's Union Descends on DC to Instruct Teachers How To Push Radical Agenda on Students. The Washington Free Beacon*, July 21, 2023. https://freebeacon.com/democrats/randi-weingartens-union-descends-on-dc-to-instruct-teachers-how-to-push-radical-agenda-on-students/.

Mek, Amy. Shocking Glimpse Into Life After The Great Reset-World Economic Forum's Sinister Plans (Videos)'. RAIR Foundation USA, October 20, 2021. https://rairfoundation.com/shocking-glimpse-into-life-after-the-great-reset-world-economic-forums-sinister-plans-videos/

MenEngage. 'Subscribe to Saathiya Launch'. UNFPA, Accessed November 15, 2024a. https://menengage.unfpa.org/en/tags/saathiya-launch.

MenEngage. 'Subscribe to Saathiya Salah App'. UNFPA, Accessed November 15, 2024b. https://menengage.unfpa.org/en/tags/saathiya-salah-app.

MGIEP. 'UNESCO MGIEP Transforming Education'. UNESCO, Accessed November 15, 2024a. https://mgiep.unesco.org/.

MGIEP. 'The International Science and Evidence Based Education (ISEE)'. UNESCO, Accessed November 15, 2024b. https://mgiep.unesco.org/iseeareport.

MGIEP. 'UNESCO MGIEP in Practice'. UNESCO, Accessed November 15, 2024c. https://mgiep.unesco.org/article/mgiep-in-practice.

MGIEP. 'SEL for SDGs | Education for Emotional Resilience'. UNESCO, Accessed November 15, 2024d. https://mgiep.unesco.org/article/sel-for-sdgs-why-social-and-emotional-learning-is-necessary-to-achieve-the-sustainable-development-goals.

MGIEP. 'UNESCO MGIEP and NIT Meghalaya Join Hands to Promote Social and Emotional Learning (SEL) in Education'. UNESCO, March 22, 2024e. https://mgiep.unesco.org/article/unesco-mgiep-and-nit-meghalaya-join-hands-to-promote-social-and-emotional-learning-sel-in-education.

MGIEP. 'Global Collective: List of Current Members'. UNESCO, Accessed November 15, 2024f. https://mgiep.unesco.org/article/global-collective-list-of-current-members.

MHRD. *National Education Policy, 2020*. Ministry of Human Resource Development, Government of India, Accessed November 15, 2024 https://www.education.gov.in/sites/upload_files/mhrd/files/NEP_Final_English_0.pdf.

Ministry of Education (@EduMinOfIndia). 'Maharashtra conducted the Periodic Assessment Test (PAT) from April 4th-6th, 2024, evaluating over 80 lakh students in grades 3-8 as part of the #STARS initiative marking a significant step in competency-based assessment'. X, April 9, 2024. https://x.com/EduMinOfIndia/status/1777654497386348702

Ministry of Education (@EduMinOfIndia). 'Smt Divya L, a National Awardee Teacher 2023 from Karnataka, is a Training Officer in Fashion Design & Technology. She has prepared the syllabus of the Competency-Based Curriculum course on Quality Control of Fabric & Accessories under DGT'. X, September 5, 2023. https://x.com/EduMinOfIndia/status/1699041930037092655

Ministry of Education, Singapore. 'Sexuality Education: Scope and Teaching Approach'. *Ministry of Education, Singapore*. Accessed November 15, 2024. https://www.moe.gov.sg/education-in-sg/our-programmes/sexuality-education/scope-and-teaching-approach.

Mochizuki, Yoko, Edward Vickers, and Audrey Bryan. *Huxleyan utopia or Huxleyan dystopia? 'Scientific humanism," Faure's legacy and the ascendancy of neuroliberalism in education. International Review of Education* 68, no. 5 (2022): 709-730.

Mochizuki, Yoko, Edward Vickers, and Audrey Bryan. *Huxleyan utopia or Huxleyan dystopia? 'Scientific humanism', Faure's legacy and the ascendancy of neuroliberalism in education. International Review of Education* 68, no. 5 (2022): 709-730.

Montana Department of Justice. World Health Organization's International Health Regulations (IHR) and New Pandemic Treaty. State of Montana, May 8, 2024. https://content.govdelivery.com/attachments/MTAG/2024/05/08/file_attachments/2871862/2024-05-08%20WHO%20Letter%20Final.pdf.

Morrison, Cassidy. *Women Who Used Contraceptive Pill as Teenagers Are 130% More Likely to Be Depressed as Adults, Study Suggests. DailyMail.com,* June 13, 2023. https://www.dailymail.co.uk/health/article-12190797/Women-used-birth-control-pills-teens-130-likely-depressed-adults.html.

Mukherjee, Ashish. *Udaan: A 360 Approach to Prevent Adolescent Pregnancies in Rajasthan.* IPEGlobal, May 2023. https://www.ipeglobal.com/wp-content/uploads/2023/05/Udaan-Brochure.pdf.

Mumah, Carrie. 'Planned Parenthood of Greater New York Announces Intent to Remove Margaret Sanger's Name from NYC Health Center'. Planned Parenthood of Greater New York. July 21, 2020. https://www.plannedparenthood.org/planned-parenthood-greater-new-york/about/news/planned-parenthood-of-greater-new-york-announces-intent-to-remove-margaret-sangers-name-from-nyc-health-center.

NACO. White Paper On Comprehensive Health-Related Services for Transgender Persons. National AIDS Control Organisation, 2023. https://naco.gov.in/sites/default/files/Whitepaper_on_Transgender_Persons_Health.pdf

Narayanan, Anju. "This Indian Woman Entrepreneur's Sextech Platform Has Won Recognition in South Korea." YourStory, November 30, 2022. https://yourstory.com/herstory/2022/11/woman-entrepreneur-sextech-platform-stand-we-speak.

National Statistical Office. Guidance on Monitoring Framework for SDGs at Sub National Level. Government of India, Ministry of Statistics and Programme Implementation, March 2022. https://mospi.gov.in/sites/

default/files/publication_reports/Guidance_on_MonitoringFramework_for_SDGs_March31_2022.pdf.

NCERT. *National Curriculum Framework for School Education 2023.* National Steering Committee for National Curriculum Frameworks, 2023. https://www.education.gov.in/sites/upload_files/mhrd/files/NCF-School-Education-Pre-Draft.pdf.

NCPCR. A Study on Implementation of Section 12(1)(c) of RTE Act, 2009 in Delhi Pertaining to Admission of Children from Disadvantaged Sections in Private Schools. National Commission for Protection of Child Rights, 2017. https://ncpcr.gov.in/uploads/165650379062bc3dee60c54_a-study-on-implementation-of-section-121-c-of-rte-act-2009-in-delhi-pertaining-to-admission-of-children-from-disadvantaged-sections-in-private-schools.pdf.

NCPCR. Impact of Exemption under Article 15(5) W.R.T. Article 21A of the Constitution of India on Education of Children of Minority Communities. National Commission for Protection of Child Rights, March 2021. https://ncpcr.gov.in/uploads/16835312236458a5d7a48c2_report-on-impact-of-exemption-under-article-155-wrt-article-21a-of-the-constitution-of-india-on-education-of-children-of-minority-communities--march-2021.pdf.

Nelson, Jelani (@minilek). '2+ yrs ago I co-authored a letter warning not offering Algebra I in public middle schools was anti-equity, as the wealthy could go private. Yesterday I discovered a great example: the main CA Math Framework author put her kids in a private school teaching Algebra I in 8th grade'. X, January 25, 2024. https://twitter.com/minilek/status/1750553300788011517.

NEON. *Sanjeev Sanyal UNFILTERED – Kolkata's Downfall & Bihar's UPSC Craze*. *NEON*, March 25, 2024. https://neon.fund/podcasts/sanjeev-sanyal-unfiltered-kolkatas-downfall/.

New Discourses. *The Origin of Queer Theory: Gayle Rubin's 'Thinking Sex'*. *New Discourses*, June 6, 2022. https://newdiscourses.com/2022/06/the-origin-of-queer-theory-gayle-rubins-thinking-sex.

New Discourses. *The Process of Marxist Consciousness*. *New Discourses*,

July 7, 2022a. https://newdiscourses.com/2022/07/process-marxist-consciousness/.

New Discourses. The Theft of Education. New Discourses, November 9, 2022b. https://newdiscourses.com/2022/11/the-theft-of-education/.

New Discourses. Resilience & Woke Brainwashing. YouTube video, 16:09. September 18, 2023. https://www.youtube.com/watch?v=CVCC_629eQo.

Nguyen, Nina. *Schools' 'Woke Agenda' Causes Children 'Climate Change Anxiety': Australian Senator. The Epoch Times,* June 28, 2022. https://www.theepochtimes.com/world/schools-woke-agenda-causes-children-climate-change-anxiety-australian-senator-4562631.

Niemi, Karen. 'CASEL Is Updating the Most Widely Recognized Definition of Social-Emotional Learning. Here's Why'. The 74, December 15, 2020. https://www.the74million.org/article/niemi-casel-is-updating-the-most-widely-recognized-definition-of-social-emotional-learning-heres-why/.

Nieuwsitems. 'WEF-Klaus Schwab (founder of The World Economic Forum): "We penetrate the cabinets"'. YouTube video. June 2, 2022. 00:00:52. https://www.youtube.com/watch?v=SjxJ1wPnkk4

NILERD. 'Roundtable on Global Evaluation Agenda for 2016-20 (September 26, 2014)'. National Institute of Labour Economics Research and Development (Formerly Institute of Applied Manpower Research), September 26, 2014. https://www.nilerd.ac.in/UserView/index?mid=1347

NIMH. *The Teen Brain: 7 Things to Know*. National Institute of Mental Health. Accessed November 15, 2024. https://www.nimh.nih.gov/health/publications/the-teen-brain-7-things-to-know.

NITI Aayog. *The Indian Model of SDG Localisation*. August 2022. https://www.niti.gov.in/sites/default/files/2022-08/The_Indian_Model_of_SDG_Localisation_13072022.pdf.

NITI Aayog. 'Education'. *NITI Aayog*. Accessed November 15, 2024. https://www.niti.gov.in/verticals/education.

North American Man/Boy Love Association (NAMBLA). Frequently Asked Questions. 2010. https://www.nambla.org/faq.htm.

NPC. Law of the People's Republic of China on Protection of Minors. The

National People's Congress of the People's Republic of China, October 17, 2020. http://en.npc.gov.cn.cdurl.cn/2020-10/17/c_674690.htm.

NRLC. Abortion Statistics: United States Data and Trends. National Right to Life, 2024. https://nrlc.org/uploads/factsheets/FS01AbortionintheUS.pdf.

Oberoi, Harjot. *The Construction of Religious Boundaries: Culture, Identity, and Diversity in the Sikh Tradition*. University of Chicago Press, 1994.

O'Connor, Ema, and Lauren Strapagiel. 'Dozens of Black Employees Said They Faced Racism at Planned Parenthood, An Internal Audit Found'. BuzzFeed News, October 10, 2020. https://www.buzzfeednews.com/article/emaoconnor/black-employees-planned-parenthood-racism.

OpIndia. Shiv Nadar School Introduces 'Non-Binary' as Child's Gender, Parents Say, 'Don't Shove Woke Politics Down Our Throat'. OpIndia. February 15, 2024. https://www.opindia.com/2024/02/shiv-nadar-school-non-binary-child-gender-feedback-form-parents-outraged/.

Padilla, Mariel. 'The 19th Explains: Why Child Marriage is Still Legal in 80% of U.S. States'. The 19th, July 5, 2023. https://19thnews.org/2023/07/explaining-child-marriage-laws-united-states/.

Pan, Bill. *UN-Developed Sex Education Curriculum Sexualizes Children, Advocates Warn. The Epoch Times,* July 27, 2021. https://www.theepochtimes.com/us/un-developed-sex-education-curriculum-sexualizes-children-advocates-warn-3920550.

Pearl, Mike. 'Whatever Happened to NAMBLA?' Vice, March 24, 2016. https://www.vice.com/en/article/7bd37e/whatever-happened-to-nambla.

Pemde, Harish Kumar, Utkarsh Bansal, Piyali Bhattacharya, Ram Niwas Sharma, Sanjiv Kumar, Poonam Bhatia, Sanjay Niranjan, Suhas Dhonde, and Jagdish Chandra Garg. *Adolescent Health Academy Statement on the Care of Transgender Children, Adolescents, and Youth. Indian Pediatrics*, May 14, 2023 [E-pub ahead of print]. https://www.indianpediatrics.net/epub052023/GUIDELINES-00534.pdf.

Pennell, Summer Melody. *Queer theory/pedagogy and social justice education*. Handbook on promoting social justice in education (2020): 2291-2311.

PFEL. Piramal Foundation for Education Leadership Signs MoU with Emory University to Implement the Social Emotional Ethical Learning Curriculum. Piramal Foundation for Education Leadership. 2020. https://www.piramal.com/wp-content/uploads/2020/04/PFEL_Partners-with-Emory-University-1-1.pdf.

PFI. 'Board & Advisory Council'. Population Foundation of India. Accessed November 15, 2024a. https://www.populationfoundation.in/board-advisory/.

PFI. Financial 2022-23. Population Foundation of India, August 2023a. https://www.populationfoundation.in/wp-content/uploads/2023/08/PFI-Financials-2022-23.pdf

PFI. Financial 2021-22. Population Foundation of India, June 2023b. https://www.populationfoundation.in/wp-content/uploads/2023/06/PFI-Financials_-202122_-with-audit-report-and-notes.pdf

PFI. Annual Report 2021-22. Population Foundation of India, June 2023c. https://www.populationfoundation.in/annual-report-2021-22

PFI. *Comprehensive Sexuality Education in India: A review of government and civil society-led curricula and strategies*. Population Foundation of India, April 2022. https://www.populationfoundation.in/wp-content/uploads/2022/07/A-review-of-government-and-civil-society-led-CSE-curricula-and-strategies-in-India-1.pdf.

PFI. *Scoping for Comprehensive Education on Adolescent Health and Wellbeing*. Population Foundation of India. Accessed November 15, 2024b. https://www.populationfoundation.in/approaches2/scoping-for-comprehensive-education-on-adolescent-health-and-wellbeing/.

PFI. *Adolescent Health and Well-being*. Population Foundation of India. Accessed November 15, 2024c. https://www.populationfoundation.in/adolescent-health-and-well-being/

PFI. Annual Report 2021-22. Population Foundation of India, June 2023d. https://www.populationfoundation.in/wp-content/uploads/2023/06/PFI_Web.pdf

PFI. *Feminist Adolescent and Youth-Led Action*. Population Foundation of India. Accessed November 15, 2024d. https://www.populationfoundation.in/approaches2/feminist-adolescent-and-youth-led-action/.

PFI. 'Educately'. Population Foundation of India. Accessed November 15, 2024e. https://www.populationfoundation.in/approaches2/educately/.

PIB. 'Comprehensive Sexuality Education'. Press Information Bureau, February 4, 2020. https://pib.gov.in/newsite/PrintRelease.aspx?relid=198908.

PIB. 'Health Secretary Launches "SAATHIYA" Resource Kit and "SAATHIYA SALAH" Mobile App for Adolescents'. Press Information Bureau, February 20, 2017. https://pib.gov.in/newsite/PrintRelease.aspx?relid=158578.

PIB. 'NITI Aayog to Draft Roadmap for Achieving Population Stabilisation'. Press Information Bureau, December 19, 2019. https://pib.gov.in/PressReleasePage.aspx?PRID=1596946.

Pipa, Anthony F., Max Bouchet, and Krista Rasmussen. 'American Leadership in Advancing the SDGs to Achieve Equity and Sustainability'. Brookings, November 12, 2020. https://www.brookings.edu/articles/american-leadership-in-advancing-the-sdgs-to-achieve-equity-and-sustainability/.

Piramal School of Leadership (@PiramalSoL). 'Excited to Share the Remarkable Success of #SocialEmotionalLearning (SEL) Samagam Series Held Across Five Districts of Jharkhand – Palamu, Chatra, Giridih, East Singhbhum, and Dumka...' X, February 9, 2024. https://x.com/PiramalSoL/status/1755955981085798729.

Portell, Mathew. '*Understanding Trauma-Informed Education*'. Edutopia, December 16, 2019. https://www.edutopia.org/article/understanding-trauma-informed-education/.

Portell, Mathew. '*Understanding Trauma-Informed Education*'. Edutopia, December 16, 2019. https://www.edutopia.org/article/understanding-trauma-informed-education/.

Pradhan, Dharmendra (@dpradhanbjp). 'Glad to be at the @IndiaToday Education Conclave. Shared my perspectives around a host of educational priorities, including on the 3 thrust areas of NEP…' X, July 30, 2024. https://x.com/dpradhanbjp/status/1818209845033451703

Pradhan, Dharmendra. *Education, a guiding light for a shared vision of G20. The Hindustan Times*, February 2, 2023. https://www.hindustantimes.com/opinion/education-a-guiding-light-for-a-shared-vision-of-g20-101675345832247.html

Press Trust of India. *1.6 Lakh Boys and Girls Will Now Be Peer Educators to Adolescents. YourStory*, February 21, 2017. https://yourstory.com/2017/02/girls-boys-educators-adolescents.

Qin, Qian, and Jiali Zhang. 'Sex Education in China: Actors and dynamics of China's policies and practices'. Cogent education 10, no. 2 (2023): 2270289.

Qin, Qian, Ziyu Li, and Xiaotong Jiao. 'Public opinion on the death penalty in Mainland China and Taiwan'. China Report 57, no. 3 (2021): 327-345.

Qingqing, Chen. *Upholding unity of loving China, the CPC vital for patriotism to be lively, genuine: top legislature, Global Times*, October 6, 2023. https://www.globaltimes.cn/page/202310/1300671.shtml

Raha, Swagata, and Shruthi Ramakrishnan. Implication of the POCSO Act in India on Adolescent Sexuality: A Policy Brief. Enfold Proactive Health Trust, UNFPA, and UNICEF, 2022. https://www.girlsnotbrides.org/documents/1960/POSCO-Act-Policy-Brief_wUlR95W.pdf.

Rasmussen Reports. 'Most Parents Oppose "Drag Queen Story Hour"'. Rasmussen Reports, November 15, 2022. https://www.rasmussenreports.com/public_content/lifestyle/general_lifestyle/november_2022/most_parents_oppose_drag_queen_story_hour.

Reigart, John Franklin. The Lancasterian System Of Instruction In The Schools Of New York City (1916)

Review the WHO. 'Attention: Elected Officials Worldwide: Demand the WHO Respect the Rule of Law', May 17, 2024. https://reviewthewho.org/.

Review The WHO. 'Demand the WHO Respect the Rule of Law'." Review The WHO, Accessed November 15, 2024. https://reviewthewho.org.

Rim, Christopher. *What To Know About The New Digital SAT. Forbes*,

February 2, 2024. https://www.forbes.com/sites/christopherrim/2024/02/02/what-to-know-about-the-new-digital-sat/.

Rim, Christopher. *What To Know About The New Digital SAT. Forbes*, February 2, 2024. https://www.forbes.com/sites/christopherrim/2024/02/02/what-to-know-about-the-new-digital-sat/.

Rimmele, Peter, and Nitya Nanda. Training Manual on SDGs for NGOs. Council for Social Development & Konrad-Adenauer-Stiftung, June 2022. https://csdindia.org/wp-content/uploads/2022/06/Training-Manual-on-SDG-for-NGOs.pdf.

Rosiak, Luke. *Leaked Files From Transgender Medical Org Show 'Medical Malpractice'. The Daily Wire,* March 6, 2024. https://www.dailywire.com/news/leaked-files-from-transgender-medical-org-show-medical-malpractice.

Rosiak, Luke. *Leaked Files From Transgender Medical Org Show 'Medical Malpractice'. The Daily Wire,* March 6, 2024. https://www.dailywire.com/news/leaked-files-from-transgender-medical-org-show-medical-malpractice.

Rubin, Gayle S. *Thinking Sex: Notes for a Radical Theory of the Politics of Sexuality.* In *Culture, Society and Sexuality*, pp. 143-178. Routledge, 2002.

Rufo, Christopher F. *The Real Story Behind Drag Queen Story Hour*. Christopher F. Rufo, October 24, 2022. https://christopherrufo.com/p/the-real-story-behind-drag-queen-story-hour.

Rutgers International. 'Scaling Up Sexuality Education: Lessons Learned and Considerations for Civil Society Organizations'. Rutgers International, Accessed November 15, 2024. https://rutgers.international/resources/scaling-up-sexuality-education-lessons-learned-and-considerations-for-civil-society-organizations/.

Rutgers International. 'Scaling Up Sexuality Education..'. Rutgers International, September 2021. https://rutgers.international/wp-content/uploads/2021/09/RUTG2102_Design_Scale-up-Report_LM_0709-1.pdf.

Saathiya. 'Welcome address by Ms Vandana Gurnani JS (RCH) MoHFW

India'. YouTube video. February 20, 2017a. 00:00:49. https://www.youtube.com/watch?v=f_D42cry9YI

Saathiya. 'Keynote address by Sh C.K. Mishra, Secretary, H&FW, MoHFW'. YouTube video. February 20, 2017b. 00:03:15. https://www.youtube.com/watch?v=OosysxoPoCk

Saavedra, Ryan (@RealSaavedra). 'Psychologist Jonathan Haidt on why he says social contagion is behind the surge in the number of cases of people claiming to be transgender: "Because it happens in clusters of girls, it happens in clusters of girls who had no previous gender dysphoria when they were young…"' X, March 31, 2024. https://twitter.com/RealSaavedra/status/1774229750409498900.

Sandhu, Amrit. 'Emotionally Intelligent Leadership w Dr. Daniel Goleman (How to Be Happy, Calm & Focused) 🧠'. YouTube video. January 8, 2023. 00:52:31. https://www.youtube.com/watch?v=sILqUB3TgTg

Sangwan, Sujata. *[Funding Alert] Pune-Based Sexual and Mental Wellness App for Teens ThatMate Raises $140K in Angel Round*. *YourStory*, May 31, 2021. https://yourstory.com/2021/05/funding-pune-sexual-mental-wellness-app-teens-thatmate-angel-round.

Sanskriti Magazine. '64 Kalas (Arts) and 14 Vidyas (Techniques) of Ancient India'. Sanskriti-Hinduism and Indian Culture Website, March 29, 2015. https://www.sanskritimagazine.com/64-kalas-arts-and-14-vidyas-techniques-of-ancient-india

Sarkar, Sonia. 'Class act: Indian drag artists spread 'strong and clear' messages of gender equality across schools'. SCMP, February 5, 2024. https://www.scmp.com/week-asia/people/article/3250733/class-act-indian-drag-artists-spread-strong-and-clear-messages-gender-equality-across-schools

Satel, Sally, and Scott O. Lilienfeld. *Brainwashed: The Seductive Appeal of Mindless Neuroscience*. Basic Civitas Books, 2013.

Saxbe, Darby. *This Is Not the Way to Help Depressed Teenagers*. *The New York Times,* November 18, 2023. https://www.nytimes.com/2023/11/18/opinion/teenagers-mental-health-treatment.html.

Scharfe, Hartmut. *The State in Indian Tradition*. E. J. Brill, 1989.

Schlott, Rikki. *We were pushed to transition as teens — now we're 'vindicated' by study showing kids grow out of it*. *New York Post*, April 16, 2024. https://nypost.com/2024/04/16/lifestyle/teen-detransitioners-weve-been-vindicated-by-fad-study/.

Seetha, and Antara Sengupta. *The Horror Called RTE: Envisaged As A Dream Project, It Is Turning Out To Be A Nightmare*. *Swarajya*, February 5, 2018. https://swarajyamag.com/magazine/the-horror-called-rte-envisaged-as-a-dream-project-it-is-turning-out-to-be-a-nightmare.

Sen, Priyadarshini, and Lubna Jerar Naqvi. *Transgender Activists Highlight the Impacts of Climate Change and Environmental Issues on the Community*. *Mongabay*, March 7, 2023. https://india.mongabay.com/2023/03/transgender-activists-highlight-the-impacts-of-climate-change-and-environmental-issues-on-the-community/.

Severino, Roger, and Jim DeMint. 'Court Should Reject Obama's Radical Social Experiment'. The Heritage Foundation, December 14, 2016. https://www.heritage.org/gender/commentary/court-should-reject-obamas-radical-social-experiment.

Severino, Roger, and Jim DeMint. 'Court Should Reject Obama's Radical Social Experiment'. The Heritage Foundation, December 14, 2016. https://www.heritage.org/gender/commentary/court-should-reject-obamas-radical-social-experiment.

SFUSD. Algebra 1 in 8th Grade Recommendations. San Francisco Unified School District, February 13, 2024. https://go.boarddocs.com/ca/sfusd/Board.nsf/files/D2APJP64985F/$file/Algebra%201%20in%208th%20Grade%20Recommendations_02-13-2024.pdf.

Shankar, Priya, Bittu K. Rajaraman, Aqsa Shaikh, Prachi Patel, Aruna Nannapaneni, Sanjay Sharma, Ricky Sharma, Amrita Sarkar, and Harish Pemde. *Decolonising Gender in India*. *The Lancet Global Health* 10, no. 2 (2022): e173-e174.

Sharma, Anchal. EdTech Promoting Social-Emotional Learning in India. Center for Sustainable Development, Earth Institute, Columbia University,

August 2021. https://csd.columbia.edu/sites/default/files/content/docs/ICT%20India/Papers/ICT_India_Working_Paper_55.pdf.

Shellenberger, Michael (@shellenberger). 'THE WPATH FILES Advocates of gender-affirming care say it's evidence-based. But now, newly released internal files from the World Professional Association for Transgender Health (WPATH) prove that the practice of transgender medicine is neither scientific nor medical...' X, March 5, 2024. https://twitter.com/shellenberger/status/1764799914918490287.

Shi-Kupfer, Kristin, and Bertram Lang. *Overseas NGOs in China: Left in Legal Limbo*. *The Diplomat*, March 4, 2017. https://thediplomat.com/2017/03/overseas-ngos-in-china-left-in-legal-limbo/.

Shrier, Abigail. *Author Reveals How 'Bad Therapy' Is Harming Children*. *Fox News* Video, February 29, 2024. https://www.foxnews.com/video/6347925836112.

Shrier, Abigail. *Author Reveals How 'Bad Therapy' Is Harming Children*. *Fox News* Video, February 29, 2024. https://www.foxnews.com/video/6347925836112.

Shrier, Abigail. *Bad Therapy: Why the Kids Aren't Growing Up*. Swift Press, 2024.

Shuo, Zou. *Inclusivity to Enhance Digital Education*. *China Daily*, February 14, 2023. https://www.chinadaily.com.cn/a/202302/14/WS63ead3f1a31057c47ebae917.html

Simple Education Foundation. Audited Balance Sheet 2023. 2023. https://drive.google.com/file/d/1HGbBCDV2S2FImCqsN09xOZTydsdOH9dF/view.

Singh, Ashish @AshishS80191136). 'With a lineup of amazing youths and decision-makers from across the globe, 🌏 we will explore the topic that matters most: 🗄 "Climate Change Anxiety Among Youth and How it Can Be Tackled through SEL...', X, June 4, 2024. https://x.com/UNESCO_MGIEP/status/1797969155565478075.

Somashekhar, Sandhya, and Danielle Paquette. *Undercover Video Shows Planned Parenthood Exec Discussing Organ Harvesting'. The*

Washington Post, July 14, 2015. https://www.washingtonpost.com/politics/undercover-video-shows-planned-parenthood-exec-discussing-organ-harvesting/2015/07/14/ae330e34-2a4d-11e5-bd33-395c05608059_story.html.

Sonika (@Sonika_Mam). 'With the right mindset, we can't lose- we either practice what we've learned or we learn what we need to practice. #professionalgrowth #socialemotionallearning #SEL @Dir_Education @SCERT2021 @UNESCO_MGIEP @GGSSS1207038n @karshan01', X, July 16, 2023. https://twitter.com/Sonika_Mam/status/1680597625693929478/photo/3.

South Asia Monitor. *Modi Government Move to Raise the Marriage Age of Women in India from 18 to 21; Task Force Recommends Sex Education in Schools. South Asia Monitor*, December 16, 2021. https://www.southasiamonitor.org/india/modi-government-move-raise-marriage-age-women-india-18-21-task-force-recommends-sex-education.

Southey, Robert, and Charles Cuthbert Southey. *The Life of the Rev. Andrew Bell:... Prebendary of Westminster, and Master of Sherburn Hospital, Durham. Comprising the History of the Rise and Progress of the System of Mutual Tuition*. Vol. 2. J. Murray, 1844.

Sriram, V. *The Egmore Redoubt – A Lost Landmark of Chennai. Madras Heritage and Carnatic Music*, August 6, 2018. https://sriramv.com/2018/08/06/the-egmore-redoubt-a-lost-landmark-of-chennai/.

Starbuck, Robby (@robbystarbuck). 'The American College of Pediatricians just put out a 🔥🔥🔥 statement calling out all the major medical associations by name for pushing the gender transition craze on kids...', X, June 8, 2024. https://x.com/robbystarbuck/status/1799281058170405320.

Stats For Gender (@statsforgender). 'Stats for Gender Provides Reliable and Accessible Information on Gender and Transition'. X.com. Accessed November 15, 2024. https://x.com/statsforgender.

Stauffer, Elizabeth. *20 Million Black Babies Have Been Aborted Since Roe v. Wade. Where Is the Equity in That?*, *Washington Examiner*, October 14, 2022. https://www.washingtonexaminer.com/news/2879870/20-million-black-babies-have-been-aborted-since-roe-v-wade-where-is-the-equity-in-that/.

stem4. 'A Third of Teenagers Say They Have Been Prescribed Antidepressants, Survey Finds'. stem4, 2022. https://stem4.org.uk/a-third-of-teenagers-say-they-have-been-prescribed-antidepressants-survey-finds/.

Stop CSE. 'A Sample of Comprehensive Sexuality Education Curriculum: Excerpts from It's Perfectly Normal'. Accessed November 15, 2024. https://www.comprehensivesexualityeducation.org/wp-content/uploads/Excerpts-from-Its-Perfectly-Natural.pdf.

Swarajya. *India's New Education Policy Will Be Based On Vedic Knowlegde-Science: HRD Minister Nishank*, May 10, 2020. https://swarajyamag.com/insta/indias-new-education-policy-will-be-based-on-vedic-knowlegde-science-hrd-minister-nishank

Tagore International School. 'Sexuality Education'. Tagore International School, Accessed November 15, 2024. https://www.vv.tagoreint.com/sexuality-education/.

Talarico, Lauren. 'Houston Public Library Admits Registered Child Sex Offender Read to Kids in Drag Queen Storytime'. KHOU 11, March 15, 2019. https://www.khou.com/article/news/local/houston-public-library-admits-registered-child-sex-offender-participated-in-drag-queen-storytime/285-becf3a0d-56c5-4f3c-96df-add07bbd002a.

Tallis, Raymond. *Aping Mankind*. Routledge, 2016.

Tang, Annie, J. Carlo Hojilla, Jordan E. Jackson, Kara A. Rothenberg, Rebecca C. Gologorsky, Douglas A. Stram, Colin M. Mooney, Stephanie L. Hernandez, and Karen M. Yokoo. *Gender-affirming mastectomy trends and surgical outcomes in adolescents. Annals of Plastic Surgery* 88, no. 4 (2022): S325-S331.

TARSHI. *What makes sexuality education comprehensive? Talking about Reproductive and Sexual Health Issues*, 2019. https://tarshi.net/downloads/What_Makes_Sexuality_Education_Comprehensive-a_Working_Paper_by_TARSHI.pdf

The Cass Review. Final Report. April 2024. https://cass.independent-review.uk/home/publications/final-report/.

The Daily Marketing (@TDailyMarketing). 'Keshav Suri Foundation (KSF), Pride Circle and Stonewall have partnered to create the India Workplace Equality Index (IWEI). This is India's first comprehensive benchmarking tool with which organisations can measure their progress on LGBT+ inclusion in the Indian context'. X, December 17, 2020. https://twitter.com/TDailyMarketing/status/1339437994474815489.

The David and Lucile Packard Foundation. 'Global Reproductive Health Initiative." Packard Foundation. Accessed November 15, 2024. https://www.packard.org/what-we-fund/global-reproductive-health/.

The Economic Times. "Mental Health for India's Young Women-Way Forward'. *The Economic Times*, February 18, 2021. https://health.economictimes.indiatimes.com/news/industry/mental-health-for-indias-young-women-way-forward/81083876.

The Hindu. *Transgender Clinics to Come Up in Many Govt. Hospitals in T.N., Says Health Minister. The Hindu*, April 11, 2022. https://www.thehindu.com/news/cities/Madurai/transgender-clinics-to-come-up-in-many-govt-hospitals-in-tn-says-health-minister/article65309216.ece.

The Nazariya Foundation. 'Funding'. The Nazariya Foundation, Accessed November 15, 2024. https://thenazariyafoundation.org/funding.

The Pioneer. *To Study Impact of 'Udaan' on Students*. *The Pioneer*, August 29, 2019. https://www.dailypioneer.com/2019/state-editions/to-study-impact-of----udaan--on-students.html.

The Pioneer. To Study Impact of 'Udaan' on Students." The Pioneer, August 29, 2019. https://www.dailypioneer.com/2019/state-editions/to-study-impact-of----udaan--on-students.html.

The Print. *National Education Policy rooted in 'Bharatiyata' while assimilating global perspective: Shah*, July 29, 2022. https://theprint.in/india/national-education-policy-rooted-in-bharatiyata-while-assimilating-global-perspective-shah/1060692

The Times of India. *State Govt Tells Univs to Bear Tuition Fees for Transgenders*. December 6, 2023. http://timesofindia.indiatimes.com/articleshow/105766793.cms.

The Times of India. Young Indians more likely to be jobless if they're educated, March 29, 2024. https://timesofindia.indiatimes.com/business/india-business/young-indians-more-likely-to-be-jobless-if-theyre-educated/articleshow/108864858.cms

The YP Foundation and Pravah. India Comprehensive Sexuality Education: The Way Forward. The YP Foundation & Pravah, February 2017. https://arrow.org.my/wp-content/uploads/2017/10/India-CSE-brief.pdf.

The YP Foundation. 'Shareer Apna, Adhikaar Apne: A Policy Brief on Comprehensive Sexuality Education'. The YP Foundation, January 2018. https://theypfoundation.org/resources/shareer-apna-adhikaar-apne-a-policy-brief-on-comprehensive-sexuality-education/.

The YP Foundation. Foreign Contribution Received for the Financial Year 2021-22. The YP Foundation, July 2021b. https://theypfoundation.org/wp-content/uploads/2021/07/FCRA-for-the-Financial-Year-2021-22.pdf.

The YP Foundation. 'Shareer Apna, Adhikaar Apne: A Policy Brief on Comprehensive Sexuality Education'. The YP Foundation, May 2021a. https://theypfoundation.org/wp-content/uploads/2021/05/Shareer-Apna-Adhikaar-Apne-A-Policy-Brief-Full-Report-English.pdf.

The YP Foundation. The YP Foundation: Organizational Profile. The YP Foundation, July 2021c. https://theypfoundation.org/wp-content/uploads/2021/07/TYPF-Organisational-Profile-2022.pdf.

Tigue, Kristoffer. *Texas Board of Education Urged to Reject Climate-Accurate Textbooks. Mother Jones*. November 14, 2023. https://www.motherjones.com/politics/2023/11/texas-board-education-climate-change-school-textbooks-vote/.

Torres, Michael. *We Thought She Was a Great Teacher. City Journal*, 2024. https://www.city-journal.org/article/we-thought-she-was-a-great-teacher.

Tripathi, Prof. (Dr.) Shruti. 'School of Employability and Holistic Development, DSEU UNIVERSITY takes pleasure to announce the MOU with UNESCO MGIEP, to implement initiatives that will help students develop their...', LinkedIn, 2023. https://www.linkedin.com/posts/hclfoundation_arsh-activity-7158701138882551808-PEJE/.

Tschurenev, Jana. *A Colonial Experiment in Education: Madras, 1789–1796.* In *Connecting Histories of Education: Transnational and Cross-Cultural Exchanges in (Post)Colonial Education*, ed. by Barnita Bagchi, Eckhardt Fuchs, and Kate Rousmaniere, 2014. Berghahn Books.

Tschurenev, Jana. *Diffusing useful knowledge: the monitorial system of education in Madras, London and Bengal, 1789–1840. Paedagogica Historica* 44, no. 3 (2008): 245-264.

U.S. Census Bureau. 'U.S. Census Bureau QuickFacts: United States'. U.S. Census Bureau, Accessed November 15, 2024. https://www.census.gov/quickfacts/fact/table/US/PST045221.

UGC. Comprehensive Accessibility Guidelines and Standards for Higher Education Institutions and Universities. University Grants Commission, Government of India, February 2022. https://www.ugc.gov.in/pdfnews/8381868_Draft-Guidelines-UGC_20-Feb-2021.pdf.

UGC. Educational Framework for Global Citizenship in Higher Education. University Grants Commission, Government of India. December, 2021. https://www.ugc.gov.in/e-book/GCED%20Book_WEB.pdf.

UN Global Compact. IPPF Communication on Engagement. UN Global Compact, May 7, 2023. https://unglobalcompact.org/participation/report/cop/detail/479286.

UN News. *Redefining Life-Long Benefits of Sexual Health–WHO. UN News*, February 11, 2022. https://news.un.org/en/story/2022/02/1111862.

UNAIDS. 'New Legal Principles Launched on International Women's Day to Advance Decriminalization Efforts'. UNAIDS, March 8, 2023. https://www.unaids.org/en/resources/presscentre/featurestories/2023/march/20230308_new-legal-principles-decriminalization.

unDivided. *'Make Sure This Email Is Deleted': How Gender Ideology Led to a Secret Teacher-Student Relationship (EXCLUSIVE). Patreon*, July 12, 2023. https://www.patreon.com/posts/make-sure-this-85986259.

UNESCO. *Healthy, happy and hot: a young person's guide to their rights, sexuality and living with HIV*. United Nations Educational, Scientific and Cultural Organization. 2010. https://healtheducationresources.unesco.

org/library/documents/healthy-happy-and-hot-young-persons-guide-their-rights-sexuality-and-living-hiv.

UNESCO. *International technical guidance on sexuality education: An evidence-informed approach*. United Nations Educational, Scientific and Cultural Organization. 2018. https://www.unfpa.org/sites/default/files/pub-pdf/ITGSE.pdf.

UNESCO. *The Journey Towards Comprehensive Sexuality Education.* United Nations Educational, Scientific and Cultural Organization 2021. https://cdn.who.int/media/docs/default-source/hrp/379607.pdf.

UNESCO. 'What is Comprehensive Sexuality Education (CSE)?', Accessed November 13, 2024. https://healtheducationresources.unesco.org/toolkit/what-comprehensive-sexuality-education-cse

UNESCO Digital Library. 'International Technical Guidance on Sexuality Education: An Evidence-Informed Approach'. UNESCO Digital Library, 2018. https://unesdoc.unesco.org/ark:/48223/pf0000260770.

UNESCO Digital Library. 'The Journey Towards Comprehensive Sexuality Education: Global Status Report'. UNESCO Digital Library, 2021. https://unesdoc.unesco.org/ark:/48223/pf0000379607.

unesco_mgiep (@UNESCO_MGIEP). 'It's only day 1 of the Global Citizenship Workshop for Teachers to promote SEL in K-12 Classrooms but the teachers from Japan, Afghanistan, Bangladesh, Sri Lanka And Maldives are already indulging in some Inter-cultural Exchanges...', Twitter, August 7, 2019. https://x.com/UNESCO_MGIEP/status/1158985559177482241

unesco_mgiep (@UNESCO_MGIEP). 'Honored to receive the certificate from @UNESCO_MGIEP for the successful completion of the course on "Climate Change: Understand, Reflect, Empathize, and Act" under the able guidance of Dr. @AnanyaM58107239...' X, January 11, 2024. https://x.com/AshishS80191136/status/1745478624432771527

UNESCO, United Nations Children's Fund, Joint United Nations Programme on HIV/AIDS, United Nations Population Fund, World Health Organization, and United Nations Entity for Gender Equality and the Empowerment of Women. *The Journey Towards Comprehensive Sexuality*

Education: Global Status Report. UNESCO Publishing, 2021. https://doi.org/10.54675/NFEK1277.

UNFCCC. Paris Agreement. United Nations Framework Convention on Climate Change. 2015. Accessed May 27, 2024. https://unfccc.int/sites/default/files/english_paris_agreement.pdf.

UNFPA. *The Evaluation of Comprehensive Sexuality Education Programmes: A Focus on the Gender and Empowerment Outcomes*. United Nations Population Fund, 2015. https://www.unfpa.org/sites/default/files/pub-pdf/UNFPAEvaluationWEB4.pdf

UNFPA. *International Technical Guidance on Sexuality Education: An Evidence-Informed Approach*. 138 pages. UNESCO, UNAIDS, UNFPA, UNICEF, UN Women, and WHO, January 10, 2018. https://www.unfpa.org/sites/default/files/pub-pdf/ITGSE.pdf

UNFPA. *Laws and Policies Impacting Young People's Sexual and Reproductive Health and Rights in the Asia-Pacific Region*: 2020 Update. UNFPA Asia-Pacific Regional Office, 2020. https://asiapacific.unfpa.org/sites/default/files/pub-pdf/case_studies_laws_and_policies_impacting_young_peoples_sexual_and_reproductive_health_and_rights_in_the_asia-pacific_region_2020_update.pdf.

UNFPA. *Country Programme Document for India*. United Nations Population Fund, July 5, 2022. https://www.unfpa.org/sites/default/files/portal-document/ENG_DP.FPA_.CPD_.IND_.10%20-%20India%20CPD%20-%20Final%20-%205Jul22.pdf.

UNFPA. *Annual Report 2022*. United Nations Population Fund, 2023. https://www.unfpa.org/sites/default/files/pub-pdf/unfpa-ar-22-en.pdf.

UNICEF. *Legal Minimum Ages and the Realization of Adolescents' Rights: A Review of the Situation in Latin America and the Caribbean*. January 2016. https://www.unicef.org/lac/media/40681/file/Legal-minimun-ages.pdf.

UNICEF. *Gender Transformative Education: Reimagining Education for a More Just and Inclusive World*. UNCF, December 2021. https://www.unicef.org/media/113166/file/Gender%20Transformative%20Education.pdf.

UNICEF. *UNICEF Does Not Endorse Conclusions of the Brief*. UNICEF,

September 2023. https://www.unicef.org/india/reports/unicef-does-not-endorse-conclusions-brief.

UNICEF East Asia & Pacific. *The Opportunity for Digital Sexuality Education in East Asia and the Pacific.* UNICEF, September 2019. https://www.unicef.org/eap/reports/opportunity-digital-sexuality-education-east-asia-and-pacific.

UNICEF India. *Adolescent Development and Participation.* UNICEF, Accessed November 15, 2024. https://www.unicef.org/india/what-we-do/adolescent-development-participation.

United Nations. 'Richa Gupta'. United Nations, Accessed November 15, 2024. https://www.un.org/youthenvoy/richa-gupta/.

United Nations. 'The 17 Goals', Department of Economic and Social Affairs, Sustainable Development. Accessed May November 13, 2024. https://sdgs.un.org/goals

Valente, K.G., *Queer(y)ing Mathematical Knowledge and Practices.* In *Handbook of the Mathematics of the Arts and Sciences*, ed. Bharath Sriraman. Cham: Springer, 2019. https://doi.org/10.1007/978-3-319-70658-0_71-1.

Vankar, Preeti. "Percentage of Teenagers in the United States Taking Antidepressants from 2015 to 2019, by Gender." Statista, November 29, 2023. https://www.statista.com/statistics/1133612/antidepressant-use-teenagers-by-gender-us/.

Vankar, Preeti. 'Percentage of U.S. Adults with Any Mental Illness in the Past Year as of 2022, by Age and Gender'. Statista, February 12, 2024. https://www.statista.com/statistics/252311/mental-illness-in-the-past-year-among-us-adults-by-age-and-gender/.

Vickers, Edward. *Rebranding Gandhi for the 21st century: Science, ideology and politics at UNESCO's Mahatma Gandhi Institute (MGIEP). Compare: A Journal of Comparative and International Education* 54, no. 5 (2024): 785-803.

Vishnoi, Anubhuti. *Smriti Irani's HRD Ministry Has Come to Agreement with Global Scholars to Teach in India. The Economic Times*, September

16, 2015. https://economictimes.indiatimes.com/industry/services/education/smriti-iranis-hrd-ministry-has-come-to-agreement-with-global-scholars-to-teach-in-india/articleshow/48978495.cms.

Walsh, Matt (@MattWalshBlog). '8/ Dr. Lawrence's writing appears to be from 1998, just a year after he resigned from a hospital after performing a non-consensual genital examination on an unconscious female patient, according to an incident report'. X, March 7, 2024b. https://twitter.com/MattWalshBlog/status/1765504207350530469.

Walsh, Matt. 'The Media's Birth Control Cover Up Is Slowly Unraveling'. YouTube video. March 25, 2024a. 00:13:08. https://www.youtube.com/watch?v=XjsrK42aoaU

Wang, Lipei. *Possibility of educating 'global citizens' through a Chinese national school curriculum. Asia Pacific Journal of Education* (2023): 1-16.

Wang, Zixu, Xin Chen, and Caroline Radnofsky. *China Proposes Teaching Masculinity to Boys as State Is Alarmed by Changing Gender Roles. NBC News*. March 5, 2021. https://www.nbcnews.com/news/world/china-proposes-teaching-masculinity-boys-state-alarmed-changing-gender-roles-n1258939.

Weed, Stan E., and Irene H. Ericksen. *Re-Examining the Evidence for Comprehensive Sex Education in Schools: A Global Research Review*. The Institute for Research & Evaluation, December 2019. https://www.institute-research.com/CSEReport/Global_CSE_Report_12-17-19.pdf.

Weiss, Bari. 'Why the Kids Aren't Alright'. Spotify, February 27, 2024. https://open.spotify.com/episode/5dyeoq59cAIlP1FpOcEW2F?si=e03e4ac4723a4594&nd=1&dlsi=aee3fc61dbc743f7.

Wexler MA JD, Kimberley,'Kim' (@KimWexlerMAJD). "If we're going to deliver on the promise of migration, we have to deliver on the promise of gender equality"'. X, August 26, 2024b. https://x.com/KimWexlerMAJD/status/1828132095425679823.

Wexler MA JD, Kimberley 'Kim' (@KimWexlerMAJD). 'UN UNInternational Office for Migration (IOM) Director General AMY POPE's Message on the Launch of the Strategic Plan 2024-2028...'. X, August 26, 2024a.

https://x.com/KimWexlerMAJD/status/1828089835564814512.

WHO Regional Office for Europe and BZgA. *Standards for Sexuality Education in Europe: A Framework for Policy Makers, Educational and Health Authorities, and Specialists*. 2010. https://www.icmec.org/wp-content/uploads/2016/06/WHOStandards-for-Sexuality-Ed-in-Europe.pdf.

Wilson, Rhoda. 2024. *Latest Pandemic Treaty Draft Has Gaping Holes Because They Daren't Reveal What They Plan to Do. The Exposé*, April 20, 2024. https://expose-news.com/2024/04/20/latest-pandemic-treaty-draft-has-gaping-holes/.

Wokal Distance (@wokal_distance). 'Trans-activists aim their trans propaganda at kids. This is why all the illustrations trans-activists use to talk about gender are things small children like...'. X, January 18, 2024. https://twitter.com/wokal_distance/status/1748005011664339228/photo/1.

World Economic Forum and The Boston Consulting Group. New Vision for Education: Fostering Social and Emotional Learning through Technology. March 2016. https://www3.weforum.org/docs/WEF_New_Vision_for_Education.pdf.

World Health Organization. 'Sexual Health'. WHO, Accessed November 15, 2024. https://www.who.int/health-topics/sexual-health.

WPATH. WPATH 2022 Award Recipients. World Professional Association for Transgender Health, 2022. https://www.wpath.org/media/cms/Documents/History/Awards/2022/2022%20Award%20Eblast.pdf.

X 'Competency Based Education, India'. X, accessed November 18, 2024. https://x.com/search?q=competency+based+education%2C+india&src=typed_query&f=live.

Xiaoliang, Chao. 'The Tenth Year of China's Proposal: A Global Community of Shared Future'. China Embassy, October 30, 2023a. http://ws.china-embassy.gov.cn/eng/xwdt/202310/t20231030_11170359.htm

Xiaoliang, Chao. '*Initiatives Proposed by China, Fruitful Outcomes Shared by World*'. May 22, 2023b. Chinese Embassy in Samoa. http://ws.china-embassy.gov.cn/eng/xwdt/202305/t20230522_11081047.htm.

Xinhua. "Xi Focus: Nurturing, encouraging China's children" Xinhuanet, June 11, 2021. http://www.xinhuanet.com/english/2021-06/01/c_139982712.htm.

Yahoo! Finance. 'Social and Emotional Learning Market Worth $10.3 Billion by 2028 - Exclusive Report by MarketsandMarkets™'. Yahoo! Finance, December 1, 2023. https://finance.yahoo.com/news/social-emotional-learning-market-worth-150100920.html.

Yenor, Scott. 'Planned Parenthood-Endorsed Sex Ed Is In These 14 Public Schools'. The Claremont Institute, November 3, 2022. https://dc.claremont.org/planned-parenthood-endorsed-sex-is-in-these-14-public-schools/.

Yu, Zhang. *Volunteers Bring Sex Education to Rural Classes After Shocking Abuse of 'Left-Behind' Kids*. *Global Times*, August 8, 2018. https://www.globaltimes.cn/page/201808/1114431.shtml.

Yu, Zhang. *Volunteers Bring Sex Education to Rural Classes After Shocking Abuse of 'Left-Behind' Kids*. *Global Times*, August 8, 2018. https://www.globaltimes.cn/page/201808/1114431.shtml.

Zguir, Mariem Fekih, Sana Dubis, and Muammer Koç. *Embedding Education for Sustainable Development (ESD) and SDGs values in curriculum: A comparative review on Qatar, Singapore and New Zealand. Journal of Cleaner Production* 319 (2021): 128534.

END NOTES

Introduction: Recruiting Our Children to Break Up India

1 Bhagavata Purana, 10.12.17-18
2 *"Acknowledging that climate change is a common concern of humankind, Parties should, when taking action to address climate change, respect, promote and consider their respective obligations on human rights, the right to health, the rights of indigenous peoples, local communities, migrants, children, persons with disabilities and people in vulnerable situations and the right to development, as well as gender equality, empowerment of women and intergenerational equity," Preamble of the Paris Agreement (UNFCCC, 2015).*
3 (Leite, 2022)
4 (Crowder 2024). Timestamp: 05:00.
5 (Crowder 2024). Timestamp: 00:30-00:41.
6 (Nieuwsitems 2022)
7 (Wexler MA JD 2024a). Timestamp: 01:19.
8 (Wexler MA JD 2024a). Timestamp: 01:33.
9 (Wexler MA JD 2024b). Timestamp: 00:04-00:21.
10 (Bell and Dinh 2024)
11 (Bell and Dinh 2024)
12 (Wilson 2024)
13 (Montana Department of Justice 2024)
14 (Montana Department of Justice 2024)
15 (Montana Department of Justice 2024)
16 (Montana Department of Justice 2024)
17 (Montana Department of Justice 2024)
18 (Montana Department of Justice 2024)
19 (Review The WHO 2024)
20 (Review The WHO 2024)
21 (Aussie17 2024). Timestamp: 01:40-02:07
22 (Aussie17 2024). Timestamp: 02:20-03:20
23 (Mochizuki et al. 2022)
24 (Bryan 2024)
25 (Bryan 2024). See: (Legrenzi & Umilta 2011; Tallis 2016; Duraiappah et al. 2021; Satel and Lilienfeld 2013)

26 (Bourn 2022)
27 (United Nations 2024a)
28 (Swarajya 2020)
29 (The Print 2022)
30 (Pradhan 2023)
31 (Pradhan 2023)
32 (AICTE 2024, 37)
33 (UGC 2021, 10)
34 (UGC 2022, 44)
35 (UGC 2021, 16)
36 (UGC 2021, 9)
37 (Wang 2023)
38 (Wang 2023)
39 (Xiaoliang 2023a)
40 (McBride et al. 2023)
41 (Xiaoliang 2023b)
42 (Xiaoliang 2023a)
43 (China Daily 2023)
44 (China SCIO 2023)
45 (Ellis 2023)
46 (Wang 2023, 3)
47 (Wang 2023, 3)
48 (Xinhua 2021)
49 (Xinhua 2021)
50 (Xinhua 2021)
51 (Xinhua 2021)
52 (Wang 2023)
53 (Wang 2023)
54 (Wang 2023). See Table 3.
55 (Wang 2023). See Table 3.
56 (Wang 2023). See Table 3.
57 (Wang 2023). See Table 3.
58 (Wang 2023)
59 (Wang 2023)
60 (Wang 2023)
61 (Wang 2023)
62 (May and Qin 2019)
63 (Wang 2023)
64 (Buckley, 2018)
65 (May and Qin 2019)
66 (Qingqing 2023)
67 (Shuo 2023)
68 (UNESCO 2024)

69 (The Times of India 2024)
70 Excerpted from: (Maher 2024).
71 Excerpted from: (Maher 2024).
72 Excerpted from: (Maher 2024).
73 Excerpted from: (Maher 2024).
74 Excerpted from: (Maher 2024).

Chapter 1: The Classroom as an Ideological Battlefield

1 (Lindsay 2022)
2 (Horowitz 2019)
3 (Lindsay 2022)
4 (Giroux 2021)
5 (New Discourses 2022a)
6 (Lindsay 2022)
7 (New Discourses 2022b). See the podcast description.
8 (França 2019)
9 (Global Education Magazine 2013)
10 (EduKitchen 2022). Timestamp: 00:07:24-00:07:45.
11 (Global Education Magazine 2013)
12 (Global Education Magazine 2013). Timestamp: 00:14-00:45.
13 (Kaushal 2023)
14 (Kaushal 2023)
15 (Goode 2011)
16 (New Discourses 2022)
17 (Big Think 2023). Timestamp: 09:47.
18 (New Discourses 2022)
19 (New Discourses 2022). Timestamp: 54:12-54:33.
20 (Rubin 2002, 158)
21 (Cornell University Library 2022. Timestamp: 01:23:09-01:32:45.
22 (Rubin 2002, 160)
23 (Rubin 2002, 160)
24 (Campbell 2021)
25 (Johnson 2021)
26 (Rufo 2022)
27 (Big Think 2023). Timestamp: 02:13.
28 (Vishnoi 2015)
29 (Doing Sociology 2020). Timestamp: 11:45-12:00.
30 (Valente 2019)
31 (Valente 2019)
32 (Carter 2023)
33 (Keenan and Hot Mess 2020)

34 (Rufo 2022)
35 (Keenan and Hot Mess 2020)
36 (Lancing and Lindsay 2024)
37 (Lancing and Lindsay 2024)
38 (Kingkade 2023)
39 (Rasmussen Reports 2022)
40 (Goode 2011)
41 (Goode 2011)
42 (Goode 2011, 132)
43 (Pearl 2016)
44 (NAMBLA 2010)
45 (Talarico 2019)

Chapter 2: The United Nations' Mandates on Sex Education

1 (Fetzer Institute 2024)
2 (Laytner 2018)
3 (Gayle 2014)
4 (Elbertson et al. 2009)
5 (Elbertson et al. 2009)
6 (Goleman 2024)
7 (Goleman 1971)
8 (Sandhu 2023). Timestamps 04:36 and 05:31.
9 (Sandhu 2023). Timestamp: 04:45.
10 (Sandhu 2023). Timestamp: 05:35-05:55.
11 (Goleman 1971)
12 (Goleman 1971)
13 (To The Best Of Our Knowledge 2014)
14 (Wilson 2014, 80-82)
15 (Goleman 1976)
16 (Wilson 2014, 80-82)
17 (To The Best Of Our Knowledge 2014)
18 (Goleman 1993, 20)
19 (Emmerling 2024)
20 (Yahoo! Finance 2023)
21 (Niemi 2020)
22 (Niemi 2020)
23 (CASEL 2024)
24 (Eden 2022)
25 (Downey 2022)
26 (Harris 2022)
27 (Borenstein et al. 2024)

28 (Chan Zuckerberg Initiative 2021)
29 (Along 2024)
30 (CZI 2021)
31 (Along 2022)
32 (Along 2022)
33 The following is a sample of questions that Along.org and other similar organizations ask students to input into their relationship management tool. Clearly, these questions are designed to map the psychological and emotional profiles of children: What do you watch on television, in movie theaters, or on other devices when you have free time? What is something or someone in your life you are grateful for and why? What's a problem you're currently facing? What is something you really value? Why do you value it? When others have disagreed with you, how respectful were you of their views? How well did you get along with students who are different from you? In your family, how clear are the rules about what you can and cannot do? How much did you care about other people's feelings? To what extent were you able to stand up for yourself without putting others down? When you get stuck while learning something new, how likely are you to try a different strategy? How often do you spend time outside (including parks, in your neighborhood, or at school)? Overall, how much do you feel like you belong at your school? How much does your opinion matter to your family? How clearly were you able to describe your feelings in the past 30 days? (CZI 2024)
34 (Bailey 2022)
35 (Boninger & Molnar 2022)
36 (Boninger & Molnar 2022)
37 (Boninger & Molnar 2022)
38 (Green 2022). Timestamp 00:07:00-00:07:57.
39 (Green 2022). Timestamp 08:13-08:22.
40 (Goldman 1993, 376)
41 (Goldman 1993, 383)
42 (Goldman 1993. 385)
43 (Goldman 1993, 386)
44 (Butler 1990, xv)
45 (World Health Organization 2024)
46 (WHO Regional Office for Europe and BZgA, 2010, 22-23)
47 (UN News 2022)
48 (WHO Regional Office for Europe and BZgA, 2010, 33)
49 (UNESCO 2018, 29)
50 (Severino and DeMint 2016, 112-113)
51 (Yenor 2022)
52 (UNESCO 2018)
53 (UNESCO 2018, 3)
54 (UNESCO 2018)

55 (UNESCO 2018, 17 and 50)
56 (UNESCO 2018, 70)
57 (UNESCO 2018, 70)
58 (UNESCO 2018, 70)
59 (UNESCO 2018, 72)
60 (UNESCO 2018, 20)
61 (UNESCO 2018)
62 (UNESCO Digital Library 2018a); For more detailed information, refer to the original publication on the website: familywatch.org.
63 (Allred 2022)
64 (Allred 2022)
65 (UNICEF 2016, 32); (Family Watch 2021a)
66 (Allred 2022)
67 (Allred 2022)
68 (McCaughey 2023a)
69 (Stop CSE 2024)
70 (Maughan 2014)
71 (WHO Regional Office for Europe and BZgA 2010)
72 (NIMH 2024)
73 (UNAIDS 2023, 2); (ICJ 2023, 2)
74 (UNAIDS 2023, 15)
75 (UNAIDS 2023, 22-23)
76 (World Economic Forum and The Boston Consulting Group 2016, 11)
77 (World Economic Forum and The Boston Consulting Group 2016)
78 (World Economic Forum and The Boston Consulting Group 2016, 5)
79 (World Economic Forum and The Boston Consulting Group 2016, 9)

Chapter 3: The Rot in American Education

1 (Eden 2022)
2 (Bryan 2024)
3 (Bryan 2024)
4 (Pennell 2020)
5 (Pennell 2020, 103)
6 (Gutstein 2005)
7 (Pennell 2020, 12)
8 (Pennell 2020, 12)
9 (Pennell 2020, 12-13)
10 (SFUSD 2024)
11 (Huang 2020)
12 (Huang 2020)
13 (Nelson 2024)

14 (Gewertz 2019)
15 (Pennell 2020, 12)
16 (Pennell 2020, 12)
17 (Pennell 2020, 12)
18 (Pennell 2020, 13)
19 (Pennell 2020, 13)
20 (Pennell 2020, 13)
21 (Pennell 2020, 14)
22 (Downey 2024)
23 (FOX 5 Washington DC 2022)
24 (Matthew 2023)
25 (Pennell 2020)
26 (Pennell 2020)
27 (Wokal Distance 2024)
28 (Dawkins, 2024)
29 (Genspect 2024). Timestamp: 3:40 and 10:58.
30 (GSA Network 2024)
31 (Lindsay 2023b)
32 (Drabinski 2013)
33 (Tang et al. 2022)
34 (Schlott 2024)
35 (Doherty 2022)
36 (Saavedra 2024)
37 (Saavedra 2024)
38 (Saavedra 2024)
39 (Dabrowski and Klingner 2023)
40 (Eden 2019)
41 (Camp 2023)
42 (Vankar 2024)
43 (Vankar 2023)
44 (Vankar 2023)
45 (Harvey et al. 2023)
46 (Kuyken et al. 2022). See also: (Saxbe 2023)
47 (Andrews et al. 2023)
48 (Dolan 2024)
49 (Shrier 2024). Timestamp: 00:30-00-40.
50 (Weiss 2024)
51 (Shrier 2024)
52 (Giordano 2023)
53 (Giordano, 2023). Timestamp: 00:54-02:21.
54 (McCaughey 2023a)
55 (McCaughey 2023a)
56 (Pan 2021)

57 (Pan 2021); (Ivey-Stephenson et al. 2020)
58 (Ericksen & Weed 2019)
59 (Biswakarma et al. 2024)
60 (Dutton & Kirkegaard 2024)
61 (Dutton & Kirkegaard 2024)
62 (Dutton & Kirkegaard 2024)
63 (Dutton & Kirkegaard 2024)
64 (Dutton & Kirkegaard 2024)
65 (Lahtinen 2024)
66 (Jamison et al., 2023)
67 (LaChance 2024)
68 (Torres 2024)
69 (unDivided 2023)
70 (unDivided 2023)
71 (Marantz & Coates 1991)
72 (Marantz & Coates 1991, 314)
73 California has over 22,000 kids between the ages of 13 and 17 who identify as transgender compared to only 800 in Iowa, which even if adjusted for population density, seems high and can be the effect of social contagion and social engineering. See: (Conron 2020)

Chapter 4: Repurposing Gandhi for Marxism

1 (MGIEP 2024a)
2 (MGIEP 2024a)
3 (Vickers 2024)
4 (Mochizuki et al. 2022)
5 (Mochizuki et al. 2022)
6 Neuroscience has previously been helpful to education especially in understanding learning disabilities such as dyslexia. But the new application has opened the door to quackery. For instance, we discussed the Stanford professor Jo Boaler, who is reducing math standards and teaching math resulting in worse outcomes than before. She claims that the latest research in neuroscience supports her claims, and MGIEF too makes similar claims. See: (Vickers 2024)
7 (unesco_mgiep 2019)
8 (Zguir et al. 2021)
9 (Zguir et al. 2021)
10 (Tigue 2023)
11 (Christodoulou et al. 2022)
12 (Christodoulou et al. 2022, 263-264)
13 (MGIEP 2024b)

14 (Christodoulou et al. 2022, 310)
15 (Christodoulou et al. 2022, 285)
16 (MGIEP 2024b)
17 (MGIEP 2024c)
18 (MGIEP 2024d)
19 (MGIEP 2024d)
20 (New Discourses 2023). Timestamp: 13:13-16:09.
21 (unesco_mgiep 2024)
22 (Singh 2024)
23 (MGIEP 2024d)
24 (Lindsay 2023a)
25 (Bryan 2024)
26 (Bryan 2024)
27 (MGIEP 2024c)
28 (MGIEP 2024c)
29 (MGIEP 2024c)
30 (Education21 2022)
31 (Sonika 2023)
32 (Tripathi 2023)
33 (Education21 2022)
34 (Education21 2022)
35 (MGIEP 2024e)
36 (MGIEP 2024f)
37 (Duraiappah et al. 2021, 2)

Chapter 5: International Planned Parenthood Federation

1 (NRLC 2024)
2 (U.S. Census Bureau 2024)
3 (Stauffer 2022)
4 (IPPF Centers & Funds 2024)
5 (IPPF 2023a)
6 (Mumah 2020)
7 (O'Connor & Strapagiel 2020)
8 (Grady & St. Fleur 2015); (Somashekhar & Paquette 2015)
9 (IPPF 2024a, 16)
10 (IPPF 2018, 19)
11 (IPPF 2024b, v)
12 (IPPF 2024b, v)
13 (IPPF 2024b, v)
14 (IPPF 2024c, 10, 17-20, and 23); https://familywatch.org/
15 (Israel 2023)

16 (Israel et al. 2023)
17 (IPPF 2023a, 60)
18 (IPPF 2023a, 24)
19 (Diller 2013)
20 (Family Watch 2024, 64) ; (CSE 2024, 2)
21 (IPPF 2020a)
22 (IPPF 2020b)
23 (UNESCO 2010)
24 (IPPF 2020b, 5)
25 (IPPF 2020b, 14)
26 (Live Action 2018). Timestamp: 01:33-01:48.
27 (UN Global Compact 2023)
28 (IPPF 2024d)
29 (Israel 2023)
30 See Annex A: (IPPF 2023a 63)
31 (Guttmacher Institute 2018)
32 (NEON 2024). Timestamp: 18:10-23:33.

Chapter 6: A Tale of Two Provinces: Jharkhand (India) and Gansu (China)

1 (Rutgers International 2024, 7)
2 (Joseph 2023)
3 (Gentleman 2007)
4 (The YP Foundation & Pravah 2017, 3)
5 (TARSHI 2019, 55)
6 (The YP Foundation & Pravah 2017, 5)
7 (The YP Foundation & Pravah 2017, 3)
8 (UNFPA 2018)
9 (TARSHI 2019, 52)
10 (TARSHI 2019, 25-26 and 56)
11 (TARSHI 2019, 56)
12 (TARSHI 2019, 57)
13 (TARSHI 2019, 56)
14 (TARSHI 2019, 22 and 57)
15 (Centre for Catalyzing Change 2024)
16 (Packard Foundation 2024)
17 (Rutgers 2021, 4)
18 (Rutgers 2021, 10)
19 (Rutgers 2021, 10)
20 (Rutgers 2021, 34)
21 (The Pioneer 2019)

22 (Rutgers 2021, 26)
23 (Rutgers 2021, 53)
24 (Rutgers 2021, 28)
25 (Rutgers 2021, 14)
26 (Rutgers 2021, 37)
27 (Chandra-Mouli et al. 2017)
28 (Rutgers 2021, 37)
29 (Rutgers 2021, 37)
30 (UNESCO 2021, 7)
31 (ASER 2022)
32 (Piramal School of Leadership 2024)
33 (NITI Aayog 2022, 119)
34 (Rutgers 2021, 34)
35 (Chandra-Mouli et al. 2017)
36 (UNESCO 2021, 47)
37 (Jin et al. 2021)
38 (Yu 2018)
39 (Jin et al. 2021)
40 (Jin et al. 2021)
41 (Jin et al. 2021)
42 (Dig Watch 2020)
43 (NPC 2020)
44 (NPC 2020)
45 (NPC 2020)
46 (UNESCO 2021, 18)
47 (UNESCO 2021, 34)
48 (Ministry of Education, Singapore 2024)
49 (Ministry of Education, Singapore 2024)

Chapter 7: Challenges Facing Indian Educators

1 (The Pioneer 2019)
2 (The Times of India 2023)
3 (Government of India 2009)
4 (NCPCR 2017, 5)
5 (Mantri 2019)
6 (Seetha & Sengupta 2018)
7 (Seetha & Sengupta 2018)
8 (Dhaliwal 2015)
9 (NCPCR 2021, 9)
10 (Rutgers 2021, 37)
11 (Rimmele and Nanda 2022)

12 (MHRD 2024, 3)
13 (Deeksha 2022)
14 (Angad 2023)
15 (MHRD 2024, 5)
16 Under the guidance of the National Assessment Centre, NCERT, and SCERTs, all states and territories will revamp student progress reports. These updated reports will be detailed, covering various aspects of each student's learning, including knowledge, emotions, and physical skills. They will also include self-evaluations, peer reviews, and different activities like projects and quizzes. To support this, a large amount of data will be gathered to monitor students' development.
17 (McCaughey 2023b)
18 (McKenna 2023)
19 (Nguyen, 2022)
20 (Anderson 2023)
21 (Anderson 2023)
22 (NCERT 2023, 359-360)
23 (NCERT 2023, 42-43 and 49)
24 (Saathiya 2017a)
25 (Saathiya 2017b)
26 (UNFPA 2023, 13)
27 (PIB 2017)
28 (Bahl et al. 2023)
29 (The YP Foundation & Pravah 2017, 4)
30 (The YP Foundation & Pravah 2017, 5)
31 (UNFPA 2022, 5)
32 (UNFPA 2020)
33 (TARSHI 2019)
34 (The YP Foundation 2021a)
35 (TARSHI 2019)
36 (UNFPA 2015)
37 (Bhattacharya 2023)
38 (Bhattacharya 2023)
39 (PIB 2020)
40 (PIB 2020)
41 (PIB 2020)
42 (UNESCO et al. 2021, 22)
43 (UNICEF East Asia & Pacific 2019, 12)
44 (Family Watch 2021b)
45 (Family Watch 2021b)
46 (Family Watch 2021b)
47 (UNICEF India 2024)
48 (Mathur and Das Gupta 2006, 1)

49 (Mathur and Das Gupta 2006, 2)
50 (The YP Foundation 2021b)
51 (Jaiswal 2023)
52 (Jaiswal 2023)
53 (Sangwan 2021)
54 (Narayanan 2022)
55 (Narayanan 2022)
56 (Rubin 2002, 158)
57 (Rubin 2002, 158-159)
58 (Raha & Ramakrishnan 2022, 15)
59 (Raha & Ramakrishnan 2022, 16)
60 (Raha & Ramakrishnan 2022, 17)
61 (Raha & Ramakrishnan 2022, 17)
62 We already discussed that the Rashtriya Kishor Swasthya Karyakram (RKSK), which was about improving nutrition and mental health, had been hijacked by the UNFPA and Population Foundation of India (PFI) by introducing a comprehensive sex education program in the form of a mobile app called *Saathy Salah*, thus by-passing parents' oversight on what kind of information is accessible to a pre-teen or a teenager. The program also by-passes adult teachers to deliver sex education and instead uses 'peer educators' to talk to young people who are also attached to Adolescent Friendly Health Clinics or AFHC (Adolescent Friendly Health Clinics).
63 (Raha & Ramakrishnan 2022, 17)
64 (Raha & Ramakrishnan 2022, 18)
65 (Law Commission of India 2023). See 4th page of the PDF.
66 (Das 2023)
67 (UNICEF 2023)
68 (South Asia Monitor 2021)
69 (South Asia Monitor 2021)
70 (Padilla 2023)
71 (González and Moreno 2022)
72 (Guttmacher Institute 2017)

Chapter 8: India's Public-Private Partnerships for Comprehensive Sexuality Education and Social Emotional Learning

1 (Balasubramanian et al. 2016, v)
2 (UNFPA 2020, 4)
3 (IPE Global 2024)
4 (IPE Global 2023)
5 (Children's Investment Fund Foundation 2024)

6 (Mukherjee 2023)
7 (Press Trust of India 2017)
8 (PFI 2024a)
9 (HCLFoundation 2022); (HCLFoundation 2024)
10 (Kissu 2024)
11 (OpIndia 2024)
12 (FPAIndia 2022, 12,35)
13 (Educately 2020); (Barik 2023)
14 Established under the leadership of the late J.R.D. Tata in 1970, PFI gets support from some of the most prominent philanthropists, including Ratan Tata who was an active board member. The prestigious J.R.D. Tata Memorial Awards for excellence in public service are hosted by the PFI. Tata Communications Ltd. is an active donor of PFI along with the Bill & Melinda Gates Foundation, David and Lucile Packard Foundation, HCL Foundation, Children's Investment Fund Foundation, DCM Shriram Foundation, United Nation Children's Fund, Facebook India Online Services Pvt. Ltd., Centre for International Development Services, Ishtar Music Pvt. Ltd., Ministry of Health and Family Welfare and others. (PFI 2023a)
15 (UNICEF, 2021)
16 (Gambini 2022)
17 (PFI 2024c, 36)
18 (Barik 2023)
19 (Educately 2020)
20 (PFI 2024e)
21 (PFI 2022, 45)
22 (PFI 2022, 15)
23 (PFI 2022, 19)
24 (PFI 2024c)
25 (PFI 2022)
26 (PFI 2022, 10)
27 (PFI 2022, 27-28)
28 (PFI 2022, 20)
29 (PFI 2022, 10)
30 (PFI 2022, 21)
31 (PFI 2022, 303)
32 (PFI 2022, 36)
33 (PFI 2022, 37)
34 (PFI 2022, 36)
35 (PFI 2022, 36)
36 (PFI 2022, 56)
37 (PFI 2022)
38 (PFI 2023d, 20)
39 (Ahuja 2022)

40 (PFI 2024d)
41 (Ahuja 2022)
42 (Ahuja 2022)
43 (Ahuja 2022)
44 Apart from the FAYA project, PFI drafted a pledge and even made the state sign a pledge to commit to CSE for youth and penetrates many agencies beyond RKSK. PFI secured commitments from the Health Minister and Women Child Development Minister in Rajasthan to promote adolescent health and well-being by making the government sign a pledge. This pledge was endorsed by four MLAs, the Chairperson of the Women & Child Committee in the state Assembly, and value bureaucrats, with media coverage amplifying its message. Additionally, PFI advanced the adolescent health agenda through various platforms beyond RKSK, including Nehru Yuva Kendra Sangathan (NYKS), Rajasthan State AIDS Control Society (RSACS), WCD, and Department of Panchayati Raj and Rural Development (PR&RD). Moreover, it successfully established Youth Resource Centres called Super Saathi Kendras (SSKs) in Dungarpur and Tonk districts, following their establishment in Bundi and Karauli in the previous year. Adolescents played a crucial role in ensuring the availability, operation, and commitment to these safe spaces, all with the blessings of local officials and RKSK counselors (PFI 2023d)
45 (PFI 2023d)
46 (FPAIndia 2024)
47 (IPPF 2024e)
48 (IPPF 2024e)
49 In 2022, the reach included 325,000 youth aged 10 to 24, 1,750 teachers, over 5900 peer educators, 1,117 schools, 1,400 school/college students sensitized to CSE, and 30,051 students reached through online mediums (FPAIndia 2022, 13)
50 (FPAIndia 2022, 12)
51 (FPAIndia 2022, 53)
52 (FPAIndia 2022, 53)
53 (FPAIndia 2022, 53)
54 (FPAIndia 2022, 53)
55 (FPAIndia 2022, 53)
56 (FPAIndia 2022, 53)
57 (FPAIndia 2022, 53)
58 (FPAIndia 2022, 53)
59 (IPPF 2023a, 21)
60 (IPPF 2024f)
61 (Israel 2023)
62 (FPAIndia 2022)
63 (FPAIndia 2022, 12)
64 (FPAIndia 2022, 47)

65 528 (FPAIndia 2022, 17)
66 (China Development Brief 2024)
67 (Littlejohn 2016)
68 (Qin & Zhang 2023)
69 (Qin & Zhang 2023, 3)
70 (Qin & Zhang 2023, 7)
71 (Qin & Zhang 2023, 9)
72 (Qin & Zhang 2023)
73 (Leavenworth 2016)
74 (Leavenworth 2016)
75 (Shi-Kupfer & Lang 2017)
76 (Lo 2024)
77 (Lo 2024)
78 (Wang et al. 2021)
79 (Qin & Zhang 2023, 9)
80 (Qian et al. 2021)
81 (Qin & Zhang 2023, 10)
82 (Girls Not Brides 2024)
83 (The YP Foundation 2021c, 7)
84 (The YP Foundation 2018, 17)
85 (The YP Foundation 2018, 8 and 18)
86 (The YP Foundation 2018, 22)
87 (The YP Foundation 2021c, 5)
88 (TARSHI 2019, 77)
89 (10to19Community 2024a)
90 (Learning4impact 2024); (10to19Community 2024b)
91 (10to19Community 2024c) (video "reflect" under glimpses from the 10to19 community)
92 (10to19Community 2024b)
93 (Ab Meri Baari 2024)
94 (10to19Community 2024c)
95 (10to19Community 2024a)
96 (Learning4impact 2024)
97 (10to19Community 2024c). See"Campaigns and initiatives".
98 (The Economic Times 2021)
99 (10to19Community 2024b)
100 (Dasra India 2021). Timestamp: 19:17-20:40.
101 (The Nazariya Foundation 2024)
102 (Bhattacharjee 2020a)
103 (Bhattacharjee 2020b)
104 (Sharma 2021, 10)
105 (TARSHI 2019, 69-70)
106 (Sharma 2021)

107 (United Nations 2024)
108 (TARSHI 2019)
109 (Hauf 2021)

Chapter 9: Institutionalizing Transgenderism

1 (Huges 2024)
2 (NACO 2023, 25)
3 Gender dysphoria is a term that describes a sense of unease that a person may have because of a mismatch between their biological sex and their gender identity.
4 Dr. Lawrence remained involved in the 'Standards of Care,' co-authoring the 6th Version (2001) by the Harry Benjamin Association, which was the last version published before a name change to WPATH in 2007. He's even cited in today's current Standards, as is Dr. Money.
5 Dr. Lawrence remained involved in the 'Standards of Care,' co-authoring the 6th Version (2001) by the Harry Benjamin Association, which was the last version published before a name change to WPATH in 2007. He's even cited in today's current Standards, as is Dr. Money.
6 (Rosiak 2024)
7 (Shellenberger 2024)
8 (Walsh 2024b)
9 (Shellenberger 2024)
10 (Shellenberger 2024)
11 (Huges 2024)
12 (The Cass Review 2024)
13 (Lewis 2024)
14 (Buttons 2024a)
15 (Buttons 2024a)
16 (Buttons 2024b)
17 (Horton 2024)
18 (Starbuck 2024)
19 (Jain 2022)
20 (Gupta et al. 2020)
21 (Stats For Gender 2024)
22 (India Today 2022)
23 (The Hindu 2022)
24 (Stats For Gender 2024)
25 (Bhuptani 2024)
26 (Pemde et al. 2023, 3)
27 (Pemde et al. 2023, 10-11)

28 Its founder and CEO is an influential retired officer of the Indian Air Force, Sanjay Sharma, with connections in the Delhi political circuit. WPATH awarded him for his successful advocacy work and describes him as an 'active member'. He serves on the board of WPATH where he lobbies the government to bring WPATH standards of care to India. His impressive resume on the WPATH website lists many accomplishments for championing the trans movement for children. He has organized webinars in collaboration with Dept. of Healthcare and Pharmaceutical Management Jamia Hamdard, on transgender healthcare. He has successfully petitioned the Delhi Commission for Protection of Child Rights (DCPCR) Government of NCT of Delhi to support WPATH's cause. He has completed the Global Education Initiative (GEI) Certified Training Courses in Best Practices in Transgender Medical and Mental Health Care. (WPATH 2022)
29 (Shankar et al. 2022)
30 (NACO 2023)
31 (NACO 2023, 22)
32 (NACO 2023, 19)
33 (NACO 2023, 25)
34 (Sarkar 2024)
35 (Sarkar 2024)
36 (Sarkar 2024)
37 (Sarkar 2024)
38 (Ghosal 2019)
39 (Keshav Suri Foundation 2020)
40 (Ghosal 2019)
41 (Give 2019)
42 (The Daily Marketing 2020)
43 (Brain 2022)
44 (KESHAV SURI FOUNDATION 2024)
45 (JPISschool 2019)
46 (Walsh 2024a)
47 (Morrison 2023)
48 (Walsh 2024a)

Chapter 10: NITI Aayog as the Gatekeeper

1 (PIB 2019)
2 (PIB 2019)
3 (PFI 2023d, 6)
4 (NILERD 2014)
5 (Rimmele & Nanda 2022, 36)
6 (Rimmele & Nanda 2022, 48)

7 (NITI Aayog 2024, 36)
8 (PFEL 2020)
9 (National Statistical Office 2022)
10 We picked the indicators for the education related SDGs to show the priorities for education as defined by the Indian government. Different indicators are measured with different frequencies. We could assume that in most cases, important indicators are measured more frequently, than those that are deemed less important. With the abysmal literacy rates among youth, the indicator 4.6.1 measures the literacy rate of 15-24 years only once in 10 years.
11 SDG Target 4.7: By 2030, ensure that all learners acquire the knowledge and skills needed to promote sustainable development, including, among others, through education for sustainable development and sustainable lifestyles, human rights, gender equality, promotion of a culture of peace and non-violence, global citizenship, and appreciation of cultural diversity and of culture's contribution to sustainable development.
12 (End Wokeness 2024)

Chapter 11: A Critique of India's Woke Education

1 (Sen & Naqvi 2023)
2 (CASEL & CIVIC 2024)
3 (CASEL & CIVIC 2024)
4 (Hylton et al. 2018)
5 (Pradhan 2024)
6 (Rim 2024)
7 (Portell 2019)
8 (Portell 2019)
9 (Bill & Melinda Gates Foundation 2024)
10 (KnowledgeWorks 2024)
11 (KnowledgeWorks 2021)
12 (KnowledgeWorks 2021)
13 (Gagnon 2024)
14 (Simple Education Foundation 2023)
15 (X 2024)
16 (ACER India 2024)
17 (ACER India 2023)
18 (Ministry of Education 2024)
19 (Ministry of Education 2023)
20 (efiletax 2023)

Chapter 12: The Vedic Philosophy of Education

1 (Ghosh & Kiparsky 2019)
2 (Scharfe 1989, 221)
3 See: (Pipa et al. 2020)
4 (Mek 2021)
5 (Mek 2021)
6 (Mek 2021)

Chapter 13: Indian Education Before the British Empire

1 (Bagchi et al. 2014, 108)
2 (Oberoi 1994)
3 (Sriram 2018)
4 (Robert and Southey 1844, 102)
5 (Robert and Southey 1844, 173)
6 (Bell 1808)
7 (Bell 1808)
8 (Robert and Southey 1844)
9 (Robert and Southey 1844)
10 (Robert and Southey 1844)
11 (Tschurenev 2014)
12 (Hogan 1989)
13 (Reigart 1916)
14 (Capital Projects 2024)
15 (Reigart 1916)
16 (Reigart 1916)
17 (Browning 1921)
18 (Hogan 1989)
19 (Hogan 1989)
20 (Tschurenev 2008)
21 (Reigart 1916)
22 (Reigart 1916)

Appendices

1 (Review The WHO 2024)
2 (PIB 2017)
3 (Government of Assam, Biswanath District 2024)
4 (Sanskriti Magazine 2015)

ACKNOWLEDGMENTS

We wish to thank several individuals who helped in the development of this book. Anurag Sharma provided research assistance. Gerald Surya did fact checking of the quotations and references. Subhodeep Mukhopadhyay built the Bibliography and ensured proper formatting of the manuscript. Swapan Dasgupta offered helpful feedback to the draft. Trisha Udumudi has designed and implemented the cover design. Rajkumar Thorat provided excellent graphics support to improve the diagrams. And most of all, we thank Sanjana Roy Choudhury for her editing and overall coordination with the publisher.

INDEX